CAREER
OPPORTUNITIES
IN THE TRAVEL INDUSTRY

JUDY COLBERT

Foreword by
DEE MINIC,
Executive Director, Tourism Works for America,
Travel Industry Association of America (TIA)

Ferguson
An imprint of ® Facts On File

Career Opportunities in the Travel Industry

Copyright © 2004 by Judy Colbert

Ferguson
An imprint of Facts On File, Inc.
132 West 31st Street
New York NY 10001

Library of Congress Cataloging-in-Publication Data

Colbert, Judy.
   Career opportunities in travel / Judy Colbert.
      p. cm. — (Career opportunities series)
Includes bibliographical references and index.
  ISBN 0-8160-4864-9
  1. Tourism—Vocational guidance. I. Title. II. Facts On File's career opportunities series.
G155.7.C65 2004
910′.23—dc21   2003049187

Ferguson books are available at special discounts when purchased in bulk quantities for businesses, associations, institutions, or sales promotions. Please call our Special Sales Department in New York at (212) 967-8800 or (800) 322-8755.

You can find Ferguson on the World Wide Web at http://www.fergpubco.com

Cover design by Nora Wertz

Printed in the United States of America

VB Hermitage 10 9 8 7 6 5 4 3 2

This book is printed on acid-free paper.

Dedicated to Saul,
who helps me find passion in my work and my travels.

CONTENTS

FOREWORD

The travel and tourism (T&T) industry is the USA's second largest employer (after health services) with one out of every seven people (or nearly 18 million) working in this important service industry, which generated a payroll of $174.5 billion in 2002. As you will learn in this publication, T&T is a good industry for preparing young people for future careers and upward mobility in a wide-range of jobs from entry level to CEO and from accountants to zookeepers.

According to research conducted by the Travel Industry Association of America, spending by resident and international travelers in the U.S. averages $1.5 billion a day, $61 million an hour, $1 million a minute, and $17,000 a second. Based on expenditures, T&T continues to be the nation's third largest retail sales industry after automotive dealers and food stores. Projected domestic and international expenditures for 2002 were $537.2 billion, a 5.8% decrease from 2000's $570.5 billion.

Each state feels the impact of travelers and the latest data available by state shows that the top five states with travel-generated employment in 2001 were California (931,700 jobs); Florida (801,300 jobs); Texas (566,100 jobs); New York (440,300 jobs); and Nevada (357,700 jobs). In a state where tourism is the number one industry, such as Florida, job creation can be tremendous; however, T&T does not have to be a state's largest industry for its impact to be felt. For example in Michigan, T&T is the sixth-largest industry, but more than 173,000 jobs are directly attributable to the dollars spent by domestic and international travelers. Overall, the T&T ranks as the first, second, or third largest employer in 29 of the 50 states. The industry is particularly attractive to students and seniors looking for part-time and seasonal work. It helps the nation where employment needs to grow: 50% of T&T employees are women, 23% of T&T businesses are owned by women, 14% of T&T businesses are owned by minorities, and 95% of T&T businesses qualify as small businesses.

According to statistics from the U.S. Dept. of Commerce's Office of Travel & Tourism Industries, 42 million international travelers spent $88 billion in the U.S. in 2002, supporting over one million jobs, generating nearly $16 billion in tax revenues and $6 billion in travel trade surplus. International travel to the U.S. is an export for the nation. Technically, it is considered a service export just like freight, insurance, telecommunications, royalties, and education.

Travel is a freedom cherished by citizens throughout the world. The U.S. travel and tourism industry supports just measures that protect this freedom for everyone, everywhere. Travel fosters understanding and understanding creates a climate that nurtures peace, stability, economic growth, and democratic rights.

For more information go to www.tia.org.

— Dee Minic
Executive Director, Tourism Works for America
Travel Industry Association of America (TIA)

INDUSTRY OUTLOOK

There is no doubt that the travel industry has had a bumpy ride since September 11, 2001, with continued terrorism attacks worldwide and the downturn in the U.S. and world economies aggravating the situation. Domestic and international travel expenditures amounted to $525.1 billion in 2002, down from 537.2 billion in 2001. Despite this fact, the 2003 projection is for $560.1 billion and for $588.2 billion in 2004.

According to the Travel Industry Association of America (TIA), travel and tourism combined form the nation's largest services export industry, the third largest retail sales industry, and one of America's largest employers. It is the first, second, or third largest employer in 29 states. Nearly 8 million people, earning nearly $174 billion in payroll, are employed in some field related to travel and tourism. That is about one out of every 18 U.S. residents in the civilian labor force employed due to direct travel spending in the United States in 2001. It is one area where we generate a trade surplus, amounting to almost $9 billion.

One of the appealing aspects of a travel-related career, other than the possibility of free or reduced-price travel to all corners of the world, is that so many positions do not require advanced degrees. People who have had on-the-job training and experience can fill even some of those positions that call for a college education.

According to TIA surveys, some of the basic changes in travel since 9/11 include more last-minute travel, fewer international visitors, more car travel, lower travel expenditures, and travel closer to home. To foster business and take advantage of these factors, travel providers have lowered prices, or at least not raised them, and added benefits. They are promoting their services to a more local market. They are also using the Internet for publicizing and advertising their products. To do so, they have increased their advertising and marketing budgets. Although 68 percent of the TIA members surveyed indicated they think business will improve in 2003, some 40 percent indicate they have had reductions in staff, salaries, or bonuses in the previous year. Yet, in the gloom of predictions saying that travel probably will not bounce back until sometime in 2004, there are bright spots.

Businesses such as hotels, resorts, restaurants, and cultural and family attractions that have changed their focus in awareness of family and business budgetary constraints, the increased inconvenience of air travel, and other factors are seeing the rewards of those changes with increased business. Those offering perceived safety and value for the dollar spent will benefit, as these are two of the main criteria travelers are now seeking.

Cruising, RV travel, and senior and leisure travel have improved in the past year. Cruising is up nearly four percent, RV rentals are up 30 percent, and leisure travel was up two percent in the first half of 2002. Business travel, while it has declined sharply overall, has picked up in more local and shorter trips.

It will be up to those who are entering travel-related businesses to revise and update the old ways of marketing and providing services. Those with creative thinking, a solid education in the travel and hospitality fields, and computer skills are sure to succeed.

Employees who approach their jobs with enthusiasm and provide clients and guests with a positive experience—whether they are security guards or general managers, flight attendants or railroad conductors, animal keepers or astronomers—will be rewarded with continued employment and promotional opportunities. Those with computer skills who can create user-friendly web pages and spreadsheets, operate audiovisual equipment, and use navigational and other software and hardware will also see plenty of opportunities in the travel industry. Those who have an excellent and knowledgeable background in the hospitality industry will benefit greatly when a strong economy returns.

HOW TO USE THIS BOOK

Career Opportunities in Travel offers information about a wide variety of occupations directly or indirectly related to travel and tourism and jobs in which travel plays a major part of the job responsibilities. The education, training, skills, and personality traits of those in many of these jobs, particularly those in travel and tourism, can transfer from one aspect of the travel industry to another. A chef can work for a restaurant, hotel, cruise ship, or spa. The same is true for a laundry manager, housekeeper, sales manager, purchasing agent, or retail supervisor. The book is designed for people just starting in the business world as well as those who have been there, done that, and want to do something different.

For each of the more than 70 jobs described in *Career Opportunities in Travel,* you will learn what you need to enter that job field, the salary range, job opportunities, and advancement prospects, and what associations or unions are available as a resource for training and job openings.

Sources of Information

The information in *Career Opportunities in Travel* comes from the following sources:

- Organizations and unions that represent the various occupations
- Major job banks
- Interviews with individuals in the various professions
- Personal experience observing the occupations
- Newsletters, books, and magazines.

Organization of Material

Career Opportunities in Travel is divided into nine employment sections: travel and transportation; cruise travel; lodging; food and beverage; tour and travel services; sales and publicity; executive and managerial; health care; and specialties. There are two parts to each career profile. The first part provides job information in chart form, giving a thumbnail idea of prerequisites; other job titles; a career ladder illustrating the common career path to a position; licensing or certification requirements; and a salary range. The second part presents more details in narrative form, including:

- The "Position Description" details a job's major responsibilities, daily tasks, and duties and provides information about working conditions.
- "Salaries" gives a general idea of the wages that workers may earn. Many salary details come from the U.S. Bureau of Labor Statistics, salary surveys done by professional associations, various state and college employment boards, and a variety of job postings.
- "Employment Prospects" lists what type of companies hire people in that career and the job outlook for today and the future.
- "Advancement Prospects" briefly covers the prospects for promotion within the field and suggestions for alternative career paths.
- "Licensure/Certification" includes any license, certification, or registration that may be required or recommended for a profession.
- "Education and Training" describes the type of diploma or degree that is needed or recommended to enter a career. This section also discusses training programs that may need to be completed.
- "Experience, Skills, and Personality Traits" itemizes the minimum experience, skills, and personality traits required for a job.
- "Unions and Associations" lists the names of some national professional organizations or unions that are open to people in each career.
- "Tips for Entry" lists suggestions for finding jobs and more information about each job.

An exhaustive list of organizations and unions, with phone and fax numbers and website URLs point to areas where you can find more detailed information. Appendixes are provided to help locate additional information about career choices. They include organizations and unions; schools that offer certificates and associates, bachelors, masters, and doctorate degrees in travel, tourism, and hospitality; lists of major hotels, cruise lines, and airlines with contact information; a bibliography; and a list of websites of interest.

Notice

Hundreds of addresses, phone numbers, and website URLs are listed in *Career Opportunities in Travel*. They are current as of this writing, but remember that associations, organizations, unions, schools, and companies move, change their phone numbers or access codes, change their names or their domain names, or cease to exist. When a connection does not work (mail is returned, phone numbers are wrong, a 404 URL error code appears), then go to a good search engine, such as Google.com or AskJeeves.com, and enter the name of the organization.

ACKNOWLEDGMENTS

My profuse thanks go to Tia Gordon at the American Hotel and Lodging Association, Mike Pina at the Travel Industry Association of America, and the National Tourism Foundation for the data, charts, lists, and other information they supplied. All associations assist the public and their members, but these three are exceptional. Gratitude also goes to Jazz Flores and Saul Fruchthendler for providing incredible support, laughs, and information.

Also, my appreciation goes to those people I questioned about their careers and who live only by their screen names on the Internet. They answered my queries with great insight and patience.

TRAVEL AND TRANSPORTATION

AIRLINE PILOT

CAREER PROFILE

Duties: Flies airplanes transporting passengers or cargo for scheduled or chartered flights

Alternate Title(s): Airline Captain

Salary Range: $32,000 to $235,000, plus per diem

Employment Prospects: Fair

Advancement Prospects: Good

Best Geographical Location(s): The West Coast, including California and Washington; the East Coast, including New York, New Jersey, Washington, D.C., Florida, and Georgia; and the Midwest, including Illinois, Michigan, and Texas for airline pilots; other locations as well for corporate pilots

Prerequisites:

Education and Training—Proper flight training through flight instruction courses or the military; at least 1,500 hours of flying time, including night and instrument flying

Experience—Position or training in the military or with a small commuter or regional airline

Special Skills and Personality Traits—Function well under pressure; able to make quick decisions; able to work well with people and supervise the flight crew; at least 23 years of age; excellent health; good hearing; 20/20 corrected vision; no physical or mental handicaps that could hamper ability to fly a plane

Licensure/Certification—Airline transport pilot's license with instrument rating and commercial pilot's license for all airline pilots; private pilot's license also required for pilots with a commercial airline

CAREER LADDER

```
┌─────────────────────────────┐
│   Pilot or Captain, Airline │
└─────────────────────────────┘

┌─────────────────────────────┐
│   First Officer, Airline    │
└─────────────────────────────┘

┌─────────────────────────────┐
│      Flight Engineer        │
└─────────────────────────────┘

┌─────────────────────────────┐
│      Military Pilot         │
└─────────────────────────────┘
```

Position Description

Pilots fly passengers and cargo for private corporations and commercial or charter airlines. Usually, two pilots, a captain and cocaptain or pilot and copilot, share the responsibilities in larger, jet-propelled aircraft. The pilot and copilot check the aircraft, including controls, engines, instruments, tires, and luggage and cargo loading to assure that all systems are operating properly. The pilot checks with the weather service to determine the fastest, safest, and smoothest flight path and files a flight plan.

Pilots monitor the instruments and various systems during the flight and keep in touch with the air traffic or flight coordinator throughout the flight to accurately maintain the flight's course, altitude, and speed. They file a flight report with the Federal Aviation Administration (FAA) and the airline upon completion of the flight.

Corporate pilots have the same responsibilities but also may be responsible for loading the luggage, supervising the fueling, and assuring that aircraft maintenance is up-to-date, either by doing it themselves or by making sure reliable maintenance personnel do it. Upon completion of the flight, the pilot must file a flight report with the FAA.

Pilots are limited to 100 hours per month and 1,000 hours per year of actual flying time. FAA regulations require airline pilots to have a minimum of eight hours of uninterrupted rest during the 24 hours before they complete the next day's flying. Flying time may be during the daytime or at night.

Pilots with more seniority are usually assigned to more desirable flight schedules, including international flights. Pilots with less seniority may be assigned to shorter commuter flights.

Many trips for commercial airlines and corporations include overnight stays away from home. The company usually pays for hotel rooms, meals, connecting transportation, and other direct expenses.

Salaries

Airline pilots are paid according to the size and type of aircraft flown, with higher salaries going to those who fly jets than for those who fly turboprops. Additional pay may be earned for international or night flights. While the average pilot earns nearly $115,000 a year, salaries with commercial airlines can range from $36,000 to a high of $235,000, each plus per diem. Corporate pilots can earn from $12,000 to $84,000. Generally, health and life insurance and retirement plans are included, along with vacation and sick pay. Commercial airline pilots and their immediate families are eligible for reduced-cost or free air transportation on their own airline and other airlines. Sometimes this is on a stand-by or space-available basis.

Employment Prospects

The availability of airline pilot positions reflects the status of the airline industry. In good economic times, there are more flights and more demand for pilots. The opposite applies when the economy is doing poorly. With increased security measures in place in commercial airports, causing travelers to spend more time in airports, more corporations have switched to private planes and jets, either by owning airplanes or chartering the flights for their executives. As such, there may be more openings for airline pilots with charter airlines. Some estimates indicate several thousand pilots will be retiring within the next 10 years, so many of those positions will have to be filled.

Advancement Prospects

Starting with a small regional or commuter airline generally leads to jobs with larger national airlines. With the decrease in commercial air flights, advancement into these higher paying jobs will be slow for the next few years. Some pilots may switch to airline business and management positions; become a flight instructor; or become a corporate, charter, test, or agricultural pilot. The mandatory federal government retirement age for commercial airline pilots is 60 years.

Special Requirements

Airline Pilots must have a commercial pilot's license (or certificate) and an airline transport pilot's license with an instrument rating.

Education and Training

Those wishing to become a commercial airline pilot or captain must obtain a private pilot's license. The Airline Pilots must be at least 23 years of age and have logged at least 1,500 hours of flying time (with some equivalency through courses in aviation school), including night and instrument flying. They must be in excellent health and pass a rigorous physical examination, have 20/20 corrected vision, good hearing, and no physical or mental handicaps that could hamper their ability to fly. They must pass a written exam covering safe flight, navigation techniques, and federal rules and regulations and a flight exam.

To receive an instrument rating, pilots must have 105 hours of flight experience, including 40 hours of instrument flying. They may also have such advanced ratings as multi-engine aircraft. To be a captain or pilot for a commercial airline, they must pass a number of flight levels, including student pilot solo, private pilot's license, cross country training, instrument rating, commercial pilot's license, multi-engine rating, certified flight instructor rating, certified flight instructor instrument rating, airline transport pilot rating, and type rating. The estimated cost for this training, taken privately, is more than $30,000. One alternative to private training is to serve as a pilot in the U.S. military. A college degree in business management or liberal arts, with studies in aviation, meteorology, or other sciences is recommended.

Experience, Skills, and Personality Traits

Pilots usually obtain flight training in the military, with a small commuter or regional airline, or through civilian flying schools that have FAA certification. They must be able to make decisions quickly and accurately under pressure as flying conditions vary, and they must be able to supervise other personnel. They must be in excellent physical condition. Even though English is the universal language of the aviation industry, knowledge of a foreign language is desirable for those who want to fly international routes or for international airlines.

Unions and Associations

Most commercial airline pilots belong to the Air Line Pilots Association, International (ALPA), or the Allied Pilots Association (American Airlines).

Tips for Entry

1. Start with civilian flying lessons or join the military, particularly the U.S. Air Force.
2. Attend a college that offers a degree in aviation or a related field or offers programs that include flight training.
3. Work part-time within the airline industry so you understand how each component contributes to an airline's success.
4. Read trade publications either by subscription or on-line.

AIRCRAFT MECHANIC

CAREER PROFILE

Duties: Services and repairs aircraft and engines

Alternate Title(s): Aircraft Engine Specialist; Aviation Maintenance Technician; A&P (Airframe and Power-plant) Mechanic; Airframe, Powerplant, and Avionics Aviation Maintenance Technician

Salary Range: $12 to $25 per hour; $26,000 to $54,000 annually

Employment Prospects: Good to excellent

Advancement Prospects: Good

Best Geographical Location(s): Anyplace where there is an airport; in California and Washington state where aircraft companies are located; near Federal Aviation Administration operations in Atlantic City, N.J.; Oklahoma City, Okla.; and Washington, D.C.

Prerequisites:

Education or Training—Training at approved two- and four-year trade schools in avionics, aviation technology, or aviation maintenance management; computer training; knowledge of engines and other mechanical applications in an aircraft

Experience—Work in an aircraft repair and maintenance shop or with the military

Special Skills and Personality Traits—Responsible; thorough; agile; able to work without constant supervision

Licensure/Certification—Aircraft Inspector's Authorization

CAREER LADDER

```
┌─────────────────────────────────┐
│    Lead Mechanic (Crew Chief)   │
└─────────────────────────────────┘

┌─────────────────────────────────┐
│            Inspector            │
└─────────────────────────────────┘

┌─────────────────────────────────┐
│         Shop Supervisor         │
└─────────────────────────────────┘

┌─────────────────────────────────┐
│        Aircraft Mechanic        │
└─────────────────────────────────┘
```

Position Description

Aircraft Mechanics service and repair aircraft and aircraft engines to ensure the safe and dependable performance of the aircraft. They perform routine maintenance and inspections as required by the Federal Aviation Administration (FAA). Planes are inspected after having been flown a specific number of hours, days, cycles of operations (take-offs and landings), or any combination of the three or when the FAA issues an inspection notice because a problem has been found in other planes of the same type.

Some Aircraft Mechanics work only on preventive maintenance, checking the accessories, engines, instruments, landing gear, and pressurized sections (brakes, valves, pumps, and air-conditioning systems). They use precision instruments to gauge parts for wear and X-ray or magnetic inspection equipment to detect cracks that cannot be seen in a visual inspection. Newer, more sophisticated aircraft have monitoring systems with electronic boxes and consoles that supply important diagnostic data to the mechanic. Should the Aircraft Mechanic find a worn part, he or she replaces or repairs it. Some Aircraft Mechanics, called aircraft engine specialists, work only on engines. Others may lubricate moving parts or replace fluids.

In some cases a pilot may mention a problem to the Aircraft Mechanic, or the mechanic may listen to an engine to "hear" how it is operating. Using blueprints and maintenance manuals they determine how the repair should be made and whether it means installing a new system or adjusting the existing one. They then run tests to ensure that the system is running correctly.

Aircraft Mechanics may work on only one type of aircraft or on several types, including jets, propeller-driven planes, and helicopters. In working for an airline, they may specialize in just one section of one type of aircraft. If the company is small, however, they may work on anything that flies. With aircraft relying more on electronic systems to help fly and land planes, more Aircraft Mechanics find a need to work on the electronic systems. Depending on the type of aircraft maintained, mechanics may need to know the newest computerized aircraft being produced as well as maintain an aging fleet.

If the aircraft can be brought into a hangar, then the work is indoors. However, if for some reason it cannot be (the hangars are too full), then the work is outdoors in all types of weather. As there is considerable noise around an airfield, ear protectors usually are worn. Once a repair or replacement is made, a report is filed detailing what was done and when, including when in the aircraft's life (how many hours flown, how many days, and how many cycles) the work was done.

Overtime is common, so the workweek may well be more than 40 hours, including evening and weekend shifts. Because so many lives are dependent upon the aircraft being safe and the mechanic works under tight time schedules, this work can be stressful.

Although most Aircraft Mechanics may not be required to travel as part of their job, the abundance of jobs in almost any part of the country means it is fairly easy to move to a different geographical location.

Salaries

Aircraft Mechanics may work on an hourly basis, with salaries ranging from $12.00 to $25.00 an hour, or an annual salary of up to $54,000 or more. Smaller, newer airlines may pay less than larger ones. Nonunion jobs tend to pay less than do those under union contracts. Aircraft Mechanics who work for commercial airlines receive free or reduced-cost travel for themselves and their immediate families.

Employment Prospects

Airlines, aircraft and parts manufacturers, airports, aircraft service companies, and various government agencies hire Aircraft Mechanics. The number of jobs, particularly at smaller, newer airlines, is expected to grow over the next decade. Competition for positions with larger airlines that pay more is keen. The number of positions available with the military depends on the size of its aircraft fleet.

Advancement Prospects

Experienced Aircraft Mechanics can advance to lead mechanic (crew chief), inspector, or shop supervisor. Airlines give exams for promotions. Other advancement possi-

bilities include executive positions and starting an aircraft repair business.

Education or Training

A high school diploma or GED is a minimum requirement, with training in airframe and powerplant (A & P) mechanics and at least 18 months of on-the-job training and experience. Courses in chemistry, computer science, electronics, math, mechanical drawing, and physics are helpful. A good command of written English is required to complete maintenance reports. Aircraft Mechanics must take at least 16 hours of training every two years to maintain their certification. Avionics trade schools must provide 1,900 actual class hours of training over a 24- to 30-month period.

Special Requirements

The Federal Aviation Administration certifies an Aircraft Mechanic as airframe mechanic, powerplant mechanic, airframe and powerplant (A & P) mechanic, or avionics repair specialist. Those who have been certified as an inspector (obtainable after three years as an A & P mechanic) can approve the work done by other mechanics.

Experience, Skills, and Personality Traits

Military experience with aircraft maintenance is a plus to civilian employers. Self-motivation, enthusiasm, and the ability to pay attention to minute details are important traits. An Aircraft Mechanic should be agile enough to reach into and around the various parts of a plane and to climb onto a plane's wing to perform some duties.

Unions and Associations

The Aircraft Mechanics Fraternal Association is a craft oriented, independent aviation union working to maintain and improve benefits, wages, and working conditions. The International Association of Machinists and Aerospace Workers and the Transport Workers Union of America are the biggest unions, although the International Brotherhood of Teamsters represents some mechanics. The Professional Aviation Maintenance Association also provides support and services to Aircraft Mechanics.

Tips for Entry

1. Become familiar with general engine repair by taking courses or reading with a specific emphasis in aircraft engine maintenance.
2. Talk with aircraft mechanics, asking their advice about career choices, internships, and apprenticeship programs.
3. Establish a network of people in the industry by attending local union functions.
4. Subscribe to trade publications or read about current trends and developments online.

AIRPORT MANAGER

CAREER PROFILE

Duties: Oversees all business functions and operations of an airport, including security, staff policies and procedures, capital improvements, retail outlets, airline sales desks, gates, and ramps

Alternate Title(s): Airport Executive Director

Salary Range: $18,000 to $220,000

Employment Prospects: Fair

Advancement Prospects: Fair

Best Geographical Location: Any location with an airport

Prerequisites:

Education or Training—Degree in aviation management, business administration, or engineering; lesser degree for assistant airport manager position

Experience—Work in management, particularly at an airport

Special Skills and Personality Traits—Creativity; strong social skills; good oral and written communication skills; time management skills; ability to handle emergencies

Licensure/Certification—Pilot's license may be helpful

CAREER LADDER

```
┌─────────────────────────────────────┐
│  Director, State Aviation Authority  │
└─────────────────────────────────────┘

┌─────────────────────────────────────┐
│           Airport Manager            │
└─────────────────────────────────────┘

┌─────────────────────────────────────┐
│      Airport Operations Manager      │
└─────────────────────────────────────┘

┌─────────────────────────────────────┐
│   Airport Management, U.S. Air Force │
└─────────────────────────────────────┘
```

Position Description

An Airport Manager administers and supervises the business of the airport, including budgeting, terminal operations, contract and grant administration, marketing and promotion, public information, ground transportation, and other matters of concern pertaining to the safe and efficient operation of the facility. Whether large or small, there are a huge variety of functions at an airport besides planes taking off and landing. The Airport Manager conducts market analyses to determine who is using the airport and who could be using it, whether it is for passenger or cargo service. After identifying the air service needs of the community, a marketing strategy is developed and implemented to obtain the required service, whether it is trying to bring in a new airline, adding a new destination, or implementing additional cargo service.

Once that service is obtained, the Airport Manager, in conjunction with the airline, promotes the new service to the public, travel agents, the business community, and others within the air transportation industry, either through the in-house public relations and marketing offices or through outside advertising and public relations firms.

The Airport Manager oversees all responses to written and verbal requests from the media and the public and is the official spokesperson for the airport (even if there is a public relations office). This may include speeches at public and private forums and dealing with any of the relevant issues on aviation and the airport. An airport almost always suffers from a NIMBY (not in my backyard) complex, so the manager must deal with neighbors who complain about noise, traffic, pollution, and other matters.

Any airport will have a number of leases, which may include car rental agencies; airlines for gate space; taxis, limousines, and courtesy shuttles; hotels; and food and other retail concessions. The Airport Manager coordinates the preparation and negotiation of these leases and agreements and makes sure all leasers comply with the contract and airport rules and regulations.

If an outside contractor has to be hired to complete airport maintenance—including expansion, renovations, or repairs—the Airport Manager develops the bid specifications (sometimes in conjunction with airport consultants and engineers) for contracts, handles negotiations, and works to assure all contracts are completed within the negotiated terms. The Airport Manager identifies sources of grant funding and meets with federal and state agencies to develop grant programs for the continued development and maintenance of the airport.

Safety is a primary concern of any airport, so the manager must oversee the proper operation of the airport facilities, storage areas, and public and private spaces to ensure compliance with regulations. An emergency plan must be developed, practiced, and implemented for times when a crisis might arise. An airport must comply with many federal, state, and local regulatory requirements, so the manager must have a thorough knowledge of these requirements and must ensure that the airport complies with them. While all of these duties come under the purview of the Airport Manager, they may be assigned to appropriate personnel, so the manager must interview, hire, and supervise qualified people to run these operations.

As military airports are converted to general aviation airports, an Airport Manager may be hired to create and perhaps implement a development plan to market the airport and convert its operation from military to commercial use.

Because the manager must attend frequent meetings with federal, state, and regional elected and appointed officials, as well as industry seminars and conferences, there can be significant travel involved with this position.

An assistant airport manager, who reports to the Airport Manager, may be in charge of such departments as airport maintenance, equipment, and general office work, including typing, filing, project management, and providing phone support.

Salaries

An Airport Manager's salary may range from $18,000 to $220,000, depending on the size, scope, and location of the airport and the manager's experience and qualifications. An airport that hires a qualified Airport Manager may pay for relocation costs. Full-time Airport Managers usually receive vacation and health leave and life and medical insurance. They may also be eligible for a retirement investment program.

Employment Prospects

Airport management is very stressful, so there is some burnout and turnover, offering a consistent, although not huge, opportunity for employment in this field.

Advancement Prospects

Assistant airport managers may look forward to advancement to a manager's position. Managers may be promoted to a position as the director of a state aviation office, overseeing the operation of several airports within the state.

Education and Training

An Airport Manager should have a college degree in aviation or airport management, business administration, marketing communications, or a related field, although in some cases previous positions that include extensive supervisory experience may be sufficient. Although not necessary, a pilot's license may be helpful.

Experience, Skills, and Personality Traits

Previous experience supervising a large number of people and in airport administration (either general, commercial, or military) is required. The manager must be able to work well with a number of people and be able to respond quickly and efficiently to emergency situations. Because many airport activities require a computer, a manager should be familiar with a number of software programs.

Unions and Associations

There are no unions for Airport Managers, but the American Association of Aviation Executives provides seminars, publications, accreditation, and assistance to those in this field.

Tips for Entry

1. Work in a management position, preferably within the travel industry.
2. Attend meetings of the American Association of Aviation Executives to meet airport managers who know about internships and job openings.
3. Keep abreast of airport and airline issues, particularly security, by reading trade publications by subscription or on-line.

FLIGHT ATTENDANT

CAREER PROFILE

Duties: Instructs passengers during boarding, flight, and arrival; tends to passengers' comfort; serves food and beverages; maintains cabin rules during flight; instructs passengers in case of emergency

Alternate Title(s): None

Salary Range: $15,000 to $85,000

Employment Prospects: Good to excellent

Advancement Prospects: Good

Best Geographical Location(s): Areas with major airline hubs are best, but attendants can commute to their "home" airport

Prerequisites:

Education and Training—At least two years of college; experience dealing with people

Experience—Jobs that require dealing with people provide an excellent background

Special Skills and Personality Traits—Must be able to handle emergencies; willing to work nights, weekends, and holidays; interpersonal skills

Licensure/Certification—Certification in CPR may be required

CAREER LADDER

> **Customer Service Specialist**

> **Lead Attendant**

> **Flight Attendant**

Position Description

Flight Attendants are charged primarily with the safety of their passengers from the moment they enter an airplane until they leave. They instruct passengers on safety procedures dealing with seat belts, seats, oxygen masks, and emergency evacuations and landings. They also try to make the flight as comfortable as possible for passengers by providing some food (less frequently these days) and beverages, pillows, blankets (also less frequently these days), and other items as dictated by the individual airline. This means attendants are on their feet for most of the flight.

Generally, Flight Attendants work 75 to 85 flight hours per month and about the same amount of time preparing the plane for the flight, writing postflight reports, and performing other nonflying duties. They are expected to work weekends, evenings, and holidays. When they have a layover away from home, the airline provides for their hotel rooms, meals, and other related expenses. Because the Flight Attendant's schedule can have predictable days home, many attendants take college courses, volunteer, or work on other long-term goals.

Because attendants work in a moving vehicle that is subject to sudden wind shifts, they are susceptible to injuries when there is unexpected turbulence. Other injuries may occur when opening overhead bin doors or from lifting heavy luggage into and out of the bins. Unusual eating and sleeping patterns and heavy stress from a high-pressure job and occasional dealings with difficult passengers can also cause adverse health reactions. Frequent pressure changes within the aircraft (during takeoffs and landings) and breathing recycled air are other factors that may take a toll on the body. Flight Attendants may be required to administer CPR or other emergency procedures when a passenger or crewmember suffers a heart attack or other ailment.

Attendants bid for the routes they want, usually on a monthly basis, with the first choice going to those with the most seniority. Attendants and their immediate family members receive free or discounted travel on their own airline and most other airlines, although it may be on a standby basis.

Salaries

Salaries are based on seniority and the contract agreed to by the union members and the individual airlines. Additional pay may be earned by working overnight or international flights, working holidays, or assuming more responsible jobs. These may include completing flight-related paperwork or serving as a purser (keeping track of all monetary transactions during the flight, including the purchase of alcoholic beverages, movie headsets, and duty-free items on international flights). A per diem is provided for meals and travel expenses. Among the best benefits are free or reduced airfares for personal travel and that of their immediate families on their own airline and on other carriers. Attendants must usually pay for their own uniforms, although cleaning and upkeep expenses may be covered by the airline. Life and health insurance and annual and sick leave are usually part of the pay package. Retirement and stock investment programs may also be available.

Employment Prospects

Employment prospects for Flight Attendants are good to excellent. Although Flight Attendants are hired starting at age 18, there is a constant turnover, either from those who retire or leave due to work-related stress or the desire to spend more time with their family. Others leave to work for private companies with their own planes.

Advancement Prospects

Advancement is primarily through seniority, as more senior attendants retire and positions of supervising or lead attendant open up. The upheaval and reduction in airline schedules in late 2001 and early 2002 brought a mixed bag of employment and advancement availability. Many positions were eliminated, and many Flight Attendants changed careers rather than face potential danger from terrorists and more stringent duty requirements. Flight Attendants can also become instructors or move into other public contact positions.

Education and Training

Most airlines prefer at least two years of college with a focus on psychology, public speaking, travel and tourism, and other human relations courses. Those who want to fly international routes or for international airlines must have proficient command of at least one language other than English.

Training ranges from four to seven weeks and can be provided by the airline (including transportation to the education center, meals, lodging, and supplies), although some airlines charge for this education. Training includes flight regulations and onboard duties, company policies, first aid, use of a portable automatic external defibrillator (for heart attacks), emergency landing procedures, water survival maneuvers, dealing with difficult passengers, and most important recently, handling terrorists and hijacking conditions. For those who plan to work international routes, there is training in passport and customs procedures.

Flight Attendants also receive practice training before being assigned to a route. Even then, most new attendants are placed on a reserve status and are called in only for sick or vacation relief or when extra flights are added. While in this reserve status, attendants must be available for service, often on short notice.

Refresher courses, usually lasting a couple of days, are given annually and as situations warrant.

Special Requirements

Certification in cardiopulmonary resuscitation (CPR) may be required.

Experience, Skills, and Personality Traits

Flight Attendants must be tactful and resourceful in possible emergency situations. Flight Attendants generally must meet height and weight specifications, have excellent vision, and be articulate. Prior work experience including extensive dealings with customers provides a good foundation for this position.

Unions and Associations

The primary unions are the Association of Flight Attendants, representing 50,000 attendants at 26 airlines, and the Association of Professional Flight Attendants, representing more than 23,000 attendants at American Airlines.

Tips for Entry

1. Work in a position that deals with the public.
2. Read trade publications in print and on-line.
3. Contact airlines for internships.
4. Attend any events held by local Flight Attendant association chapters to establish networking contacts and possible mentoring situations.

AIR COURIER

CAREER PROFILE

Duties: Accompanies time-sensitive packages and shipments; carries shipping papers

Alternate Title(s): Traveling Messenger

Salary Range: None

Employment Prospects: Good

Advancement Prospects: Good

Best Geographical Location(s): New York, Miami, San Francisco, Los Angeles, Chicago, Boston, and Orlando in the United States; Toronto, Vancouver, and Montreal in Canada

Prerequisites:

Education and Training—None

Experience—None

Special Skills and Personality Traits—Able and eager to travel to domestic and foreign destinations; neat appearance and dress

Licensure/Certification—Valid passport

CAREER LADDER

```
┌─────────────────────────────┐
│   Independent Air Courier   │
└─────────────────────────────┘

┌─────────────────────────────┐
│    Contract Air Courier     │
└─────────────────────────────┘
```

Position Description

Most Air Couriers work for one or more courier associations. Annual fees run about $50 a year, or a lifetime membership costs about $175. Some courier companies also sell companion (spouse) memberships, ranging from $65 for one year to $199 for lifetime membership.

Once an Air Courier has been accepted by a courier company, he or she specifies which destinations are of interest and when he or she is available or wants to fly. Assignments may be at a moment's notice (often at no ticket expense for the courier) or may be scheduled as early as a few months in advance. Tickets are almost always for round-trip airfare—priced at 30 to 85 percent off regular fares (last minute special or LMS)—and the trips are usually for seven days or more. Sometimes the Air Courier accompanies a shipment on the return flight. Some examples of recent ticket prices are $400 from Los Angeles to Bangkok, $300 from New York to Hong Kong, $74 from Miami to Chicago, and $200 from New York to Rio de Janeiro. Airfare bargains reflect the regular travel

season, with lower fares available off-peak and higher fares in the summer. The tickets are for coach seats, but couriers can upgrade at their own expense.

At check-in, the Air Courier meets with an agent from the courier company and receives the necessary paperwork (shipping manifest) that is presented to a customs agent. Upon arrival at the destination, the courier presents the documentation to the firm's representative, who then assumes responsibility for the shipment. The courier company is responsible for clearing customs at both ends of the trip. The Air Courier is then free to spend time as he or she wishes until the return flight. They may fly on to other countries at their own expense if they wish. During the trip, the courier is responsible for all lodging, meals, and rental car expenses.

There should be no concern about escorting illegal materials. The courier companies are respectable (FedEx, DHL, etc.) and expect their shipments to be examined by airport customs officials. Courier companies employ Air Couriers for several reasons: cargo travels less expensively as passenger baggage than as cargo; material being shipped is time-sensitive and cannot languish in a cargo storage area; and the courier company may not have enough items to ship in one of their own planes.

Although there may be some restrictions on the amount of luggage an Air Courier can take (because the shipment is traveling as the courier's baggage), some companies allow two suitcases for trips that last two weeks or longer. Others may request a small fee to take luggage other than a carry-on bag. Air Couriers are expected to dress neatly, and business attire is desirable.

Salaries

Air Couriers are unpaid. Instead, they receive transportation to foreign countries at greatly reduced prices or even for free. Some courier associations provide a mileage club with benefits, and airlines generally award miles toward their frequent-flier programs.

Employment Prospects

There is always a need for Air Couriers, with many companies shipping to destinations on a daily basis.

Advancement Prospects

An Air Courier can advance to management within a courier company or start his or her own business by contracting with one or more shipping companies.

Education and Training

There are no educational or training requirements to be an Air Courier.

Experience, Skills, and Personality Traits

Air Couriers should be flexible in their time schedules, polite, and interested in domestic and foreign travel.

Unions and Associations

Among the associations and companies operating Air Courier businesses are the International Association for Air Travel Couriers, the International Association of Air Travel Carriers, Courier Travel, and the Air Couriers Association.

Tips for Entry

1. Talk with Air Couriers, asking their advice about their experiences.
2. Subscribe to trade publications or read about current trends and developments on-line.

AIR TRAFFIC CONTROLLER

CAREER PROFILE

Duties: Controls the movement of aircraft safely through the skies, between airports, and on the ground

Alternate Title(s): Airfield Operations Specialist

Salary Range: $40,000 to $130,000

Employment Prospects: Fair

Advancement Prospects: Fair

Best Geographical Location: Herndon, Va. (location of the Federal Aviation Administration's Traffic Control Systems Command Center); Atlantic City, N.J. (the FAA's national experimental center); Oklahoma City (the FAA's academy); areas with a large concentration of commercial air traffic

Prerequisites:

Education and Training—College degree, followed by training at the FAA academy

Experience—Background as a pilot, navigator, or military flight controller is helpful

Special Skills and Personality Traits—Controllers must be articulate to assure pilots can understand their instructions; intelligent; have a good memory and be able to concentrate despite numerous distractions

Licensure/Certification—FAA license

CAREER LADDER

```
┌─────────────────────────────────┐
│  Manager, Flight Service Station │
└─────────────────────────────────┘

┌─────────────────────────────────┐
│   Arrival, Departure, Local, or  │
│        Ground Controller         │
└─────────────────────────────────┘

┌─────────────────────────────────┐
│    Pilot, Navigator, or Military │
│        Flight Controller         │
└─────────────────────────────────┘
```

Position Description

Air Traffic Controllers are in charge of assuring the safe movement of commercial and private (or general aviation) aircraft on the ground and through the air. These flights carry more than 1 million passengers a day. They must concentrate on safety by keeping the aircraft a prescribed distance apart horizontally and vertically (2000 feet vertically between planes at 29,000 feet or above, flying along or near the same flight path), and make sure they operate efficiently to avoid flight delays. They rely on radar and visual observation, communicating with pilots about other traffic in the area and any changing weather conditions, including any sudden changes in wind speed and direction.

Different controllers handle different parts of the aircraft's movement. One controller may direct an inbound or arriving pilot to a runway or into a holding pattern, depending on other traffic and conditions in the area when the aircraft is many miles away. He or she remains in contact with controllers in other centers to make sure planes keep a safe distance from one another and do not arrive at the airport at the same time, at the same speed and altitude, or on the same flight path.

Another controller takes over as the pilot nears the airport and places the plane into the landing pattern. Finally, a ground controller directs it to the appropriate taxiway and its assigned airport gate. The reverse is true for departures, with such responsibilities as notifying the pilot of the wind and weather conditions, assigning an altitude and direction, and notifying the controller in the next tower along the route that the plane is about to leave one control center and enter the next.

There are 21 control centers across the country with 300 to 700 controllers. Busy airports may have 150 controllers or more on duty during peak travel times. Each team of controllers handles several planes at the same time: those approaching the airport's airspace and those about to land.

Other controllers work in more than 100 flight service stations around the country, providing pilots with weather and routing information, terrain information, and any other data that will help assure the safety of the aircraft. Although flight service station specialists may assist in emergency situations, they do not actively direct air traffic. The entire system is under the control of the David J. Hurley Air Traffic Control System Command Center in Herndon, Va., a suburb of Washington, D.C. Controllers there keep watch over the entire system to eliminate traffic jams and provide guidance when there is a problem, such as fog or a bad storm system that could adversely affect traffic going into a specific geographical area.

Controllers use glowing green computer radar displays to track all aircraft. By the end of 2010, they will use larger full-color monitors with zoom capabilities and touch screen options for changing radio frequencies to communicate with pilots and others.

Controllers must pass a physical examination each year and a job performance examination twice each year. Failure to become certified in any position at a facility within a specified time may result in dismissal. Controllers also are subject to drug screening as a condition of continuing employment.

Salaries

Air Traffic Controllers enjoy high salaries and excellent benefits. In the year 2000, most flight controllers earned between $62,000 and $101,000 plus overtime pay. The U.S. Federal government employs nearly 90 percent of all flight controllers. Controllers generally work a 40-hour week, but there may be overtime, particularly in the busiest centers that operate around the clock. Night and weekend shifts are rotated.

Controllers at the busiest facilities earn more pay than those at quieter centers. Paid vacation is based on years of service and runs from 13 to 26 days per year, plus 13 days of sick leave. Other benefits include life and medical insurance. Controllers may retire at age 50 with 20 years of active service or after 25 years at any age. This is younger than most federal employees. Those who manage air traffic must retire by age 56.

Employment Prospects

Although the demand for Air Traffic Controllers is not high at the moment, about half of the nation's controllers are due to retire by 2010, so employment opportunities will increase.

Advancement Prospects

Air Traffic Controllers can be promoted to a management position, overseeing the operation of a control center. This can be done by transferring to a position at a different location and by taking on additional responsibilities, continuing classroom instruction, and independent study.

Education and Training

The Federal Aviation Administration is in charge of administering a series of written and psychological tests, over a week's period of time, at the Mike Monroney Aeronautical Center in Oklahoma City to determine how appropriate a candidate is for a flight controller position. Applicants generally are expected to have a college degree or a comparable number of years of work experience, or a combination of both. Candidates for towers and other centers must be younger than 30 years of age. Those who are older may qualify for flight service stations.

The first phase of the FAA Academy's multiyear training program lasts seven months, covering the fundamentals of the system, agency regulations, aircraft performance characteristics, and the equipment. Prospective controllers must then pass another series of examinations that test their judgment, problem-solving skills, aircraft recognition, and other skills that may be involved in the performance of the job. Students can choose between en route or terminal operations for their training.

The military is another avenue for the necessary training, with opportunities in the U.S. Air Force, Army, Marine Corps, Navy Coast Guard, and Air National Guard. In addition, there are 14 colleges that offer degrees in aviation administration with an emphasis on air traffic control.

Special Requirements

All Air Traffic Controllers must have an FAA license, which is awarded after successful completion of one of the training programs described above.

Experience, Skills, and Personality Traits

Experience as a pilot, navigator, or military aircraft controller is helpful. Controllers must be able to think quickly, handle the stress of controlling several planes and functions simultaneously, and be able to work different shifts. Three-dimensional spatial capabilities, decisiveness, and a good memory are prime requirements. All applicants must pass drug screening tests. Controllers should be articulate so pilots can understand the instructions they are given.

Unions and Associations

The National Air Traffic Controllers Association is the exclusive bargaining representative for Federal Aviation Administration Air Traffic Controllers, representing more than 15,000 Air Traffic Controllers throughout the United States, Puerto Rico, and Guam.

Tips for Entry

1. Study aviation, meteorology, and other related sciences.
2. Take flying lessons to become familiar with airplanes and airport functions.
3. Meet other Air Traffic Controllers to learn about internships and job openings.
4. Read such trade publications as *Aviation Weekly*, either by subscription or on-line, to keep abreast of industry news.

TRAIN CONDUCTOR

CAREER PROFILE

Duties: Oversees and coordinates all operations of a train under the supervision of the engineer

Alternate Title(s): Pullman Conductor; Sleeping Car Conductor; Yard Conductor; Assistant Brakeman; Trainman

Salary Range: $18 to $21 per hour; $37,000 to $44,000 annually

Employment Prospects: Fair

Advancement Prospects: Fair

Best Geographical Location(s): Wherever trains operate

Prerequisites:

Education and Training—High school diploma; conductor trainee courses

Experience—Work as a brakeman/woman is required; mechanical experience

Special Skills and Personality Traits—Conscientious; able to lift weights of 85 pounds or more

Licensure/Certification—None

CAREER LADDER

```
┌─────────────────────────────┐
│       Train Engineer        │
└─────────────────────────────┘

┌─────────────────────────────┐
│       Train Conductor       │
└─────────────────────────────┘

┌─────────────────────────────┐
│      Conductor Trainee      │
└─────────────────────────────┘
```

Position Description

A Conductor's most visible duties involve the train's passengers. He or she assists them boarding the train, assuring they are on the right train, directing them to their car or seat, and helping them stow their luggage. He or she answers questions about the time schedule and railroad operation. The Conductor also announces the train's arrival at each station and opens and closes the train's doors. After the passengers have boarded or disembarked the train, the Conductor signals the train operator when to start the train.

When passengers occupy a sleeping or Pullman car and lounge cars, the Conductor supervises the duties of the employees who provide services to the passengers. This may include porters, maids, and meal servers.

Before the passengers board, the Train Conductor reads the train orders and checks the timetable and other written instructions from the train dispatcher. These items are discussed with the engineer and other train crewmembers. The engineer and Train Conductor make sure their watches are in agreement so the train will arrive and depart on schedule.

The Train Conductor also supervises the workers who inspect various operating parts of the train including air brakes, air hoses, couplings, and journal boxes and the workers who regulate air-conditioning, lighting, and heating to ensure safety and comfort to passengers. At the end of the run, the Train Conductor prepares reports, describing and noting the reason for any accidents, unscheduled stops, or delays. Other reports note the number of passengers and the destinations of and accommodations occupied by each passenger.

Because many trains use the same tracks in some parts of the country (particularly the Northeast corridor between Boston and Washington, D.C.), it is important to maintain the proper speed. A train that goes too fast, besides possibly jeopardizing the safety of the train and passengers, could catch up with another train, enter track that should be occupied by another train, or arrive at a station while another train is there. A train leaving a station too early could leave some passengers stranded. With hand signals, a radiotelephone, or a lantern, the Train Conductor lets the engineer know that all passengers are clear of the doorways and that it is safe to proceed to the next station.

On a freight train, the Train Conductor supervises the duties of the train crew involved in moving the freight. Many of these duties are the same as on a passenger train, including reading train orders (where the train is going and the time schedule) and other written instructions from the train dispatcher.

The freight Train Conductor inspects or supervises those who inspect the couplings and air hoses, making sure they are securely fastened; the journal boxes to make sure they are lubricated; and the handbrakes on cars, making sure they are released before the train begins to run. He or she inspects freight cars to ensure that they are securely sealed. He or she records the number of cars and corresponding seal number and compares the listings with the waybill to ensure accuracy of routes and destinations. A yard conductor supervises the activities of the railroad yard crew and has very little (if any) contact with the traveling public.

Conductors work indoors (on trains) and outdoors, in all types of weather. They must be able to lift 80 pounds, the weight of the knuckle that connects two rail cars. They also travel extensively, although often covering the same routes and destinations, and often are away from home for days or weeks at a time. Conductors may be asked to be available for work 24 hours a day, seven days a week, with mandatory rest periods. Their work schedules can be irregular. Beginning Conductors may be required to work evening, weekend, and holiday shifts. Once a new Conductor has worked enough hours to earn seniority, he or she may be given a regularly scheduled assignment.

Because safety is such a primary issue, Conductors are subject to random alcohol and drug testing, per Federal Railroad Administration Guidelines, which demand a zero tolerance policy.

Salaries

Trainees are paid about $400 to $500 a week during training and some expenses, including lodging and meals; some transportation costs usually are covered during this training. Once past training, Conductors receive a portion (about 80 to 95 percent) of full salary increased annually for the first five years. The daily hourly rate for a Conductor averages between $18 and $21 per hour, while annual salaries range from $37,000 to $44,000. Medical and life insurance and annual and sick leave are provided, and Conductors usually may participate in a retirement plan, with company contributions to the Railroad Retirement Program.

Employment Prospects

Job opportunities are not abundant, due to consolidation of railroads and job duties. As salaries are fairly high and come with good benefits, and most train workers stay with this job as a lifelong career, competition is keen. The economy is another factor, and when it improves and intermodal (train and truck) transportation increases, then employment opportunities should improve.

Advancement Prospects

Some Conductors may want to or may be required to accept compulsory promotion to locomotive engineer and attend locomotive engineer training.

Education and Training

A high school diploma generally is required. Conductor trainees attend classroom and field instruction courses for sixteen weeks. Written exams are administered at the end of the training session and employees are placed on a probationary period for two months.

Experience, Skills, and Personality Traits

Work in other railroad jobs is essential, as people who have passed their tests on signals, timetables, operating rules, and related subjects almost always fill Conductor positions.

Conductors must have good oral and written communication skills and be able to make quick decisions. Passenger Train Conductors should be pleasant and have a good interpersonal and management aptitude.

Unions and Associations

The Train Service Union or Engineer's Union represents Train Conductors and works on safety and other issues of importance to conductors.

Tips for Entry

1. Talk with Conductors, asking their advice about career choices, internships, and apprenticeship programs.
2. Establish a network of people in the industry by attending local union functions.
3. Subscribe to trade publications or read about current trends and developments on-line.

TRAIN ENGINEER

CAREER PROFILE

Duties: Operate trains carrying cargo and passengers between stations

Alternate Title(s): Locomotive Engineer

Salary Range: $47,000 to $81,000 plus overtime pay

Employment Prospects: Good

Advancement Prospects: Fair

Best Geographical Location(s): Wherever trains operate, particularly cities with major terminals

Prerequisites:

Education and Training—High school diploma

Experience—Work as a brake operator or conductor

Special Skills and Personality Traits—Conscientious; excellent eyesight and hearing; must have excellent color vision

Licensure/Certification—Certification by the Federal Railroad Administration

CAREER LADDER

```
┌─────────────────────────────────────┐
│   Train Dispatcher or Train Master   │
└─────────────────────────────────────┘

┌─────────────────────────────────────┐
│           Train Engineer             │
└─────────────────────────────────────┘

┌─────────────────────────────────────┐
│           Train Conductor            │
└─────────────────────────────────────┘

┌─────────────────────────────────────┐
│             Yardmaster               │
└─────────────────────────────────────┘
```

Position Description

Train Engineers operate trains carrying cargo and passengers between stations. Before starting a trip, the engineer inspects the train, reporting major defects and implementing necessary adjustments. The engineer receives information about stops, delays, and train locations by communicating with the conductor and traffic control center personnel.

Once in operation, the engineer controls the throttle to start and accelerate the train and applies the air brakes or dynamic brakes to slow and stop it. To assure the smooth and safe operation of the train, he or she monitors gauges and meters that measure the speed, fuel, temperature, battery charge, and air pressure in the brake lines.

It is important that trains keep to a schedule or timetable. If a train is operated too fast or too slowly, it can interfere with other train traffic and impair the schedule of an entire track system. The Train Engineer must be thoroughly familiar with the signal systems, train yards, and terminals along his or her route. He or she should also be aware of the train's condition and makeup to allow for differences in reaction time depending on the number of cars, whether some or all of the cars are filled, the grade and condition of the rail, and other factors.

As trains run around the clock, a Train Engineer may have to work nights, weekends, and holidays and sometimes be away from home for days or weeks at a time. More senior engineers have some choice in selecting the shift they prefer.

Train Engineers must wear a uniform that is supplied by the company. Some Train Engineers work for municipal transportation systems (subways and streetcar operators), and while most of their duties are identical to those of passenger and freight trains, they may also be in charge of announcing stations, opening and closing doors, and making station and other announcements to the passengers. These engineers have slightly more contact with the public than Train Engineers who operate passenger and freight trains. All railroad employees are subject to periodic and random drug and alcohol tests while on duty.

Railroad engineers who handle passenger and freight trains have the most opportunity to travel. Railroad employees receive free or discounted travel options when on leisure travel.

Salaries

Of the four basic types of Train Engineer, those in charge of passenger trains earn the most, followed by through-freight engineers, local-way freight engineers, and then yard engineers. The range is from $47,000 to $81,000 plus overtime pay. Subway and streetcar engineers earn up to $24 an hour. Workers in the Northeast earn more than do those in other regions.

Employment Prospects

Although there has been some consolidation of railroad companies, the opportunity for employment is steady, particularly for Train Engineers. While lower-level jobs require little formal education, the position of Train Engineer requires additional education and continuing training courses. These additional requirements tend to limit the number of applicants for the position of Train Engineer.

Advancement Prospects

Train Engineers, with an appropriate education, may advance to management positions.

Education and Training

Beyond a high school diploma (or GED), a Train Engineer must take courses in locomotive operations. This can be done after several years of experience in the railroading business. Some colleges, like the National Academy of Railroad Sciences at Johnson County Community College in Kansas, offer an associate degree in railroad operations.

Special Requirements

A classroom and hands-on instruction course in locomotive operations, lasting about six months, is required by the Federal Railroad Administration. Certification includes passing tests covering the equipment, air brake systems fuel economy, train-handling techniques, and operating rules and regulations.

Experience, Skills, and Personality Traits

Train Engineers must be in good physical condition with excellent hearing and eyesight and perfect color vision. They also should have good hand–eye coordination, manual dexterity, and mechanical aptitude.

Unions and Associations

Most Train Engineers belong to the Brotherhood of Locomotive Engineers. Some belong to the United Transportation Union. Subway and streetcar engineers usually belong to the Amalgamated Transit Union or the Transport Workers Union of North America. Each union works toward improving salaries and working conditions and offers such benefits as legal counsel, continuing education, and retirement programs.

Tips for Entry

1. Become familiar with the railroad industry: try an entry-level position such as working as a yard laborer. Further training and advancement can lead to conductor and engineering jobs.
2. Talk with Train Engineers, asking their advice about career choices, internships, and apprenticeship programs.
3. Establish a network of people in the industry by attending local union functions.
4. Subscribe to trade publications or read about current trends and developments on-line.
5. If you are interested in finding a college offering courses in railroad operations, try entering associate degree railroad operations in an Internet search engine.

TOUR MOTORCOACH DRIVER

CAREER PROFILE

Duties: Drives passengers around a city for sightseeing or from one destination to another

Alternate Title(s): Tour Bus Operator

Salary Range: $10 to $20 an hour

Employment Prospects: Good

Advancement Prospects: Fair

Best Geographical Location(s): Anywhere across the country with a charter bus company

Prerequisites:

Education and Training—High school diploma; two to eight weeks of classroom and behind-the-wheel instruction; first aid; emergency evacuation procedures; able to read and speak English

Experience—Work experience as a Motorcoach Driver for a school system or municipal bus company; work experience as a truck driver

Special Skills and Personality Traits—Excellent driver; strong customer service skills; good sense of direction; able to read road maps and schedules; detail-oriented; able to manage large groups of people with varying needs; good oral and written communications skills; able to handle mental stress

Licensure/Certification—Commercial driver's license (CDL) for interstate bus trips on any bus with a capacity of 16 or more passengers

CAREER LADDER

```
┌─────────────────────────────┐
│     Owner, Bus Company      │
└─────────────────────────────┘

┌─────────────────────────────┐
│   Supervisor or Dispatcher  │
└─────────────────────────────┘

┌─────────────────────────────┐
│    Tour Motorcoach Driver   │
└─────────────────────────────┘

┌─────────────────────────────┐
│      Motorcoach Driver,     │
│    Local Transit Company    │
└─────────────────────────────┘
```

Position Description

By the very nature of the position, Motorcoach Drivers travel extensively. A Tour Motorcoach Driver transports passengers who are touring a city or region on special chartered tours and excursions. He or she picks up and drops off passengers at a predetermined spot, helps load luggage, and checks the number of passengers on the charter.

Safety is the primary concern, so the Motorcoach Driver must operate the bus safely. Meeting time schedules is another important concern, as the bus should not arrive late (thus missing the start of a ballgame, tour, concert, or other event) nor depart before the scheduled time (possibly causing passengers to miss the bus).

Even if there is a maintenance department for a fleet of buses, the driver should check the vehicle's brakes, fuel, lights, oil, tires, water supply, and windshield wipers before each departure. A Motorcoach Driver should also check for such safety equipment as fire extinguishers, first aid kits, and emergency flares. Motorcoach Drivers who drive across state or national boundaries must fulfill U.S. Department of Transportation (USDOT) regulations, including vehicle inspection reports, and record distances traveled and the time spent driving. A Motorcoach Driver usually works with a tour guide, so that their guests enjoy both a comfortable and informative trip.

The driving schedule may include holidays, weekends, and evenings, but drivers must still comply with Federal regulations that stipulate that they may drive only for 10 hours and work up to 15 hours (including driving and such nondriving duties as completing forms) before having eight hours off duty. A driver may not drive after working 70 hours within any eight-day period. The hours worked must be documented in a logbook. Many charter companies have equipped their buses with ergonomically designed seats and controls to make sitting for many hours more comfortable.

Because tour companies do not always have the maximum number of tours booked every day of the year, the work schedule can be part time and irregular. Although many tours last only one day, without an overnight stop, most last more than one day, and some may last a week or more. The Motorcoach Driver may be away from home for weeks at a time, with only a day or two to visit home every week, or may not have an assignment for weeks at a time, depending on seniority. Depending on the location of the company and where it schedules trips, the busy season most likely will be from May through August, when most people go on vacations.

Salaries

As part-time employees, Motorcoach Drivers start at about $10 an hour and with seniority may receive $20 an hour or more. Salaries are highest in the Northeast and much lower in the South. Some drivers are paid from the time they check in until the bus is parked for the night; others are paid a per diem rate, regardless of the hours worked. Motorcoach Drivers are given a limited per diem or are reimbursed for lodging and meal costs (but not personal phone calls or other personal expenses). That may mean the driver stays at a different hotel and eats at different restaurants, both of which will be less expensive than where the tour stays and eats. Motorcoach Drivers also may receive a uniform allowance to help defray or cover the costs of uniforms. They may also receive tips from the passengers on the trip. Motorcoach Drivers may receive vacation and sick leave and retirement investment options. Generally, Motorcoach Drivers receive free admission to museums and other attractions. Senior Motorcoach Drivers often are assigned their own coach (bus) so they are familiar with its operation.

Employment Prospects

Bus (municipal and school) and Motorcoach Drivers accounted for more than 650,000 jobs in 2000, with almost two-thirds of them employed by school districts. More than a third of them worked part time, so many of them often move to a company that offers more hours or higher pay or into other fields. Hence, employment prospects are good. Full-time Motorcoach Drivers are not affected by a downturn in the economy as quickly as are part-time drivers.

Advancement Prospects

Motorcoach Drivers can advance to supervisory or dispatcher positions or buy their own bus(es) and start their own motorcoach company. As most tour companies are small family businesses, advancement within these companies is limited.

Education and Training

Generally, the hiring company will give Motorcoach Drivers two to eight weeks of classroom and behind-the-wheel instruction, teaching Department of Transportation and company work rules, safety regulations, state and municipal driving regulations, safe driving practices, first aid, and emergency evacuation procedures. Driving practice on closed courses and on the road includes turns and other maneuvers, backing up, and driving on narrow roads. They may be asked to drive a scheduled trip with an experienced driver who evaluates driving performance and interaction with the passengers.

Although federal regulations govern how many hours a driver may work during a day and during an eight-day period, driving through heavy traffic, on monotonous interstate highways, and through busy city streets can be very stressful.

Special Requirements

Motorcoach Drivers must have a commercial driver's license (CDL) from the state where they live for interstate bus trips on any bus with a capacity of 16 or more passengers. They must pass a written test on the motor carrier safety regulations of the U.S. Department of Transportation.

They must be at least 21 years of age (although many companies prefer that drivers be at least 24 years of age with several years of bus or truck driving experience) and pass a physical exam once every two years that includes good hearing (ability to hear a forced whisper in one ear at not less than five feet, with or without a hearing aid); 20/40 vision (with or without glasses or corrective lenses) and a 70-degree field of vision in each eye; they must not be colorblind; they must have normal use of arms and legs and normal blood pressure; they may not use controlled substances unless prescribed by a licensed physician; and they may not have epilepsy or diabetes controlled by insulin.

Motorcoach Drivers must be tested for alcohol and drug use as a condition of employment and must take random tests while on duty. They must not have been convicted of a felony involving the use of a motor vehicle, a crime involving drugs, or a hit-and-run driving charge that resulted in injury or death. For international travel (between the United States and Canada), they must have two forms of picture identification, which may be a driver's license and a passport, or original birth certificate.

Experience, Skills, and Personality Traits

Motorcoach Drivers should have experience driving for a school district (or contract company) or municipal bus system.

They should be considerate, courteous, even-tempered, and conscientious. They should have good oral and written communications skills. They should be able to administer basic first aid and emergency resuscitation procedures. Motorcoach Drivers must be able to read and speak English well enough to read road signs, prepare reports, and communicate with law enforcement officers and the public.

Unions and Associations

The Amalgamated Transit Union represents more than 175,000 members, including bus, subway, light rail, and ferry operators. It lobbies Congress and other bodies about proposed legislation, offers a scholarship program to union members and their dependents for those interested in union issues, and negotiates contracts for its members.

Tips for Entry

1. Take courses in business, geography, and community relations.
2. Talk with Motorcoach Drivers, asking their advice about your career choices and career opportunities.
3. Establish a network of people in the industry by attending local union functions, if allowed.
4. Subscribe to trade publications or read about current trends and developments on-line.

CAR RENTAL MANAGER

CAREER PROFILE

Duties: Develops and manages all operations involved with a car rental agency

Alternate Title(s): None

Salary Range: $20,000 to $35,000, plus bonus

Employment Prospects: Fair to good

Advancement Prospects: Good

Best Geographical Location(s): Positions available throughout the country

Prerequisites:

Education and Training—College degree; communications and sales background; additional training provided by the hiring company

Experience—Customer service or sales background

Special Skills and Personality Traits—Manage stressful situations well; good oral and written communications; excellent interpersonal skills; basic computer skills; foreign language fluency is an asset; detail-oriented

Licensure/Certification—Valid driver's license

CAREER LADDER

```
┌─────────────────────────────┐
│      District Manager       │
└─────────────────────────────┘

┌─────────────────────────────┐
│     Car Rental Manager      │
└─────────────────────────────┘

┌─────────────────────────────┐
│        Rental Agent         │
└─────────────────────────────┘
```

Position Description

A Car Rental Manager is responsible for all activities at a car (and truck) rental agency, including the rental of cars to customers; selling optional coverages (e.g., insurance), services (e.g., cell phones, a future rental reservation), and logo merchandise (e.g., key chains, baseball caps, coffee mugs, umbrellas, watches, duffel bags, car safety kits, and car repair kits); answering telephone calls and e-mails; responding to customers' questions; and maintenance of the fleet.

The Car Rental Manager develops (or receives from a regional office) a sales objective detailing how many rental contracts and additional sales they want to make within the coming year. Then, a marketing plan is developed to promote the agency (sometimes in conjunction with other offices of the same rental company and sometimes with the assistance of a marketing company). A revenue and expense budget is developed that includes anticipated rentals and sales balanced against such overhead costs as utilities, staff salaries, repairs, and taxes to assure profitability.

Although the local office may have sales agents who visit local businesses, the Car Rental Manager may also make sales calls. The manager may also be required to negotiate all contracts with outside vendors of gasoline, auto repair parts, and office supplies.

A fair amount of time is spent on administrative duties, including interviewing, hiring, training, career coaching and management, performance reports, supervising, and firing employees. Such employees are sales agents, administrative staff, and repair and maintenance technicians. The manager or an assistant handles and tries to resolve all customer complaints. The manager must also handle the rental car inventory, coordinating the movement of cars among offices to assure the most efficient use of the rental car fleet. Because car rental agencies can be open 24 hours a day at busy airports, night, weekend, and holiday work can be expected.

Salaries

Salaries range from $20,000 to $35,000, plus bonuses for office performance above goals. Benefits may include health and life insurance, retirement account and investment opportunities, vacation and sick leave, free uniforms, and discounts on travel, including car rental and accommodations. Managers usually receive a company car and may receive tuition reimbursement and a car purchase/lease plan for family members. Relocation expenses are rarely covered.

Employment Prospects

While most car rental company offices are located at airports and in major cities, additional locations are opening in suburban communities, providing additional employment opportunities.

Advancement Prospects

Advancement opportunities are good as companies tend to promote from within, so rental agents can be promoted to assistant managers, managers, and regional or district managers. Other opportunities occur by switching from one company to another, or by opening a franchise.

Education and Training

A college degree in management or business is usually required. Good communication and computer skills are necessary, with some training in the sales and customer service fields. The company will supply additional paid training specific to that company's policies.

Experience, Skills, and Personality Traits

At least two years' experience in a high-volume managerial position in the retail, travel, car rental, or restaurant industry is required. The Car Rental Manager must be able to handle stressful situations well, particularly at times of high rental demand, such as during a convention. He or she must have good oral and written communication skills to be able to express the company's objectives to the employees, to deal with customers and vendors, and to complete daily reports to the regional or national office. This also requires excellent interpersonal skills. Because the environment can be fast-paced, it is important that the manager be able to work on multiple projects simultaneously, pay attention to details, and be able to define work priorities. Basic computer skills are essential. The command of a foreign language is helpful in many areas of the country. When a car rental agency is located at an airport, the Car Rental Manager must function as the liaison with the airport commission or board to ensure effective communication and to resolve any issues that may arise.

Unions and Associations

There is no union for Car Rental Managers. The Association for Car and Truck Rental Independents and Franchisees provides information of interest to the industry.

Tips for Entry

1. Learn the car rental business from the ground up, starting at a small suburban franchise and transferring to larger offices.
2. Talk with Car Rental Managers, asking their advice about career choices, internships, and apprenticeship programs.
3. Establish a network of people in the industry by attending local functions with auto rental personnel.
4. Subscribe to trade publications or read about current trends and developments on-line.

CRUISE TRAVEL

SHIP CAPTAIN

CAREER PROFILE

Duties: Directs all activities aboard ship; directs and navigates the ship

Alternate Title(s): None

Salary Range: $48,000 to $100,000

Employment Prospects: Fair to good

Advancement Prospects: Fair

Best Geographical Location(s): Major port cities; anywhere ships sail

Prerequisites:

Education and Training—Bachelor's degree from maritime school, with an emphasis on mathematics, physics, computers, and electronics

Experience—Previous work on a ship, with progressively more responsible positions

Special Skills and Personality Traits—Detail oriented; good oral and written communication skills; able to operate under pressure; good interpersonal skills

Licensure/Certification—Ship Captains on U.S. flagged (registered) vessels must be licensed by the Coast Guard

CAREER LADDER

```
┌─────────────────────────────┐
│       Ship Captain          │
└─────────────────────────────┘

┌─────────────────────────────┐
│     Chief or First Mate     │
└─────────────────────────────┘

┌─────────────────────────────┐
│ Second Mate or Second Officer│
└─────────────────────────────┘
```

Position Description

Ship Captains direct and navigate all kinds of ships. Some operate cruise ships, while others operate barges, ferries, dredges, freight and cargo ships, and other vessels. Ship Captains may be civilian or military employees.

The Captain sets the course and speed of a ship with the help of navigational aids, charts, celestial observations, compass, sexton, computers, and observations. They avoid hazards and other ships by using buoys, depth finders, lighthouses, lights, ship pilots, and radar. He or she directs the crew in steering the ship, operating the engines, signaling to other vessels, performing maintenance, and loading and unloading passengers or cargo. The Captain's primary concern is the safety of the ship, its crew, and its passengers.

On large ships, such as ocean liners, Captains may assign some duties to assistants, but they are ultimately responsible for the ship's business, including the logs of the ship's activities, weather, fuel consumption, navigational decisions, pollution control records, and cargo. They interview, hire, instruct, and coordinate the activities of such crewmembers as the mates, engineers, deckhands, electricians, machinery mechanics, and the radio officer.

On a cruise ship, the Captain socializes with the passengers on a daily basis, including a Captain's reception to which all passengers are invited and a Captain's cocktail party that may be limited to a select invitation list. He or she entertains an even smaller number of guests at the Captain's table in the dining room. The Captain may also invite passengers to take a tour of the bridge, where all the navigational work is done.

Although the situation may vary, the Captain usually is on duty seven days a week while at sea, standing watch in four-, eight-, or twelve-hour shifts during calm and inclement weather. A cruise Ship Captain works for two months and then is off for a month. The cruise line pays for transportation between the Captain's home and the ship. Ship Captains who work on freighters and other vessels in the Great Lakes area may not work in the winter when the lakes are frozen. Ship Captains who work in harbors and rivers may go home every night. Besides the benefit of possibly visiting exotic ports, the cruise's Ship Captain has the privilege of having his or her family travel with him or her, thus easing the months away from home.

Employment Prospects

There are few vacancies for Ship Captains aboard cruise ships. Commercial ships and the military have a fair number of openings for Ship Captains.

Advancement Prospects

A Ship Captain can move into cruise or freighter line management or start his or her own shipping or charter company.

Education and Training

A degree from the U.S. Merchant Marine Academy (USMMA) or one of six state Maritime academies (Texas, California, Maine, Massachusetts, New York, and Michigan) and the Paul Hall Center for Maritime Training and Education in Piney Point, Md., for Seafarers International Union membership is often required.

The USMMA is a military school in Kings Point, N.Y. It is run by the U.S. Department of Transportation and requires an appointment by a member of Congress. This four-year training leads to a bachelor of science degree and a U.S. Coast Guard license as a third mate or third assistant engineer or both. The Great Lakes Maritime Academy in Michigan trains officers for vessels that ply the Great Lakes only. The six state maritime academies offer a four-year bachelor's degree with programs in nautical science, marine transportation, or engineering.

Special Requirements

A ship Captain must possess a U.S. Coast Guard (USCG) master's license. All officers and operators of watercraft must have one or more of the nearly 60 different licenses issued by the U.S. Coast Guard.

Experience, Skills, and Personality Traits

Captains must have years of shipboard experience and be able to command a large number of crewmembers. He or she must be able to operate under extreme pressure, be social when dealing with cruise passengers, and be able to be away from home for long periods of time.

Unions and Associations

The Cruise Lines International Association and the International Council of Cruise Lines have information about various cruise lines. The American Maritime Officers Union was chartered in 1949 as the Brotherhood of Marine Engineers, an affiliate of the Seafarers International Union of North America. Today American Maritime Officers is an independent national union representing licensed officers in all sectors of the U.S.-flag merchant fleet, including oceangoing, Great Lakes, and inland-waters commercial, military support, and cruise vessels.

Tips for Entry

1. Visit, volunteer, or apply to work at your local marina or boat club to become familiar with boats and maritime rules and regulations.
2. Talk with Ship Captains, asking their advice about your career choices, internships, and apprenticeship programs.
3. Contact cruise lines for employment information.
4. Apply early to a merchant marine academy or other schools with maritime studies.

PURSER, CRUISE SHIP

CAREER PROFILE

Duties: Supervises all financial business functions of the ship

Alternate Title(s): None

Salary Range: $19,000 to $56,000

Employment Prospects: Fair to good

Advancement Prospects: Good

Best Geographical Location(s): Cruise ships leave from numerous ports along the U.S. coastline

Prerequisites:

Education and Training—A degree in hotel administration, finance, or accounting is required; one or more foreign languages are helpful

Experience—Must have several years of hotel or cruise ship management experience, with administration and accounting responsibilities

Special Skills and Personality Traits—Outgoing; open-minded and flexible; able to work with an international crew; able to perform well under pressure; Word, Excel, Power-Point, and Micros-Fidelio software knowledge may be required

CAREER LADDER

```
┌─────────────────────────────────┐
│  Chief Purser or Hotel Manager  │
└─────────────────────────────────┘

┌─────────────────────────────────┐
│            Purser               │
└─────────────────────────────────┘

┌─────────────────────────────────┐
│          Crew Purser            │
└─────────────────────────────────┘

┌─────────────────────────────────┐
│        Assistant Purser         │
└─────────────────────────────────┘
```

Position Description

The Cruise Ship Purser manages all administrative personnel on a cruise, answering to the Chief Purser and/or hotel manager, depending on the cruise line. The Purser and his or her staff ensure smooth and accurate onboard financial operations, including auditing, revenue, and money transactions; prompt processing of legal documents with port authorities; budgeting; coordination of payroll for onboard employees; and dealing with general accounting for the ship's food and beverage operation. This involves considerable bookkeeping, thus the need for familiarity with computer software programs. Pursers also take part in interviewing, hiring, training, promoting, and firing personnel. The Purser usually spends some time interacting with the passengers, particularly during meals and shore excursions.

The Purser's office spends a great deal of time with immigration and customs issues, completing port papers for clearance. Until this work is done, neither passengers nor crew can disembark from the ship. Each country—and sometimes, different ports within the same country—can have different clearance requirements. The Purser must maintain an excellent rapport with the various port authority personnel to help speed up the clearance in each port. Whenever a ship docks at a port for the first time (or for the first time of a new season), the clearance process can take an hour or more while the port authorities check the paperwork and have breakfast. With tighter security on cruise ships these days, this may also involve a shipboard search by drug-sniffing dogs.

Maintaining good relationships with dockside workers is also important to facilitate loading and unloading hundreds, or even thousands, of suitcases when the ship reaches a turnaround port where passengers will be embarking and disembarking. This helps ensure that luggage being loaded onto the ship is the right luggage, something that can be a problem when there are a number of ships departing on the same day.

On a large cruise ship, deputy and assistant Pursers aid the Chief Purser and may be assigned to specific jobs, including the direct operation of the front desk where they handle accommodation problems, complaints, changing currency, selling postage, mailing correspondence, handling safe deposit boxes, and keeping track of the passengers' statement (folio) of onboard charges (gift shop purchases, alcoholic beverages, spa treatments, or other items). They may also track credit card accounts and currency used onboard.

Many ships now use a cashless credit program, and all items and services purchased onboard are charged to the passenger's account. All passengers must register with the Purser's office during embarkation, completing an application form with a major credit card or checking account debit card that is registered with a major credit card. Those passengers who do not wish to use a credit card may leave a cash deposit and must be notified whenever their charges are near the limit of that deposit. The Purser's office provides an up-to-date balance to the passenger when requested at any time during the cruise.

The Crew Purser handles the administration of the crew, including sign-on and sign-off, cabin assignments, and crew identification cards. Because employees may be from many countries and the ship visits numerous countries, payroll may be done in cash that can run into the thousands or tens of thousands of dollars. If a crewmember is disembarking because of illness or is at the end of his or her contract, then special paperwork must be completed for that employee. Occasionally a passenger will die onboard, and it may be up to the Purser's office to complete the paperwork so the body can be taken ashore and to help comfort the family. Because this job requires weeks and months at sea, the Purser must not be prone to motion sickness (or take medication or wear seabands to offset the effects of motion sickness) and must be able to be away from friends and family for long periods of time.

Salaries

A Chief Purser can earn from $48,000 to $56,000, depending on experience, the size of the ship (and number of passengers and crew), and the cruise line. The salary range for a Purser is $25,000 to $36,000; Assistant Purser $19,000 to $35,000; Junior Assistant Purser $15,600 to $31,000; and Crew Purser $20,000 to $26,000.

The cruise line pays for almost all expenses, including food (dining with the passengers or in the officer's mess), accommodations (single cabin or stateroom), medical care, laundry, and roundtrip airfare between home and the port of embarkation. Additionally, under certain circumstances, U.S. citizens do not pay income tax if they are working on a ship that is not based in the States. In many cases, the Purser's office is open 24 hours a day, so a Purser or an assistant must be available at all times. Many shops and services in port cities offer discounts to crewmembers who show their ship identification card.

Employment Prospects

The cruise industry expects to grow as more cruise ships are constructed and brought into service, so there should be greater demand for Pursers, assistant pursers, and others in the Purser's office.

Advancement Prospects

Because of a fair amount of turnover in the cruise business, advancement is fairly easy, particularly for someone with the right background and a willingness to learn and be a team player. Pursers can advance to become a chief purser or hotel manager.

Education and Training

A degree in accounting or business management, with related studies in the hospitality field, is almost mandatory. Awareness of customs in various countries is helpful, as is a proficiency in at least one foreign language.

Experience, Skills, and Personality Traits

Hotel and bookkeeping experience (particularly in the hospitality industry) provide a good background. A Purser should be outgoing and detail-oriented. Computer skills are essential. Pursers must be comfortable dealing with large amounts of money and the responsibility that comes with it.

Unions and Associations

There are no unions or associations for Pursers.

Tips for Entry

1. Work in the hospitality industry, particularly in the payroll or accounting department.
2. Work in a travel agency, particularly one that specializes in cruises, to become familiar with dealing with passengers and cruise lines.
3. Meet as many Pursers as possible, perhaps by taking a cruise or two, to establish a network of people who know about job openings.

CRUISE DIRECTOR

CAREER PROFILE

Duties: Oversees all entertainment on a cruise ship

Alternate Title(s): Activities Mate

Salary Range: $3,800 to $7,500 per month; $45,000 to $90,000 annually

Employment Prospects: Good

Advancement Prospects: Good

Best Geographical Location(s): Anywhere a cruise ship berths

Prerequisites:

Education and Training—No formal education or training required, although a background in the hospitality and entertainment industry is helpful

Experience—Professional entertainment background; cruise ship staff position

Special Skills and Personality Traits—Fluent English (second language desirable); excellent public speaking skills; strong organizational skills; cheerful and energetic

Licensure/Certification—SCUBA and lifeguard certificate desired on some ships

CAREER LADDER

```
┌─────────────────────────────┐
│      Cruise Director        │
└─────────────────────────────┘

┌─────────────────────────────┐
│   Assistant Cruise Director │
└─────────────────────────────┘

┌─────────────────────────────┐
│     Social Host/Hostess     │
└─────────────────────────────┘
```

Position Description

A Cruise Director oversees all onboard entertainment, including creating, coordinating, and implementing all daily activities, and acting as a master of ceremonies (emcee) at social activities and evening shows. These activities include bingo games, scavenger hunts, beach volleyball, mock Olympics games, cocktail parties, passenger briefings, and onboard and offshore excursions. The Cruise Director is social butterfly, accountant, politician, and entertainer, always working to ensure that passengers have a good time.

Briefing passengers about possible offshore activities and coordinating these activities is a major function of the Cruise Director, not only because the entertainment is there for passengers to enjoy, but because the ship derives a part of its income from selling shore excursions. The Cruise Director must be a walking, talking guidebook to the various port stops and answer any questions about the stop that passengers may have, whether about currency, operating hours, special exhibitions, dining suggestions, or shopping options (what

and where the best bargains are). The Cruise Director also informs passengers about the ship's departure time and the last launch time back to the ship when the passengers have to use a launch between the ship and the port activities.

He or she prepares a list of possible activities for every port the ship will visit, using brochures, photographs, maps, and descriptions of the tours. This may include a sightseeing tour, SCUBA diving or snorkeling, deep-sea fishing, a helicopter flight, or some time at a secluded beach. He or she must remember that some passengers will have physical limitations, so provisions should be made to accommodate them.

The Cruise Director will be required to contact individual vendors in the various parts, letting them know when the ship will arrive and depart and confirming the number of passengers booked for the excursion and the time and place for meeting the passengers. Following the excursion, the Cruise Director pays the vendors and resolves any complaints.

The Cruise Director should know how to sing and dance and be willing to be a clown. Although larger ships have staff photographers, the Cruise Director will almost certainly be asked to take pictures of the passengers or be in them. At the end of the cruise, the Cruise Director gives a disembarkation talk about customs and immigration requirements and suggestions for the amount of money passengers should tip the various shipboard staffmembers (although some ships have a no-tipping policy).

A Cruise Director usually starts working on a cruise ship (or in a resort) as a social host or hostess, introducing the captain to passengers at such functions as the Captain's welcoming reception or cocktail party, acting as an emcee, and performing other social functions as directed by the Cruise Director. From there, the social hostess or host may be promoted to an Assistant Cruise Director, taking on additional responsibilities, including the planning and creation of the daily programs.

A Cruise Director on a small ship, with few or no assistants, must be visible and accessible to the passengers from breakfast through the evening entertainment, both on shore and at the beach. The hours can be long and include weekend work. He or she may be responsible for maintaining such activities gear as snorkeling and diving equipment and teaching passengers how to use them. On a larger ship, the Cruise Director will have assistants, thus easing the demands on his or her time. A Cruise Director is usually hired for a season or longer, working on the ship for several months at a time and enjoying vacations that are a month or more long. One of the best benefits of being a Cruise Director—besides enjoying what you do—is meeting people and making friends from around the world.

Salaries

Salaries for a Cruise Director vary according to the ship's size and the Cruise Director's experience. It may run from $3,800 to $7,500 a month and include room, board, and uniforms. Passengers may tip the Cruise Director (if allowed by the cruise line). Full-time Cruise Directors receive salaries ranging from $45,000 to $90,000 and may receive health and life insurance, sick and vacation leave, and an opportunity for retirement and investment programs. The cruise line provides airfare between the ship and home.

Employment Prospects

As more cruise ships are brought into service and as Cruise Directors retire, change jobs, or are promoted, there is a fairly constant need for new Cruise Directors. Usually they are hired from within the company, as Assistant Cruise Directors are promoted into the position.

Advancement Prospects

Advancement is almost always a possibility as a Cruise Director gains more experience, either within the company, for another cruise line, or at a resort.

Education and Training

Although no formal education or training is required, a background in the hospitality and entertainment industries is helpful. Command of one or more foreign languages is helpful so that the Cruise Director can communicate with guests and staff who do not speak English as their first language. Bookkeeping may be required, depending on the ship and the Cruise Director's duties.

Special Requirements

On smaller ships, the Cruise Director may be required to be a certified SCUBA diver and have a lifeguard certificate because he or she is personally involved with water-related activities.

Experience, Skills, and Personality Traits

Experience as an Assistant Cruise Director is helpful. Computer skills may be required. A Cruise Director has to be efficient, organized, outgoing, and, most of all, customer-oriented to ensure all passengers enjoy their cruise experience.

Unions and Associations

There are no unions or associations for Cruise Directors.

Tips for Entry

1. Learn the cruise business from the ground up, working in the Cruise Director's office or other position on a cruise ship.
2. Talk with Cruise Directors, asking their advice about career choices.
3. Subscribe to trade publications or read about current trends and developments on-line.

ENTERTAINER, CRUISE SHIP

CAREER PROFILE

Duties: Performs aboard cruise ships

Alternate Title(s): Comedian; Dancer; Magician; Musician; Juggler; Puppeteer; Singer

Salary Range: $350 to $750 a week

Employment Prospects: Good

Advancement Prospects: Good

Best Geographical Location(s): Anywhere that a cruise ship berths

Prerequisites:

Education and Training—Performing arts training, formal or informal

Experience—Performances in school, community, or professional theater

Special Skills and Personality Traits—Talent; good interpersonal skills; personal magnetism; ability to perform in front of large groups; foreign language knowledge helpful

Licensure/Certification—None

CAREER LADDER

```
┌─────────────────────────────┐
│   Entertainment Director     │
└─────────────────────────────┘

┌─────────────────────────────┐
│       Show Producer          │
└─────────────────────────────┘

┌─────────────────────────────┐
│        Entertainer           │
└─────────────────────────────┘
```

Position Description

Entertainers—including musicians, bandleaders, dancers, singers, magicians, jugglers, puppeteers, comedians, and other performers—are employed on cruise ships in a variety of venues, including showrooms, bars or lounges, and nightclubs. Musicians, singers, and dancers usually are signed to contracts that may run as long as six months, while specialty and featured acts may be signed on for only one or two performances.

Musicians are expected to be familiar with a variety of musical styles, including rock, jazz, Motown, popular, country, blues, classical, ballroom, show, and other types of music. Although the musicians will have rehearsals, musicians are expected to be able to sight-read music. The piano, electric bass, drums, trumpet, saxophone, trombone, and guitar are the instruments most often used on board, with the saxophone player doubling on clarinet and flute.

A musical director leads the ship's main orchestra, which backs all shows and performers on the main stage. A typical cruise might consist of three different hour-long Broadway-style revue shows and four variety shows. Usually there are two shows each evening.

Musicians are expected to have their own tuxedos for work on larger ships. Ships may provide a day uniform. Cruise lines rarely insure musical instruments, so entertainers should carry their own coverage.

Depending on the venue, a performer may be a featured act or may be part of an ensemble or revue. As part of the ensemble company, a show director usually coordinates all the acts, scheduling who will appear in what order and how long the act will be. He or she coordinates with musicians, lighting and special effects technicians, and costume designers to create a theme throughout the entire evening's entertainment.

Singers may be required to perform pop, country, classical, Broadway, rock, and other genres. Similarly, dancers may be asked to perform hip-hop, tap, ballet, or other styles of dance. In the case of chorus singers and dancers, the show producer, director, or choreographer will create the production numbers, teach them to the performers, and guide them through rehearsals until the show is ready to present to an audience.

Performances usually are scheduled in the evening, with some specialty Entertainers (balloon artists, magicians, jugglers) performing and interacting with the passengers during the day. Shipboard Entertainers must be able to perform onstage in possibly rough sea conditions. Entertainers, other than musicians, may be asked to do cruise staff duties, including assisting in shipboard activities.

Entertainers should have a passport that is good beyond the end of their contract. They may also be required to obtain visas and vaccination certificates, which the cruise line or hiring company will help obtain, although they do not cover these costs.

Ships provide meals and accommodations. Entertainers usually share a cabin with another Entertainer (where one smokes and the other does not, the no-smoking rule applies). Maid service is provided on larger ships. Known performers receive better accommodations than those who are just starting in the business.

Modern ships come equipped with a gym, theater, pool, and Internet access. At times the Entertainers will use the same facilities as the passengers; at other times they will have their own facilities, including a 24-hour lounge for night owls. All Entertainers are expected to participate in passenger and staff boat drills. There may also be special training periods for staff and crew that Entertainers must attend.

Although the schedule can be demanding, there is still time for sightseeing at the various ports of call and for pursuing other leisure activities such as learning a new skill or language, establishing and maintaining a fitness routine, SCUBA diving, reading, and writing.

Some showrooms, bars and lounges, and other entertainment venues still allow guests to smoke, so the Entertainer has to be willing to be exposed to second-hand smoke. Entertainers should assume all ships have a no-tolerance policy regarding controlled substances and overindulging in alcoholic beverages. It is not uncommon for cruise ships to conduct random drug tests or cabin inspections. Possession of illegal substances or testing positive on a drug test can lead to immediate dismissal at best and imprisonment at the worst. Most ships also prohibit Entertainers from visiting passengers' cabins and passengers from visiting Entertainers' cabins.

Salaries

Salaries vary depending on the Entertainer's experience and reputation, the venue, the length of the contract, and other factors. A bandleader may earn from $500 to $750 a week on a cruise ship, while a sideman may earn from $350 to $500 a week. Salaries for dancers and other performers may range from $350 to $400 a week. Headliners can earn from $800 to $2,000 a week or more. Cruise salaries include room and board. Salaries generally are paid in cash, but in cases where a check is issued, the chief purser or on-board banker will cash the check.

The Internal Revenue Service has started taxing Entertainers who perform on ships that have corporate offices in the United States, so the cruise line may withhold applicable federal taxes from U.S. residents. Booking or employment services may deduct between 12 and 15 percent commission.

Most Entertainers are considered independent contractors and are not provided with any benefits, although some ships provide full medical coverage once the performer has passed a physical exam (including a chest X-ray for tuberculosis; a urinalysis for drugs, alcohol, and diabetes; and a blood test for sexually transmitted diseases) prior to departure. Paid vacations are not included, but Entertainers may have a contract that assures they will have a job when they return from their vacation.

Employment Prospects

With an increase in the number of cruise ships, employment prospects for Entertainers are good. Entertainers may live anywhere in the United States, since the cruise ship will pay their transportation costs between home and the ship and back again. Ships depart from ports along the Atlantic and Pacific Oceans, the Mississippi River, the Gulf of Mexico, and other foreign ports. Jobs may be obtained through unions or companies that hire Entertainers for cruise lines.

Advancement Prospects

Entertainers can advance by moving from the chorus to being a featured performer and from smaller venues to larger ones. From there, they can advance to film and television or become a show producer for an entertainment venue.

Education and Training

A formal education is not required to be an Entertainer. However, specialized training in the specific talent area is important. This may include classes in theater, dance, music, or the performer's specialty. As many passengers and crewmembers do not speak English as a first language, a foreign language can be helpful.

Experience, Skills, and Personality Traits

Previous experience in a performing venue is helpful with a wide variety of experiences. Musicians should be able to sight-read and improvise. Performers should have excellent interpersonal skills and be able to "connect" with the audience easily. Performers should be physically fit, although there are some jobs for performers with physical and mental disabilities. Because Entertainers bunk with one another and are at sea for long periods of time, it is essential that an Entertainer exhibit extreme cooperation and common courtesy, both with the guests and the other performers.

Unions and Associations

Among the associations and unions available for Entertainers is the American Federation of Musicians (AFM), American Federation of TV and Radio Artists (AFTRA), Screen Actors Guild (SAG), and Actors Equity. Each provides information about the industry, offers advice and seminars, and works to protect their members regarding pay and benefits. Not all cruise ships, however, sign the necessary agreements with these unions for performers, other than for headliners.

Tips for Entry

1. Learn the entertainment business from the ground up, perhaps starting at a community theater, in college, or some other venue.
2. Have a videotape created of performances to present to casting directors or show producers, as a personal audition is not always possible.
3. Talk with Entertainers, asking their advice about career choices and possible openings.
4. Subscribe to trade publications or read about industry news on-line.

DECKHAND

CAREER PROFILE

Duties: Performs maintenance duties and operates equipment on the deck of a ship

Alternate Title(s): Seaman

Salary Range: $86 to $106 per day

Employment Prospects: Fair

Advancement Prospects: Fair

Best Geographical Location(s): Wherever ships navigate rivers, lakes, oceans, or other bodies of water

Prerequisites:

Education and Training—No formal education or training required; able to read and comprehend instructions and manuals

Experience—No experience necessary for entry-level positions

Special Skills and Personality Traits—Able to lift heavy lines (ropes) and other equipment; able to follow instructions and be willing to work all shifts in all types of weather

CAREER LADDER

```
┌─────────────────────────────┐
│      Vessel Manager         │
└─────────────────────────────┘

┌─────────────────────────────┐
│        Boatswain            │
└─────────────────────────────┘

┌─────────────────────────────┐
│       Head Seaman           │
└─────────────────────────────┘

┌─────────────────────────────┐
│        Deckhand             │
└─────────────────────────────┘
```

Position Description

Deckhands work on all types of ships, from river barges to ocean liners. Under the direction of the ship's officers, they are charged with keeping the nonengineering areas of a ship in good order, making up cables, rigging barges, laying wires, handling lines (including cutting, splicing, and tying), and assisting with locking boats and barges onto river barges. They must safely operate manual and electronic winches to help load supplies and cargo on to the ship. They aid navigation by standing watch to look out for other vessels and obstructions in the ship's path, steering the ship, measuring the water depth in shallow waters, and maintaining and operating such deck equipment as anchors, lifeboats, and cargo handling gear.

Safety is a primary concern onboard any ship, so the Deckhand must be aware of and comply with all safety rules and regulations. He or she may be required to wear a life vest, hearing protection devices, steel-toed shoes, work gloves, safety glasses, and splash goggles. Familiarity with all safety equipment is imperative, including alarms, fire

fighting apparatus, and life rings and jackets. As ships are exposed to all types of weather, they are in constant need of maintenance, so a Deckhand usually is required to clean the deck and exteriors of the ship, chip off rust and old paint, and apply new paint.

Depending on the type of ship and the length of the voyage, a Deckhand may work 30 days on and 30 days off, or 28 days on and 14 days off, or other variations that may include months at sea with a month or more off for vacation. A Deckhand may work two six-hour or two eight-hour watches a day. Deckhands working on ships in a harbor usually go home every day. The work takes place 24 hours a day, seven days a week, in pleasant and inclement weather. Those working on ships in the Great Lakes may be laid off during the winter when the lakes freeze over.

Deckhands who work on ocean-going vessels usually experience extensive travel to foreign ports. Deckhands on cruise ships rarely have any contact with the passengers. Those who work on canals and rivers may travel a great deal between the same ports. Those who work in harbors do not travel as part of their job descriptions. However, they may relocate to other harbors.

Salaries

Deckhands earn from about $86 to $106 per day, plus room (usually shared with other Deckhands or ship crewmembers) and board (meals). They usually are considered full-time, permanent employees, but they are not paid on their days off.

Employment Prospects

Deckhands can find employment depending on the location and the time of the year. However, deep-sea shipping has been declining among U.S.–manned ships, and automation has eliminated a number of jobs on foreign freighters. Civilian jobs with the U.S. Navy offer some good prospects.

Advancement Prospects

There are a number of positions a Deckhand can advance to, including boatswain and vessel manager. However, as long as there is a shortage of jobs there will be fewer opportunities for advancement.

Education and Training

Deckhands do not need a high school or college degree, but they must be able to read and understand ship policies and procedures and follow safety instructions and bulletins.

Experience, Skills, and Personality Traits

A Deckhand must be able to stoop and climb up and down high masts or other structures of a ship. The Deckhand must be able to lift heavy weights, including lines (ropes) during docking and departing and handling buoys, and must be able to maintain good balance on ships that may traverse rough seas. A resistance to motion sickness is desirable. It also helps to be able to swim, although that skill is not required.

Unions and Associations

The Seafarers' International Union and the International Organization of Masters, Mates, and Pilots are two unions that provide information about training and working conditions. As jobs are scarce, the unions are not accepting many memberships.

Tips for Entry

1. Become familiar with the nonengine parts of a ship, including how to tie the various knots used in securing a ship to a pier and for other uses.
2. Talk with Deckhands and harbormasters, asking their advice about career choices and training and apprenticeship programs.
3. Establish a network of people in the industry by attending local union functions.
4. Subscribe to trade publications or read about current trends and developments on-line.

BOAT PILOT

CAREER PROFILE

Duties: Guides ships in and out of harbors, along rivers, and through straits and other confined waterways

Alternate Title(s): Canal Pilot; River Pilot; Harbor Pilot

Salary Range: $350 to $1,000 per week; $18,000 to $52,000 annually

Employment Prospects: Fair to good

Advancement Prospects: Fair to good

Best Geographical Location(s): Any waterway or harbor

Prerequisites:

Education and Training—On-the-job training from work experience on boats or ships; degree from the U.S. Coast Guard Academy or other state academy

Experience—Work on a ship as deckhand, learning on-the-job skills

Special Skills and Personality Traits—Ability to stoop, bend, climb up and down to and from high elevations; ability to communicate via radio, phone, and computer; ability to maintain balance

Licensure/Certification—A Boat Pilot must possess a U.S. Coast Guard (USCG) license of OUTV (Operator of Uninspected Towing Vessels) rank or higher

CAREER LADDER

```
┌─────────────────────────────┐
│          Captain            │
└─────────────────────────────┘

┌─────────────────────────────┐
│         Boat Pilot          │
└─────────────────────────────┘

┌─────────────────────────────┐
│        Able Seaman          │
└─────────────────────────────┘
```

Position Description

There are two types of Boat Pilots: harbor pilots and river or canal pilots. A harbor pilot is usually an independent contractor who boards a vessel and guides it as it enters or leaves the port. The pilot must be familiar with local water depths, winds, tides, currents, and such hazards as reefs and shoals, so that the boat can be safely navigated into and out of the harbor.

When a ship is ready to enter a harbor, the harbor pilot rides out to the ship (this may be as far as seven miles or more) in a pilot boat and boards the ship. He or she then guides it safely to the harbor. When the ship is ready to depart, the harbor pilot boards it, takes it out to sea, and then boards the pilot boat to return to the harbor. Harbor pilots may work from early morning through late evening.

River or canal pilots generally are members of their vessel's crew and stay with the vessel on its voyage, alternating between being away from home for extended periods and being on leave for extended periods. Because there is so much potential for injury from falling overboard or working with machinery, heavy loads, and dangerous cargo, a major portion of the river or canal pilot's job is involved with safety procedures and compliance. Among other duties, a river or canal pilot may be required to maintain the vessel and equipment to the company's standards, maintain proper deck watches, and use proper deck watch change procedures. Crew discipline and assuring that the ship and crew comply with all applicable government and company rules, regulations, policies, and laws may also be part of the job.

He or she uses effective routine and emergency communications, reports traffic, incidents, and problems, and participates in incident investigations. A river or canal pilot may also assist in the selection of deck employees for promotion or permanent employment, participate in new employee orientation, and conduct on-the-job training for steersmen.

A river or canal pilot may work two six-hour watches per day or stand watch for four hours and be off for eight hours. They may work 30 days on, 30 days off; 28 days on, 14 days off; 20 days on, 10 days off; or some other combination. Those employed on Great Lakes ships tend to work 60 days and have 30 days off, but they do not work in the winter because the lakes freeze. In other locations, river or canal pilots usually work all year in all types of weather, during storms, damp and cold conditions, and hot and humid spells.

Older vessels may not have air conditioning, soundproofing, or comfortable living accommodations, but newer vessels usually do have these appointments.

Salaries

Salaries vary greatly and depend upon such things as whether a Boat Pilot is working all year or seasonally. River or canal pilots tend to earn less than do harbor pilots. However, because river or canal pilots are provided with lodging and meals, their on-board expenses are minimal.

Weekly salaries for Boat Pilots range between $350 and $1,000, while full-time salaries range from $18,000 to $52,000.

Employment Prospects

About 40 percent of all water transportation workers are employed on merchant marine or U.S. Navy ships operating on the oceans or Great Lakes. Another 40 percent are in such transportation services as dredges, ferries, towboats, tugs, and other watercraft in harbors, rivers, and canals. The rest are employed on cruise ships, sightseeing and excursion boats, and ferries.

Competition for these jobs is intense, with some decline in the number of available positions for the next few years, particularly as the percentage of cargo carried by U.S.–manned ships decreases. Another factor is the design of newer ships that can be operated by smaller crews than can older vessels.

As all graduates of the U.S. Merchant Marine Academy are commissioned as ensigns in the U.S. Naval Reserve, they may go on active duty in the U.S. Navy. Graduates may also take jobs with foreign ships.

Advancement Prospects

Because the number of jobs is shrinking, advancement can be difficult. Some licensed officers are even taking jobs under their level of licensure. However, senior officers will be retiring within the next decade, so some advancement will be possible.

Education and Training

A Boat Pilot needs at least a high school diploma and years of working on boats with independent study to be able to pass a written Coast Guard exam. A faster route is to obtain a degree from the U.S. Merchant Marine Academy (USMMA) in King's Point, N.Y.; from one of six state academies (Texas, California, Maine, Massachusetts, New York, and Michigan); or from the Paul Hall Center for Maritime Training and Education in Piney Point, Md., for Seafarers International Union members.

The USMMA is a military academy overseen by the U.S. Department of Transportation, and admission requires appointment by a member of Congress. This four-year training leads to a bachelor of science degree and a U.S. Coast Guard license as a third mate or third assistant engineer or both. The Great Lakes Maritime Academy in Michigan trains officers for just the vessels that ply the Great Lakes. The other schools offer a four-year bachelor's degree with programs in nautical science, marine transportation, or engineering.

Special Requirements

All officers and operators of watercraft must have one or more of the 60 different licenses issued by the U.S. Coast Guard. A Boat Pilot must possess a U.S. Coast Guard (USCG) license of OUTV (Operator of Uninspected Towing Vessels) rank or higher.

Experience, Skills, and Personality Traits

A Boat Pilot should have experience working on boats or ships, be able to communicate well, and withstand possible pressures exerted by time constraints and weather conditions.

Unions and Associations

Shipping companies hire Boat Pilots through union hiring halls or directly. The Seafarers International Union, Atlantic, Gulf, Lakes and Inland Waters District, AFL-CIO, represents unlicensed U.S. merchant mariners sailing aboard U.S. vessels in the deep sea, Great Lakes, and inland trades. The union also represents licensed U.S. mariners in the Great Lakes and inland sectors. It works to protect job security, but because of the decreasing number of jobs, union membership can be difficult to obtain.

The International Organization of Masters, Mates & Pilots (MM&P) is the international marine division of the International Longshoremen's Association, AFL-CIO. With 6,800 members, it represents licensed deck officers, state pilots, and other marine personnel on U.S. commercial vessels sailing in international waters, the inland waterways and Great Lakes of the United States, the Panama Canal, and the Caribbean, and crews sailing civilian-crewed military vessels of the United States.

Tips for Entry

1. Talk with Boat Pilots, asking their advice about career choices, internships, and apprenticeship programs.
2. Establish a network of people in the industry by working part-time or full-time around a boatyard or harbor.
3. Attend union functions to develop a network of people informed about job openings.
4. Subscribe to trade publications or read current trends and developments on-line.

GENTLEMAN HOST

CAREER PROFILE

Duties: Accompany and dance with guests aboard cruise ships

Alternate Title(s): Dance Host; Ambassador Host

Salary Range: $28 to $38 per day, plus cruise and airfare

Employment Prospects: Good

Advancement Prospects: Good

Best Geographical Location(s): Wherever cruise ships sail

Prerequisites:

Education and Training—Dance training (may be informal)

Experience—None required

Special Skills and Personality Traits—Must be between 45 and 72 years of age; able to ballroom dance; very outgoing; good social skills

CAREER LADDER

```
┌─────────────────────────────────────┐
│   Owner, Gentleman Host Agency       │
└─────────────────────────────────────┘

┌─────────────────────────────────────┐
│          Gentleman Host              │
└─────────────────────────────────────┘
```

Position Description

Single gentlemen (may be divorced) are invited aboard cruise ships to dance with women passengers, join them at dinner, play board games, go on shore excursions, and otherwise mingle. There are three primary requirements: age (the Gentleman Host must be between 45 and 72), ability to ballroom dance (fox trot, swing, waltz, rumba, and cha-cha are required; tango, samba, quick step, merengue, salsa, two-step, and polka are desirable), and a very social personality. Approximately four to 12 hosts may be present on a cruise, and most often the cruise has a dance theme.

Potential Hosts, usually retired or semiretired, are interviewed and judged on their dancing ability before they are hired. They are expected to be healthy and sufficiently physically fit to dance and be involved in the various shipboard activities.

Because the ships that hire Gentlemen Hosts tend to have a stricter dress code, the Gentleman Host is expected to have a tuxedo, white dinner jacket, three tuxedo shirts, and appropriate accessories. They should also have such traditional informal attire as navy blue blazers, tan dress trousers, ties, and other accessories.

The Hosts dance an equal amount of time with each passenger and are forbidden from becoming romantically involved with any passenger (at least while at sea). Hosts may sail almost as much as they wish, with some men cruising as much as 60 percent of the year. To some extent, they can select where they want to sail and on which cruise line. Cruise lines that use Gentlemen Hosts are Crystal, Celebrity, Cunard, Holland America, Norwegian, Orient, Radisson Seven Seas, Regal, Royal Olympic, Silversea, and World Explorer.

Salaries

Gentlemen Hosts receive free passage on the cruise, accommodations, meals, and beverages. They often receive free air transportation to and from the ship and free shore excursions while in port. They are paid between $28 and $38 per day.

Employment Prospects

As 10 cruise lines use Gentlemen Hosts, there are good employment opportunities for men who are socially adept and can dance well.

Advancement Prospects

Gentlemen Hosts can start their own businesses, establishing contracts with cruise lines and screening applicants.

Education and Training

The only training necessary is in dancing, which most Gentlemen Hosts have learned by practice over the years.

Experience, Skills, and Personality Traits

Gentlemen Hosts must be very social, should be able to play some card or table games (bridge, hearts, etc.), and be able to dance.

Unions and Associations

There are no relevant unions or associations for this position.

Tips for Entry

1. Take a cruise or two where Gentlemen Hosts are employed to observe their roles on the cruise.
2. Talk with Gentlemen Hosts, asking their advice about the various cruise lines and destinations.

LODGING

GENERAL MANAGER, HOTEL

CAREER PROFILE

Duties: Oversees the entire operation of a hotel, motel, resort, or cruise ship (other than line officers)

Alternate Title(s): Hotel Manager; Resident Manager

Salary Range: $20,000 to $126,000

Employment Prospects: Good

Advancement Prospects: Good

Best Geographical Location: Almost every area in the country has a hotel, motel, or resort with job possibilities; major port cities

Prerequisites:

Education and Training—College degree in hotel or restaurant management or hospitality

Experience—Managerial positions in hotels, motels, resorts, food service operations, sales and marketing, and other related positions

Special Skills and Personality Traits—Able to deal with a variety of personalities; good oral and written communication skills; ability to deal with a multiplicity of assignments simultaneously

CAREER LADDER

```
┌─────────────────────────────┐
│      General Manager        │
└─────────────────────────────┘

┌─────────────────────────────┐
│      Assistant Manager      │
└─────────────────────────────┘

┌─────────────────────────────┐
│       Sales Manager         │
└─────────────────────────────┘

┌─────────────────────────────┐
│  Food and Beverage Manager  │
└─────────────────────────────┘
```

Position Description

A General Manager has overall control of the day-to-day operation of a hotel, resort, motel, cruise ship, or other lodging. Depending on the size of the facility, the manager may be responsible for budget planning, payroll, room rates, nightly audits, personnel, advertising, marketing, food and beverage, catering, meetings, maintenance, housekeeping, and all the other duties that are involved in running the property. Larger facilities will have department heads for each of these areas, all of whom answer to the General Manager. Although most General Managers work in hotels and resorts, some may work in boarding houses, camps, dude ranches, and inns.

Some managers (resident managers) live on the property, while others reside elsewhere. Although assistant managers may act as the manager-on-duty or manager of the day (MOD), the General Manager can still be on call 24 hours a day in case of an emergency, illness, vacation relief, or other

unexpected event. Night and weekend shifts are commonplace, and the workweek generally runs more than 40 hours.

Usually, there is a day manager and a night manager, except in small motels where either the front office is closed for the night or the night auditor works as the manager. As most people check in during the day, the day manager is usually the more prestigious of the two positions, generally garnering a slightly higher salary. Assistant Managers help run the property, usually taking charge of specific functions, delegating responsibility to department heads, and otherwise taking over the duties of the hotel manager when the manager is not available.

Because of the nature of the business, there can be a large amount of travel for corporate meetings, conventions and trade shows, and other functions. Although there has been some change in the market, hotel chains often move managers to new properties or to those having problems, or managers are given the option of requesting relocation.

Salaries

Major hotels, whether independent or part of a chain, usually offer medical and life insurance, retirement plan, vacation (at no or low cost at other hotels within the chain), and sick leave. Many provide lodging and meals, laundry, and other services as part of the manager's salary package. Within chains, there is often a chance to participate in a profit-sharing plan and continuing education at the chain's expense.

Employment Prospects

Employment options vary with the economy as individuals open a hotel and as chains open and close properties. The hotel industry has changed drastically in the past few years, adding numerous segments, including economy, long-stay, all-suites, midrange, family, full-service, upscale, resorts, and residential spas, and each has its own method of operation. Someone who wants to specialize in one of these categories can create a niche specialty and be highly valuable as an employee, particularly during good economic times when many hotels are being constructed. During downturns in the hospitality industry, a generalist might fare better.

Advancement Prospects

There are always excellent advancement opportunities, particularly in good economic times. Promotions almost always come from advancing through the ranks, so advanced degrees or continuing education courses in hotel operations will be an asset.

Education and Training

A bachelor's degree is almost mandatory, and advanced degrees and courses in hotel or restaurant operations, business, advertising, marketing, international relations, public speaking, journalism, and logistics are becoming more important. Almost all hotels use computers for reservations, supply ordering, payroll, and other functions, so the manager should be computer literate. There are more than 800 colleges that offer aspects of travel and tourism courses, and some high schools are now offering these classes as well.

Experience, Skills, and Personality Traits

Previous experience in hotel jobs with progressively greater responsibilities is beneficial. A General Manager should be able to adjust quickly to a changing and challenging situation, be flexible, and understand that their position usually involves long, late, and weekend hours. They must be personable, patient, and possess good communication skills.

Unions and Associations

The American Hotel and Lodging Association is the largest organization for hotel personnel, providing frequent conferences and seminars of interest to those who want to advance in a hotel management career.

Tips for Entry

1. Check with a hotel chain for training courses, internships, and apprentice programs.
2. Get experience at progressively more well-known hotels and lodging establishments.
3. Attend as many industry functions as possible, both to learn what is new and to establish a network of others in the field who know when there are job openings.
4. Read trade publications, either by subscription or on-line.

CHIEF ENGINEER

CAREER PROFILE

Duties: Oversees mechanical, electrical, plumbing, and fire protection operations

Alternate Title(s): Director of Engineering; Building Engineer

Salary Range: $9+ per hour; $19,000 to $85,000 annually

Employment Prospects: Excellent

Advancement Prospects: Good to excellent

Best Geographical Location(s): Any area with hotels or resorts

Prerequisites:

Education and Training—Bachelor's degree in electrical engineering or equivalent

Experience—Several years' work in such trades as electrical operations, plumbing, carpentry, and maintenance

Special Skills and Personality Traits—Technical, maintenance, repair, and mechanical skills; leadership ability; organized; able to handle multiple projects and tasks simultaneously

Licensure/Certification—Requirements vary according to local jurisdictions for electricians, plumbers, and other maintenance personnel

CAREER LADDER

```
┌─────────────────────────────┐
│   Director of Maintenance   │
└─────────────────────────────┘

┌─────────────────────────────┐
│       Chief Engineer        │
└─────────────────────────────┘

┌─────────────────────────────┐
│     Apprentice Engineer     │
└─────────────────────────────┘
```

Position Description

Chief Engineers oversee the installation, operation, and maintenance of the mechanical, electrical, plumbing, and fire protection components of a hotel, resort, casino, or other lodging facility. Their responsibilities might include negotiating with local utility companies; coordinating safety and risk management personnel to ensure compliance with insurance underwriter requirements for all new projects and renovations, and reviewing individual projects to comply with MEP (mechanical, electrical, and plumbing) guidelines. The Chief Engineer ensures that all regulations are met, including those from the Occupational Safety and Health Administration (OSHA): the Americans with Disabilities Act (ADA); national and regional building, fire, and electrical codes; and Building Officials Code Administrators, Inc. (BOCA).

The Chief Engineer may prepare requests for proposals (REPs) and contracts for various construction projects, according to company policy and procedures manuals. This includes outlining plans and specifications for new construction and renovations, working with subcontractors, and completing purchase orders, submittals, and change orders.

The Chief Engineer interviews, hires, trains, and supervises the maintenance staff. The Chief Engineer makes sure that every light bulb, toilet, and shower/tub works; the sprinkler system is functional; the heating, ventilation, and air conditioning and heating plants (HVAC) perform properly; all locks are functional (and rekeyed after each guest checks out); supplies are ordered and stocked; walls are painted and repaired; carpentry is maintained; and that anything else that needs it receives the attention of the maintenance department.

As part of the hotel management, the Chief Engineer takes part in the manager of the day or manager on duty (MOD) program, meeting and dealing with the guests to assure any problems are prevented or resolved. As a hotel operates 24 hours a day, a Chief Engineer can expect work that includes evening, weekend, and holiday shifts.

Most Chief Engineers do not have travel as part of their job description, although they may travel for industry and corporate meetings. Jobs are sufficiently available, so transferring to another part of the country is fairly easy.

Salaries

Engineers may start at minimum wage; generally earn $9 an hour or more as an hourly employee, and may earn up to $85,000 plus bonuses annually as full-time employees. Benefits usually include health and life insurance and sick and vacation leave and may include retirement and investment programs. When working for a hotel chain, the Chief Engineer receives free or discounted lodging, food, beverages, dry cleaning, and laundry. Educational assistance may be provided. Engineers working at a resort may have use of the resort amenities. Relocation expenses are rarely covered.

Employment Prospects

Hotels, resorts, conference centers, and other public and private buildings are almost always looking for engineers who can handle all aspects of building maintenance and for tradespeople who specialize in electrical, plumbing, carpentry, and heating and air conditioning.

Advancement Prospects

Engineers can advance to more supervisory positions, such as directory of maintenance, or start their own businesses.

Education and Training

A degree in electrical engineering or similar training usually is required for managerial positions.

Experience, Skills, and Personality Traits

The Chief Engineer of an establishment must have the ability to give and follow directions, supervise personnel, and notice and repair problems before they become serious. Chief Engineers should have an excellent background in electrical, HVAC, and plumbing maintenance work, and a history of increasingly more responsible supervisory positions.

Special Requirements

Local jurisdictions may require and issue licenses for HVAC, plumbing, and electrical personnel.

Unions and Associations

The Building Officials Code Administrators association provides training, code updates, conferences, and other information to all engineers in the various trades. Some areas have unions for specific trades, including the International Brotherhood of Electrical Workers and the National Association of Plumbing-Heating-Cooling Contractors.

Tips for Entry

1. Learn the maintenance business from the ground up, taking courses in electrical engineering, plumbing, air conditioning, carpentry, and related fields.
2. Talk with Chief Engineers, asking their advice about career choices, internships, and apprenticeship programs.
3. Establish a network of people in the industry by attending local functions of the Building Officials Code Administrators.
4. Subscribe to trade publications or read about current trends and developments on-line.

ROOMS DIVISION MANAGER

CAREER PROFILE

Duties: Oversees management of front office, housekeeping, and reservations

Alternate Title(s): Rooms Manager; Assistant General Manager; Rooms Executive

Salary Range: $35,000 to $73,000, plus bonus

Employment Prospects: Fair to good

Advancement Prospects: Good

Best Geographical Location(s): Wherever there are large hotels, resorts, and cruise ships

Prerequisites:

Education and Training—Bachelor's degree or higher in hotel management, business, communications, computer skills, or some aspect of the hospitality field; foreign language fluency for hotels and resorts with a large number of guests and employees who do not speak English as a first language

Experience—Several years of experience in a related management position

Special Skills and Personality Traits—Interpersonal skills; able to study, analyze, and interpret complex information; strong verbal and written communication skills; able to deal with a variety of personality types

Licensure/Certification—Certified Rooms Division Executive certification is desirable

CAREER LADDER

```
┌─────────────────────────────┐
│      General Manager         │
└─────────────────────────────┘

┌─────────────────────────────┐
│   Rooms Division Manager     │
└─────────────────────────────┘

┌─────────────────────────────┐
│     Front Office Manager     │
└─────────────────────────────┘
```

Position Description

The Rooms Division Manager provides operational support to the general manager by overseeing some or all of the following departments: the front office, desk agents, guest service representatives, bell and door staff, concierges, housekeeping, maintenance, and reservations. Based on forecasts, occupancy, and budgets, the Rooms Division Manager schedules employees to effectively and efficiently handle existing and incoming guests. He or she works to achieve customer satisfaction, quality service, and compliance with the owner's policies and procedures while meeting or exceeding the established financial goals.

The Rooms Division Manager resolves customer complaints; anticipates potential problems by reviewing and monitoring complaints, operation issues, business flow, and associate performance; and manages the human resources within the departments to attract, retain, and motivate the employees. There is a lot of guest contact in this position. For small properties, the Rooms Division Manager may oversee the operation of several hotels or motels.

The work schedule of a Rooms Division Manager often involves weekends, holidays, and evenings. As part of the upper management team, he or she will work as manager on duty or manager of the day (MOD). Some positions, particularly at remote locations, will include housing. Generally, travel is not a major part of this position. However, some travel may be involved to attend trade functions and corporate meetings.

Salaries

Salaries depend on the size and location of the property; what price segment the hotel represents; experience; the ability to speak more than one language; and whether a Certified Rooms Division Management certificate has been earned. Jobs in the Northeast, South Atlantic, and Pacific regions pay better than do those in the Midwest, South Central, and Mountain regions. A Rooms Division Manager may earn from $35,000 to $73,000, plus bonuses (paid quarterly or annually for meeting or exceeding job performance standards and revenue projections). Most benefits packages include life and health insurance and a retirement savings plan.

Rooms Division Managers working for a hotel chain receive discounted or free accommodations, food, and beverages. Relocation expenses may be covered, depending on the location of the property and the experience of the applicant.

Employment Prospects

Employment options vary with the economy. In a healthy economy, new lodging facilities open, creating jobs, but a poor economy often brings layoffs, consolidations, and closings. There is high turnover in the hotel business, both because of new construction and promotions and because of the long hours and intense pressure that causes people to choose another career or industry.

Advancement Prospects

The position of Rooms Division Manager is in an excellent situation for promotion into the position of general manager. With a fairly constant turnover of hospitality personnel, there are usually ample advancement opportunities.

Education and Training

A bachelor's degree or higher in hotel management or a combination of a degree and experience is required. Additional studies in public relations, management, computers, and related fields are helpful. Fluency in a foreign language is helpful for dealing with other hotel employees and guests.

Special Requirements

The Education Institute arm of the American Hotel and Lodging Association offers a Certified Rooms Division Executives recognition program based on years of experience as a Rooms Division Manager and participation in the lodging industry or in a teaching capacity.

Experience, Skills, and Personality Traits

Previous experience in hotel jobs with progressively greater responsibilities is beneficial. A Rooms Division Manager should be able to adjust quickly to a changing and challenging situation and be flexible. They must be personable, patient, and possess good communication skills.

Unions and Associations

The American Hotel and Lodging Association is the largest organization for hotel personnel and provides frequent conferences and seminars of interest to those who want to advance in a hotel management career.

Tips for Entry

1. Check with a hotel chain for training courses, internships and apprenticeship programs.
2. Get experience at progressively more important hotels and lodging establishments.
3. Talk with Rooms Division Managers asking their advice about career choices.
4. Attend functions sponsored by the local chapter of the American Hotel and Lodging Association if possible, both to learn what is new and to establish a network of others in the field who can let you know when openings are available.
5. Read trade publications, either by subscription or on-line.

RESERVATIONS MANAGER

CAREER PROFILE

Duties: Supervises and monitors the daily operations, systems, and programs in the reservations department; communicates rates, room inventories, and strategies to the appropriate departments to maximize occupancy, revenue, and profit goals

Alternate Title(s): None

Salary Range: $20,000 to $48,000

Employment Prospects: Good

Advancement Prospects: Good

Best Geographical Location(s): Major cities and areas with a large number of outstanding hotels, resorts, restaurants, and cruise ships

Prerequisites:

Education and Training—High school diploma, at a minimum; some college-level courses in business administration and hospitality are helpful; computer literacy required

Experience—Work in a reservations office and front desk, either at a hotel, resort, or travel agency

Special Skills and Personality Traits—Supervisory and customer service skills; well-organized; good interpersonal skills

CAREER LADDER

```
┌─────────────────────────────────┐
│      Front Office Manager        │
└─────────────────────────────────┘

┌─────────────────────────────────┐
│      Reservations Manager        │
└─────────────────────────────────┘

┌─────────────────────────────────┐
│       Reservations Clerk         │
└─────────────────────────────────┘
```

Position Description

The Reservations Manager is responsible for overseeing the daily operations, systems, and sales in the reservations department. This includes supervision of reservations clerks or agents to ensure price quotes for room rates are accurate and that the staff is efficient, friendly, and helpful. The Reservations Manager is called in when a guest has a complaint about his or her reservation or how it was filled.

Reservations clerks usually are the first human contact a potential guest has with a hotel or cruise line, and the first impression should be an excellent one. The clerk should know the availability of rooms that are handicapped-accessible, nonsmoking, child-proof, adjoining, and have a special view or other feature, including those that may be nearer or farther from the elevators or any construction and renovation that is taking place. The clerk also should be familiar with all amenities in the rooms, including robes, hair dryers, toiletries, iron and ironing board, and whatever else the booking guest may request.

The Reservations Manager may be involved with direct correspondence or conversations with individuals, groups, and travel agents, particularly when it comes to filling special requests (e.g., a family reunion needing rooms on the same floor). The manager trains agents in handling reservations and cancellations for individual and group bookings, although the sales staff rather than the reservations clerks may handle groups.

Reservations may be made over the phone, directly through the hotel, through a chain-wide toll-free number, by travel agents, over the Internet, or by clients walking in at the last minute. All reservations clerks must be familiar with handling all these reservation methods and making sure they are entered into a common database. This will ensure, to some degree of certainty, that there are enough rooms available for incoming guests. (In the days before computer systems, it was not unusual for a hotel to have many more reservations than rooms.) As some hotels deliberately accept more reservations than they have rooms to compensate for cancellations or no-shows, the Reservations Manager, in conjunction with other hotel personnel, will determine what percentage of overbooking should be accepted. Where desired, the clerks may be trained to upsell or upgrade a reservation, suggesting a suite or concierge/club-level room instead of a basic room.

The Reservations Manager provides a list of registered guests to the front desk personnel and assures that a folio (listing of the hotel room charges) has been created for each guest room. Daily and monthly reports are generated showing reservations and cancellations for the previous and current period. The Reservations Manager may work with other hotel personnel to lower the reservation-to-cancellation ratio. Working in conjunction with the sales and marketing departments, Reservations Managers try to accurately predict future occupancy by coordinating advertising and promotional specials. With the increased popularity of Internet booking, a Reservations Manager should be familiar with on-line capabilities, dealing with Internet technology personnel, and on-line reservation software.

As many large hotels, resorts, and cruise ships may have 2000 or more rooms or cabins, many of them catering to groups and conferences, the Reservations Manager may see up to 80 percent of the rooms and all of a ship's cabins booked for the same time, with room inventory rates changing during a short few hours. For example, guests in 1,500 or more of the 2,000 rooms may check in on the opening day of a conference and check out on the closing day.

Although some travel may be required to industry conferences, the Reservations Manager usually does not travel extensively. There are opportunities, however, to transfer to other hotels within a chain or to larger properties with more job responsibilities in other geographic areas.

Salaries

The larger and more luxurious the property and the more experience a Reservations Manager has, the higher the salary. This is mitigated, to some extent, by location, with the Midwest paying the least ($21,000 to $31,000) and the Northeast paying the most ($36,000 and more). Hotels with union employees tend to pay more than do those without union employees, even though the Reservations Manager is not a union employee.

Full-time Reservations Managers usually receive vacation and health leave and life and medical insurance. They may also be eligible for retirement investment and stock buying programs. As an employee of a hotel, resort, or cruise line, the Reservations Manager usually receives free or discounted accommodations at other hotels within the chain or on cruises.

Employment Prospects

As new hotels are constructed, there will be a need for onsite reservation personnel. Employment will be governed to a large extent by the employee's knowledge of the current software and database systems and by the economy.

Advancement Prospects

The managerial skills necessary to be a Reservations Manager are easily transferred to other positions, either laterally or climbing up the corporate ladder. Because of the high rate of turnover and promotions in the lodging industry, advancement can be an almost automatic assumption for qualified and hard-working employees. A Reservations Manager may advance to a position such as front office manager.

Education and Training

A high school diploma is necessary, with some advanced education in computers and software systems, including Delphi, PMS (Property Management Systems), and MARSHA (Marriott Automated Reservation System for Hotel Accommodations). Bookkeeping, accounting, and personnel management may also be required.

Experience, Skills, and Personality Traits

An ability to multitask and handle difficult situations is essential. Previous experience in reservations and personnel management is indispensable.

Unions and Associations

The American Hotel and Lodging Association provides information and support about Reservations Managers' duties and responsibilities.

Tips for Entry

1. Take courses in computer languages and software applications.
2. A hospitality degree, or courses, cover the different aspects of the field and reveal how the reservations office coexists with other offices.
3. Meet with Reservations Managers for career advice and networking about job openings and advancements.
4. Read trade publications, either by subscription or online, to keep up with industry news and trends.

FRONT OFFICE MANAGER

<table>
<tr><td>

CAREER PROFILE

Duties: Oversees all operations in the front office of a hotel, resort, or cruise ship, including guest registration, guest checkout, complaint resolution, accurate completion of the nightly audit, and supervision of bell stand, reservations, and concierge

Alternate Title(s): Front Desk Manager

Salary Range: $17,000 to $59,000

Employment Prospects: Fair to good

Advancement Prospects: Excellent

Best Geographical Location(s): Major cities and tourist destinations with large numbers of hotels and resorts; cruise ships

Prerequisites:

Education and Training—College degree, focusing on hotel management, business, communications, and computer skills; on-the-job training as part of the educational program; foreign language

Experience—Work experience as a desk clerk and in other hotel positions is imperative

Special Skills and Personality Traits—Able to handle a number of different functions simultaneously; able to deal with a variety of personality types; good communication skills; organized

</td><td>

CAREER LADDER

```
┌─────────────────────────────────┐
│   Assistant Manager, Hotel      │
└─────────────────────────────────┘

┌─────────────────────────────────┐
│     Front Office Manager        │
└─────────────────────────────────┘

┌─────────────────────────────────┐
│  Assistant Front Office Manager │
└─────────────────────────────────┘

┌─────────────────────────────────┐
│      Front Office Clerk         │
└─────────────────────────────────┘
```

</td></tr>
</table>

Position Description

The Front Office Manager oversees all functions that ensure all guests are registered promptly and efficiently, keeping track of rooms that are available as cleaned and vacated (and what type of rooms are available, including accessible, smoking/nonsmoking, single or double) and seeing that luggage is taken to the guest rooms, cars are valet-parked (if that option is available and the guest chooses to have the car parked), and that mail and messages are delivered to the guests. The front desk also is responsible for guest checkout and assuring that all statements (folios) are settled promptly and accurately. If there is a dispute, the Front Office Manager may step in to resolve the problem.

Hotels may overbook (accept more reservations than they can accommodate) based on a history that shows a per-centage of people will reserve a room and then not show up or cancel at the last minute and that some guests stay longer than they originally planned. The Front Office Manager must be prepared to handle guests who arrive late only to find a room is not available, or a guest who reserves a specific type of room (smoking/nonsmoking, accessible, scenic view, etc.) that is not available. The manager must either upgrade the room request or "walk" the guest to another hotel with comparable accommodations. The manager may decide that the guest does not have to pay for that evening's lodging.

The manager is responsible for ensuring that there is a sufficient number of employees to handle the number of guests registering and checking out during busy hours; for training front office employees; and for coordinating communications among the various offices (e.g., accounting, housekeeping, reservations) to ensure efficient, organized, and courteous front office procedures. Other than the telephone reservations clerks, the front office personnel provide the first impression a guest receives when visiting a hotel, and it should be perfect.

Salaries

Salaries depend on the size and location of the property, what price segment the hotel represents, previous experience, and often the ability to speak more than one language. As with other positions in the hospitality field, jobs in the Northeast, South Atlantic, and Pacific regions pay better than do those in the Midwest, South Central, and Mountain regions. Larger, more luxurious hotels and resorts pay more than do budget and economy motels. Starting salaries at establishments with fewer than 75 rooms may be as low as $17,000 a year. At hotels with 500 or more rooms, a Front Office Manager may earn $59,000 or more. A boutique hotel may pay as much as 25 percent more than does a chain hotel for the same position.

Major hotels, whether independent or part of a chain, usually offer medical and life insurance, a retirement plan, vacation (at no or low cost at other hotels within the chain), and sick leave. Within chains, there is often a chance to participate in a profit-sharing plan and continuing education at the hotel's expense. There is little travel involved in the position of Front Office Manager, but one may be transferred or request a transfer to another location.

Employment Prospects

Employment options vary with the economy, with more hotels and facilities opening in good economic times and layoffs and closings in an economic downturn. The hotel industry has changed drastically with the advent of numerous specialty segments, including economy, long-stay, all-suites, midrange, family, full-service, upscale, resort, and residential spas, so there is a constant need for good qualified Front Office Managers. There is frequently a high turnover in the hotel business, both because of new construction and promotions and because of burn-out from the long hours and intense pressure.

Advancement Prospects

Advancement possibilities are excellent, particularly as chains open more properties and promote from within their own ranks of employees. These promotions may be at the same property, within the same geographic area, or to another geographic region entirely. Promotions may also be to another hotel within the chain's brand or to a more upscale brand within the chain.

Education and Training

The level of education required for this position varies with the type of hotel (resort, cruise ship) its location, size, and the responsibilities involved. While it is possible to attain this position without a college degree, anyone who wants to be a Front Office Manager with a major property should have taken college courses in public relations, management, computers, and other related fields. Extensive training in previous front desk and other hotel departments may be substituted for a college degree. Fluency in a foreign language is helpful for dealing with other hotel employees and guests.

Experience, Skills, and Personality Traits

Previous experience in hotel jobs with progressively greater responsibilities is beneficial. A Front Office Manager should be able to adjust quickly to a changing and challenging situation, be flexible, and understand that their position usually involves long, late, and weekend hours. They must be personable, patient, and possess good communication skills.

Unions and Associations

The American Hotel and Lodging Association is the largest organization for hotel personnel, providing frequent conferences and seminars of interest to those who want to advance in a hotel management career.

Tips for Entry

1. Check with a hotel chain for training courses, internships, and apprenticeship programs.
2. Get experience at progressively more well-known hotels and lodging establishments.
3. Attend as many industry functions as possible, both to learn what is new and to establish a network of others in the field who can let you know when there is an opening for which you might qualify.
4. Read trade publications, either by subscription or on-line.

CONCIERGE

CAREER PROFILE

Duties: Provides special services for hotel, resort, or cruise ship guests

Alternate Title(s): None

Salary Range: $20,000 to $50,000

Employment Prospects: Good

Advancement Prospects: Fair

Best Geographic Location(s): Major resort and upscale hotel areas, including Las Vegas, New York, Washington, D.C., New Orleans, Chicago, Orlando, Los Angeles, and on cruise ships

Prerequisites:

Education and Training—College degree; foreign language competency; computer literacy

Experience—Work in a customer service related field, particularly in the travel industry

Special Skills and Personality Traits—Good written and oral communication skills; detail oriented; problem-solving abilities; customer service skills

CAREER LADDER

```
┌─────────────────────────────────────┐
│ President, Private Concierge Service │
└─────────────────────────────────────┘

┌─────────────────────────────────────┐
│           Head Concierge            │
└─────────────────────────────────────┘

┌─────────────────────────────────────┐
│             Concierge               │
└─────────────────────────────────────┘

┌─────────────────────────────────────┐
│          Front Desk Clerk           │
└─────────────────────────────────────┘
```

Position Description

A Concierge at a resort or upscale hotel prides himself or herself on being able to obtain whatever a guest needs, from tickets to a sold-out Broadway show or sports event to formal attire for the guest whose luggage went astray. The Concierge is the employee who lives to serve and help people. A Concierge finds the perfect restaurant and makes reservations, sends a New York deli corned beef sandwich to someone across the country, finds a restaurant that will create a special dish for a guest, books a baby-sitter at the last minute, shops for the ideal birthday or anniversary present, gets a tee time at a popular golf course, locates someone who speaks (and translates) a foreign language, books a corporate jet, or finds an astronomer to give a guest an evening star tour.

A Concierge may even (without being asked) find a newspaper with a discount coupon when he or she learns a guest will be shopping at a specific store or visiting a nearby tourist attraction. The Concierge will know where there is an after-hours pharmacy or a doctor who will make a call to the hotel or resort or see a patient in other than regular office hours. At other times, a Concierge may be asked to arrange a wedding or even a funeral. In other words, through a wide range of contacts, the Concierge assists a guest with whatever reasonable, or sometimes unreasonable, requests the guest may have.

To help educate the Concierge, new restaurants extend invitations to sample the food (or when a restaurant hires a new chef), theaters provide tickets, and new local attractions send passes. Concierges visit the best and most unusual shops and see all the new exhibits at galleries and museums. They are expected to know the names of frequent guests and sometimes what their favorite flowers, fruits, and beverages are.

Other Concierges may work in a corporate setting (helping an employee relocate to a new city, planning special meetings or events, or obtaining such special services as interpreters); a residential context (personalized shopping, errand running, or arranging special dinners or weekend getaways); or as an entertainment Concierge (specializing in obtaining the impossible ticket, making party arrangements, or planning events). Wherever there are a large number of hotels or resorts with a Concierge staff, there is usually an association of Concierges who help one another whenever there is an unusual request. They have national and local meetings to discuss issues and meet one another to develop a network of contacts in other areas.

In some areas, where there is not enough demand for each hotel to have a Concierge on staff, the property will use the service of a "virtual concierge" who may be miles or cities away. The guest uses an interactive computer monitor in the hotel lobby to request a special need. Alternatively, when there are a number of brands of a hotel line in one area, the most upscale will have a Concierge, and guests staying at the other properties can use that person's services (e.g., a guest at a Marriott Courtyard, Residence Inn, or Fairfield Inn would use the services of the Marriott hotel or resort Concierge).

Salaries

The salary range varies according to the property and the location but starts at about $20,000 and goes to $50,000 plus gratuities. These tips range from $5 to $10 or higher, as a percentage of the price of the theater tickets or other purchases made for a guest, or as a guest otherwise sees fit to reward the Concierge depending on the difficulty of fulfilling the request. A guest will often tip even when the Concierge cannot fulfill a request.

Full-time Concierges generally receive health and life insurance, annual vacation and sick leave, and other benefits offered to other full-time employees. They may be eligible for retirement and stock option programs.

Employment Prospects

Major cities, including Chicago, Dallas, Las Vegas, Los Angeles, New Orleans, New York, Orlando, and Washington, D.C., are the areas where most Concierges are located. The best place to seek employment is in metropolitan areas like these experiencing high hotel or business development.

Wherever there is a major resort or upscale hotel, there is bound to be a Concierge. However, many of them stay at the same property for years and are a source of pride at the property, so there is not much turnover or promotion. In the United States, the majority (57%) of Concierges are female; in foreign countries, it is a more male-dominated field.

Advancement Prospects

Concierges advance when a senior Concierge retires or is hired away by another property.

Education and Training

Any training within a hotel operation is helpful, as are courses in the hospitality field, public relations, communications, and foreign languages. The International Concierge Institute (in association with Les Clefs d'Or), with schools in Montreal and Fort Lauderdale, offers a nine-week course followed by a nine-week internship. A Concierge should learn about visa and passport requirements, particularly when working in an area with foreign visitors or business people who do a lot of foreign travel.

Experience, Skills, and Personality Traits

Concierges should have a comprehensive knowledge of their local area and be able to network with the people and businesses they will be using and referring to their guests. They should have superior interpersonal skills and excellent oral and written communication skills. A Concierge must be impeccably groomed, tactful, discreet, and have a zest for helping others.

Unions and Associations

There are no Concierge unions, but there are two major associations. The National Concierge Association has chapters in Arizona, Baltimore, Northern California, Colorado, Chicago, Minnesota, Nevada, central Texas, and Wisconsin. Les Clefs d'Or meaning "Keys of Gold" in French) grants membership only after an applicant meets specific requirements, including at least five years of experience in the hotel industry, of which three years must be as a full-time lobby-level Concierge. Its membership is restricted to hotel lobby Concierges only, whereas the National Concierge Association represents Concierges in other fields as well.

Tips for Entry

1. Meet with other Concierges, attend their meetings, and network with them as much as possible to learn about position openings.
2. Learn as much as possible about the area around a hotel. Be able to name restaurants (and the maitre d's name), boutiques, and current museum exhibits when an interview is scheduled.
3. Work in other hotel positions, particularly the front desk, where there is a lot of contact with hotel guests.

MAITRE D'

CAREER PROFILE

Duties: Oversees the efficient operation of a dining room, either in conjunction with a dining room manager or alone

Alternate Title(s): Dining Room Manager; Maitre d'Hotel

Salary Range: $30,000 to $75,000, plus gratuities

Employment Prospects: Fair

Advancement Prospects: Fair

Best Geographical Location: Major cities and areas with a large number of outstanding hotels, resorts, upscale restaurants, and cruise ships

Prerequisites:

Education and Training—A college degree in hotel management or food and beverage service or several years of experience in progressively more important positions in restaurants

Experience—Experience in fine dining rooms is necessary

Special Skills and Personality Traits—Must enjoy working with people; friendly and outgoing; eager to do whatever necessary to make guests happy

CAREER LADDER

```
┌─────────────────────────────┐
│         Maitre d'           │
└─────────────────────────────┘

┌─────────────────────────────┐
│      Banquet Manager        │
└─────────────────────────────┘

┌─────────────────────────────┐
│          Waiter             │
└─────────────────────────────┘
```

Position Description

A Maitre d' makes sure that each dining room guest feels welcomed and comfortable and is served properly, politely, and efficiently. The position involves supervising and managing the reservations desk, hostess station, dining room captains, wait staff, bus people, and any others who work in the dining room. This includes greeting each guest and sometimes escorting him or her to a table, making sure they are attended to efficiently and promptly (but not in a hurried, officious, or smothering manner), and that the wait staff are properly attired or uniformed. The Maitre d' may explain the day's specials or brief the wait staff to do so and then instruct the sommelier (wine steward) to visit the table in a timely manner. Training and developing personnel for promotions is also an important function. The Maitre d' should be familiar with and comply with all U.S. public health rules and regulations.

When a restaurant does not have a wine steward, the Maitre d' should be familiar with the wine cellar, be able to recommend an appropriate wine to go with a meal, and serve the wine properly. This may be done in conjunction with recommendations from the chef.

Without being obsequious or intrusive, the Maitre d' should visit each table to determine that the service and menu selections are equal to (or better than) the guests' expectations. If not, any problems should be resolved immediately.

Management is a large portion of this job, including scheduling employees, forecasting revenue, arranging for large parties and events, and ensuring that employees have fresh flowers arranged properly, candles lit, napkins folded, and tables set properly. It helps to have an understanding and a flair for the dramatic for such special occasions as a birthday parties, marriage proposals, anniversary celebrations, and other festive occasion.

The job usually requires evening and weekend hours. In some restaurants, such as those specializing in French or

Italian cuisine, it may be desirable to have a good command of that language.

Salaries

Salaries are on the high side because upscale, expensive restaurants are the facilities that use the services of a Maitre d'. Salaries range from $30,000 to 75,000, an income of $60,000 or more, plus gratuities and sometimes bonuses (up to another 10 percent or more) is common. Boutique hotels may pay as much as 25 percent more than do chain hotels for the same position.

A full-time Maitre d' usually receives vacation and sick leave and life and medical insurance. Retirement and stock investment programs may also be offered. Free meals are included, and the full use of other resort amenities are often made available. If working for a chain of restaurants or at a restaurant in a hotel chain, a Maitre d' may receive discount travel options.

Other than attending industry functions (food and wine seminars), there is not much travel involved in this position. However, with lateral transfers and promotions, it is possible to relocate to other parts of the country, the world, or to a cruise ship. Some companies will pay relocation costs for an experienced Maitre d'.

Employment Prospects

When the economy is down, there are fewer first-class restaurants using Maitre d's. Conversely, when the economy is good, there are more options available. In general, there are a reasonable number of openings at any given time for an experience Maitre d'.

Advancement Prospects

The management skills acquired by a Maitre d' from dealing with a variety of guests and employees makes it possible to transfer into other hotel or restaurant management positions or into managerial positions in other industries, travel-related or otherwise.

Education and Training

A college degree in a hospitality field is desirable, but on-the-job experience may qualify. A foreign language is helpful, as is a firm knowledge of wines, wineries, and viticulture.

Experience, Skills, and Personality Traits

Generally, a Maitre d' must have a number of years of experience as a senior banquet captain or banquet manager, must demonstrate leadership capabilities, and be able to manage numerous responsibilities simultaneously. A keen sense of follow-up, making sure all details are attended to, and the ability to handle crises are necessary. Excellent communication and interpersonal skills also are required.

Unions and Associations

There is no union or association specifically for Maitre d's, but information can be obtained through the Educational Foundation of the National Restaurant Association and the Council on Hotel, Restaurant and Institutional Education.

Tips for Entry

1. Talk with as many Maitre d's as possible to establish a network of experts who can provide you with information about the industry, internships, and leads toward job openings.
2. Attend any lectures or courses offered about restaurant management, food, and wines.
3. Read trade publications, either by subscription or online.

RECREATIONAL INSTRUCTOR

CAREER PROFILE

Duties: Teaches and trains novices in various recreational activities

Alternate Title(s): Activities Instructor

Salary Range: Minimum hourly wage to $25,000 a year

Employment Prospects: Good to excellent

Advancement Prospects: Good

Best Geographical Location(s): Any resort or vacation destination; cruise ships

Prerequisites:

Education and Training—Specific training in the activity

Experience—Work or volunteer time spent in the area of expertise

Special Skills and Personality Traits—Excellent physical condition for athletic instruction; interpersonal skills; even-tempered

Licensure/Certification—Varies according to the subject taught; CPR and higher certificates for some fields; passport

CAREER LADDER

```
┌─────────────────────────────────────┐
│        Activities Coordinator        │
└─────────────────────────────────────┘

┌─────────────────────────────────────┐
│   Educational Sports Trainer or Coach │
└─────────────────────────────────────┘

┌─────────────────────────────────────┐
│       Recreational Instructor        │
└─────────────────────────────────────┘
```

Position Description

Many people want to do or learn something during their vacations, so they look at their time away as a chance to learn how to ski, snowboard, toboggan, scuba dive or snorkel, water ski, hang glide, sail, kayak, canoe, white water raft, windsurf, surf, shoot skeet or trap, knit or cro- chet, dance, quilt or sew, play basketball, baseball, football, golf, tennis, or other sports, ride a horse, or any number of other activities that may lead to a pleasant hobby.

In many cases, such as cake-decorating or lei-making, this could be as little as a one-hour session per week. In other cases, it could be a series of lectures on investments or writing during the length of a cruise. It could be a full-time job that is either seasonal or all year, with different "stu- dents" every day or a week-long (or longer) course. When seasonal, it could mean at least an eight-hour day every day of the week. It depends on the activity and the location.

These activities can be conducted in all types of weather, although ski instruction would not take place during a mas- sive snowstorm, water-based activities would not be held in

rough seas, and airborne endeavors would not take place during a storm. Nevertheless, they do take place outdoors, so sun block is an essential preventive measure. Some sea- sonal instruction can be made into a year-long occupation by moving from one hemisphere to another as the seasons change. Other instructors work in other fields during the off months. The students may have varying levels of aptitude, so it is important that the instructor be able to present the course in its basic form, progressing to more detailed work.

As a guest lecturer on a cruise ship, one must have exper- tise in a specific field that the cruise line thinks will interest its passengers. In some cases, the cruise line will pay a salary; in others, they exchange the cruise for the lecture series. (An alternative is to organize a group of people inter- ested in a topic and coordinate all the details involved in booking the cruise arrangements, or by becoming involved with an organization that wants to sponsor a cruise lecture series.)

The main advantage to being a recreational instructor, of course, is being paid for doing something that one would pay to do. Because of the potential of personal injury in some activities, the instructor must be concerned about safety, both by making sure the students are using the correct form and that the equipment is in excellent condition. These would include lessons in snow, water, and air. These instructors must know all the rules and regulations and be extremely proficient in the activity. Although some athletic activities require a young, agile body, other activities, including skiing and scuba instruction, have no upper-age restrictions.

Salaries

Salaries vary according to the activity, responsibilities, and the time involved. Someone managing an entire training program will earn more than an instructor. Some activities, such as scuba, can be a full-time, permanent position, with salaries ranging up to $25,000 a year or more, particularly with courses in management. Full-time instructors are usually provided with health insurance. Resorts located in remote areas generally provide room and board, but the salary will be lower than at places that do not.

Employment Prospects

As people want to spend their leisure time and retirement days involved in a significant or interesting pastime, there will be more demand for special-interest instructors. Most are excellent opportunities for students between semesters or retired people who want a second, perhaps part-time, career.

Advancement Prospects

Advancement depends on the type of activity. Teaching a craft (e.g., lei-making, quilting) at a resort might lead to a position coordinating all leisure activities. Athletic coaching could lead to a full-time job as a professional team coach.

Education and Training

The nature of the activity being taught determines required education and training. Generally, the more physical the activity, the more training required. However, an expert lecturing on a cruise ship probably will need either advanced degrees or years of experience in the field.

Experience, Skills, and Personality Traits

Recreational Instructors should be extremely patient to deal with the various personalities of their students. They should have excellent written and oral communication skills. In some cases, they will need computer skills. A background in the subject being taught, either as a participant or assistant instructor, is helpful.

Special Requirements

Certain activities, such as scuba diving, may require certification (e.g., Master Diver and Resort Operations Specialist [ROS]) with CPR (cardiopulmonary resuscitation) and first aid training. When working in a foreign country, a passport is almost always required. Some locations will also require a visa. The associated fees for these documents may or may not be paid for by the hiring company. When working in a foreign country, married couples have a better chance of finding employment if both spouses work in the same field.

Unions and Associations

Almost every sports activity has an association, but there is no overall organization for Recreational Instructors.

Tips for Entry

1. Become familiar with and proficient in the specific sport or activity.
2. Talk with Recreational Instructors, asking their advice about career choices, internships, and apprenticeship programs.
3. Establish a network of people in the industry by attending local organization or club functions.
4. Contact local resorts and similar destinations to determine what needs they have for talented instructors.
5. Subscribe to trade publications or read about current trends and developments on-line.

BELLHOP

CAREER PROFILE

Duties: Assists guests with luggage and escorts them to their rooms in resorts and on cruise ships and trains; assists with luggage and check-in at airports and bus terminals

Alternate Title(s): Porter; Doorman; Skycap; Station Agent

Salary Range: $5.75 to $18 per hour, plus tips; $12,000 to $37,000 annually

Employment Prospects: Good

Advancement Prospects: Good

Best Geographical Location(s): Wherever there is a large hotel, resort, airport, major train station, or cruise ship

Prerequisites:

Education and Training—No formal education is required, although a high school diploma is desirable

Experience—Work as a bellhop at other places where luggage is handled for travelers

Special Skills and Personality Traits—Friendly; reliable; able to carry heavy luggage

Licensure/Certification—A driver's license might be required for Bellhops who also work as valets

CAREER LADDER

```
┌─────────────────────────┐
│      Bell Captain        │
└─────────────────────────┘

┌─────────────────────────┐
│        Doorman           │
└─────────────────────────┘

┌─────────────────────────┐
│        Bellhop           │
└─────────────────────────┘
```

Position Description

A Bellhop at a hotel or resort, on a train, or on a cruise ship greets a traveling guest and helps transport his or her luggage to a room, cabin, or compartment, either carrying them by hand or using a luggage cart. As the Bellhop is the first person the guest deals with (other than the reservations agent), it is up to the Bellhop to give a good first impression to the guest. The Bellhop must make the guest feel welcome and comfortable in surroundings away from home. They explain the features of the room, including how the air conditioning and heat controls work, how to operate the television, how to set the safety lock on the door, where the ice supply is, and any other aspect of the room that might present a problem to the traveler. If there are special tourist attractions nearby or in the hotel (e.g., the dining room is open late, there is an ice rink nearby, horseback riding is available), particularly attractions that the hotel is promoting, the Bellhop explains those as well. The Bellhop offers to hang luggage in the closet and get ice or other items that the guest might want.

Bellhops may also deliver messages, deliver room service, and provide laundry pickup and delivery. The Bellhop or bell captain may call a taxicab or shuttle for a guest and provide some security against nonhotel guests who are loitering in the lobby or other areas of the hotel. They assure the security of luggage left with them when a room is not available for a guest or when the guest has to check out of the hotel room before he or she is ready to leave the hotel.

Because guests can arrive and depart at all hours on all days, a Bellhop may be required to work evenings, weekends, and holidays. As the Bellhop is often stationed outdoors to receive visitors, they work in all types of weather conditions. Bellhops generally are required to wear a uniform that is provided by the company.

Although a Bellhop rarely has to complete a large amount of paperwork, the bell captain does. The bell captain also interviews, hires, and trains new employees and provides performance appraisals, conducts staff meetings, and may have to oversee time slips and payroll.

Skycaps work for an airline (but not the airport where they work). They check a passenger's luggage, confirm the passenger's destination and flight number, issue a boarding pass, prepare the appropriate luggage destination tags and attach them to the luggage, and then put the luggage on a conveyor belt or take it into the terminal. At the other end, skycaps collect luggage for passengers from the conveyor belts, take it outside the terminal, and place it in the passenger's car. The company that hires them provides them with uniforms.

Pullman porters work for Amtrak and assist passengers boarding and disembarking. They help the boarding passenger find a seat and stow the luggage, or they assist the passenger disembarking by removing their luggage from the train and taking it to the passenger's vehicle. Amtrak provides Pullman porters with their uniforms.

Salaries

Bellhops generally work for hourly wages, which can range from $5.75 to $18 per hour, plus tips. Salaries and tips will be more substantial at upscale resorts and onboard a cruise ship or a train. Other factors include whether the Bellhop belongs to a union whose the contract calls for higher wages than nonunion employees receive and whether the property (or ship, etc.) has a lot of conventions and group travel for which the contract calls for an automatic payment to the Bellhop of up to $2 a bag. Other factors include seniority and shift schedule, with evening shifts generally paying more than daytime. A full-time Bellhop may earn between $12,000 and $37,000 annually, receive paid vacation and sick leave, receive life and health insurance, and be eligible for retirement investment programs.

Bellhops may be eligible for free or discounted accommodations or transportation. Resorts and hotels rarely pay for relocation expenses, but transferring from one area of the country to another is relatively easy.

Employment Prospects

As long as people travel there will be a need for Bellhops. With more resorts opening almost daily, there will be a constant availability of jobs. Many Bellhops work their way through college, getting hospitality experience, and leave the job once they graduate.

Advancement Prospects

Advancement possibilities are good as people leave the job to take a Bellhop position at a more prestigious property or are promoted to bell captain or other more senior positions within the hospitality industry.

Education and Training

There are no formal education or training requirements, but a background in foreign languages is helpful in places visited by people who speak a language other than English.

Special Requirements

A Bellhop who also works as a valet must have a valid driver's license.

Experience, Skills, and Personality Traits

A Bellhop must be thorough and accurate to assure that the proper luggage is delivered to the right place in a timely manner. As they deal with the guests and other employees, they must have good interpersonal skills. The Bellhop must speak clearly, stand for long periods of time, and be interested in anticipating a guest's needs.

Unions and Associations

The Hotel Employees and Restaurant Employees (HERE) International Union represents Bellhops in negotiating contracts and benefits.

Tips for Entry

1. Become familiar with the hospitality industry.
2. Learn to drive a variety of cars, including standard and automatic transmission, learning where trunk levers are and other idiosyncrasies of the various makes and models.
3. Talk with Bellhops, asking their advice about career choices.
4. Establish a network of people in the industry by attending local union functions.
5. Subscribe to trade publications or read about current trends and developments on-line.

EXECUTIVE HOUSEKEEPER

CAREER PROFILE

Duties: Supervises the housekeeping of a hotel, resort, spa, cruise ship, or other lodging

Alternate Title(s): Housekeeping Manager; Director of Environmental Services

Salary Range: $18,000 to $68,500

Employment Prospects: Good

Advancement Prospects: Good

Best Geographical Location(s): Major cities and areas with a large number of outstanding hotels, resorts, restaurants, and cruise ships

Prerequisites:

Education and Training—Degree in hotel management or equivalent experience; foreign language; computer literacy

Experience—Several years in progressively more responsible positions within the housekeeping department of a hotel or resort, motel, cruise ship, or other lodging facility

Special Skills and Personality Traits—Supervisory and management skills; detail-oriented; very organized

Licensure/Certification—Certified Executive Housekeeper (C.E.H.) and Registered Executive Housekeeper (R.E.H.)

CAREER LADDER

```
┌─────────────────────────────────┐
│   Manager, Other Departments    │
└─────────────────────────────────┘

┌─────────────────────────────────┐
│     Executive Housekeeper       │
└─────────────────────────────────┘

┌─────────────────────────────────┐
│       Floor Supervisor,         │
│   Housekeeping Department        │
└─────────────────────────────────┘

┌─────────────────────────────────┐
│         Housekeeper             │
└─────────────────────────────────┘
```

Position Description

The Executive Housekeeper must ensure that every visible part (and those parts that are not) of a lodging facility is as spotlessly clean as possible, from ceilings to floors. Although courtesy, design, décor, and attentive staff are very important factors in a pleasant stay, nothing turns a guest off more quickly than a dirty guest room. Unkempt public spaces are also displeasing because the guest wonders "if the housekeeping staff can't keep the public spaces clean, what are they not cleaning in the guest rooms?" A guest who is not satisfied with the cleanliness of a property not only will not return but will tell others who might otherwise have stayed at the property.

Housekeepers who clean the guest rooms must vacuum, change the linens and towels, and refresh the toiletries and amenities (e.g., shampoo, conditioner, bathroom tissue, glassware, shower caps, mouthwash, soap, bathrobes, stationery, magazines, note paper and pen, ashtrays). They clean the bathroom, wash the windows and mirrors, dust the furniture and walls, and replace or report any nonworking lightbulbs. They also check that room service menus and other printed matter (e.g., weekly magazines, hotel literature) are freshly stocked in each room. Housekeepers should also note any repairs that need to be made (e.g., a leak in the bathroom) and report them to maintenance. Housekeepers may also be charged with replenishing and billing for a minibar. Other housekeepers are responsible for similar duties in such public areas as lobbies, ballrooms, hallways, and sometimes the restaurants and bars.

The Executive Housekeeper schedules work hours (day-time and nighttime in those properties that have a nighttime turndown service) and which rooms each housekeeper must clean, provides necessary training, and ensures sufficient stock is in inventory so each housekeeper has the cleaning materials and other supplies necessary. This may include overseeing such housekeeping vehicles as golf carts or licensed vehicles. The Executive Housekeeper may be responsible for ordering linens and housekeeping supplies, and working with vendors to ensure proper pricing, delivery, and maintenance.

After each guestroom is cleaned, the Executive House-keeper reports the status of vacant rooms to the front check-in desk so the desk clerks know which rooms can be assigned to newly arriving guest. Some Executive House-keepers are also responsible for the laundry of all guest room linens, housekeeping uniforms, tablecloths, and nap-kins to make sure all linens are clean and a clean emergency supply is available in inventory. They also supervise the col-lection and distribution of any items the guest may wish to have the valet service clean. The Executive Housekeeper, working with the catering or food and beverage department, schedules regular cleaning of all carpets at a time that will cause the least inconvenience to the hotel staff and guests. An annual budget and weekly or monthly report must be established and maintained by the Executive Housekeeper. The Executive Housekeeper also must ensure that all Occu-pational Safety and Health Administration (OSHA) and Americans with Disabilities Act (ADA) polices are adhered to. These functions usually can be completed in a 40-hour week, but often the workweek includes evening and week-end hours.

Salaries

The Northeast and Pacific regions generally pay the high-est average salaries ($38,000 and up), depending on the size and location of the property. An Executive House-keeper at a hotel with 500 or more rooms can earn approx-imately $68,500. Luxury resorts with many guest rooms and banquet facilities will pay more than a highway motel. A boutique hotel may pay as much as 25 percent more than a chain hotel for the same position. Because there can be an extremely high turnover in the housekeeping depart-ment, qualified Executive Housekeepers who can motivate employees and boost the employee retention rate may be offered relocation costs. Full-time Executive Housekeep-ers usually receive vacation and sick leave and life and medical insurance. They may also be offered tuition assis-tance, retirement, and stock investment plans.

There is very little travel associated with the position of Executive Housekeeper, other than to association meetings and conferences. It is possible to transfer to a similar posi-tion in another hotel in the chain located in another area.

As a full-time employee, the Executive Housekeeper gen-erally receives free or reduced-cost meals and lodging at the property and is eligible to receive free or discounted accommodations at other properties in the hotel chain or on cruise ships.

Employment Prospects

Because of the high turnover rate in the hospitality industry and the increased number of hotels and lodging facilities (and cruise ships) being built, there is always a demand for Executive Housekeepers.

Advancement Prospects

Advancement for an Executive Housekeeper is primarily to larger, more luxurious properties, to a position overseeing other housekeepers at a number of properties within a chain, or by transferring management skills to other departments within a lodging facility or to the corporate office.

Education and Training

A degree in hotel management is desirable, but someone with a high school diploma, additional courses in hotel or business administration, and years of experience may be hired as an Executive Housekeeper. Computer literacy, par-ticularly with spreadsheet applications, is desirable. Because a large number of housekeepers do not speak En-glish as their first language, a foreign language is helpful.

Special Requirements

The Certified Executive Housekeeper (C.E.H.) and Regis-tered Executive Housekeeper (R.E.H.) programs, as admin-istered by the International Executive Housekeepers Association, Inc., are helpful in obtaining top positions in this field. A C.E.H. applicant must have completed high school or have a GED. An R.E.H. candidate must have a B.A. or B.S. degree from an accredited college or university.

Experience, Skills, and Personality Traits

The Executive Housekeeper should have excellent time management, scheduling, and organizational skills; be able to work without constant supervision; deal well with cus-tomers and employees; and be able to resolve conflicts with fairness and confidence.

Unions and Associations

The International Executive Housekeepers Association (I.E.H.A.) is a professional and educational organization of about 6,000 members dedicated to a cleaner, safer, and healthier environment. It offers an educational program leading to industry certification.

Tips for Entry

1. Contact Executive Housekeepers to establish a network of professionals who can keep you informed of changes within the industry, internships, and possible job openings.
2. Work as a housekeeper in progressively larger and more luxurious properties, assuming more responsibility whenever possible.
3. Attend any workshops available that deal with housekeeping computer software and housekeeping management.
4. Read trade publications, either by subscription or on-line.

LAUNDRY MANAGER

CAREER PROFILE

Duties: Maintains the cleanliness of all linens for a hotel, resort, cruise ship, or theme park

Alternate Title(s): Linen Director

Salary Range: $20,000 to $60,000

Employment Prospects: Good

Advancement Prospects: Good

Best Geographical Location(s): Any area with large hotels, resorts, theme parks, or cruise ships

Prerequisites:

Education and Training—High school diploma; studies in laundry cleaning techniques and management

Experience—Work in a hotel or commercial laundry

Special Skills and Personality Traits—Mechanical aptitude; foreign language; good oral and written communication skills; knowledge of wash cycle, stain removal, reclamation, and ironing processes; inventory management

Licensure/Certification—Registered Laundry and Linen Director (RLLD); Certified Laundry/Linen Manager (CLLM)

CAREER LADDER

```
┌─────────────────────────────────┐
│     Director of Housekeeping     │
└─────────────────────────────────┘

┌─────────────────────────────────┐
│         Laundry Manager          │
└─────────────────────────────────┘

┌─────────────────────────────────┐
│        Laundry Assistant         │
└─────────────────────────────────┘
```

Position Description

Every hotel, resort, cruise ship, and theme park has laundry needs. These include bed linens, towels, dining linens, draperies, and wardrobe (costumes or uniforms). Some places send some or all of their laundry to a commercial facility, but others do it in-house. The executive housekeeper may be in charge of laundry if the hotel or resort is small enough, but for larger hotels and resorts, cruise ships, and theme parks, there may be a Laundry Manager.

The duties of a Laundry Manager include collection of the dirty laundry, washing and ironing, distribution, supervision of laundry personnel, budgeting, needs forecasting, and ordering. When a theme park has hotels associated with it, there may be a central plant that handles laundry from all the restaurants, hotels, and the theme park. Therefore, trucks have to be scheduled to take the laundry to the central location and return it when clean.

Close coordination with the housekeeping and sales staffs is needed to anticipate laundry needs. It is also important to communicate with other departments to determine how many sets (called the par level) of linen are needed for each bed, how many uniforms for each performer, and how many sets of linens for each of the restaurants. Many properties are trying to be environmentally sound by asking guests if they want their linens changed daily or less frequently, thus saving water, limiting the amount of laundry chemicals from entering the environment, and lowering the use of materials. The Laundry Manager must include the potential and realistic calculation of how much less laundry this produces.

The Laundry Manager must work with the maintenance department to schedule regular preventive maintenance and the engineering department to learn what to watch for to anticipate equipment maintenance problems. A good Laundry Manager will stay current on laundry products and equipment that can simplify and reduce the cost of laundry. A Laundry Manager may be brought in when a property or cruise ship is in the development stage to determine the amount of storage space needed for all linens, uniforms, and laundry equipment.

It is important that all Occupational Safety and Health Administration (OSHA) and Americans with Disabilities Act (ADA) policies are adhered to. This is particularly true when training and developing employees with limited education and experience.

A Laundry manager works with computers, tracking linen use, monitoring costs, and determining the amount of laundry to be done each day, the supplies that must be ordered, and the amount of inventory on hand, because linens and uniforms must be ordered weeks and sometimes months ahead of time. Usually, a Laundry Manager will work a regular 40-hour week even though the laundry facilities may operate all day every day. When there is an emergency, however, such as machinery breaking down or an unusual demand for laundry, the manager may have to work evenings and weekends.

Salaries
Laundry Managers can earn from $20,000 to $60,000, depending on the place of employment and the responsibilities assumed. Benefits usually include health and life insurance and sick and vacation leave. At properties where the public has to pay for parking (such as a theme park), free parking is usually included. As with other hospitality positions, accommodations in other hotels in the chain usually are free or discounted, as are meals.

Employment Prospects
Laundry workers are always needed wherever linens and uniforms are used daily, so employment prospects are good.

Advancement Prospects
Laundry workers can be promoted to the position of Laundry Manager, who in turn can be promoted to executive housekeeper or into other management positions. With new properties opened almost daily, there are good prospects for advancement.

Education and Training
Although a high school diploma and years of on-the-job training may be sufficient, courses in hotel and hospitality studies, laundry service, textiles, environmental issues, and business management are extremely helpful.

Special Requirements
The National Association of Institutional Linen Management, following the required years in service and training, bestows the Registered Laundry and Linen Director (RLLD) and Certified Laundry/Linen Manager (CLLM) designations.

Experience, Skills, and Personality Traits
Because the housekeeping staff may not speak English as a first language, it is important that the Laundry Manager speak at least one foreign language. He or she should possess mechanical aptitude; a knowledge of washing, stain removal, and ironing; strong communication skills; and the ability to keep track of inventory and supplies.

Unions and Associations
The National Association of Institutional Linen Management works to improve laundry technology and management through the exchange of information and educational programs. The American Hotel and Lodging Association also provides information of use to Laundry Managers.

Tips for Entry
1. Learn the laundry business from the ground up, starting as a laundry assistant at a hotel or resort.
2. Talk with Laundry Managers, asking their advice about career choices, internships, and apprenticeship programs.
3. Establish a network of people in the industry by attending local functions of the associations and organizations.
4. Subscribe to trade publications or read about current trends and developments on-line.

BED-AND-BREAKFAST OWNER

CAREER PROFILE

Duties: Oversees all functions and operations of a bed-and-breakfast establishment

Alternate Title(s): Innkeeper

Salary Range: $20,000 to $100,000

Employment Prospects: Good

Advancement Prospects: Fair

Best Geographical Location(s): Most areas of the country, particularly near tourist attractions, business areas, and picturesque locations

Prerequisites:

Education and Training—High school diploma; courses in hospitality and business management; innkeeping training

Experience—Previous experience in the hospitality industry, in a hotel, resort, or bed-and-breakfast; innsitting for other bed-and-breakfast owners

Special Skills and Personality Traits—Good oral and written communication skills; good time and business management; computer skills

Licensure/Certification—Local and state zoning and occupancy licenses

CAREER LADDER

```
┌─────────────────────────────────────┐
│      Bed-and-Breakfast Owner         │
└─────────────────────────────────────┘

┌─────────────────────────────────────┐
│  Assistant Manager, Bed-and-Breakfast │
└─────────────────────────────────────┘

┌─────────────────────────────────────┐
│      Assistant Manager, Hotel        │
└─────────────────────────────────────┘
```

Position Description

A Bed-and-Breakfast Owner is the host to guests in his or her home as a home-away-from-home for business and leisure travelers. These lodging facilities are very attractive for the executive who might be on the road for days or weeks at a time and be tired of cookie-cutter hotels that often provide impersonal service and every-day food. They are attractive to leisure travelers who want to really learn about a destination and perhaps make friends who will last for a lifetime.

This segment of the lodging industry has grown from 1,000 properties in 1980 to more than 19,000 inns in 2001. Nearly half of them are run as a "hobby" or part-time business (e.g., open seasonally), using reservation services and the Internet for bookings. In the early days, most Bed-and-Breakfast Owners were retired couples looking for something to do with their big, empty, multibedroomed homes.

Today, many owners are entering the business at a younger age as a lifetime career instead of a retirement occupation. They also take courses in business management, food services, marketing, and other subjects so they can make wise business decisions. Others, young and old, enter the business by buying an existing bed-and-breakfast.

Among the decisions an owner must make is whether the bed-and-breakfast will be open daily or just weekends, all year, seasonally, or closed so the owners can take a vacation. The owners also have to decide if children will be allowed and if pets will be permitted.

The Bed-and-Breakfast Owner must perform or oversee every aspect of the operation, including acquiring the zoning permits, complying with local and state regulations, meeting health department standards, decorating, doing the maintenance, marketing, gardening, housekeeping, setting room rates, bookkeeping and payroll, computing and paying travel agent commissions, entertaining, shopping for supplies, meal planning and preparation, and a dozen other things. As the Bed-and-Breakfast Owners may wish to hire a housecleaner, chef, gardener, receptionist, and other staff, they have to interview potential employees and initiate taxes, social security, and bonding paperwork.

When guests arrive, the owner, receptionist, host, or hostess helps the guests with their luggage, offers a tour of the property and perhaps a glass of tea, lemonade, wine, or a cup of coffee to the travelers (even if they are not weary).

The day starts early with breakfast, set either to the owners' time preference or as the guests are ready for it. Some offer to serve breakfast on a tray and set it outside the guest room door. Some serve a Continental breakfast (beverage and Danish or croissant), and some serve a full breakfast including a choice of cereal, eggs, and breakfast meat (or vegetarian options).

Many Bed-and-Breakfast Owners enjoy an afternoon tea or evening wine-and-cheese session with their guests. A few bed-and-breakfast establishments also offer dinner to their guests and outsiders (for a fee), so menus must be planned and food purchased, prepared, and served.

As area residents, the owners may be asked for recommendations for restaurants, sightseeing, and shopping. They should have a good supply of brochures about the area and know the owners of several good restaurants to help ensure last-minute reservations. The owners must decide if they are going to wait up until their last guests have returned, give the guests a house key, or leave the front door open so the guests can enter without disturbing the owners.

If the bed-and-breakfast is particularly attractive and in a scenic area, the owners might consider renting the property for weddings, thus providing the setting, lodging, and perhaps meals as an attractive all-in-one package for the bride and groom. Some properties are promoted as a small meeting site, and others are marketed to such specific segments as dog lovers, gay and lesbian travelers, and romantic getaways. Special events, including mystery weekends, quilting lessons and sessions, cooking seminars, and birding excursions attract many guests who might not otherwise visit. Another revenue source is from a gift shop that can stock locally made crafts and artwork, sundries, guidebooks, and other items travelers might want to purchase for daily use or as a souvenir.

If the owners are planning to take their own vacation, travel for business, or get away for weddings or other family events, they must hire a manager or an innsitter or program a time when the bed-and-breakfast will be closed. An alternative to a bed-and-breakfast is a boat-and-breakfast for those who live on the water.

Salaries

In determining the costs and fees for a bed-and-breakfast, it is important to establish a salary and not just "take what's leftover." Net profits depend on many factors, including whether the bed-and-breakfast home had to be purchased or was already owned. Considering the operating costs, it is easy to see why annual expenses for a new facility with one to four rooms can have annual expenses of more than $70,000. The average revenue for small inns in 2000 was about $100,000 (not including the mortgage and owners' salary). By the time the bed-and-breakfast has been operating for seven years the expenses are up to nearly $147,000, with total revenues at nearly $250,000 (with the major increases in advertising and promotion, business taxes and fees, food and beverage, and repairs and fixtures). Expenses and relative profits are higher in establishments with more bedrooms than in those with four or fewer rooms.

Employment Prospects

Bed-and-breakfast establishments are found throughout the country, with the most (36 percent) in the Northeast, followed by the West (28 percent), South (20 percent), and Midwest (15 percent). Although some are located in urban areas (20 percent), most are located in small resort villages (49 percent) and rural areas (31 percent).

Advancement Prospects

Advancement tends to come from a fairly high turnover as people sell their bed-and-breakfast establishment or by purchasing more than one property.

Education and Training

Although a degree in hospitality studies is not necessary for a couple to open a bed-and-breakfast, courses in bookkeeping, marketing, public relations, and hospitality-related subjects are helpful. The Professional Association of Innkeepers International offers frequent basic and advanced seminars useful to innkeepers.

Special Requirements

Local and state zoning and occupancy licenses are required to operate any commercial lodging establishment, including a bed-and-breakfast.

Experience, Skills, and Personality Traits

Good written and oral communication skills, interpersonal skills, and the ability to handle a number of tasks simultaneously are all necessary, both in dealing with employees and guests. Computer skills are helpful for bookkeeping and maintaining an Internet presence. Previous experience in the hospitality industry, whether at a hotel or restaurant, is beneficial.

Unions and Associations

There are no unions for Bed-and-Breakfast Owners, but the Professional Association of Innkeepers International is the largest association of innkeepers (large and small properties). They offer seminars, training, and pertinent publications to members and nonmembers.

Tips for Entry

1. Learn the bed-and-breakfast business from the ground up, perhaps starting as a receptionist or other staff member of a bed-and-breakfast, as an innsitter, or working at another type of lodging facility.

2. Talk with Bed-and-Breakfast Owners, asking their advice about career options.

3. Establish a network of people in the industry by attending local functions held by Bed-and-Breakfast Owners.

4. Subscribe to trade publications or read about current trends and developments on-line.

INNSITTER

CAREER PROFILE

Duties: Oversees all functions and operations of a bed-and-breakfast establishment or inn on a temporary basis

Alternate Title(s): None

Salary Range: $100 to $250 a day, plus expenses

Employment Prospects: Good

Advancement Prospects: Fair

Best Geographical Location(s): Any tourist destination with bed-and-breakfasts or inns

Prerequisites:

Education and Training—Courses in bookkeeping, hospitality, and computer software are helpful

Experience—Experience in assisting bed-and-breakfast and inn owners in their daily operations; former owner of a bed-and-breakfast; work experience in the hospitality field

Special Skills and Personality Traits—Must be flexible; able to deal with a variety of personality types; able to handle emergencies; able to cook, at least breakfast; personable; organized; good communication skills

CAREER LADDER

```
┌─────────────────────────────────┐
│     Bed-and-Breakfast Owner     │
└─────────────────────────────────┘

┌─────────────────────────────────┐
│            Innsitter            │
└─────────────────────────────────┘

┌─────────────────────────────────┐
│   Bed-and-Breakfast Employee    │
└─────────────────────────────────┘
```

Position Description

Many people are in the bed-and-breakfast and inn business. Many people would like to be but do not relish the thought of all the demands of a full-time bed-and-breakfast business. Some people are not sure they can earn a sufficient income in return for the work and time involved. Others have owned a bed-and-breakfast, retired, but do not want to give up the bed-and-breakfast life completely. These people become Innsitters. When innkeepers have to go out of town for a wedding, graduation, or just to get away, they hire Innsitters. Innsitters go from one bed-and-breakfast to another, staying as little as one week to a month or more, and take over the operation of the bed-and-breakfast while the owners are away. They love the idea of entertaining and being involved with all the minutia of operating a bed-and-breakfast or inn, but they do not necessarily want to do it 365 days a year because they want to travel. For them, innsitting is the best of both worlds. To some extent they can choose the location where they want to go and find a bed-and-breakfast establishment or inn that needs sitting.

Their responsibilities are the same as if they owned the bed-and-breakfast or inn. They must take reservations, greet guests and show them to their rooms (offering to carry their luggage), take guests on a tour of the home if they want, offer a welcoming beverage or snack, and suggest things for them to see and do in the area. Innsitters collect and distribute brochures about the area, collect local restaurant menus, prepare the rooms for the guests, order and stock supplies, buy groceries, make breakfast, and host the afternoon wine and cheese reception if there is one. They also make minor repairs, mow the lawn, weed the garden, handle any business issues that arise (with the permission of or on instructions from the owner), get up early to make the first pot of coffee, and go to bed late after everything is locked up. The Innsitters have to plan meals, grocery shop, clean up after meals, organize social activities, coordinate day-to-day activities, do the laundry, vacuum the house, clean all the guestrooms and bathrooms, purchase and arrange flowers, and whatever else comes up.

In exchange, the Innsitters receive a place to stay (possibly in a part of the country they like visiting), payment for their services, and perhaps the use of the innkeeper's car. From payment and transportation costs to whether they can bring their children or a pet, everything is negotiable. Depending on how much work the Innsitters want to do, their experience, and abilities, they can work as many weeks a year as they wish.

Salaries
Pay for Innsitters ranges from about $100 a day to $250 a day and can be based on a flat salary or a percentage of the room rate multiplied by the number of rooms available to rent or the number of rooms actually rented. Full-time Innsitters rarely receive any benefits.

Employment Prospects
Employment prospects are good to excellent because more bed-and-breakfast establishments open every year, and their owners invariably want their own vacation or need to get away for weddings, graduations, or other events. Therefore, they either have to shut down their inn while gone or hire Innsitters.

Advancement Prospects
Innsitters may go on to manage an inn, open their own bed-and-breakfast, or start an Innsitter booking service through which they coordinate between bed-and-breakfast owners and people who want to be Innsitters.

Education and Training
Hospitality training, whether as a hotel manager, chef, or previous bed-and-breakfast or inn owner, is excellent training. Computer literacy and a bookkeeping background are helpful, as is a formal education in hospitality or hotel management.

Experience, Skills, and Personality Traits
Experience as an innkeeper is not necessarily essential but is desirable. Innsitters should be flexible and enjoy working with a variety of people. They should be gracious and enjoy handiwork, minor repairs, and entertaining. They must be well organized and possess good communication skills.

Unions and Associations
There are no unions for Innsitters, but the Professional Innsitters Association provides education, training, conferences, and networking and makes Innsitter listings available to bed-and-breakfast owners.

Tips for Entry
1. Work for a bed-and-breakfast or other property in the hospitality field.
2. Meet with bed-and-breakfast owners and Innsitters to establish a network of people who can let you know about job openings and training sessions.
3. Read trade publications, either by subscription or online.

CASINO MANAGER

CAREER PROFILE

Duties: Oversees all activities within a casino

Alternate Title(s): Casino Floor Manager

Salary Range: $60,000 to $92,000

Employment Prospects: Good

Advancement Prospects: Good

Best Geographical Location(s): Las Vegas, Reno, Sparks, Laughlin, Atlantic City, California, and other places with casinos, including the Caribbean, United Kingdom, Canada, and Australia; on cruise ships

Prerequisites:

Education and Training—High school diploma at a minimum; college degree in business administration or related field suggested

Experience—Work experience in a casino, as a dealer, pit boss, or in other managerial positions

Special Skills and Personality Traits—Supervisory and interpersonal skills; organized; able to do multiple tasks simultaneously

Licensure/Certification—Many areas require some form of licensure; bonding

CAREER LADDER

```
┌─────────────────────────────┐
│       Casino Manager        │
└─────────────────────────────┘

┌─────────────────────────────┐
│        Shift Manager        │
└─────────────────────────────┘

┌─────────────────────────────┐
│       Floor Supervisor      │
└─────────────────────────────┘

┌─────────────────────────────┐
│          Pit Boss           │
└─────────────────────────────┘
```

Position Description

A Casino Manager oversees the daily operations of a casino under the guidance of the casino owner, a board of directors, or other management board. The Casino Manager is responsible for all the employees working in the casino, the table games, the maintenance and repair of all the gaming machines, and the security of the casino's money, employees, and guests.

Besides possessing excellent management skills, the Casino Manager should be completely familiar with all federal and state regulations for land-based casinos, and any pertinent regulations affecting casinos aboard cruise ships. A Casino Manager, working with other department heads, makes sure there is sufficient staffing, that staff is well-trained, and that all safety regulations are observed.

Depending on the size of the casino, the Casino Manager may also be responsible for any restaurants or food service operations, gift shops, the entertainment center, and hotel or motel operations.

Guest satisfaction is an important part of a casino's operation. Special attention must be paid to frequent visitors and high-rollers (those who wager large amounts frequently), to ensure they are given the best available accommodations, dining options, spa treatments, and other benefits. Day-trippers, those who take buses to a casino and home again in one day (particularly to the Atlantic City casino market), are another large audience that must be attended to.

And, of course, it is important that a casino make money, so the Casino Manager must work closely with the accountants, marketing specialists, and other personnel involved in the daily operations.

Salaries

Casino salaries tend to be based on the number of slot machines and games rather than the number of hotel rooms.

Therefore, a casino with up to 1,500 slots might pay a Casino Manager $60,000; one with 1,500 to 3,000 slots might pay $74,000; one with 3,000 or more might pay as much as $92,000.

Employment Prospects

Casino employment opportunities are abundant, particularly as new casinos are opening across the country. Lower positions are the easiest to obtain, but there are good prospects for Casino Managers as well.

Advancement Prospects

As more casinos open there will be a constant need for Casino Managers to move from one casino to a more prestigious casino or one that pays more. Casino Managers can move up to managing a number of casinos or by advancing into other executive positions.

Education and Training

A high school diploma is the minimum educational requirement for Casino Managers, although a college degree in business administration or a related field is suggested. A foreign language is essential in working for casinos in other countries and is helpful in U.S. casinos as well. Learn the various casino games, and take courses in computers, math, and management.

Experience, Skills, and Personality Traits

Although many Casino Managers now have a college degree in business management or other related field, they may also have climbed the ranks, starting as a money carrier (taking money between the games and the cashiers), then rising to be a dealer in blackjack, baccarat, roulette, Caribbean poker, and other games. From there they rise to assistant pit boss (overseeing the dealers) and next to pit boss, followed by assistant floor manager and finally Casino Manager.

Casino Managers must possess excellent supervisory and interpersonal skills to deal with customers and employees. Good oral and written skills are helpful in filing reports and dealing with employees. They also need to be able to stand and walk for long periods of time.

Unions and Associations

There are no unions or associations specifically for Casino Managers. However, membership in the American Hotel and Lodging Association can be helpful in increasing management skills.

Tips for Entry

1. Learn the casino business from the ground up, perhaps starting as a change person, then a dealer, and taking additional instruction in the various games.
2. Talk with Casino Managers, asking their advice about career choices, internships, and apprenticeship programs.
3. Establish a network of people in the industry by attending local functions of the American Hotel and Lodging Association chapters and similar organizations.
4. Subscribe to trade publications or read about current trends and developments on-line.

FOOD AND BEVERAGE

RESTAURANT MANAGER

CAREER PROFILE

Duties: Oversees the operation of a restaurant, including staff supervision, training, hiring and firing, setting work schedules, creating and maintaining standards, handling customer satisfaction

Alternate Title(s): None

Salary Range: $25,000 to $60,000+

Employment Prospects: Good to excellent

Advancement Prospects: Good to excellent

Best Geographical Location(s): Major cities and areas with a large number of outstanding hotels, resorts, restaurants; cruise ships

Prerequisites:

Education and Training—College degree in restaurant management, business, public relations, or other related subject is desirable for high visibility restaurants; high school diploma with some college-level courses in same areas is helpful for lower-profile establishments

Experience—Supervisory experience in a restaurant environment or in another field, with some restaurant background

Special Skills and Personality Traits—Supervisory skills; good written and oral communication skills; business skills; able to handle multiple tasks simultaneously

CAREER LADDER

```
┌─────────────────────────────────────┐
│     Food and Beverage Manager       │
└─────────────────────────────────────┘

┌─────────────────────────────────────┐
│         Restaurant Manager          │
└─────────────────────────────────────┘

┌─────────────────────────────────────┐
│         Assistant Manager           │
└─────────────────────────────────────┘
```

Position Description

A Restaurant Manager, depending on the size of the restaurant and its staff, may be responsible for hiring, firing, training, and scheduling staff members; overseeing purchases through the food and beverage department, including supplies, furniture, accessories, and food items; and assuring customer satisfaction. The manager may also be responsible for all advertising and public relations activities, equipment repair scheduling, and state and local regulation compliance for the safety and health of the restaurant's employees and customers. Other tasks controlled by the manager are the budget, sales projections, and the nightly audit and bank deposit. This requires knowledge of accounting software

programs. In a large restaurant, the manager may oversee some or all of these duties; in a smaller operation, the manager is usually responsible for all of them.

Because customer satisfaction is one of any restaurant's main goals, the manager must do whatever is possible to assure the customers are pleased with the service, the appearance of the restaurant, and the meal. If something is wrong, the manager works to resolve the problem so that the customer will return. This may mean offering a free dessert or after-dinner beverage, reducing the price of the dinner, offering it for free, or offering the customer one or more free meals on the next visit. Since giving away food and beverages is detrimental to the profit of the restaurant, it is important that the customer be satisfied and not have a complaint.

Hiring new staff is expensive considering the cost of placing a classified ad and providing training and any new uniforms, so it is important that the Restaurant Manager keep the employees happy as well. A good training program and frequent recognition for a job well done help retain good employees. Because restaurants are open late, may open early, and are open seven days a week, a Restaurant Manager can expect long hours, including evening and weekend shifts.

Aside from attending trade shows, Restaurant Managers usually are not required to travel extensively. However, restaurants that are part of a chain may offer a transfer from one restaurant location to another. The larger the chain or the wider the geographic distribution of its outlets, the more chance there is to travel or move. Cruise ships offer the best chance for consistent travel.

Salaries

Depending on the size, eminence, and location of the restaurant, the responsibilities assumed by the manager, and his or her experience and education, a Restaurant Manager can earn from $25,000 to $75,000 and up. Some restaurants offer salary increases or bonuses based on restaurant performance.

Full-time Restaurant Managers usually receive vacation and sick leave and life and medical insurance. Some restaurants offer retirement plans and stock investment options. Some restaurants also offer tuition reimbursement for work-related courses taken while employed with them. One or more free meals a day, although not necessarily at regular eating times, are included. Reduced free meals or price may be offered to family members.

Employment Prospects

Restaurants are always looking for qualified managers, since existing managers are often promoted within a company to a higher corporate position or transferred to open a new restaurant. Other new restaurants and resorts, hotels, and cruise ships with one or more dining options are opening on a daily basis.

Advancement Prospects

As the number of restaurants increases, the potential for advancement is good to excellent. Also, because of the long hours, there is a fair amount of burnout, requiring replacement. A good manager may be promoted to oversee a number of restaurants or be hired away by larger or more prestigious restaurant.

Education and Training

The more prestigious the restaurant, the higher the education level required. A five-star dining room will require at least a bachelor's degree in management, preferably related to food service, and sometimes advanced degrees. Computer literacy is essential, as almost every restaurant today uses a computer for ordering, inventory, billing, employee time cards, maintaining schedules, contacting the company and regular customers via email, and other aspects of the restaurant business. Other courses in advertising, public relations, and human resources are desirable. A foreign language is helpful at almost every type of restaurant, because the manager must deal with employees, customers, and suppliers who speak a foreign language.

Experience, Skills, and Personality Traits

Restaurant Managers should have held progressively more responsible supervisory management positions in more prestigious restaurants or other food- and beverage-related operations (e.g., cafeteria, catering). They should have excellent oral and written communication skills and good management skills. They should be able to interact well with people and be able to teach. Flexibility is required because of frequent long, late, and weekend hours and the potential for problems because of late or no food delivery, equipment malfunction, or customer dissatisfaction.

Unions and Associations

The Council on Hotel, Restaurant and Institutional Education (CHRIE) and the National Restaurant Association Educational Foundation (EFNRA) offer additional training and courses to help advance a career, including certification as a foodservice management professional (FMP).

Tips for Entry

1. Learn the restaurant business from the ground up, perhaps starting at a fast-food operation and working up to a full-service restaurant or the food and beverage department of a hotel or resort.
2. Talk with Restaurant Managers, asking their advice about career choices, internships, and apprenticeship programs.
3. Establish a network of people in the industry by attending local functions of the National Restaurant Association chapters and similar organizations.
4. Subscribe to trade publications or read about current trends and developments on-line.

FOOD AND BEVERAGE DIRECTOR

CAREER PROFILE

Duties: Oversees all food and beverage services in a hotel, resort, or on a cruise ship; coordinates staff, food preparation, and ordering to ensure profitable sales

Alternate Title(s): Food and Beverage Manager

Salary Range: $28,000 to $85,000

Employment Prospects: Good

Advancement Prospects: Excellent

Best Geographical Location(s): Major cities and areas with a large number of outstanding hotels, resorts, restaurants, or cruise ships

Prerequisites:

Education and Training—High school diploma; degree from a culinary school with courses in business management and hospitality-related topics

Experience—Managerial training in food and beverage departments

Special Skills and Personality Traits—Must be detail oriented; organized; able to negotiate and communicate well

CAREER LADDER

```
┌─────────────────────────────────┐
│   Food and Beverage Director    │
└─────────────────────────────────┘

┌─────────────────────────────────┐
│      Restaurant Manager         │
└─────────────────────────────────┘

┌─────────────────────────────────┐
│       Assistant, Food and       │
│      Beverage Department         │
└─────────────────────────────────┘

┌─────────────────────────────────┐
│   Wait Staff, Restaurant or Bar  │
└─────────────────────────────────┘
```

Position Description

A Food and Beverage Director coordinates everything that goes on in all food and beverage venues within a hotel, resort, or cruise ship, including room service, bars, catering, restaurants, and snack bar. The responsibilities include ordering food items that may range from ordinary staples for the regular menu to exotic mushrooms or specific-flavored ice cream cones for a private banquet, from the breakfast cafe to the ballroom dining experience of 600 people or more. This is done in conjunction with the chef(s), catering manager, sales manager, and individual restaurant managers. Coordination with other hotel personnel is essential, so a chef can have enough of an item he or she wants to feature on a menu, and a large party can be assured that the catering department has acquired ingredients that do not conflict with food restrictions (dietary or religious).

The beverage side of this position includes alcoholic and nonalcoholic beverages for all food venues and bars. It is important to keep a large and varied inventory to handle almost all requests in a bar, but not so diverse that an exotic bottle will take up space for an extended period of time and not make back the cost of the beverage.

For special functions, the Food and Beverage Director may meet with the client and personnel from other departments to make sure all the arrangements can be met or to suggest alternatives to food items that may be out of season or otherwise difficult or exceedingly expensive to purchase. In some cases, the Food and Beverage Director will continue to meet with staff and client and even attend the function to make sure all is going smoothly.

It is important that the Food and Beverage Director, or whoever is handling the ordering, knows which providers specialize in specialty items and who offers the best price, quality, and delivery options. These are all important considerations that can improve or harm the profit of the operation and please or disappoint a client.

Storage space—in lockers or coolers—is a major consideration, as is the timing of orders so that perishable items are used at their peak. Delivery times must be coordinated to use the appropriate space and when there are people available to transfer the items from the delivery truck to the kitchen and pantry. In a large establishment many of these duties will be assigned to other people, with the Food and Beverage Director coordinating all activities. In smaller properties, the Food and Beverage Director will have to orchestrate all these functions alone. The Food and Beverage Director may also work with the property's web designer and manager to promote special meals for holidays or provide on-line menus for prospective guests to view. Some websites also include recipes of the restaurant's signature dishes. Although most of the Food and Beverage Director's functions are managerial, it helps to have some food preparation background to better understand the demands and restrictions that affect an efficient and profitable food and beverage department.

With more hotels, resorts, and cruise ships adding additional properties, there is an excellent chance for transfer to another location. Some travel may be required to attend conferences, trade shows, and training seminars.

Salaries

The larger and more luxurious the establishment, the higher the salary, with small budget or economy hotels paying from $19,000 to $45,000 annually and larger, more luxurious properties paying from $61,000 to $85,000. In higher cost-of-living areas, including the Northeast, Pacific, and South Atlantic, salaries are a little higher than in other areas. A lower salary does not necessarily mean less responsibility, as a smaller property may ask a Food and Beverage Director to also function as chef and restaurant manager. A boutique hotel may pay as much as 25 percent more than does a chain hotel for the same position.

Full-time Food and Beverage Directors usually receive vacation and sick leave and life and medical insurance. They are often eligible for retirement savings and stock investment plans. Free or discounted meals and lodging at the property are often made available to the Food and Beverage Director. Discounted stays at other hotels within the chain or on another cruise ship are also possible.

Employment Prospects

Employment options should be good to excellent in the near future, particularly as hotels of all sizes and almost all price ranges are offering meeting facilities and small function rooms that provide catering services. More locations are also offering at least a Continental breakfast, and more resorts are adding top-notch eating experiences. All areas of the country should have opportunities for employment, with most positions available where there is a large concentration of lodging establishments.

Advancement Prospects

Advancement potential is excellent for those who want progressively more responsible jobs and for those who are interested in relocating to other areas, as Food and Beverage Directors are promoted or move to other locations or properties. There is always a strong demand for good Food and Beverage Directors. From this position, it is relatively easy to advance to become a general manager of a hotel or to oversee the Food and Beverage Directors at a number of properties owned by the same chain.

Education and Training

A basic understanding of the various components of the food and beverage industry is essential, and a degree in restaurant management is helpful. A foreign language is helpful in negotiating with other hotel staff members and the various food and beverage provisioners.

Experience, Skills, and Personality Traits

Previous experience in running a bar or restaurant or as an assistant in a food and beverage department is essential, particularly with a background in supervising other employees. The ability to negotiate fair prices and a willingness to work long evening and weekend hours are important.

Unions and Associations

A Food and Beverage Director may join the Hotel Employees and Restaurant Employees International Union, which represents more than 250,000 people. The American Hotel and Lodging Association is the primary association for additional industry information.

Tips for Entry

1. Take courses in business administration and food services.
2. Work as a waitperson (server) or bartender or in the kitchen.
3. Stay informed by reading trade publications, either in print or on-line.
4. Meet with Food and Beverage Directors to establish a network of employers who are eager to promote hard-working and dedicated employees. Check with them about internships and apprenticeships.

CATERING SALES MANAGER

CAREER PROFILE

Duties: Solicits, books, plans, and coordinates meetings and functions for catering facilities

Alternate Title(s): Banquet Sales Manager

Salary Range: $36,000 to $100,000, plus commission or bonus

Employment Prospects: Good

Advancement Prospects: Good

Best Geographical Location: Major cities and areas with a large number of outstanding hotels, resorts, restaurants, or cruise ships

Prerequisites:

Education and Training—Computer training, particularly in Excel, Outlook, Delphi, and word processing; bachelor's degree, preferably in hotel management

Experience—Prior sales experience; restaurant experience

Special Skills and Personality Traits—Excellent business development skills; determination; menu-pricing skills; strong oral and written communication skills; sales ability

CAREER LADDER

```
┌─────────────────────────────┐
│   General Sales Manager     │
└─────────────────────────────┘

┌─────────────────────────────┐
│   Catering Sales Manager    │
└─────────────────────────────┘

┌─────────────────────────────┐
│   Catering Sales Assistant  │
└─────────────────────────────┘

┌─────────────────────────────┐
│   Restaurant or Hotel Sales │
│        Representative        │
└─────────────────────────────┘
```

Position Description

A Catering Sales Manager solicits, books, plans, and coordinates meetings and functions that use a banquet space to meet or exceed sales goals. This includes surveying the local community and creating the collateral material (e.g., brochures with room layouts and seating arrangements) necessary to sell the space. The manager may work for a restaurant, a chain of restaurants, a hotel or resort, a convention center, or other establishment that offers banquet facilities and services and may oversee other catering sales personnel. Catering sales may be directed to local organizations or associations, inbound groups (conventions, reunions, etc.), or local residents (weddings, bar/bat mitzvahs, parties). When dealing with local organizations, it helps if the Catering Sales Manager is very involved with the community and its organizations.

After soliciting business, the Catering Sales Manager meets with the clients to discuss their needs, including the number of people who will be attending, any special dietary needs, choice of menu and beverage selections, prices, whether audiovisual equipment or a band is needed, and then prepares and presents the contract. Once signed, the Catering Sales Manager blocks the appropriate space for the function. The manager may also work with the hotel sales manager to reserve accommodations.

The Catering Sales Manager monitors the cut off dates by which time reservations or a head count must be made and arranges for any VIPs, limo requests, and other special needs, including assistance for those who have physical disabilities. It is up the manager to enforce the sales contract and to work with the client in case of emergencies that might affect the stipulations in the contract.

Catering Sales Managers work with the banquet or food and beverage department to determine menu options and prices. They also work with the housekeeping and engineering departments to assure a high level of service and happy clients. Because sales are involved, there is a lot of work with spreadsheets and other computer software, possibly including Delphi, Excel, Outlook, and word processing. Unlike many hotel and hospitality positions, the Catering Sales Manager rarely has to work weekends or holidays, although some late hours may be required.

Salaries

Full-time Catering Sales Managers may earn up to $100,000 or more including bonuses, depending on the size of the property or restaurants. They usually receive vacation and sick leave and life and medical insurance and may be eligible for retirement and stock investment plans and educational assistance. They may also receive free or reduced-price meals and, if they work for a hotel chain or a company that caters to airlines, reduced-cost travel accommodations. Relocation expenses usually are not covered.

Employment Prospects

With people living farther apart and in smaller homes and with couples both working so they have no time for large entertainment, there is more demand for places where families can gather for holidays and special events. Similarly, organizations and associations are downsizing their office and meeting spaces and catering staff, so they are looking for spaces for meetings with catering facilities. Therefore, there will be a fairly steady demand for salespeople who can book these events.

Advancement Prospects

A Catering Sales Manager may advance to other sales positions in a hotel chain or other areas of the travel industry, including room sales, convention sales, and general managerial positions.

Education and Training

Computer training, particularly in Excel, Outlook, Delphi, and word processing and a bachelor's degree, preferably in hotel management, are important prerequisites for this position.

Experience, Skills, and Personality Traits

A sales background, predominantly in the food or hospitality industry, is beneficial. Interpersonal, math, menu pricing, computer, and business development skills are required. Because catering sales require a lot of cold calls, the Catering Sales Manager should have determination to find likely clients and to make sales. Strong oral and written communication skills are necessary.

Unions and Associations

The National Association of Catering Executives, with chapters throughout the country, holds annual conferences and facilitates continuing education for catering professionals. The International Association of Convention and Visitors Bureaus (IACVB) provides meeting and support services for Catering Sales Managers.

Tips for Entry

1. Work at a convention center or hotel with conference and banquet services.
2. Contact Catering Sales Managers about job potential and internships.
3. Attend local functions and trade shows to develop a network of people who can provide information about job openings and internships.
4. Read trade publications, either in print or on-line.

CHEF

CAREER PROFILE	CAREER LADDER

Duties: Coordinates all components of meal service, including creating recipes and menus, overseeing food preparation, estimating and ordering supplies and provisions, and cleanliness of the kitchen

Alternate Title(s): Executive Chef; Master Chef; Chef de Cuisine

Salary Range: $40,000 to $125,000+

Employment Prospects: Fair to good

Advancement Prospects: Good

Best Geographical Location: Major cities and areas with a large number of outstanding hotels, resorts, restaurants and cruise ships and also in train diner cars

Prerequisites:

Education and Training—Fine restaurants usually require a degree from an accredited culinary school, although extensive experience including progressively greater responsibilities may substitute

Experience—Several years of work as an assistant chef or in other restaurant positions

Special Skills and Personality Traits—Ability to multitask and solve problems; staff motivation skills; computer literacy; cooking creativity if position includes menu creation

Licensure/Certification—Certification from the American Culinary Federation as a master chef, chef de cuisine, executive chef, culinarian, or culinary educator

```
┌─────────────────────────────────┐
│   Restaurant Owner and Chef     │
└─────────────────────────────────┘

┌─────────────────────────────────┐
│             Chef                │
└─────────────────────────────────┘

┌─────────────────────────────────┐
│           Sous Chef             │
└─────────────────────────────────┘
```

Position Description

Restaurants, hotels, resorts, cruise ships, airlines (although fewer of them these days), and some trains all employ one or more cooks under the direction of a Chef or executive chef. A Chef usually holds a managerial position and may oversee several kitchens (in hotels, resorts, and cruise ships with more than one dining location), each with its own Chef. Responsibilities include the planning of menus, portion sizes, and control; meeting the quality standards of the restaurant and any governmental offices that may have jurisdiction over the restaurant; and employee training. The Chef should keep track of the number of employees, their competency, and the amount of payroll involved in the efficient operation of the kitchen.

A Chef may or may not decide the type of cuisine offered—whether it is fare from Italy, Spain, France, the United States, or elsewhere—and the type of service (including table cloth, fast-food, or buffet). The Chef must have excellent culinary skills to ensure that the food is appetizing in taste and appearance. Another major requirement is budgeting knowledge, including the cost of the food used in preparation, the availability of seasonal products, the amount of waste involved, and the price charged for the meal so the restaurant shows a profit (an exception might be in a casino operation where the restaurant is used to entice people into the casino, which produces the majority of the income).

A Chef creates new dishes, either from scratch or by modifying existing recipes to reflect the tastes of the customers and the availability of ingredients. When there are sous or assistant chefs, the Chef must train each of them in the preparation of these dishes and then supervise their work.

A Chef may also be called on to compete in local, regional, or national culinary contests or be available to represent the restaurant at charity and community events, thus requiring some travel. Seminars and trade conferences can also mean travel to distant locations. Chefs who work for a restaurant or hotel chain may have an opportunity to transfer to another location, although the chain may not pay moving costs unless the position involves supervision or management of a number of properties.

Cruise ships offer the best chance for travel. Because restaurants are generally open seven days a week and are busiest at dinner, this job often requires long and late hours and weekends. A cruise ship Chef may be on board for weeks or months at a time and then receive several weeks' vacation.

Cross-country (Amtrak) and excursion trains also employ a few Chefs. Generally, the menu is fairly limited and often determined by the season and foods available. The kitchen, or galley space, on a train is very restricted, and the train is moving and rocking, so the Chef has to be very selective in what and how food is prepared. Cross-country trains offer the most opportunity to travel, while excursion trains allow a Chef to go home every day.

Salaries
Depending on the size of the restaurant, the menu, the location, and other factors, a Chef can earn from $45,000 to more than $125,000. Other personal factors such as the Chef's training and experience, reputation, and responsibilities can affect the salary. Boutique hotels may pay as much as 25 percent more than does a chain hotel for similar positions.

Full-time Chefs usually receive vacation and sick leave and life and medical insurance. Some companies also offer savings and retirement plans and stock purchase programs. Companies may provide uniforms, or a Chef may be required to purchase them. One or more free meals a day are included, although not necessarily at regular eating times (when the restaurant is the busiest). Reduced meal prices may be offered to family members.

Employment Prospects
With new restaurants, hotels and resorts, and cruise ships coming on-line almost daily, there is a fairly constant need for Chefs. Also, openings are created when Chefs move from one restaurant to another.

Advancement Prospects
Restaurants see a very high turnover at the lower levels, thus offering a good potential for advancement from cook to specialty chef to executive chef. Good Chefs are often hired away by larger, newer, or more prestigious restaurants, thus leaving a vacancy. Other Chefs may decide to open their own restaurants once they have a loyal following.

Education and Training
A degree from an accredited culinary school, whether from the Culinary Institute of America, Wales and Johnson, or another school recognized by the American Culinary Federation, is almost always required at prestigious restaurants. Chefs can also acquire their knowledge by working through all the positions in a kitchen, perhaps developing a specialty in appetizers, entrees, soups, sauces, or desserts.

A foreign language is helpful for those who want to work abroad or with a multinational staff. Some knowledge of chemistry is good to facilitate an understanding of what ingredients react with others, and a strong knowledge of wines (domestic and imported) may be required to recommend which wine best accompanies a particular menu creation.

Special Requirements
The American Culinary Federation offers certification as a master chef, master pastry chef, chef de cuisine, executive pastry chef, executive chef, culinarian, culinary educator, and in other areas.

Experience, Skills, and Personality Traits
Besides having a great deal of culinary knowledge, a Chef must have management and administrative skills. The ability to teach is helpful, as is the ability to handle a multitude of assignments simultaneously.

Unions and Associations
The American Culinary Federation is the largest association of its kind, with 25,000 members. It offers certification and other career advancement options.

Tips for Entry
1. Take as many cooking, budgeting, and management courses as possible.
2. Spend time as an intern in a restaurant, learning about the many restaurant-related positions.
3. Check the classified advertisements in newspapers and on-line for position openings. Look under Chef, hotels, resorts, cruise ships, and other categories.
4. Talk with as many Chefs as possible, asking their advice on career goals and apprenticeship programs, and establishing a network of people who hear about many openings that are never advertised.
5. Be prepared to "show your stuff" when applying for a position, in that factors such as taste, ease of preparation, and appearance are involved in the selection of a Chef.
6. Contact a headhunting firm that specializes in culinary positions for advancement in the industry.

BARTENDER

CAREER PROFILE

Duties: Mixes and serves alcoholic and nonalcoholic beverages; stocks and manages a bar

Alternate Title(s): Dining room attendant

Salary Range: $15,000 and up, plus tips

Employment Prospects: Excellent

Advancement Prospects: Fair to good

Best Geographical Location(s): Any city or town with hotels, resorts, restaurants, and cruise ships

Prerequisites:

Education and Training—High school diploma for regular bars; at least some college for more upscale properties; training at a bartending school; some computer literacy

Experience—Restaurant service or bartending

Special Skills and Personality Traits—Great memory; knowledge of recipes for common and exotic mixed drinks; good social and math skills

CAREER LADDER

```
┌─────────────────────────────────────┐
│      Food and Beverage Manager       │
└─────────────────────────────────────┘

┌─────────────────────────────────────┐
│      Assistant Beverage Manager      │
└─────────────────────────────────────┘

┌─────────────────────────────────────┐
│              Bartender               │
└─────────────────────────────────────┘
```

Position Description

A bartender's most obvious outward function is to take and prepare drink orders from customers at a bar or from the waitstaff who have taken orders from customers. To do this, the bartender must be familiar with dozens of cocktail recipes and names or create drinks to a customer's specifications. Often drink names are regional, so an awareness of the variability of drink names is desirable. The bartender then collects the money, makes change, and keeps track of tips (particularly when tips are distributed among bartenders, waitstaff, and other restaurant employees).

Beyond mixing drinks, the bartender has to maintain an inventory of the alcoholic beverages, mixes, and other bar supplies, making sure the items are ordered, received, and stocked. The bartender also washes the glassware and mixing implements, arranges them attractively, and keeps snacks on hand (usually salty so customers get thirsty quickly) in dishes on the bar.

Many customers will frequent a bar on a regular basis, so the bartender should get to know the customers and their regular drink orders. The bartender should be able to recommend nearby restaurants and attractions and offer some advice about the area. Occasionally a bar is themed, be it sports, Irish, or wine, so the bartender may want to be familiar with what is happening in the world of sports, particularly home team standings and accomplishments; have a repertoire of Irish songs ready to sing; or have a near encyclopedic knowledge of wines, vintages, vineyards, and trends in the wine industry.

Because of the possibility of a lawsuit or criminal charge, the bartender should make sure all customers are of a legal drinking age and make sure they do not overly imbibe. Although some jurisdictions have enacted legislation prohibiting smoking in bars, it is still allowed in many. Therefore, the bartender is exposed to second-hand smoke.

Bartenders have few travel obligations other than attending industry conferences and seminars unless they work on a cruise ship. However, the skills are easily transferable whenever a bartender wants to move to a different location. One way to assure travel and celebrity is to develop a specialty, such as being known as the martini master or by creating as many unusual but tasty drinks as possible. Bartenders can specialize in one ingredient (e.g., vodka, Scotch, rum, wine), or dessert drinks, or even mocktails (cocktails without alcohol). Bartenders with such a reputation may be invited to demonstrate their specialties at trade shows, food and wine festivals, on television shows, and in other venues. Transportation, accommodations, and meals usually are paid when bartenders are invited to these events.

Salaries

Salaries are notoriously low in most bars, often below minimum wage, because it is assumed the majority of income will be from tips, which are often shared with other employees of a restaurant/bar or club. Some bars and bartenders do not always report an accurate accounting of tips, thus prompting the IRS to establish a rule-of-thumb of what bartenders should take home in tips. However, many bartenders, such as those who have been at an establishment for years, may take home $200 or more a night in tips. In general, bartenders earn more than those who work on the waitstaff. A bartender working in a restaurant may also receive free meals.

Full-time bartenders usually receive vacation and sick leave and life and medical insurance. Part-time bartenders rarely receive any benefits.

Employment Prospects

Employment opportunities for experienced bartenders are excellent and even very good for new bartenders. Even the smallest town will have a bar or bar service at a restaurant. Many people tend bar part-time to support themselves while pursuing other goals, guaranteeing steady turnover and regular openings in the field.

Advancement Prospects

A bartender can be hired by a more prestigious bar or be promoted to a food and beverage manager for those who want to go into that area. Some might open their own restaurant or bar.

Education and Training

A high school diploma (and being of legal age to serve liquor) may be the only requirements for a beginning bar-

tender. For those who want to work at more prestigious bars or go on to a career in management, additional training and education is helpful. This might include attending a school for bartending or additional courses in business management, food and beverage management, or other secondary education. A foreign language is helpful for those who want to work on a cruise ship or at a bar with a large international client base.

Experience, Skills, and Personality Traits

While some bars require previous experience at a bar, obviously a bartender has to start somewhere, and there are bars that will provide on-the-job training. Bartenders should be friendly and have an excellent memory, not just for the drinks that are ordered but for the ingredients in each cocktail ordered. Computer programs and books are available that provide recipes and mixing instructions for various drinks.

Unions and Associations

Depending on the area and the bar, bartenders may be eligible (or required) to join a bartenders' union such as the Bartenders and Beverage Union or the Hotel Employees and Restaurant Employees International Union (HERE). The National Restaurant Association provides information about bartending schools and other programs of interest to bartenders.

Tips for Entry

1. Meet bartenders for ideas about working in a bar setting and for information about job openings.
2. Read trade publications, either by subscription or online, to keep up with industry trends and legislative issues that might affect the industry.
3. Work as a waitperson to learn about drink orders, wines, and other information that will be helpful as a bartender.

BANQUET MANAGER

CAREER PROFILE

Duties: Plans, organizes, and manages the food and beverage service for an organization or business

Alternate Title(s): Caterer; Catering Manager

Salary Range: $17,600 to $70,000+

Employment Prospects: Good

Advancement Prospects: Good

Best Geographical Location(s): Wherever food service is catered to small or large groups

Prerequisites:

Education and Training—Hotel and catering management; dietetics and nutrition; food science and technology; bachelor's degree in hospitality management or a related field

Experience—Supervising and managing people; good oral and written communication skills; good business and finance skills are valued

Special Skills and Personality Traits—Proficient in Windows, spreadsheet, and word processing; able to handle multiple tasks simultaneously; active participation in community and civic activities to establish contacts; great interpersonal and management skills

Licensure/Certification—Voluntary designation as a certified professional catering executive

CAREER LADDER

```
┌─────────────────────────────────┐
│    Owner, Catering Business     │
└─────────────────────────────────┘

┌─────────────────────────────────┐
│      Director of Catering       │
└─────────────────────────────────┘

┌─────────────────────────────────┐
│        Banquet Manager          │
└─────────────────────────────────┘
```

Position Description

A catered event may mean a meal for a dozen or several hundred people. Unlike a restaurant meal, where each diner selects an appetizer, salad, entree, and dessert, from a full menu, the catered meal may include a number of hors d'oeuvres presented by the waitstaff circulating through the room, and then one choice of each course (although there may be a selection of two or three entrees due to dietary considerations) or a series of food stations. At a sit-down dinner that means each course of all dozen or several hundred meals has to be ready to serve at one time. The Banquet Manager makes sure the quality, consistency, eye appeal, and taste meet or exceed the standard for the property.

The Banquet Manager controls and organizes the work of the catering team to provide good quality food within budgeted costs. He or she selects and trains staff, monitors

and evaluates the service provided; budgets to ensure maximum profitability of the operation, while following health and safety regulations; and maintains a high level of customer contact. The Banquet Manager may also be in charge of audiovisual services. If the banquet hall or facility has union contracts with some or all of the employees, the Banquet Manager must be aware of all union policies.

A Banquet Manager may provide catering services at banquet facilities, hotels and resorts, conference centers, houses of worship, schools, and other venues. He or she may need to supervise several banquets at the same time.

Working with the catering sales, culinary, and food and beverage staffs, the Banquet Manager develops both standard and creative menus and marketing strategies to deliver quality food at the least expensive price and most profit for the catering service. The Banquet Manager may make sales calls to potential clients and develop a "most wanted" or "top 20" client list. He or she works with outside planners and vendors for special events and may participate in community and civic activities to establish a network of people and companies that could create booking opportunities.

Supervising the work of dozens of people, including the waitstaff and bartenders who set up, serve, and clean up after the function and overseeing the preparation of hundreds of meals to be served as simultaneously as possible can be extremely stressful.

Travel may be involved if the Banquet Manager attends meetings and trade shows to discuss their catering capabilities with meeting planners from various organizations and associations. Working hours often include weekends, holidays, and evenings because banquets are frequently held at those times.

Salaries

Banquet Manager salaries depend on the size of the operation, the level of responsibility, and experience. Starting pay at small operations may be $17,600 and range to $70,000 or more at the upper level. Benefits usually include life and health insurance, retirement and investment programs, sick and vacation leave, and tuition reimbursement. Meals and accommodations may be free when working for a hotel or resort. Discounts on golf, tennis, and merchandise may also be available when working for a hotel or resort. A highly experienced Banquet Manager may be paid relocation expenses. In some remote resort locations, lodging may be included.

Employment Prospects

Banquet Managers are always in demand at convention centers, banquet facilities, hotels and resorts, colleges, hospitals, and other venues. Almost any place in the country has such facilities, so there is a wide selection of beach, mountain, city, and country settings.

Advancement Prospects

A Banquet Manager with a good food and beverage background combined with sales and management can advance to overseeing several banquet facilities or open his or her own banquet and catering business.

Education and Training

A degree in hospitality or sales and management as well as training in banquet operations are essential.

Special Requirements

The National Association of Catering Executives awards a voluntary Certified Professional Catering Executive designation.

Experience, Skills, and Personality Traits

A Banquet Manager should have a flair for customer service and be able to train and manage the people he or she supervises. Strong organizational and computer skills are required.

Unions and Associations

The International Caterers Association, the National Association of Catering Executives, and the Leading Caterers of America are educational organizations for the catering industry, with publications, seminars, workshops, and demonstrations.

Tips for Entry

1. Become familiar with food and beverage and banquet operations by working as a server or in the office of a banquet facility.
2. Talk with caterers and Banquet Managers, asking their advice about career choices, internships, and apprenticeship programs.
3. Establish a network of people in the industry by attending local association functions.
4. Subscribe to trade publications or read about current trends and developments on-line.

TOUR AND TRAVEL SERVICES

RECEPTIVE TOUR COMPANY MANAGER

CAREER PROFILE

Duties: Conducts local tours for traveling charter tour companies

Alternate Title(s): Receptive Tour Operator; Step-on Tour Company Manager

Salary Range: $30,000 to $100,000

Employment Prospects: Good

Advancement Prospects: Good

Best Geographical Location(s): Areas with attractions for tourists, including Branson, Mo., New York City, Washington, D.C., New England, and Orlando in the United States, and Toronto, Niagara Falls, Montreal, Nova Scotia, and Quebec in Canada

Prerequisites:

Education and Training—High school diploma with advanced education courses in business, travel and tourism, history, geography, computers, administration, math, and sales; college degree is helpful for managerial positions; fluency in one or more foreign languages is helpful

Experience—Managerial positions, particularly in tour operations, travel agencies, or suppliers (e.g., hotels or resorts, airlines, convention and visitors bureaus), with experience in sales, negotiations, and the Internet

Special Skills and Personality Traits—Good organizational and, interpersonal skills; oral and written communication proficiency; negotiating and business management ability

Licensure/Certification—Voluntary certification can be helpful; some states require licensure following one or more training courses

CAREER LADDER

```
┌─────────────────────────────────────┐
│   President/Owner, Tour Company      │
└─────────────────────────────────────┘

┌─────────────────────────────────────┐
│     Manager, Tour Company            │
└─────────────────────────────────────┘

┌─────────────────────────────────────┐
│ Director of Operations, Tour Company │
└─────────────────────────────────────┘

┌─────────────────────────────────────┐
│          Tour Guide                  │
└─────────────────────────────────────┘
```

Position Description

The main goal of a receptive tour company is to provide a tour that goes beyond, "And on the left side of the bus is . . . " A receptive tour company is usually located in a specific geographic area of which its tour guides have an encyclopedic knowledge. The manager and most of the employees have inspected the hotels, eaten in the restaurants, seen the shows, and taken the tours of historic and cultural attractions so that they can assure the quality and appropriateness of these facilities and attractions.

The company may go beyond the normal sightseeing options by contracting for a behind-the-scenes tour of a theater or museum restoration department or a meal in the kitchen of a fine restaurant. They eliminate the possibility of a group scheduling a visit to a museum that is closed for renovation, missing a once-in-a-lifetime exhibit at a small out-of-the-way gallery, or losing out on the chance of seeing a theatrical production.

Working with tour operator companies that schedule trips into the local area, the receptive tour company helps design a tour that will interest the clients and be within their physical limitations. These groups may come from a school sponsoring a "spring trip" or from a senior citizens center. Their interests may be cultural, musical and theatrical presentations, sports, grandparent/grandchild travel, historical, or whatever is of special interest in that geographical area.

The receptive tour company may specialize in groups for seven, eight, 12, 15, or nearly 50 people, depending on the size of the vehicles they own or lease, or, they may own or lease vehicles based on the size of the groups they want to escort. Clients may be Americans or international travelers.

A Receptive Tour Company Manager deals with the same issues as does the manager of any tour company, including hiring, firing, training, budgeting, and promotion, with an added emphasis on knowing a specific geographic area inside out. The Receptive Tour Company Manager supervises all staff to determine the operating budget; conducts market research to determine what interest there is in particular tours; prices and sells the tours and services (negotiating for a discount admission, lodging, or meal price and including taxes, gratuities, and profit margin); and may be requested to make sure all required lodging, transportation, and ticket arrangements are made. Oftentimes, however, the inbound tour company makes most of those arrangements. He or she also may arrange meals and other entertainment, either as part of the package or as options. Managers meet with meeting planners and convention and visitors bureau representatives to sell tour services to inbound meeting attendees or to learn what is new and interesting and should be included in upcoming tours. They also prepare or oversee the preparation of all necessary materials for the tourguides and then evaluate the comments from guests regarding future trips, including what should be deleted or added to make the trips more enjoyable.

It is important that Receptive Tour Company Managers belong to an organization, such at the National Tour Association, that has strict requirements regarding insurance, number of tours conducted, and employee experience. The reputation of this association improves the reputation of the receptive tour company. All NTA members are covered by the association's consumer protection plan, which protects client deposits in the event the receptive tour company files for bankruptcy.

Salaries

General managers average $45,000 annually, with vice presidents earning about $52,000. Operation managers/tour planners make an average of $34,000. Most tour operations offer reimbursement for additional training of their full-time employees. Almost all full-time employees are provided with health insurance covering all or part of medical, prescription, and dental costs. About half of tour operations companies offer life insurance, and the majority provide a retirement or pension plan. Generally, employees receive two weeks paid vacation, with an additional week of sick days and personal time.

As receptive tour companies feature local tours, there is not much national or international travel connected directly with the job. However, national and international tour operator conferences, where such a company would go to solicit business and keep abreast of the industry, call for some travel.

Employment Prospects

About one-third of tour operation companies have between one and three full-time employees, while 13 percent have up to 20 full-time employees. More than 50 percent have another one to three part-time employees. With an employee turnover rate of about seven percent, there are not many openings for upper-level management personnel, especially within small operations. Larger operations offer more opportunities and a chance to learn the various aspects of the business while gaining experience for more important positions. Convention and visitors bureaus offer excellent ground-floor experience.

Advancement Prospects

As most companies are family owned and small, there is very little room for advancement among full-time employees. Larger companies offer some room for advancement.

Education and Training

Upper-level management personnel are expected to have at least some college, with most companies preferring a college degree and a small percentage requiring a postgraduate degree.

Special Requirements

The National Tour Association offers a Certified Tour Professional official recognition program. A Certified Travel Counselor program or a Destination Specialist program, offered by the Institute of Certified Travel Agents, is helpful.

Experience, Skills, and Personality Traits

Strong oral and written communication skills are essential for managerial positions and for tour guides. Management experience is helpful. It helps to have a flexible and detail-oriented personality to handle all the aspects of a tour.

Unions and Associations

The most active associations in the tour business are the National Tour Association and the U.S. Tour Operators Association. They have strict guidelines for membership and sponsor frequent regional, national, and international conferences and shows for training and one-on-one discussions with contacts from destinations, attractions, and service providers.

Tips for Entry

1. Learn the travel and tourism business from the ground up, perhaps starting as a tour guide.
2. Learn about the area, it's geography, history, culture, sports, and other special features and attractions.
3. Talk with receptive tour companies, asking their advice about career choices, internships, and apprenticeship programs.
4. Establish a network of people in the industry by attending local and National Tour Association functions.
5. Subscribe to trade publications or read about current trends and developments on-line.

TOUR OPERATOR

CAREER PROFILE

Duties: Arranges group tours to visit attractions and events

Alternate Title(s): Tour Operation Owner; Tour Operation Manager

Salary Range: $30,000 to $100,000 for tour operator president/owner

Employment Prospects: Fair to good for management positions

Advancement Prospects: Poor

Best Geographic Location: Every region of the country has tour operations, so job prospects are good; top destinations as of 2000 in the United States are Branson, Mo.; New York City; Washington, D.C.; New England; and Orlando and Toronto, Niagara Falls, Montreal, Nova Scotia, and Quebec in Canada

Prerequisites:

Education and Training—High school diploma with advanced education courses in business, travel and tourism, history, geography, computers, administration, math, and sales; college degree is helpful for managerial positions; fluency in one or more foreign languages is helpful

Experience—Managerial positions, particularly in tour operations, travel agencies, or suppliers (e.g., hotels or resorts, airlines, convention and visitors bureaus), with experience in sales, negotiations, and the Internet

Special Skills and Personality Traits—Good organizational and interpersonal skills; oral and written communication skills; negotiating and business management proficiency

Licensure/Certification—Voluntary certification can be helpful; some states require licensure following one or more training courses

CAREER LADDER

```
┌─────────────────────────────────────┐
│  Tour Operator or Tour Operation     │
│  President/Owner/Manager             │
└─────────────────────────────────────┘

┌─────────────────────────────────────┐
│  Director of Operations              │
└─────────────────────────────────────┘

┌─────────────────────────────────────┐
│  Tour Planner                        │
└─────────────────────────────────────┘
```

Position Description

A Tour Operator arranges long and short tours, lasting from a half-day (as part of a convention package or city sightseeing tour) to several weeks, with the average trip lasting about five days. The average tour operations company conducts approximately 200 tours a year for individuals (sometimes) or busloads of people (more frequently) throughout the year. While the senior market is constantly growing, more than 1 million student/youth travelers account for approximately $1 billion in travel expenses annually. A number of tour operations sell airline, cruise, and other travel-related services. For the most part, tour operations are family-owned businesses.

Tours may have a focus on historic spots, art galleries and museums, musical and theater presentations, spectator sports, hiking, adventure, ecotourism, boating, cruising, grandparent/grandchildren travel, band or class trips, or any other interest a group of people might have. They may be domestic or international or serve international visitors who are touring the United States. They may be budget tours or upscale.

The Tour Operator supervises all staff to determine the operating budget; conducts market research to determine what interest there is in particular tours; promotes the trips; sells the tours and services; and arranges all lodging, transportation, and ticket purchases. He or she may also arrange meals and other entertainment, either as part of the package or as options.

Tour Operators meet with meeting planners and convention and visitors bureau representatives to sell tour services to inbound meeting attendees or to learn what is new and interesting that should be included in upcoming tours. They negotiate prices (factoring in overhead) with hotels, restaurants, attractions, bus or airline companies, and all other providers, as well as with their customers. They also prepare or oversee the preparation of all necessary materials for the tour guides and then evaluate the comments from guests regarding future trips, including what should be deleted or added to make the trip more enjoyable. The Tour Operator should know about passport/visa requirements, any State Department travel advisories (if international travel is involved), and pertinent legislation pending at the local, regional, state, and national levels.

Salaries

General managers average $45,000 annually, with vice presidents earning about $52,000. Operation managers/tour planners make an average of $34,000. Most tour operations offer reimbursement for additional training of their full-time employees. Almost all full-time employees are provided with health insurance. About half the companies offer life insurance, and the majority provide a retirement or pension plan. Generally, full-time employees receive two weeks of paid vacation, with a week of sick days and personal time.

Employment Prospects

About one-third of tour operation companies have between one and three full-time employees, while 13 percent have up to 20 full-time employees. More than 50 percent of companies have another one to three part-time employees. With an employee turnover rate of about seven percent, there are not many openings for upper-level management within small operations. Larger operations offer more opportunities and a good way to learn the various aspects of the business while

gaining experience for more important positions. Convention and visitors bureaus offer excellent ground-floor experience.

Advancement Prospects

As most companies are family owned and small, there is very little room for advancement among full-time employees. Larger companies offer some room for advancement.

Education and Training

Tour Operators are expected to have at least some college, with most companies preferring a college degree and a small percentage requiring a postgraduate degree. Tour planners should have some college. The National Tour Association offers a program toward a Certified Tour Professional certification. A Certified Travel Counselor program or a Destination Specialist program, offered by the Institute of Certified Travel Agents, is helpful.

Experience, Skills, and Personality Traits

Strong oral and written communication skills are essential for managerial positions such as Tour Operator and for tour guides. Management experience is helpful. It helps to have a flexible and detail-oriented personality to handle all the aspects of a tour.

Unions and Associations

The most active associations in the tour business are the National Tour Association and the U.S. Tour Operators Association. They have strict guidelines for membership and sponsor frequent regional, national, and international conferences and shows for training and one-on-one discussions with contacts from destinations, attractions, and service providers.

Tips for Entry

1. Travel as much as possible through school trips, study abroad programs, and interning with Tour Operators.
2. Start part-time with a tour company and be willing to accept new responsibilities to gain additional experience. Determine which aspect of the travel industry is most desirable.
3. Attend as many travel and tourism conferences and trade shows as possible (check websites, the local convention and visitors bureau, and travel trade publications) and develop as many contacts as possible within the industry. Network as much as possible to learn about internships and job opportunities.
4. Talk with the owners and employees of local tour operations to receive career advice.
5. Develop an expertise and contact Tour Operators who specialize in that area (e.g., classical music, sports, history).

TOUR GUIDE

CAREER PROFILE

Duties: Controls all minute-by-minute operations of a sightseeing tour within one city or geographic area, narrating the sightseeing details

Alternate Title(s): Tour Host; Tour Escort; Step-on Guide

Salary Range: $115 a day (average)

Employment Prospects: Good to excellent

Advancement Prospects: Poor

Best Geographic Location(s): Every region of the United States and Canada; such top tourist destinations as Branson, Mo., New York City, Washington, D.C., New England, Orland, Toronto, Niagara Falls, Montreal, Nova Scotia, and Quebec

Prerequisites:

Education and Training—High school diploma; additional courses in travel and tourism, local history, business, and a foreign language are helpful

Experience—Previous work with a tour operation

Special Skills and Personality Traits—Good organizational skills; interpersonal skills; oral and written communication proficiency; flexibility; able to deal with a variety of personality types

Licensure/Certification—A license may be required in some locations

CAREER LADDER

```
┌─────────────────────────┐
│   Tour Operator or      │
│  Tour Company Manager   │
└─────────────────────────┘

┌─────────────────────────┐
│      Tour Guide         │
└─────────────────────────┘

┌─────────────────────────┐
│    Office Assistant     │
└─────────────────────────┘
```

Position Description

Tour Guides manage tours lasting from half a day to several days depending on the itinerary. These duties include accounting for all passengers and luggage (for multiday tours); confirming that bus, meal, and hotel reservations are accurate; awareness of the day's route and driving instructions; ensuring all guests have paid any incidental expenses at the hotel; and providing assistance to any passengers with special needs (e.g., making sure that a requested nonsmoking hotel room is a nonsmoking room). They make sure passengers know the bus or flight number and what time they are scheduled to depart and distribute admission tickets. They may be asked to check out other hotels, restaurants, and attractions for future trips. The hours are long, from early-morning wake-up calls and luggage pull until after the evening's activities, and frequently include weekends.

Step-on guides may concentrate on giving tours of a specific city or area, meeting groups at prearranged locations or picking them up at designated stops. They usually stay with their group only for the duration of the tour and do not assist with general travel matters.

Tours may have a focus on historic spots, art galleries and museums, musical and theater presentations, trekking across glaciers, spotting baby seals, spectator sports, hiking, adventure, ecotourism, boating, cruising, grandparent/grandchildren travel, or any other interest a group of people might have. They may be domestic or international or serve international visitors who are touring the United States. They may be budget tours or upscale.

In exchange, Tour Guides are paid to travel and sightsee and may receive discounts on other travel not associated with the company's tours. They also get to meet some interesting people who are taking the tours.

Salaries

Tour Guides' salaries average $115 a day, including gratuities and a meal allowance. Other incidental expenses directly related to the trip usually are covered, including transportation to and from the starting and ending points of a trip when the trip is not local. Personal incidental expenses are not covered. A full-time Tour Guide may be provided with vacation and sick leave and health and life insurance. Part-time guides rarely receive these benefits.

Employment Prospects

Small tour operators generally run fewer tours than do larger companies, so the turnover can be high as Tour Guides move to companies that can offer full-time employment. Therefore, there are generally plenty of vacancies depending on the location and the type of touring an employee wants to do.

Advancement Prospects

As most tour companies are family owned and small, there is very little room for advancement from part-time to full-time employment for Tour Guides, other than starting their own tour company. Larger companies offer some room for advancement into management positions.

Education and Training

Less than half of tour companies require a college degree from their part-time employees. Additional courses in travel and tourism, foreign languages, math, geography, and other subjects can make a Tour Guide more employable.

Special Requirements

Some jurisdictions require Tour Guides to take an exam and be licensed.

Experience, Skills, and Personality Traits

Tour Guides must have strong oral and written communication skills, and be able to handle a variety of personality types. They should be flexible and detail oriented and possess problem-solving skills to handle all aspects of a tour. Management experience is helpful for those aiming for managerial positions or planning to open their own tour companies. Any prior experience with a tour company, as an office assistant or such is beneficial for those who want to become a Tour Guide.

Unions and Associations

The most active associations in the tour business are the National Tour Association and the U.S. Tour Operators Association. They have strict guidelines for membership and sponsor frequent regional, national, and international conferences and shows for training and one-on-one discussions with contacts from destinations, attractions, and service providers. Although Tour Guides are rarely paid to attend these events, they can be helpful in the pursuit of a full-time career in a tour operation or in planning to open one's own tour company.

Tips for Entry

1. Travel as much as you can through school trips, study abroad programs, and interning with tour operators.
2. Start part-time with a tour operator and be willing to accept new responsibilities so you can learn on the job.
3. Attend as many travel and tourism conferences and trade shows as possible (check websites, local convention and visitors bureau, and travel trade publications) and develop as many contacts within the industry as possible. Network as much as possible to learn about internships and job openings.
4. Talk with the owners and employees of local tour operations to receive career advice.
5. Develop an expertise in an area you like and contact tour operators who specialize in that area (e.g., classical music, sports, history).

GENERAL MANAGER, ATTRACTION

CAREER PROFILE

Duties: Manages the operation of an attraction, including theme parks, museums, zoos, waterparks, circuses, and aquaria

Alternate Title(s): None

Salary Range: $25,000 to $110,000

Employment Prospects: Fair

Advancement Prospects: Good

Best Geographical Location(s): Tourist areas with tourist attractions

Prerequisites:

Education and Training—Bachelor's degree in park and recreation management, business and marketing, travel and tourism, or related field

Experience—Work in an attraction in progressively more responsible positions

Special Skills and Personality Traits—Interpersonal skills; budgeting and management skills

CAREER LADDER

```
┌─────────────────────────────────┐
│  General Manager, Larger or      │
│  More Prestigious Attraction     │
└─────────────────────────────────┘

┌─────────────────────────────────┐
│  General Manager, Attraction     │
└─────────────────────────────────┘

┌─────────────────────────────────┐
│  Assistant Manager, Attraction   │
└─────────────────────────────────┘

┌─────────────────────────────────┐
│  Director of Sales and           │
│  Marketing, Attraction           │
└─────────────────────────────────┘
```

Position Description

A General Manager of an attraction oversees the management and financial control of the attraction for safe and enjoyable family entertainment. This starts by developing a projected income and expense budget and hiring and training upper-level staff members who hire and train other employees. Admission fees, fundraising (for non-profit attractions), salaries, and overhead costs (e.g., mortgage or rent, utilities, maintenance, and cleaning) have to be projected so the attraction will show a profit at the end of the fiscal year.

Working with an effective marketing plan that promotes a park to local and distant travelers, the manager must estimate the number of guests who will visit the attraction each day so enough personnel can be hired and sufficient supplies (e.g., food and beverages, souvenirs) can be on hand. Too many employees puts a drain on the budget; too few leaves visitors disappointed by not receiving prompt and attentive service.

Maintenance has to be scheduled, both in prevention and repair, so that it causes only minimal disruption to the operation of the attraction. Major repairs may sometimes be made on the days the attraction is closed, in the evening, or in the winter for attractions that are open only in the summer. It is important to have as little disruption as possible.

Some attractions, particularly theme parks, are open only seasonally; some are open all year. A typical workweek may indicate forty hours of work, but late and weekend hours are not unusual. The job can be stressful because of the need to meet projected budget and guest numbers. Other than corporate and industry meetings, there is little travel involved with this position.

Salaries

Small, family-operated amusement parks offer lower salaries than do corporate theme parks, with salaries ranging from a low of $25,000 to a high of $110,000. Benefits can include a company car, health and life insurance, sick and vacation leave, and investment and retirement plans. A bonus for families is free admission to the park and other parks within the corporate structure.

Employment Prospects

Employment prospects at the top level are not stellar, but as more amusement and theme parks and attractions open, there will be steady, if not abundant, possibilities.

Advancement Prospects

A General Manager may move to larger, more prestigious attractions, become regional manager of several attractions, or open a consulting business offering advice to other attractions regarding exhibits, rides, marketing, and operations.

Education and Training

A degree in travel and tourism, perhaps with special studies in theme park and attraction management, contemporary issues relating to attractions, or other similar courses is helpful. Other courses should include human resources, public relations, management, accounting, and business practices.

Experience, Skills, and Personality Traits

Several years of work with progressively more responsible positions at an attraction are required for management positions. An ability to do multiple tasks simultaneously is helpful. Interpersonal skills are essential.

Unions and Associations

The International Association of Amusement Parks and Attractions and the American Association of Museums provide information about careers and training.

Tips for Entry

1. Learn the attraction business from the ground up, starting as an hourly employee at a local museum or theme park of interest.
2. Talk with employees at several attractions to obtain advice about career choices, internships, and apprenticeship programs.
3. Establish a network of people in the industry by attending local functions of the International Association of Amusement Parks and Attractions, the American Association of Museums, and similar organizations.
4. Subscribe to trade publications or read about current trends and developments on-line.

EXECUTIVE DIRECTOR, CONVENTION AND VISITORS BUREAU

CAREER PROFILE

Duties: Oversees all functions and operations of a city, area, or state convention and visitors bureau to attract business and leisure visitors to that area

Alternate Title(s): President, convention and visitors bureau

Salary Range: $30,000 to $125,000

Employment Prospects: Good

Advancement Prospects: Fair

Best Geographical Location: Major cities and areas with a large number of attractions for leisure visitors or a convention center and hotels to attract business travelers

Prerequisites:

Education and Training—Degree in business administration, marketing, communications, hospitality, or travel and tourism or related field or work experience equivalency; foreign language and computer literacy are helpful

Experience—Progressively more important positions in convention and visitors Bureaus in progressively larger bureaus

Special Skills and Personality Traits—Must be able to handle relationships with a range of public and private organizations; organized; able to oversee a variety of functions simultaneously; personable; able to handle a variety of personality types

CAREER LADDER

```
┌─────────────────────────────────┐
│  Executive Director, Convention  │
│       and Visitors Bureau        │
└─────────────────────────────────┘

┌─────────────────────────────────┐
│  Director of Sales and Marketing,│
│   Convention and Visitors Bureau │
└─────────────────────────────────┘

┌─────────────────────────────────┐
│ Account Representative, Sales and│
│ Marketing Office, Convention and │
│         Visitors Bureau          │
└─────────────────────────────────┘
```

Position Description

The Executive Director of a convention and visitors bureau oversees the daily operation of the bureau, including marketing, sales, and business plans. He or she promotes the convention facilities as a meeting location to associations and organizations, while promoting the area as a vacation destination to leisure travelers.

When promoting the convention center, the director acts as the official contact point for associations, organizations, and companies that have meetings of regional, national, and international interest. With the sales and marketing office, the Executive Director contacts the prospective organiza-tions to determine a group's specifications, including the amount of meeting space and the number of hotel rooms needed, audiovisual needs, catering requirements, meeting dates, transportation, and other requirements.

The Executive Director and the sales and marketing team present information to the potential client and explain why their convention center and destination are ideal for their requirements. During this presentation, they provide floorplans of the convention center, costs, dates available, transportation options, and other pertinent information. This may include a slide show, videotape, model of the convention center, and printed materials. Often the information will be contained on a CD (including photographs) that the convention and visitors bureau staff can leave with the prospective client, or it may be mailed to them.

As large conferences and trade shows are planned five to 10 years in advance, it is important that the director know what other conferences or events are planned in the area to make sure there will be sufficient hotel rooms and transportation services available. Sometimes there are holes in the convention center bookings, so the director and sales and marketing staff must keep a current list of companies or industries that can be contacted to fill in those dates with their meetings. There must also be a contingency plan for last-minute meeting cancellations, with a list of prospective clients who may be able to take advantage of the bargains that will be available for renting space and other needs.

Sometimes the sales meetings are done on a one-to-one basis, at the association or organization office or at a board meeting. At other times the director and staff members attend trade shows with other convention and visitors bureaus so they can introduce themselves and their center to many meeting planners in one or two days.

When promoting the area to leisure visitors, the bureau prepares collateral material that includes brochures of things to do and see; a calendar of events (quarterly or annually); and a list of lodging and dining options, airport convenience, and other items that will interest prospective visitors. Other special interest brochures may cover such themes as Latino or African-American culture, accessibility, history, or sports. These days, most convention and visitors bureau offices have a website with this information along with a place to request information and perhaps a place to make hotel reservations or buy tickets to an upcoming event.

The staff also prepares and creates advertising and public relations materials (or hires a company to do this) and directs these efforts to the population most likely to drive, fly, or take a train or bus to their destination. This will include print and electronic media that cover travel topics and sometimes direct mailings. The bureau may also be involved with inviting the media to the destination to promote the area and the convention center to the trade and the public. Usually, the Executive Director will oversee the media or press office as they create and execute these media visits.

All of these items must be budgeted for the upcoming year and beyond, and it is the Director's responsibility to create the budget or oversee the department that does. On the other side of the ledger, the Director must calculate income from meetings and events, dues paid by members of the bureau, and other sources.

The Executive Director also oversees interviewing, hiring, training, and sometimes firing of employees. Knowledge of the Americans with Disabilities Act (ADA) and other government rules and regulations is essential. In areas where international travelers or large ethnic populations visit, a foreign language can be helpful and may even be required to deal with incoming visitors or staff members.

A Convention and Visitors Bureau Director can expect to work more than 40 hours a week, including evenings and weekends. Extensive travel to visit prospective clients and other convention bureaus and to attend trade shows and conferences is to be expected. Some Directors stay with the same bureau for years, while other make fairly frequent moves to achieve promotions within the industry.

Salaries

Depending on the size and scope of the convention and visitors bureau, salaries can range from $25,000 to $120,000, plus bonuses. An outstanding Executive Director will most likely receive relocation costs when hired by another bureau.

Full-time convention and visitors bureau directors usually receive vacation and sick leave and life and medical insurance. They may also be eligible for retirement and stock investment programs.

Employment Prospects

As areas build convention centers and initiate visitors bureaus and as more areas of similar size with similar attractions compete against one another, there will be an increasing demand for experienced Convention and Visitors Bureau Directors. Openings will also be found where a Director is not performing satisfactorily or where a Director transfers, retires, or resigns.

Advancement Prospects

Promotions usually are made from within, with more important advancements made by transfers to other bureaus. Due to the limited number of positions, opportunity for advancement is fair.

Education and Training

A degree in sales and marketing, hospitality, or travel and tourism is almost always required, and advanced degrees are helpful. On-the-job training in lower-level positions often is required. Executive Directors should also be familiar with the city or area in which they operate.

Experience, Skills, and Personality Traits

Years of experience in positions with progressively greater responsibilities and with progressively larger convention and visitors bureaus or within other areas of the hospitality industry are essential. A good Convention and Visitors Bureau Director should be able to deal with a variety of personality types and be able to oversee a variety of functions simultaneously. He or she should also be organized and personable.

Unions and Associations

There is no union for Convention and Visitors Bureau Directors, but the International Association of Convention and Visitors Bureaus is a large organization dedicated to promoting professional practices in the field. It provides educational resources and networking opportunities and organizes conferences where meeting planners can talk with representatives from convention and visitors bureaus.

Tips for Entry

1. Work for a convention and visitors bureau or in the meetings and conferences office of an association or organization to learn about sales and tourism.

2. Meet as many convention and visitors bureau staff and Directors as possible to establish a network of people who can give career advice and information about job openings.

3. Read trade publications, either by subscription or on-line, to keep abreast of industry news and trends.

4. Read literature from various convention and visitors bureaus to see how they approach the business and leisure travel markets.

EXECUTIVE DIRECTOR, TRAVEL TRADE ASSOCIATION

CAREER PROFILE

Duties: Oversees all functions and operations of a travel trade association

Alternate Title(s): Vice President; President

Salary Range: $25,000 to $70,000+

Employment Prospects: Fair to good

Advancement Prospects: Poor

Best Geographical Location(s): Travel trade association offices can be located in any part of the country

Prerequisites:

Education and Training—Bachelor's degree; advanced degree in management, liberal arts, business administration, marketing, travel and tourism, or related field; foreign language and computer literacy

Experience—Work in a trade association with progressively more responsible positions

Special Skills and Personality Traits—Strong written and verbal communication skills; organized; computer skills; able to work with a variety of people; able to handle a number of assignments simultaneously

CAREER LADDER

```
┌─────────────────────────────┐
│     Executive Director       │
└─────────────────────────────┘

┌─────────────────────────────┐
│     Department Director      │
└─────────────────────────────┘

┌─────────────────────────────┐
│   Administrative Assistant   │
└─────────────────────────────┘
```

Position Description

A travel trade association is made up of member organizations. For example, a group of tour bus or tour packaging companies will belong to a tour bus association. Other associations are comprised of tourism destinations, lodgings, and travel agents and are usually run as nonprofit operations. As membership in these associations is voluntary, the associations depend on membership dues to keep them going. The Executive Director is primarily charged with promoting the cause of the association and recruiting and retaining membership.

For example, an association of tour bus owners and tour packagers may prepare a campaign to recognize a national tour bus month, encouraging people to take a bus tour of various parts of the country. The association's function includes compiling data on how many people take bus tours, how many days (on average) they spend on the tour, and how much money they spend (for the tour and such other items as meals, souvenirs, and attractions). They then use this information to prepare and distribute promotional and advertising materials for print and electronic media, showing the value of the members of this association for the local economy. They also come up with ideas that members can use to promote their "special" month.

This information may also be useful when a federal or local governmental body is considering legislation that would affect the members of the association. Someone from the association, either the Executive Director, the president, or chairman of the board of directors uses this information when discussing the proposed rules or regulations with elected officials and governmental staff members. Theoretically, nonprofit associations are not allowed to lobby members of Congress and some other elected officials, but they are allowed to discuss and explain the issues as the association sees it. To accomplish these goals, the Executive Director oversees the management, fund-raising, planning and budgeting, research, program development, communications and marketing, and human resources of the association.

The members have regular meetings and conferences with training seminars, exhibit booths, and social functions. The Executive Director must coordinate scheduling these meetings, speakers, hotel and transportation arrangements, exhibit space and rental, meals, spouse activities, and whatever else the members need at these gatherings.

Most associations also have one or more publications with articles about marketing, legal issues, industry news, and other items, so the Executive Director must have a staff to write, edit, and publish these papers or magazines. Membership directories, governmental rules and regulations, and other business practices may be published as a book and sold to members and nonmembers, providing another source of income to the association. With today's reliance on the Internet, the association must also have a website and someone to manage it.

An auxiliary function of some associations is a scholarship program to help deserving students (or children of association members) study in this or a related field. To raise funds for these scholarships, the Director might promote and coordinate such events as a golf tournament or a trip abroad to meet with foreign associations with similar interests or to discuss how foreign operations are different or similar to theirs.

Some associations may use the services of an Executive Director on a part-time basis, and some association executives work for more than one association at a time. As a travel-related association, there can be an extensive amount of travel involved, visiting various members across the country and attending industry conferences.

Salaries

Executive Directors may earn $15,000 a year for a part-time position and up to $70,000 or more as a full-time director. Full-time Executive Directors usually receive vacation and sick leave and life and medical insurance. They may be eligible for retirement investment programs. Some associations will pay relocation costs for newly hired, experienced association Directors.

Employment Prospects

There are relatively few travel trade associations, so employment as an Executive Director is limited. Other positions within such associations are more plentiful.

Advancement Prospects

As an Executive Director of an association, it is fairly easy to transfer these skills and experience to other associations. Someone who has been a part-time Director for a number of smaller associations may take a position as a full-time Director of a larger association, thus leaving an opening for someone to become the Director of a smaller association. Directors of travel associations may also move to other fields for advancement.

Education and Training

A degree in travel and tourism, management, public relations, or a related field is required, and an advanced degree is helpful. Training in other associations is necessary.

Experience, Skills, and Personality Traits

Progressively more important positions in nonprofit or for-profit associations is usually compulsory, although managing a business may provide the experience necessary to run a travel trade association. Candidates should be outgoing and well organized. They should have good communication skills and knowledge of the industry served by the association.

Unions and Associations

There are no unions for association executives, but the American Society of Association Executives, with 25,000 members in 10,000 associations, and Association Management Companies, representing companies that manage more than one association, offer seminars and other benefits. The Travel Industry Association of America also provides similar services.

Tips for Entry

1. Work in a travel or other association to learn how they function.
2. Meet with travel trade personnel to learn the specific needs of these types of associations and to develop a network of people who can provide information about internships and positions.
3. Read publications, either by subscription or on-line, to keep abreast of travel trends and developments.

TRAVEL AGENT

CAREER PROFILE

Duties: Consults with clients about travel plans and needs

Alternate Title(s): Travel Counselor; Independent Agent; Outside Agent

Salary Range: $16,000 to $60,000

Employment Prospects: Fair to good

Advancement Prospects: Fair

Best Geographical Location(s): Most regions and major cities in the United States offer job possibilities, with New York City at the top of the list, followed by Anchorage, Atlanta, Chicago, Dallas, Los Angeles, and Honolulu

Prerequisites:

Education and Training—High school diploma required, with math and geography courses helpful; training in computer systems; completion of a travel agent program in a recognized travel academy

Experience—Direct sales, customer relations, or work experience in another segment of the travel industry (e.g., hotels, tours)

Special Skills and Personality Traits—Sales ability; attention to detail; organizational skills; problem-solving ability; strong oral and written communication skills; interpersonal skills

Licensure/Certification—Certification from the Airlines Reporting Corporation as a Certified ARC Specialist (ARCS) and the International Airlines Travel Agent Network; bonding required; there are no federal licensing requirements for travel agents but some states require registration or certification

CAREER LADDER

```
┌─────────────────────────────────────┐
│   Travel Agency Manager or Owner     │
└─────────────────────────────────────┘

┌─────────────────────────────────────┐
│            Travel Agent              │
└─────────────────────────────────────┘

┌─────────────────────────────────────┐
│               Clerk                  │
└─────────────────────────────────────┘
```

Position Description

Travel Agents consult with business and leisure travel clients about their travel plans and make and confirm transportation (plane, train, or ship), accommodations, dining, recreation, and rental car reservations. Generally, an agent working for an agency earns an income from the commission received from the various providers of these services or a base salary plus commission. However, with reduced commissions from the airlines, more Travel Agents are starting to charge clients for some services. An Agent working for a corporation usually works on a salaried basis.

The Agent may make reservations at places the client requests or make suggestions based on a personal visit, on the reputation of the various hotels and cruise lines, and on the numerous brochures (print or CD) and videos sent to the agent from the providers. He or she may also make suggestions according to which airline flies to the destination and offers the best price or the most convenient schedule.

Almost all the information an agent needs is on the Internet, including thousands of flight itinerary and price changes that occur daily, so good computer skills are critical.

Once the reservations are completed, the Travel Agent secures the necessary documents, including airline tickets and hotel reservation confirmation numbers, and collects payment from the client to be forwarded to the provider. It is very important to be detailed oriented and to proofread all the documents to assure their accuracy. It is also necessary to be aware of visa and passport requirements for foreign travel.

Some agents specialize in niche markets such as incentive, conference, adventure, business or corporate, upscale, ecotourism, family, package tours, cruise, group, weddings, spas, leisure, disabled, senior, and grandparent/grandchild travel. Others specialize in specific geographic areas, including the Pacific, Caribbean, and Europe. While many bookings are made because a client has contacted the Agent, often the Agent will contact a client when a favorite destination offers a special package. As more people are using the Internet to book their own travel arrangements, many Agents are involved in cold-calling potential clients to solicit their business.

A beginning Agent may be assigned to do general office work of filing brochures, making copies of travel documents, and notifying a client if an itinerary changes as well as selling travel. Outside sales agents often work in this field as a part-time job, holding down another full-time career in another field. They work through a travel agency but usually from their home.

Salaries

Agents who are paid by commission earn an average annual salary of $29,500; salary plus bonuses amount to an average of $35,200 a year; and salary plus commission, $38,100. Travel Agents with Certified Travel Counselor (CTC) status earn an average of $33,100, while non-CTCs earn an average of $27,400. The salaries of 95 percent of agents who participated in any kind of training averaged $11,000 more than of those who did not take any training. Agents working for agencies with sales less than $1 million earned an average of $20,000, while those working for agencies with sales of more than $20 million earned $38,000.

Agents who deal with a special niche market average between $27,200 (mature market) and $36,800 (incentive travel), an average of 10.5 percent more than agents who are considered generalists. Small town market agents must be all things to all clients, yet, they earn smaller salaries that reflect a lower cost of living. Agents in large cities with five to ten years' experience working for corporations can earn from $39,000 to $60,000. Agents in general must sell more than $700,000 in travel to earn more than $30,000.

The main benefit of being a Travel Agent is being able to travel at reduced rates. Cruise Travel Agents also receive reduced-rate cruises. Sometimes the travel is arranged by the Travel Agent, but there are times when a resort, cruise line, or destination will invite Travel Agents on "fam" (familiarization) trips that include a whirlwind tour of an area, one or more hotels, and restaurants. Although the travel agency pays the Agents during these trips, the Agent is not in the office selling and earning commissions while away on trips.

Eighty percent of all U.S. travel agencies provide health insurance to their full-time staff, and more than 50 percent provide 401K plans and life and dental insurance. Almost 50 percent provide disability insurance, with fewer agencies providing pension and retirement plans and maternity/paternity leave. Less than 25 percent have profit sharing. Nearly 60 percent pay for airline CRS (central reservation system) training, and more than 50 percent offer supplier/product seminars, computer/office technology training, and CTC certification. The averages drop to just below 50 percent for travel industry conferences/trade shows, the ICTA Destination specialist course, the CLIA (Cruise Line International Association) cruise training program, and destination training. More than 20 percent pay for college-level courses related to travel.

Outside sales agents generally work for commissions and are not on a regular salary. They usually do not receive any benefits.

Employment Prospects

Although most areas in the United States have travel agencies, it is anticipated that many travel agencies will be out of business within the next five years due to increased use of the Internet for booking travel arrangements. Opportunities will still be available in corporate travel agencies and those agencies that specialize in the niche markets of corporate and cruise travel.

Advancement Prospects

Travel Agents can advance to management positions within travel agencies or corporate offices, but the competition will be tough as many Agents in the market lose jobs as agencies close. Some Agents may choose to start their own agencies.

Education and Training

The Institute of Certified Travel Agents offers Certified Travel Counselor and Destination Specialist programs. Either one will benefit a Travel Agent's ability to obtain employment and stay employed. Computer literacy training, including courses in developing agency websites, is an added educational factor. A good knowledge of geography is also helpful, as are courses in salesmanship. Other training options include airline CRS (central reservation system) and CLIA (Cruise Line International Association) cruise training. Advanced courses from the Institute of Certified Travel Agents (ICTA) lead to the Certified Travel Counselor (CTC) rating.

Special Requirements

Travel agents must obtain certification from the Airlines Reporting Corporation as an ARCS (Airlines Reporting Corporation Specialist) and must be either a U.S. citizen or national, an alien authorized to work in the United States, or a foreign corporation authorized to do business in the area where the agency is located. Acquiring Certified Travel Counselor or Destination Specialist status from the Institute of Certified Travel Agents helps obtain and keep a position.

While there are no federal licensing requirements for Travel Agents, the states of California, Florida, Hawaii, Illinois, Iowa, Ohio, Oregon, Rhode Island, and Washington require a form of registration or certification for travel agents.

Experience, Skills, and Personality Traits

Travel Agents must have strong interpersonal skills, be highly organized, and be willing to work long hours. They must have problem-solving skills for those times when a hotel, resort, car rental company, or other supplier has not provided the product or service the client has booked. As the agent for that supplier, although not legally bound to repay the client for the service, he or she should work to resolve the complaint or risk losing the customer. Other last-minute problems might include a lost passport or wallet, illness or injury, or a severe storm. The agent must be able to help resolve the problems that arise from these situations.

Unions and Associations

Two major associations are open to Travel Agent membership: the ASTA (American Society of Travel Agents) and the ARTA (Association of Retail Travel Agents). Both offer seminars, government representation (lobbying Congress about issues of importance to Travel Agents and agencies), and marketing assistance to agents and agencies.

Tips for Entry

1. Take courses in Travel Agent training at a recognized travel academy, college, or university.
2. Take sales and computer training courses.
3. Study world geography so you will know the location and climate of various vacation and business destinations, and stay abreast of the world's political climates to be sure you do not recommend a destination in the middle of a civil war.
4. Work as an intern or volunteer with travel suppliers, including tourism bureaus.
5. Offer to volunteer or intern with a travel agency to determine if this is the type of work you want or if you are interested only in the travel benefits.

INCENTIVE TRAVEL AGENT

CAREER PROFILE

Duties: Arranges travel for employees or customers who meet or exceed business goals

Alternate Title(s): Travel Account Executive

Salary Range: $20,000 to $150,000

Employment Prospects: Fair

Advancement Prospects: Good

Best Geographical Location(s): Major cities; near corporate centers

Prerequisites:

Education and Training—High school; travel agent training; courses in sales, marketing, and computers

Experience—Travel agent experience; direct sales; customer relations

Special Skills and Personality Traits—Strong oral and written communication skills; able to work well with various types of people; organized; able to handle emergencies

Licensure/Certification—Certification from the Airlines Reporting Corporation as a Certified ARC Specialist (ARCS) and the International Airlines Travel Agent Network; bonding required; some states require certification or registration

CAREER LADDER

```
┌─────────────────────────────┐
│    Owner, Travel Agency     │
└─────────────────────────────┘

┌─────────────────────────────┐
│   Incentive Travel Agent    │
└─────────────────────────────┘

┌─────────────────────────────┐
│        Travel Agent         │
└─────────────────────────────┘
```

Position Description

An Incentive Travel Agent works in a singular area of the travel industry that rewards employees and customers for meeting or exceeding performance or purchasing minimums. For example, a radio or television station may offer an incentive trip to advertisers who buy a certain amount of advertising time within a specific calendar period; an employer may reward a salesperson for selling a specific amount of a product or service; and a factory may recognize employees who produce products in a more efficient way, have a perfect attendance record, or have an accident-free period. These incentive trips may be fully paid or greatly discounted for the recipients. The trips may be for one recipient (and a guest, usually) or for as many as 60 or more recipients.

The Incentive Travel Agent must find the companies that want to sponsor an incentive trip. He or she asks the sponsor a lot of questions, including where they have been before and what they liked or disliked about the trip. Then the Agent assembles one or more suggested itineraries, including transportation, lodging, free-time activities, and any meals and receptions if it is a group. It is important that the agent not present too many options, as this may make it difficult for the client to decide. Often, the sponsoring company is looking for a new and exotic destination, resort, or cruise ship more than a less expensive trip that goes somewhere "everyone" has been. A trip may be a weekend at an exclusive hotel or a week in Hawaii.

The Incentive Travel Agent negotiates prices with the potential suppliers, including airlines, hotels, restaurants, auto rental companies, golf courses, and any other components of the trip. He or she assembles the costs and presents the alternatives to the sponsoring company. If the prices do not include a commission to the agent, then an appropriate amount of money must be added to the price so the agent can receive payment for the work done.

Once the incentive package is chosen, the Agent makes and confirms the reservations, acquires the necessary confirmations and documents, and arranges the payments from the client.

If the Agent does not go on the incentive trip, he or she may arrange for an escort to make sure everything goes as planned or to help resolve problems that may arise.

Incentive travel, particularly for a group, involves a great number of details, as the incentive winners may come from various parts of the country or have a variety of needs (handicapped-accessible facilities, nonsmoking rooms, baby-sitters, special dietary restrictions, etc.). Airlines may change flight schedules after the reservations have been made, desired hotel rooms and rental cars may become unavailable due to other group bookings or demands, or a cruise ship may go out of service. Not only must these problems be resolved, but the Incentive Travel Agent must calm jittery and panicky clients. Although a beginning Incentive Travel Agent probably will work with all types of clients going to a variety of destinations, more experienced agents may work for specific companies or have a specialty in the types of trips arranged (e.g., cruises, golf vacations, or theater trips).

Salaries

Incentive Travel Agent salaries may start as low as $20,000 and rise as high as $150,000 plus incentives. They may be paid a base salary plus commissions or work only for commissions paid by the suppliers. Many specialists also attend some or all of the incentive trips they organize. They also receive the benefits of travel agents, including reduced-cost transportation and lodging and invitations to familiarization trips. Relocation expenses are usually paid for highly experienced and accomplished Incentive Travel Agents. Full-time agents may receive sick and vacation leave and participation in retirement plans.

Employment Prospects

The recent economic downturn has caused some very large incentive travel companies to go out of business. The companies that still exist are trying hard to improve employee efficiency and sales. As these companies expand and new companies open, there will be a fair number of openings for experienced Incentive Travel Agents. Other openings will occur as agents retire or transfer to other occupations.

With so many suppliers having an Internet presence, it is possible for an Incentive Travel Agent to live almost anywhere. However, because of the potential for so much travel, it helps to live near a major airport.

Advancement Prospects

Good Incentive Travel Agents can advance from general incentive travel to dealing with a specific market segment or to working for a single corporation. Beyond progressing to management positions within a travel agency, they could open their own agencies.

Education and Training

An Incentive Travel Agent must have training as a general travel agent with Certified Travel Counselor credentials as issued by the Institute of Certified Travel Agents. If an agent plans to specialize in a specific destination, he or she should have more advanced training to be certified as a Destination Specialist. Other advanced agent training and computer training are helpful.

Special Requirements

Travel agents must obtain certification from the Airlines Reporting Corporation as an ARCS (Airlines Reporting Corporation Specialist) and must be a U.S. citizen or national, an alien authorized to work in the United States, or a foreign corporation authorized to do business in the area where the agency is located. Acquiring Certified Travel Counselor or Destination Specialist status from the Institute of Certified Travel Agents helps obtain and keep a position.

California, Florida, Hawaii, Illinois, Iowa, Ohio, Oregon, Rhode Island, and Washington require a form of registration or certification for travel agents.

Experience, Skills, and Personality Traits

An Incentive Travel Agent must have outstanding sales skills, have an ability to handle a multiplicity of details, be extremely organized, and have excellent oral and written communication skills. Computer competency is necessary. Experience working for meetings and incentive travel company is helpful.

Unions and Associations

The Society of Incentive and Travel Executives offers publications, seminars and conferences, contacts with other Incentive Travel Agents in foreign countries, and numerous publications regarding the industry.

Tips for Entry

1. Learn the travel business from the ground up, starting at a general travel agency and then working for an agency that specializes in incentive travel.
2. Talk with travel agents, asking their advice about career choices, and attend events sponsored by the Society of Incentive and Travel Executives.
3. Subscribe to trade publications or read about current trends and developments on-line.

TRAVEL ACADEMY INSTRUCTOR

CAREER PROFILE

Duties: Teaches students the skills necessary to pursue a career as a travel agent

Alternate Title(s): Travel Instructor

Salary Range: $14,000 to $35,000

Employment Prospects: Fair to good

Advancement Prospects: Good

Best Geographical Location(s): Travel academies are located in most parts of the United States

Prerequisites:

Education and Training—High school diploma required; bachelor's Degree recommended, with studies in travel and tourism, geography, business management, and hospitality

Experience—Work experience in a travel agency or travel-related industry; teaching or training experience

Special Skills and Personality Traits—Interpersonal skills; strong oral and written communication skills; computer literacy

CAREER LADDER

```
┌─────────────────────────────┐
│   Dean, Travel Academy      │
└─────────────────────────────┘

┌─────────────────────────────┐
│ Travel Academy Instructor   │
└─────────────────────────────┘

┌─────────────────────────────┐
│     Teacher's Aide          │
└─────────────────────────────┘
```

Position Description

A Travel Academy teaches prospective travel agents the information they need to work a computer reservation system (CRS) with such computer software programs as APOLLO (United Airlines) and SABRE (American Airlines); how to sell travel; how to deal with the airlines, trains, and cruise lines; how to make cold calls; customer service; and how to handle emergency travel problems. Using computers, lectures, audiovisual aids, visiting travel agents, and others in the industry, the students are taught a wide perspective of the business.

The agent learns about encoding, decoding, obtaining fare quotes, special requests, pricing and ticketing, advanced seat selection, car rentals, and hotel reservations. Other courses include the history of the travel industry, U.S. and international geography particularly relating to travel and commerce, and such special topics as foreign independent tours, escorted tours, and motor coach rentals. They also learn about international time zones and currency conversion.

Job counseling is an integral part of this career. From the courses they teach students resume writing and successful interviewing. Travel Academy Instructors show their students how to find a suitable position after graduation. With so many travel agencies closing and merging because of decreased commissions from airlines, it is important to teach and coach the students about the options available within the travel industry, including reservations and such specialties as corporate, group, and senior travel. Instructors may travel to attend job fairs for high school and college students, talking to them about careers in the travel agent business.

Salaries

Travel Academies are considered technical schools. Thus, they do not pay as much as a community college or university, but they also do not require the educational degrees that colleges do. Other teaching options include a school-to-work program or travel studies in a community college or university. Salaries can range from $14,000 to $35,000 depending on the type of school (school-to-work program, designated travel academy, community college, etc.). Teaching, particularly via the Internet, provides an excellent second job for travel agents.

Employment Prospects

Instructors with travel agency experience usually can find employment as a Travel Agency Instructor. With the decrease in the number of travel agents, there has been a slight decrease in the demand for instructors.

Advancement Prospects

Travel Agency Instructors can advance to training for a national travel agency or progress to such positions as dean or director of the academy or to a similar management job. They may also transfer from a travel academy to a college or university to teach travel studies.

Education and Training

Generally, Travel Academy Instructors need a bachelor's degree in a related field, but several years' experience and training in a travel agency could be more important than a degree in an unrelated field. Computer literacy, a foreign language, and an excellent knowledge of world geography can be very helpful.

Experience, Skills, and Personality Traits

Work experience as a travel agent is desirable. Strong teaching and interpersonal skills are required as are excellent oral and written communication skills. An interest in helping people advance, particularly at-risk students in a school-to-work program, is indispensable.

Unions and Associations

The American Society of Travel Agents, the National Tour Association, and the American Hotel and Lodging Association are helpful for industry news, seminars, and other support services.

Tips for Entry

1. Learn the travel industry by working at a travel agency, hotel, or in another hospitality trade.
2. Talk with Travel Academy Instructors, asking their advice about career choices, internships, and apprenticeship programs.
3. Establish a network of people in the industry by attending local functions of the American Society of Travel Agents chapters and similar organizations.
4. Subscribe to trade publications or read about current trends and developments on-line.

CORPORATE TRAVEL MANAGER

CAREER PROFILE

Duties: Makes travel arrangements for a corporation's employees, including airline or train, car service, and lodging; negotiates fares with airlines and rates with hotels; maintains travel budgets

Alternate Title(s): Business Travel Manager; Corporate Business Travel Planner

Salary Range: $25,000 to $80,000

Employment Prospects: Excellent

Advancement Prospects: Good

Best Geographic Location(s): Major cities and areas with a large number of major corporations or travel management companies

Prerequisites:

Education and Training—Business administration and accounting are strong assets; knowledge of airline and hotel reservation programs is required

Experience—Progressively more important travel booking positions with a travel agency, travel office, or travel provider, particularly dealing with business and corporate travelers

Special Skills and Personality Traits—Excellent analytical and computer skills; ability to function well during an emergency

Licensure/Certification—Certification from the Airlines Reporting Corporation as a Certified ARC Specialist (ARCS) and the International Airlines Travel Agent Network; bonding required; some states require certification or registration

CAREER LADDER

```
┌─────────────────────────────────┐
│   Corporate Travel Manager      │
└─────────────────────────────────┘

┌─────────────────────────────────┐
│   Corporate Travel Specialist   │
└─────────────────────────────────┘

┌─────────────────────────────────┐
│   Travel Agent                  │
└─────────────────────────────────┘
```

Position Description

A Corporate Travel Manager oversees all travel arrangements for the employees of a company or corporation or works for a company that manages such arrangements. The manager starts by reviewing the previous year's travel, including how many trips went to specific cities or countries; which airlines, hotels, rental car companies, and other suppliers were used most frequently; and the costs for these and other aspects of each trip. The manager then consults with department heads to project the upcoming year's travel plans and works to negotiate favorable rates with the airlines, hotels, automobile rental agencies, and other frequent travel service providers to effect as much savings as possible. If enough employees are attending a meeting or conference, the manager may decide that a charter flight on a commercial airline or private plane may be more economical or a more efficient use of time and money than using a scheduled airline.

Corporate Travel Managers must consider many factors, such as who, if anyone, in the corporation travels first class;

who receives the points and benefits from frequent traveler programs and how they are used; whether some or all employees are required to stay over a Saturday evening as required by some airlines to receive reduced airfares; and whether a train might be faster than a plane because of downtown train station locations and lack of weather complications. Other considerations might be whether airline courtesy clubs are included (so employees have a quiet work environment where they can wait during long flight layovers) and whether flights are to be booked on a lowest price or a shortest flight time (and no connecting flights). It is up to the travel manager to communicate these policies to the employees and make sure they are followed.

All travel arrangements for conferences, sales calls, meetings, or other reasons are booked through the travel office as the need arises. These arrangements may include a car service to pick up the employee and drive him or her to the airport; airline reservations; car rental; hotel reservations; and car service for the return from the airport to the employee's home or office.

Because travel plans can be interrupted or changed for any number of reasons—from inclement weather causing cancelled flights to security violations that close an airport terminal—the Corporate Travel Manager (or staff member) must be on call 24 hours a day, particularly when an employee is traveling, to quickly make alternate arrangements, whether it is booking a flight on another airline or booking a hotel room until the next flight is available. The Corporate Travel Manager handles all requests for refunds, rebates, and whatever other issues may stem from problems experienced by employees who are traveling for the company.

When necessary, the Corporate Travel Manager will deal with an outside travel agency, so the manager must analyze the type of business an agency does and select one that is most appropriate. Sometimes it may be one in the same office building rather than in another city or one that is open 24 hours a day, seven days a week, regardless of its location.

Weekly travel reports must be submitted to the appropriate ruling body and an expense report of all travel costs and reimbursements filed with the corporate comptroller or someone in a similar position. Much of the Corporate Travel Manager's work is done via the Internet, but in emergency situations it may be done by telephone. The Travel Manager must be resourceful and have a number of alternatives available—a thorough list of suppliers who are available or who provide services at the last minute. The Travel Manager oversees the operations of the travel office, interviewing, hiring, training, scheduling, and firing personnel. At times, the Travel Manager may also make travel arrangements of a personal nature for employees, if that is within corporate policy.

Travel Managers may travel a little or extensively to attend trade conferences or as part of the office traveling to corporate meetings. The Travel Manager may also be required to visit potential sites to inspect the meeting, hotel, and transportation facilities and services available.

Salaries

Because of soaring travel costs, the functions of a Corporate Travel Manager have become significantly more important. Therefore, although some salaries may start in the mid-$20,000 range, a salary of $80,000 plus relocation costs is not unusual for a truly qualified manager who can show years of travel cost reduction.

Full-time Corporate Travel Managers usually receive vacation and sick leave and life and medical insurance. They may also be eligible for retirement and stock investment plans.

Employment Prospects

As more travel agencies merge and go out of business, there will be fewer travel agents to handle travel arrangements. Therefore the importance of travel managers will increase, so employment prospects are excellent.

Advancement Prospects

With all the management skills developed and honed as a Corporate Travel Manager, promotion to other management positions is a strong possibility. They may also decide to work for a travel supplier in a management or sales position. Until recently, Corporate Travel Managers might have opened their own travel agency, but with the decline in commissions and the large number of travel agency mergers these days, that option probably will not be exercised as much in the future.

Education and Training

A college degree with a strong emphasis on business management, finance, or travel and tourism is highly recommended. Those who wish to move on to other management positions should continue their education with an advanced degree in a related field.

Experience, Skills, and Personality Traits

Negotiating skills, perfected through years of work in a travel agency or office or with a supplier, are essential. The ability to persuade corporate employees to work within company policy guidelines is important, as is the ability to react quickly when travel arrangements must be rearranged.

Unions and Associations

There are no unions for Corporate Travel Managers, but the National Business Travel Association (NBTA) and the Association of Corporate Travel Executives (ACTE) provide their members with information about the business travel industry and offer numerous education and training opportunities.

Special Requirements

Travel agents must obtain certification from the Airlines Reporting Corporation as an ARCS (Airlines Reporting Corporation Specialist) and must be a U.S. citizen or national, an alien authorized to work in the United States, or work for a foreign corporation authorized to do business in the area where the agency is located. Acquiring Certified Travel Counselor or Destination Specialist status from the Institute of Certified Travel Agents helps obtain and keep a position. California, Florida, Hawaii, Illinois, Iowa, Ohio, Oregon, Rhode Island, and Washington require a form of registration or certification for travel agents.

Tips for Entry

1. Work with a corporate business travel agency or in the travel office of a corporation.
2. Establish a network of corporate business travel planners or agents to keep up on industry news and trends and to learn about internships and job openings.
3. Read travel trade publications, either by subscription or on-line, to keep abreast of current trends.

MEETING PLANNER

CAREER PROFILE

Duties: Coordinates all functions of an organization's or company's meeting

Alternate Title(s): Conference Planner; Convention Planner

Salary Range: $18,000 to $75,000

Employment Prospects: Good to excellent

Advancement Prospects: Fair

Best Geographical Location(s): Major cities across the country

Prerequisites:

Education and Training—College degree in hospitality, marketing, or business management

Experience—Previous experience working for a convention bureau or in a meeting planning office of an association, organization, or company

Special Skills and Personality Traits—Strong planning, organizational, and negotiation skills; written and oral communication skills; detail oriented; personable; computer literacy

Licensure/Certification—A Certified Meeting Professional designation is helpful, but not compulsory

CAREER LADDER

```
┌─────────────────────────────┐
│      Meeting Planner        │
└─────────────────────────────┘

┌─────────────────────────────┐
│  Assistant Meeting Planner  │
└─────────────────────────────┘

┌─────────────────────────────┐
│       Meeting Staff         │
└─────────────────────────────┘
```

Position Description

A Meeting Planner works for an organization or company using the facilities of a hotel/resort, convention center, or cruise ship to hold meetings, trade shows, exhibits, and other functions. Meeting Planners must coordinate the selection of a destination and meeting place, ensuring there will be enough meeting space, break-out rooms (for smaller committee meetings), hotel rooms, dining space, and exercise rooms. They also schedule free time for golf, shopping, theater, sightseeing, and other activities for spouses to accommodate all who will be attending the meeting.

It is important that the Planner create a budget for the meeting and make sure everything comes in at or under budget. For some organizations, the annual meeting is the biggest fundraiser of the entire year. The Planner negotiates with the hotel(s) for room rates and with the convention center for the cost of the exhibit and meeting space, all meals that are sponsored by the conference, audiovisual equipment, and any special events needs (e.g., awards banquet, product demonstration). The Planner may also negotiate transportation arrangements and costs to make sure attendees can get between a hotel and a meeting place and between their home cities and the meeting destination.

Exhibit space is sold as a way to earn funds for the sponsor of the meeting and as a way to help educate the attendees about new trends and products they can purchase and use. The Meeting Planner may be in charge of contacting possible exhibitors and selling that space.

Additionally, the planner must keep track of all those who plan to attend, usually through a computer database; oversee preparation of all collateral material including conference description brochures, name badges, tent cards, certificates, and evaluation sheets; and ensure timely mailings of brochures and registration confirmation. In some cases, the Meeting Planner is in charge of hotel room reservations. At other times, a reservation service is used, or the hotel maintains a separate list for the conference's block of rooms.

The Planner must create a timeline budget according to which all functions must be met. The Meeting Planner may be working on a dozen or more meetings at one time, some of which may not take place for another five years. Some of these meetings may be national or international in scope and attendance; others might be executive board meetings in the headquarters office. Usually at the direction of the executive director or executive committee, the Planner may be responsible for arranging for the guest speaker(s) and entertainer(s) and all transportation and lodging details for the guests.

This job may or may not involve extensive travel. The Meeting Planner may have to travel to various locations for site inspection tours or to trade shows where dozens or hundreds of convention and visitors bureaus have booths to promote their meeting facilities. Some associations, organizations, or companies, particularly those that meet within their own community, do not require any travel.

Salaries

Association Meeting Planners can earn from $18,000 to $75,000, depending on the size of the association, the number of meetings, the complexity of the arrangements, and experience. Full-time Meeting Planners usually receive vacation and sick leave and life and medical insurance. Some Meeting Planners may be eligible for retirement investment plans and tuition toward work-related continuing education courses.

Although visiting other locations for site inspection tours usually creates a very busy schedule, it is sometimes possible to take a spouse or companion (at the Planner's expense) and add an extra day for sightseeing and pleasure. This is particularly true when an airline requires a Saturday night stay and the inspection is scheduled for a Friday or Monday.

Employment Prospects

There are more than 2,000 associations and countless other organizations in the United States, of which more are hiring Meeting Planners to schedule meetings. Even high school and college classes hire a Planner to arrange a reunion. Technology has entered this field, so some meetings will be done by video conferencing, but even that requires coordination and planning. Thus, there is excellent potential for Meeting Planners, even in midsize towns. With so many associations, organizations, companies, and convention centers, finding a job in a new geographic area—either by transferring to a lateral position or receiving a promotion—is usually a fairly easy procedure. Certified Meeting Professional Planners earn up to $10,000 more annually than do those who do not have this recognition.

Advancement Prospects

Because some Planners travel frequently and work very long and hard hours, there is a certain amount of turnover, leaving room for advancement from an assistant Meeting Planner to Meeting Planner.

Education and Training

A degree in marketing, hospitality, or a related field is usually required, although enough years of experience in progressively more important conference and convention planning positions with greater responsibilities may be sufficient.

Special Requirements

The Certified Meeting Professional (CMP) Program acknowledges advanced training in the field and is awarded by Meeting Professionals International. Applicants must complete a three hour-exam with 150 multiple-choice questions on the functions of a Meeting Planner, have at least three years of meeting management experience, and be currently employed as a Meeting Planner.

Experience, Skills, and Personality Traits

Several years' experience in convention and conference planning is important, as are good written and oral communication skills. A proficiency in a foreign language is helpful for those planning international meetings or meetings where foreigners will attend or exhibit. The ability to work on multiple assignments simultaneously is essential, as is a willingness to work long hours and weekends.

Unions and Associations

Meeting Professional International (MPI) is an association that represents more than 20,000 Meeting Planners around the globe, providing publications, seminars, and the Certified Meeting Professional program.

Tips for Entry

1. Work at a convention center to help with registration and other assignments.
2. Contact Meeting Planners about potential job openings and internships.
3. Attend local Meeting Planner functions and develop a network of Meeting Planners who can help you achieve your career goals.
4. Read trade publications, either in print or on-line.

SALES AND PROMOTION

SALES MANAGER, MEETING FACILITY

CAREER PROFILE

Duties: Sells and coordinates all functions of a meeting at a hotel, resort, convention center or on a cruise ship

Alternate Title(s): Director of Sales, Convention Center; National Sales Manager; Group Sales Manager

Salary Range: $18,000 to $75,000

Employment Prospects: Good to excellent

Advancement Prospects: Good

Best Geographical Location(s): Major cities and areas with a convention or conference center, a large hotel, resort, or cruise ships

Prerequisites:

Education and Training—College degree in hospitality or marketing

Experience—Previous experience working for a convention bureau or in a meeting planning office of an organization or association

Special Skills and Personality Traits—Strong planning, organizational, and written and oral communication skills; computer literacy

CAREER LADDER

```
┌─────────────────────────────────┐
│         Sales Manager           │
└─────────────────────────────────┘

┌─────────────────────────────────┐
│    Assistant Sales Manager      │
└─────────────────────────────────┘

┌─────────────────────────────────┐
│         Staff Member            │
└─────────────────────────────────┘
```

Position Description

A meeting Sales Manager, whether working for a convention and visitors bureau, a hotel or resort, or a cruise line, works with meeting planners from associations, organizations, and companies to sell the space and services available in that convention center, hotel or resort, or cruise ship. The Sales Manager starts by developing (or having an advertising, marketing, or public relations firm develop) collateral material, including news releases and sales literature. This features a layout of the meeting space, with measurements and the number of people or exhibit booths each venue will hold in different configurations (e.g., a room will hold more people at a cocktail party than it will at a sit-down dinner). Other materials might include a brochure from the convention and visitors bureau highlighting the number of hotels and hotel rooms available for a meeting and attractions of the area including theater, golf courses, tennis courts, children's activities, and museums. A hotel or resort or cruise ship Sales Manager will prepare similar materials featuring the property or facility.

Each Sales Manager will target a specific audience or potential client to attract to their meeting facility based on the size of their function, the length of time for the meeting, and where they have held previous meetings. The Sales Manager will meet with the clients and distribute the materials they have produced or develop a direct mail marketing campaign or place advertisements in the appropriate publications (e.g., trade magazines, in-flight magazines). Most often meetings are planned years in advance, so the Sales Manager must know about any planned changes, renovations, or additions to the meeting space, highway or airport expansion or construction, and any other factors that could influence a decision to meet at their convention center or facility. Together, the Sales Manager and the association meeting planner work to create interesting meetings, exhibits, and other functions for the association's members.

As the representative of a place with meeting and event space, the Sales Manager coordinates all the details for booking meeting space, including break-out rooms, special events areas, audiovisual equipment, catering, directional signs and easels, and whatever else a meeting might need. The meeting planner helps negotiate the price for the facilities and services and, if necessary, arranges shuttle transportation between the hotel(s) and the convention center. The planner has a list of providers who can help with floral arrangements, create special events, and meet other special needs. A hotel meeting Sales Manager does much of the same, coordinating the meeting rooms, hotel rooms, catering, tee times for golf or tennis court reservations, spouse and family activities, theater and sightseeing tickets, and whatever else the association, organization, or company might need.

The Sales Manager keeps in constant contact with the meeting planner from the association, organization, or company to make sure everything will be in smooth operating order for the meeting. The efficient Sales Manager has a list of contacts who can provide back-up services and facilities in case there is an emergency that prohibits or restricts the use of the meeting or function space.

The Sales Manager creates a financial budget and a timeline budget for the meeting and makes sure everything comes in at or under budget and on time. Additionally, the Sales Manager or staff may help the association with attendee registration by providing temporary staffing, computers for printing name badges, handout materials, and whatever else may be necessary.

This job usually involves an extensive amount of travel. A Sales Manager working for a convention center or event venue may have to travel to trade shows and conferences that promote a variety of meeting options and enable representatives from associations, organizations, and companies to compare locations and facilities. The Sales Manager may also have to travel to make sales calls to these associations, organizations, and companies.

Salaries

Sales Managers who work for large conference and convention centers in the Northeast and big cities can earn the most at large luxury resorts, with salaries of $45,000 or more. Salaries throughout the rest of the country are lower. Full-time Sales Managers usually receive vacation and sick leave and life and medical insurance. Some Sales Managers may be eligible for retirement investment plans.

Employment Prospects

As more cities of all sizes build convention centers and as more hotels add meeting space, the demand for Sales Managers will continue to grow.

Advancement Prospects

With additional meeting spaces and event venues hiring away experienced Sales Managers, there will be room for sales representatives to become assistant sales managers and assistant sales managers to advance to the position of Sales Manager. Sales Managers may be promoted to a higher management position within the convention center, hotel, or cruise line for whom they work.

Education and Training

A degree in marketing is helpful, as is a foreign language. This is especially true as the Latino market continues to grow and as more foreign visitors come to this country for international meetings.

Experience, Skills, and Personality Traits

Several years in convention and conference planning are important. Sales Managers should possess good written and oral communication skills (including public speaking), and proficiency in a foreign language is helpful. The ability to work on multiple assignments simultaneously is essential, as is a willingness to work long hours and weekends.

Unions and Associations

The International Association of Convention and Visitors Bureaus (IACVB) provides meetings and support services. Other organizations for Meeting Facility Sales Managers include the Hospitality Sales and Marketing Association and Sales and Marketing Executives International, Inc.

Tips for Entry

1. Work at a convention center to help with registration and other assignments.
2. Contact Sales Managers about job potential and internships.
3. Attend local Sales Manager functions and trade shows to develop a network of people who can provide information about job openings and internships.
4. Read trade publications, either in print or on-line.

RETAIL SUPERVISOR

CAREER PROFILE

Duties: Oversees all functions and operations of a hotel or resort or cruise ship gift shop

Alternate Title(s): Store Manager

Salary Range: $17,000 to $45,000, plus bonus

Employment Prospects: Excellent

Advancement Prospects: Good

Best Geographical Location(s): Major cities and areas with a large number of outstanding hotels, resorts, and cruise ships

Prerequisites:

Education and Training—Degree in retail marketing or the equivalent experience; computer literacy

Experience—Several years in progressively more important positions in retail sales; foreign language fluency is helpful, particularly on cruise ships and at resorts with a large international clientele

Special Skills and Personality Traits—Supervisory and customer service skills experience; good written and oral communication skills

CAREER LADDER

```
┌─────────────────────────────────────┐
│  Retail Supervisor or Store Manager  │
└─────────────────────────────────────┘

┌─────────────────────────────────────┐
│         Assistant Manager            │
└─────────────────────────────────────┘

┌─────────────────────────────────────┐
│         Buyer, Retail Store          │
└─────────────────────────────────────┘

┌─────────────────────────────────────┐
│         Clerk, Retail Store          │
└─────────────────────────────────────┘
```

Position Description

The Retail Supervisor oversees all aspects of a retail store operation. This includes interviewing, hiring, training, scheduling, and, when necessary, firing employees; maintaining inventory and suggesting new items for inventory; ensuring the store is neat and items are convenient; establishing and maintaining a budget; enforcing merchandise control procedures to eliminate fraud, theft, and other losses; and assuring customer satisfaction.

Keeping track of the merchandise available is a primary concern, so the Retail Supervisor must be aware of what is selling and what is not, and what customers request that is not in stock. Logo items are always big sellers, but seasonal items and souvenirs also represent a large part of the inventory. Enough must be kept in stock, in sizes and colors that are current and popular, without keeping too much inventory on hand. The gift store also carries such items as the bathrobe provided in the guest rooms. Recently, many hotels have added such brand items as mattresses, linens, pillows, lamps, ashtrays, throw pillows, artwork, and even dishes and flatware used in the dining room. Large items usually are not kept in stock at the hotel, but the store might be asked to handle the sale of these items.

Hotel or resort retail stores generally are open for more than 40 hours a week, so the Supervisor must be available to work evenings and weekends. Some properties, particularly casino hotels, have stores open 24 hours a day. Work schedules for clerks must account for predictably busy times so there is sufficient staff to provide satisfactory service.

Travel is not usually a large part of the Retail Supervisor's job when working for a hotel or resort other than attending trade shows and conferences. As the manager or director of a chain's retail stores, periodic visits to the other properties will require some travel. When working for a hotel or resort chain or cruise ship, it is possible to transfer to other locations or different ships. Of course, when managing a retail store on a ship, travel is expected. Gift stores generally are closed when a ship is in port.

Salaries

Depending on the size and location of the property and his or her experience in retail sales and merchandising, a Retail Supervisor may earn from $17,000 to $45,000 and more, plus bonuses based on sales and performance. Corporate-level oversight of a number of stores at a number of locations should mean additional pay.

Full-time Retail Supervisors usually receive vacation and sick leave and life and medical insurance. They may also be available for retirement and stock purchase programs.

Employment Prospects

Every resort, large hotel, and cruise ship has a gift shop. There are pro shops connected with golf courses and tennis courts, and sales counters in spas. As more hotels or resorts and cruise ships are built, and as more hotels or resorts add additional retail outlets (besides the standard gift and sundries shop), there will be more demand for qualified supervisors. These will be found most easily in areas with a large concentration of upscale hotels and resorts, but also in other areas where conference centers and hotels or resorts are being constructed.

Advancement Prospects

Advancement opportunities are plentiful as more hotels or resorts and cruise ships come on line and existing managers are promoted up the corporate ladder. There is a fair amount of attrition, particularly among the clerks and hourly employees and as some supervisors leave for other careers or promotions outside the company.

Education and Training

A degree in marketing usually is required, although progressively more important positions in a number of retail outlets may be substituted.

Experience, Skills, and Personality Traits

Previous corporate hotel gift shop merchandising experience is a plus. Retail Supervisors must have good interpersonal and management skills and should be organized, efficient, and detail oriented. They should be able to motivate their employees and have a good marketing sense.

Unions and Associations

The National Retail Federation offers advice, publications, and news of the industry.

Tips for Entry

1. Work in a retail establishment to learn about merchandising and other aspects of retailing.
2. Meet retail managers who can help you learn about internships and tell you about job openings.
3. Attend as many conferences and meetings of retail operators, including chamber of commerce functions, as possible.
4. Read trade publications, either by subscription or online, to keep abreast of industry news and trends.

PUBLIC RELATIONS MANAGER

CAREER PROFILE

Duties: Defines and maintains an image of a company or service (e.g., hotel or resort, convention center, airline, or cruise line) to be distributed to the employees, stock holders, government officials, the public, the media, and others

Alternate Title(s): Public Affairs Specialist; Press Secretary; Publicist

Salary Range: $35,000 to $150,000

Employment Prospects: Fair to good

Advancement Prospects: Fair

Best Geographical Location(s): Major cities and areas with a large number of outstanding hotels, resorts, restaurants, convention centers, airlines, and cruise ships; New York, Los Angeles, and Florida

Prerequisites:

Education and Training—A degree in public relations, marketing, journalism, hospitality, or other related subject

Experience—Several years' work in a public relations firm, for a publication, or with a travel-related industry

Special Skills and Personality Traits—Excellent written and oral communication skills; creativity; ability to deal with emergency and high-pressure situations

CAREER LADDER

```
┌─────────────────────────────────────┐
│      Public Relations Manager        │
└─────────────────────────────────────┘

┌─────────────────────────────────────┐
│  Public Relations Account Manager    │
│           or Supervisor              │
└─────────────────────────────────────┘

┌─────────────────────────────────────┐
│  Public Relations Account Executive  │
└─────────────────────────────────────┘

┌─────────────────────────────────────┐
│  Public Relations Research Assistant │
└─────────────────────────────────────┘
```

Position Description

A Public Relations Manager can work for a firm that represents travel clients (an attraction, destination, or property) or work at the attraction (museum, theme park), destination (city or state), or property (hotel, resort, cruise ship, airline). The Public Relations Manager creates and maintains communications with the media and public (including employees, stockholders, and government officials). Ideally, the public relations department issues news releases when something good or interesting happens and suggests stories to print and electronic publication writers and editors who might feature the property or service the manager represents. The Public Relations Manager must keep company officials informed of what is happening and of the results of public surveys, focus groups, or other news that might affect the company or the industry.

A Public Relations Manager should create a crisis management manual that defines who does what and who contacts who in the event of a major accident or disaster. This could include who will represent the company to the media and the families of the employees if there is a fire, flood, cruise ship accident, airline crash, or major criminal activity. Everyone should know who is responsible for contacting family members and communicating the status of the incident.

The Public Relations Manager oversees the design and creation of news releases, background papers (e.g., biographies of major employees, history of the company, how many meals are served every day, how much caviar is consumed on a cruise ship), articles for trade publications, annual reports, slide presentations, and speeches. The public relations department may be in charge of creating special events that will draw favorable media coverage. As part of these duties, the Public Relations Manager will create an annual budget and keep track of all coverage received. Part of this will be creating an estimated value of the editorial coverage, figuring out how much it would have cost to pay for the amount of advertising space in a publication or how much the amount of air time on a radio or television show would have cost.

Occasionally, the Public Relations Manager may be charged with teaching and training company executives how to talk to the media. The Public Relations Manager or his or her assistant handles queries from the media about the company's operations and for opinions on what is happening in that segment of the business. Requests for interviews with company representatives are handled through this office. A Public Relations Manager must have an extensive list of contacts to whom to pitch ideas, from sports writers to beauty editors (not just travel editors). It is important to keep this list up-to-date and communicate with these reporters even when the Public Relations Manager is not trying to pitch an idea.

Working with a public relations firm, a convention and visitors bureau, or other entity, the public relations office will initiate or assist with media tours so journalists can experience their facility (e.g., hotel or resort, airline, cruise ship) firsthand. This may include qualifying journalists (making sure they have the knowledge and outlets or publication credits to present the facility to the general public or trade members), arranging transportation to and from the facility, scheduling all activities that will take place during the visit, and arranging interviews and photographs or photo shoots of interest to the journalist.

The public relations office may submit articles and photographs of the facility or event(s) held there to publish in a company publication, either for internal distribution to employees or external use for guests and clients. The office may also be responsible for creating or maintaining a website. The public relations office also keeps in contact with others in similar positions through professional associations, conferences, and other networking opportunities.

At times, the public relations and sales and marketing offices will coordinate their activities to provide prizes (e.g., free stay, meal, flight, cruise) for sweepstakes or contests, either as a tie-in for a product used in the facility or along with such media events as National Tourism Week or National Cruise Vacation Month in May or with charity events. The Public Relations Manager should deal with the sales and marketing department to make sure they are sending the same message to the public, whether it is in an advertising or a public relations campaign.

Although some in public relations consistently work a 40-hour week, more are likely to work long hours (evenings and weekends) meeting tight deadlines and responding to emergencies. As the Public Relations Manager for any travel-related operation, there is a great chance the job will include extensive travel, visiting properties, setting up interviews with the media to try to generate articles, and attending professional conferences and trade shows. Relocation possibilities are excellent, either to branch offices of a public relations firm that specializes in travel accounts, to another branch office of a hotel chain, or even freelancing with travel-related accounts.

Salaries

Salaries depend on the location of the job and the duties involved, with a manager's pay ranging from $35,000 to $100,000 or more. Because the public relations field is often considered a "glamour industry," beginning salaries for assistant account managers at a public relations firm are notoriously low, even in cities with a high cost of living. Some say this is offset because of the many freebies (meals, specialty advertising items, travel) involved in managing a travel-related account. Salaries increase dramatically with additional responsibilities and experience.

Full-time Public Relations Managers usually receive vacation and sick leave and life and medical insurance. They may be eligible for retirement investment accounts and stock purchases plans. They also may receive discounts for themselves and their families at other properties or on airlines and cruise ships within the company and sometimes on other airlines and cruise ships.

Employment Prospects

Employment in the public relations field is always best when the economy is good. Because it is difficult to put a bottom line figure to the results of a public relations campaign (other than the space valuation of an article in a magazine or on radio or television), many companies will cut the PR department and rely strictly on advertising, which gives more visually quantitative results. The upside of this is that as public relations staffs are cut, there are more opportunities for freelance work.

Advancement Prospects

When the economy is good, advancement opportunities are abundant. Because the hours can be long and grueling and the need for creativity is constant, there is a large amount of burnout.

Education and Training

A degree in public relations, English, marketing, or hospitality is desirable, with plenty of summer internships that include working in a public relations office. A foreign language is helpful in obtaining employment with companies that have international offices and clients.

Experience, Skills, and Personality Traits

Computer literacy, particularly word processing, desktop publishing, and database management, is beneficial. The ability to work on a number of assignments and withstand pressure is essential, as are good verbal and written communication skills. A sense of what makes a good news story can also be important.

Unions and Associations

The Public Relations Society of America (PRSA) offers seminars and training and after five years an accreditation course and test (APR—Accreditation in Public Relations). There is also a special student membership category with chapters on college and university campuses where public relations is an accredited major.

Tips for Entry

1. Attend local Public Relations Society of America (PRSA) meetings. Develop a network of experts who hear about internships and job openings.
2. Take as many communications, business, and computer courses as possible.
3. Intern at public relations offices where the client base is strong in travel accounts or in travel-related industries.
4. Read as many trade publications (in print and on-line) as possible to keep up with trends and ideas within the industry.

ADVERTISING DIRECTOR

CAREER PROFILE

Duties: Oversees the promotion of a product or service through advertising in a variety of media

Alternate Title(s): None

Salary Range: $15,000 to $200,000

Employment Prospects: Good

Advancement Prospects: Good

Best Geographical Location(s): New York and major cities

Prerequisites:

Education and Training—College degree in advertising and marketing with other studies in tourism and management; fluency in a foreign language, particularly Spanish; knowledge of computer software programs

Experience—Internships during high school and college in an advertising agency or the advertising office of a large corporation

Special Skills and Personality Traits—Creativity and great attention to detail; good communication skills; willingness to work long hours, including weekends and evenings

CAREER LADDER

```
┌─────────────────────────────┐
│    Advertising Director      │
└─────────────────────────────┘

┌─────────────────────────────┐
│      Assistant Manager       │
└─────────────────────────────┘

┌─────────────────────────────┐
│       Creative Director      │
└─────────────────────────────┘

┌─────────────────────────────┐
│         Art Director         │
└─────────────────────────────┘
```

Position Description

Advertising Directors are responsible for coordinating all facets of an advertising campaign, from creating a concept to implementing the ideas to placing the advertising and ensuring that it runs when and where it was scheduled. They make sure tasks are executed on time and that clients are satisfied. Often, they set the general tone for the type of work done at an advertising agency.

A resort, hotel chain, cruise line, airline, or other travel-related industry may have an in-house advertising department, or they may do some of the work themselves and use the services of an advertising agency, media buyer, or other specialty firm. Alternatively, the work may be done entirely by a full-service advertising agency that develops an advertising campaign, creates the advertisements or commercials, plans where the ads should go, develops a budget, buys the advertising space and time, tracks the placements, and gives a report to the client. Ads appear in newspapers, magazines, and other publications; on the Internet; on television (broadcast or cable) and radio; by direct mail; and in out-of-home placements (e.g., billboards, taxi and bus signs, bus shelter signs, etc.).

In a large agency or in-house operation, the Advertising Director has a number of assistants, including a media planner, media buyer, account executive, and creative director. Because the Advertising Director usually works up the ranks, he or she knows the importance and function of each position.

A media planner recommends where advertising dollars should go, starting with the geographic area where the ads will be placed. The planner then checks reference books and calls the various advertising options (newspapers, magazines, TV and radio stations, out-of-home locations) to obtain the cost of placing the ad or running the spot, depending on size, length, or frequency (how many times on a TV station and what times of day, how many editions of a magazine or newspaper, and other variables). The plan is presented to the client for approval.

A media buyer (often combined with the media planner job in a shop that specializes in media buying or in-house shop) executes the plan by placing insertion or run orders for the ads and making sure the ads or commercials are delivered in a timely manner. The buyer then checks that the ads ran when and where they were supposed to and handles replacement ads ("make-goods") for those that were not run correctly.

An account executive works for an advertising agency and is charged with the responsibility of handling one or more accounts for the firm and coordinating all aspects of the advertising campaign from creation to placement.

The creative director oversees the creative department, from helping generate ideas for advertisements to creating a storyboard or sample ad for client approval. This includes the advertising copy (what announcers or actors say or the text in an ad), film, video or animation, music, and special effects. The creative director or the account executive may also supervise the shooting of commercials, both in still format for print publications and online, and in motion for television and movie placements.

Long hours, usually 50 hours or more a week, including weekends and evenings, are almost a given, and employees must deal with clients, bosses, and many last-minute deadlines and changes. Depending on the position, the Advertising Director's position may entail extensive travel. This could be to meet the client, visit the hotel or resort properties, home office, or branch offices, or attend industry-related conferences and trade shows. A larger firm—whether a national or international advertising agency or hotel or resort company—may have a number of regional offices that offer job assignments in other parts of the country or world.

Salaries

Advertising Directors in large cities and in large firms may earn $150,000 or more a year, plus bonuses. Starting salaries are very low, a particularly hard fact to deal with in major cities with a high cost of living. However, promotions in a large firm can come rapidly. For 2001, the average CEO earned $167,000; chief financial officer, $92,000; and lead account planner, $70,000. All these averages are down from the previous year due to pay cuts, deferred raises, days off without pay, and increased cost of benefits to employees. Approximately half the major advertising agencies are located in the New York area. Salaries in the Midwest are slightly higher than in the rest of the country.

Employment Prospects

During the hard economic times of 2001 and 2002, advertising agencies reduced the number of employees by 20 percent, particularly in the creative director, art director, and account executive positions. With so many Internet and dotcom businesses failing, the West Coast agencies were particularly hard hit with loss of business. When the economy improves, agencies anticipate hiring again. Women in general advertising positions slightly outnumber men, but men have an almost three-to-one ratio over women in senior positions.

Advancement Prospects

Advancement tends to come quickly and frequently for those who are dedicated and talented. A media planner or buyer can move up to an account executive position and consequently may be promoted to a group executive overseeing a number of accounts. Further promotion may lead to heading a department and then lead either to the senior executive level, starting another branch of a large firm, or opening an independent advertising agency.

Education and Training

An Advertising Director almost always needs a bachelor's degree, and post-graduate work is helpful. Almost all advertising positions above clerical require at least a bachelor's degree in one of the following concentrations: advertising, marketing or marketing research, consumer behavior, liberal arts, business management or administration, art history and theory, hospitality and tourism, computer competency, or other related fields, including sociology, psychology, literature, journalism, and philosophy. Additional degrees, often in business law, economics, accounting, finance, or statistics are usually required for top management positions.

Familiarity with such software programs as PageMaker, PhotoShop, PowerPoint, and QuarkExpress is desirable for web design, development, and editing. Because of the extensive use of calculations, knowledge of database, spreadsheet, and billing software (Control G, Silent Partner, SmartPlus, Donovan Media) is essential. Fluency in a foreign language can be very helpful, particularly Spanish due to the growing Latino population.

Experience, Skills, and Personality Traits

Internships during high school and college are recommended at advertising agencies, television and radio stations, cultural attractions, and convention and visitors bureaus or with a hotel, tour company, or other travel-related business. Creativity and excellent verbal and written communication skills are essential for the creative positions—those who conceive and execute the advertisements. Financial and business skills are important for those who will be working in planning and management positions.

Unions and Associations

There are no unions for advertising personnel, but there are numerous advertising associations, including local and national advertising clubs coordinated by the American Advertising Federation and the American Association of Advertising Agencies. Each can provide helpful information and useful contacts.

Tips for Entry

1. Intern with an advertising company or agency or within the advertising department of a travel-related company.

2. Determine what area of advertising is preferred, whether creative, administrative, marketing, research, direct sales, media buying and planning, or other.

3. Read advertising trade publications, either by subscription or on-line, to follow the trends.

4. Attend advertising club functions to establish a network of contacts within the field who know about internships and job openings.

MARKET RESEARCHER

CAREER PROFILE

Duties: Studies public interest and reaction to travel products and goods; computes and analyzes research results and recommends changes or modifications to client, if necessary

Alternate Title(s): Secret Shopper; Mystery Shopper

Salary Range: $5 per hour to $60,000 a year

Employment Prospects: Good

Advancement Prospects: Good

Best Geographical Location(s): Major cities and areas with a large number of hotels, resorts, restaurants, and cruise ships

Prerequisites:

Education and Training—College degree in marketing or economics and computer literacy for a Market Researcher; high school for a mystery/secret shopper

Experience—Market research and statistical analysis for a Market Researcher; shopping experience for a mystery/secret shopper

Special Skills and Personality Traits—Analytical mind and ability to discern trends for Market Researcher; keen observation skills and ability to complete extensive questionnaires for a mystery/secret shopper

CAREER LADDER

```
┌─────────────────────────────────┐
│   Director of Market Research    │
└─────────────────────────────────┘

┌─────────────────────────────────┐
│       Market Researcher          │
└─────────────────────────────────┘

┌─────────────────────────────────┐
│      Secret/Mystery Shopper      │
└─────────────────────────────────┘
```

Position Description

There are two types of functions within the market research field—a market researcher studies and analyzes a market, while a secret or mystery shopper visits a property unannounced to determine the quality of its services or product. Market Researchers interview typical travelers in focus groups (people most likely to use the service or product), distribute questionnaires and survey comment cards in hotel rooms, and assign mystery/secret shoppers to hotels, resorts, spas, airlines, cruise ships, and any other provider of services or products. Whether it is choosing a mattress, a new commercial for an entire chain of hotels, or analyzing the potential market for a new attraction, Market Researchers determine how customers perceive the new product or service. This combination of subjective and objective opinions and findings is combined with field research from other studies on the topic, analyzed, and then presented to the client with a recommendation to modify, approve, or discard the proposed idea.

Generally, it takes years to develop the understanding and the matrix (a chart itemizing the various aspects of the research compared with comments from the users about how important or satisfactory those aspects are) necessary to analyze the original request (the questions the customer wants answered), create the means to test the idea or item (weighing such components of a market as gender, race, religion, age, marital status, income, number and age of children, country of origin, and other factors), and interpret the results. It requires a great deal of computer work and the ability to work well with a variety of people. Normally Market Researchers work a 40-hour week, although focus group sessions may be held in the evening or on the weekend.

Mystery or Secret Shoppers visit a spa, cruise on a ship, check into a hotel, or stop by a restaurant or bar in a hotel to notice how customers or guests are treated, the appearance of the place, the promptness of service, the thoroughness, whether the clerk tried to "upsell" (suggesting a glass or bottle of wine with dinner, offering gift wrapping in the sundry shop), and other matters of interest to the company. In a hotel setting, a Secret Shopper will check that the room is thoroughly cleaned, that room service delivers an accurate order in a timely and courteous manner, and all other aspects of a property. A detailed report is filed and returned to the market research company that hired the mystery/secret shopper. The company compiles the results from all their Secret Shoppers and submit a summary to the company that hired them. The information gathered is considered proprietary, and the company that hired the shopper may require the shopper not to work for any other secret/mystery shopping companies.

Companies around the country and the world hire Market Researchers, so travel can be minimal or extensive.

Assignments for secret shoppers are irregular, depending on the contracts the market research company has. Theoretically, this could be a full-time job, but usually it is not.

Salaries

Market Researchers can earn annual salaries of $60,000 or more, depending on the location and size of the company, the type of research done, and the companies that hire them. Full-time Market Researchers usually receive vacation and sick leave and life and medical insurance. They may also be eligible for retirement and stock investment programs.

Mystery/Secret Shoppers generally receive no benefits other than the price per shopping experience, the meal they may purchase, the movie they may see, or the items they have bought. A shopping event may pay $5 to $25, and sometimes includes mileage.

Employment Prospects

As travelers spend their travel dollars cautiously and more options become available to them, the information gathered by Market Researchers about how travelers spend will continue to be valuable to corporations whose decisions are based on that research. Therefore, employment prospects for Market Researchers and Mystery/Secret Shoppers should remain good to very good for at least the next decade.

Advancement Prospects

Market Researchers can advance from working on various market research projects to manager or director of marketing or research.

Mystery/secret shoppers could work in the office of the company that hires shoppers or start their own marketing research or mystery/secret shopping business.

Education and Training

A college degree focusing on market research or marketing, with a strong emphasis on economics and computer database programs, is essential for a Market Researcher.

Mystery/secret shoppers do not need a degree but should have a high school diploma or equivalency. They also should have a valid driver's license and an automobile in good working condition at their disposal.

Experience, Skills, and Personality Traits

Market Researchers should have experience with focus groups, statistics, and work as an assistant in a market research firm. A keen analytical mind is essential. They must be well organized, detail oriented, and able to clearly communicate their findings to their clients. A strong sense of the consumer market is helpful.

Unions and Associations

There is no union for Market Researchers, but the American Marketing Association (AMA) and the Marketing Research Association (MRA) provide seminars, publications, and other materials of interest.

Tips for Entry

1. Intern for a market research company, either working with the statistics or out in the field with surveys and focus groups.
2. Meet as many Market Researchers as possible to establish a network of people who can provide career advice and news about job openings and internships.
3. Read trade publications, either by subscription or online.
4. Attend marketing meetings and events to keep up with trends and current research.

EXECUTIVE AND MANAGERIAL

HUMAN RESOURCES DIRECTOR

CAREER PROFILE

Duties: Recruits, interviews, and assists in hiring and firing employees; trains and motivates employees; administers compensation and benefit programs

Alternate Title(s): Director of Human Resources; H.R. Director, Director of Personnel; Human Resources Manager

Salary Range: $14,000 to $80,000+

Employment Prospects: Good to excellent

Advancement Prospects: Excellent

Best Geographical Location(s): Major cities and areas with a large number of outstanding hotels, resorts, restaurants, convention centers, cruise ships, and other travel-related industries

Prerequisites:

Education and Training—College degree in human resources, personnel administration, industrial and labor relations, liberal arts, business management, or a related field; a foreign language is helpful

Experience—Progressively greater responsibilities in human resources offices, including employee supervision

Special Skills and Personality Traits—Verbal and written communication skills; excellent interpersonal skills; knowledge of federal and state employment rules and regulations; computer literacy

CAREER LADDER

```
┌─────────────────────────────────────┐
│   Vice President, Human Resources    │
└─────────────────────────────────────┘

┌─────────────────────────────────────┐
│      Human Resources Director        │
└─────────────────────────────────────┘

┌─────────────────────────────────────┐
│     Benefits, Compensation, or       │
│       Recruitment Manager            │
│       (or related position)          │
└─────────────────────────────────────┘
```

Position Description

The Human Resources Director oversees all the steps necessary to hire a potential employee, including creating and placing the advertisements announcing position openings, interviewing, testing, reference and background checking, and completing the necessary paperwork. The director usually does not actually hire the more senior or executive positions and may not even hire mid-level employees, but is used to forward the most promising candidates for the position. Those prospective employees who bypass the interview stage with the human resources department will need to deal with this office as it processes and maintains the required paperwork. The Human Resources Director compiles an annual budget to administer the various programs, including the cost of new recruitment to fill vacancies or newly created jobs.

The human resources office creates a handbook of company policies and forms and makes sure each employee is familiar with its content and that the handbook is updated either annually or whenever policies are changed, added, or deleted. The director will oversee the creation and distribution of materials explaining the employee benefits program. When union employees are involved, the Human Resources Director may handle the company's side of union issues and participate in contract negotiation, although that work may be assumed by a union negotiator, either on staff or hired for that purpose.

In a large company, the human resources department can be charged with training and development, coordinating English as a second language and other courses, and career counseling. The office can also be responsible for creating and managing job fairs (to attract many new employees) and such programs as employee retention, internships and apprenticeships, training, employee suggestions, accident prevention, car-pooling incentives, and daycare options. The human resources office also may advise employees who have been terminated or transitioned (due to mergers and acquisitions) in locating new work or filing unemployment forms. When the company hires foreign employees, the Human Resources Director must be familiar with the rules and regulations, including foreign holidays and tax laws, to make sure the company complies with international rules and regulations, particularly if the foreign employee works in a foreign office rather than in the United States.

Much of this work involves extensive use of the computer, including word processing, desktop publishing, and database management. Technical updating and employee training programs administered by human resources help employees keep up-to-date with technological advances. In a large company, the Human Resources Director may supervise specialists in compensation and benefits, job analysis, equal employment opportunity (EEO) regulations, tuition reimbursement programs, training specialists, employee welfare programs, affirmative action guidelines, and other fields, each of whom may be charged with resolving grievances, analyzing corporate policies for possible violations, and filing the appropriate paperwork.

Generally, Human Resources Directors work a standard 40-hour week, but there may be exceptions during emergencies and contract negotiations. Job-related travel can be minimal or extensive and may include attending work-related conferences, and, in smaller companies, participating in job fairs and visiting college campuses to interview prospective employees.

Salaries

A Human Resources Director who works for a corporation or a large, luxury property will earn up to $70,000, while someone who works for a budget or economy property may earn $14,000 a year. Additionally, properties with union employees tend to pay more than do those without unions. Salaries also depend on the experience and other functions performed by the Human Resources Director. A boutique hotel may pay as much as 25 percent more than does a chain hotel for the same position.

Full-time Human Resources Directors usually receive vacation and sick leave and life and medical insurance. They also may participate in retirement investment programs and stock investment plans. As an employee of a hotel or chain, the manager may receive free or discounted travel benefits.

Employment Prospects

With changing federal and state regulations in the workplace and the ever-present need for employee retention, more companies are hiring specialists in human resources.

Thus, even if the economy is down, there is still a constant need for experts in this field.

Advancement Prospects

The chances for advancement from entry-level to managerial positions such as Human Resources Director are excellent, particularly when the employee has taken job-related courses in administration, compensation, organizational structure, performance appraisal, psychology, recruitment, sociology, training and development, administration, and other areas. Human Resources Directors may advance to a number of positions including vice president of human resources, president of human resources, and executive vice president of a company.

Education and Training

A well-rounded college education that includes several interdisciplinary approaches to the field of human resources is desirable. Training in negotiations, public speaking, and other specialties is helpful. A degree in such related fields as economics or business management is desirable. Knowledge of EEO (Equal Employment Opportunity), OSHA (Occupational Safety and Health Administration), ADA (Americans with Disabilities Act), COBRA (Consolidated Omnibus Budget Reconciliation Act of 1986), HIPAA (Health Insurance Portability and Accountability Act of 1996), anti-discrimination, immigration, and other applicable regulations is required. In companies with union employees, experience with unions is beneficial. Some positions require advanced college degrees in areas such as economics, business management, and negotiations.

Experience, Skills, and Personality Traits

Human Resources Directors must have excellent people skills, be able to resolve disputes, and want to assist people in making the most of their careers. Jobs in human resources offices with progressively more responsibility provide excellent experience.

Unions and Associations

The major association for this field is the Society for Human Resources Management (SHRM), which offers assistance and advice in all areas of human resources.

Tips for Entry

1. Take a broad range of subjects in school as part of a liberal arts major or minor.
2. Meet with Human Resources Directors to establish a network of experts who can offer advice about internships, apprenticeship programs, and entry-level or promotional job openings.
3. Attend meetings of human resources officials.
4. Read trade publications, either in print or on-line.

SECURITY DIRECTOR

CAREER PROFILE

Duties: Supervises the security department that patrols the property and grounds of a hotel, resort, or a cruise ship

Alternate Title(s): Security Manager

Salary Range: $16,000 to $45,000+

Employment Prospects: Good to excellent

Advancement Prospects: Good to excellent

Best Geographical Location(s): Major cities and areas with a large number of outstanding hotels, resorts, restaurants, and cruise ships

Prerequisites:

Education and Training—High school diploma; on-the-job training

Experience—Prior law enforcement or military experience

Special Skills and Personality Traits—Attentive; courteous; conscientious; able to work well with both employees and guests; observant; discreet; no criminal record

Licensure/Certification—Some states require licenses

CAREER LADDER

```
┌─────────────────────────────┐
│     Security Director        │
└─────────────────────────────┘

┌─────────────────────────────┐
│  Assistant Security Director │
└─────────────────────────────┘

┌─────────────────────────────┐
│  Security Shift Supervisor   │
└─────────────────────────────┘

┌─────────────────────────────┐
│     Security Guard           │
└─────────────────────────────┘
```

Position Description

Security is a critical part of the operation of any hotel, resort, or cruise ship. Guests must be safe and feel safe when they visit, comforted by the thought that they will not be harmed (accidentally or otherwise) or their belongings stolen. The property must ensure that items, whether cash or furnishings, will not be stolen or vandalized. Both scenarios can cost the property money either in lawsuits for personal injury or theft or in their bottom line should room furnishings (televisions, linens, furniture, decorative items) or office equipment be stolen.

The Security Director or manager is responsible for creating a security policy if one is not already in place. He or she must hire security guards, provide any training necessary, assign work shifts, file and monitor any minor incident reports, and be the liaison with local police departments. Other duties include ensuring that all guards have taken and passed any required courses and exams and possibly other administrative duties, including payroll. Generally, the Security Director or manager keeps in contact with the security guards on duty through a two-way radio system.

Security guards protect the property partly through being seen by potential thieves and vandals because the guards are wearing uniforms, by observing what is happening as undercover guards without uniforms, and by monitoring security cameras. Security guards regularly patrol the exterior and interior of the property, either on a regular schedule or by focusing on areas that might be highly subject to theft. Other responsibilities of the security department might include inspecting life safety devices, checking various mechanical systems, monitoring critical operations equipment, and checking for any other irregularities.

At times, security guards may also be called upon to escort guests and employees to and from parking areas and other parts of the property and to escort or transport the nightly deposit to the bank. They also may be asked to negotiate difficult situations between guests, particularly in a bar, or to escort guests off the property.

Some security guards must carry a firearm that usually requires special training and licensing. Security guards are usually required to pass a drug test before being hired.

Salaries

Security guards receive notoriously low pay, usually barely more than minimum wage, and rarely more than $10 an hour. This means a lot of people take on a position as a security guard as a second job and for the benefits. Security Directors are salaried employees and earn higher pay, ranging from $16,000 to $45,000 or more.

Unlike other lodging positions, salaries for Security Directors are relatively higher in the Mountain region of the United States, although they are also strong in the Northeast, South Atlantic, and Pacific regions, followed by the Midwest and South Central sections of the country. Other factors include responsibilities, the size of the property, and experience.

Full-time Security Directors usually receive vacation and sick leave and life and medical insurance. They may be offered a retirement investment plan and stock options if they work for a large enough company. Full-time personnel may also be eligible for hotel stay discounts and tuition reimbursement for career-related courses. Some jurisdictions require that security guards be bonded and have liability insurance.

Employment Prospects

As security forces are increased in almost every type of lodging facility, the need for experienced security personnel with management experience is going to be good to excellent.

Advancement Prospects

Relatively low pay for security guards makes for steady turnover, creating regular openings. Also, travelers are more security conscious than ever, and thus security has been beefed up at almost every hotel and resort and on cruise ships. Employment prospects for Security Directors are good to excellent.

Education and Training

A law enforcement degree can be helpful in securing a position as a Security Director, but it is rarely required. Usually a high school diploma and some job-related courses are sufficient. Retired law enforcement officers often pursue a second career in security.

Several state police departments, many community colleges and other educational venues, and many private companies offer security guard training, which may include instruction in handgun use, first aid, working with guard dogs, rules for search and seizure, laws of arrest, and other topics. Some jurisdictions require annual firearm training and testing.

Special Requirements

At least 33 states require security guards to be licensed. The International Association of Security and Investigative Regulators is working toward full reciprocity agreements with other state licensing bureaus. Until then, someone who wants to transfer to another geographic location, within a chain or independently, may have to be licensed in that jurisdiction. The previous training and experience will still be taken into account, however.

Experience, Skills, and Personality Traits

Experience on a recognized police force or in the military can be beneficial. Good written and oral communication skills are required, and a foreign language is helpful in dealing with employees and guests. As these positions generally require a great deal of walking, security guards and managers should be in good physical condition.

Security Directors should be friendly but authoritative and be able to react promptly to unexpected situations. They must be able to work shift hours and weekends.

Unions and Associations

An association of security guard companies, the International Association of Security and Investigative Regulators, represents 35 states and four Canadian provinces and works to help educate, lobby legislators, develop and enforce model laws and regulations, and other functions.

Tips for Entry

1. Take any law enforcement courses you can to help give you a broad background of local rules and regulations.
2. Contact the Security Director of one or more companies to determine what courses and experience you should have and to start establishing a network of people who will let you know when a position is available.
3. Experience in a military or civilian police force will help secure a job within private industry.

CREDIT MANAGER

CAREER PROFILE

Duties: Tracks and manages receivables and monthly reporting; analyzes bad debt ratio and cash collections; supervises credit and collection department

Alternate Title(s): Collection Manager

Salary Range: $30,000 to $90,000, plus bonuses

Employment Prospects: Good to excellent

Advancement Prospects: Good

Best Geographical Location(s): Any location with hotels or resorts, cruise ships, or casinos

Prerequisites:

Education and Training—Computer software, including Excel, Showcase, MS Access, SAP, or Saville; bachelor's degree or higher in business, accounting, or finance

Experience—Several years of credit and collections experience; staff management experience

Special Skills and Personality Traits—Confident, organized, articulate, and analytical; good oral and written communication skills

Licensure/Certification—Certified Credit Executive (CCE), Credit Business Association (CBA), Credit Business Fellow (CBF), or Certified International Credit Executive (CICE)

CAREER LADDER

```
┌─────────────────────────────┐
│   Vice President, Finance    │
└─────────────────────────────┘

┌─────────────────────────────┐
│       Credit Manager        │
└─────────────────────────────┘

┌─────────────────────────────┐
│      Credit Assistant       │
└─────────────────────────────┘

┌─────────────────────────────┐
│    Collection Supervisor    │
└─────────────────────────────┘
```

Position Description

Almost any hotel, resort, or cruise ship can fill every bed and every restaurant seat and theoretically be successful. A casino can have plenty of people playing their table games and slot machines and appear to be thriving.

In reality, the management needs to know what the income and expenses are, and in a timely manner. Although much of the business of a hotel or resort is with individuals who use credit cards, other business is derived from corporations, organizations, and companies (e.g., tour operators) that want to establish their own account because of the amount of regular business they will be doing.

The Credit Manager starts with a presale credit risk evaluation, including financial statement analysis and analysis of data obtained from bank and trade references, including

Dun & Bradstreet. He or she establishes credit guidelines by determining the appropriate risk levels. The Credit Manager supervises the collection, cash applications, and general ledger reconciliation. He or she also manages the collection and resolution of outstanding invoices. Among the duties and functions of the credit office is the preparation of recommendations and credit approval on new accounts to make sure the client has the ability to pay and a good credit record, establishment and maintenance of credit and collection guidelines with updated collection policies and procedures, monitoring collection efforts by auditing accounts and reports, and tracking and managing of company receivables and payables. Should an account be delinquent, the Credit Manager calls and writes to the delinquent account to collect the past due amount, keeping in mind the stipulations of the Fair Debt Collection Act and federal and state regulations concerning collection activities.

A Credit Manager may travel to make customer visits and attend sales and industry meetings. Generally, this is a 40-hour workweek, with little evening or weekend work required. The hiring company may pay relocation expenses.

Salaries

A Credit Manager may earn from $30,000 to $90,000 a year, plus bonuses. A full-time Credit Manager also may receive vacation and sick leave, health and life insurance, tuition reimbursement, and retirement and investment options.

Employment Prospects

With the downturn in the economy, many companies are folding or merging, so the essential component to staying in business is having a good idea of where a company's assets and liabilities are and making sure defaulting accounts are brought up to date and that risky accounts are kept to a minimum. Employment prospects and promotional opportunities are very good.

Advancement Prospects

The potential for advancement is good, either through moving up the company ladder or by starting a consulting business for companies that may need someone to evaluate their credit accounts and establish guidelines and policies for future business.

Education and Training

A bachelor's degree in accounting, business administration, economics, or finance is vital, with a master's in any of those subjects or risk management almost a requirement. With changing federal and state laws and regulations, continuing education is imperative.

Special Requirements

At a minimum, a Credit Manager must be bonded. Such programs as the Certified Credit Executive (CCE), Credit Business Association (CBA), Credit Business Fellow (CBF), or a Certified International Credit Executive (CICE) help individuals obtain and keep a job.

Experience, Skills, and Personality Traits

Credit Managers should be thorough, pay great attention to details, and be number-oriented. It helps to have good oral and written communication skills, and computer literacy is compulsory.

Unions and Associations

There is no union for Credit Managers, but the National Association of Credit Management provides educational seminars, works with various government agencies regarding credit policies and practices, and offers advice about the industry.

Tips for Entry

1. Work in a bank, a financial institution, or the credit office of a company to become aware of the work involved in this career.
2. Become familiar with financial software programs, credit policies, and federal and state regulations.
3. Talk with Credit Managers, asking their advice about career choices, internships, and apprenticeship programs.
4. Establish a network of people in the industry by attending local organization functions.
5. Subscribe to trade publications or read about current trends and developments on-line.

NIGHT AUDITOR

CAREER PROFILE

Duties: Prepares revenue reports; reconciles supporting documents; posts transaction information to the appropriate folios; closes the registers from the front office and any point-of-sale registers (bar, restaurant, gift shops)

Alternate Title(s): Auditor; Bookkeeper

Salary Range: $7 to $12 per hour

Employment Prospects: Good to excellent

Advancement Prospects: Good

Best Geographical Location(s): Anywhere in the United States with hotels and resorts

Prerequisites:

Education and Training—A degree in accounting is generally required, although extensive experience in the field may substitute for a formal education; computer literacy, including a knowledge of various spreadsheet programs; knowledge of a foreign language is helpful

Experience—Work experience in an accounting office, preferably for a hotel

Special Skills and Personality Traits—Able to work nights and weekends; detail-oriented; able to function with little supervision; must enjoy reconciling a balance sheet at the end of every night's work

CAREER LADDER

```
┌─────────────────────────┐
│        Auditor          │
└─────────────────────────┘

┌─────────────────────────┐
│      Night Auditor      │
└─────────────────────────┘

┌─────────────────────────┐
│     Weekend Auditor     │
└─────────────────────────┘

┌─────────────────────────┐
│    Front Desk Clerk     │
└─────────────────────────┘
```

Position Description

A Night Auditor, as the title implies, works nights, generally from 11 P.M. to 7 A.M. Duties may include checking the front office accounting records for accuracy, summarizing and compiling information for the hotel's financial records; tracking room revenues and occupancy percentages; performing a food and beverage audit; preparing a summary of cash, check, and credit card activities; posting room charges and room taxes to guest accounts (folios); processing guest charge vouchers and credit card vouchers; verifying all account postings and balances made during the day; and monitoring the current status of coupons, discounts, and other promotional programs.

At some properties, the Night Auditor also works as the front desk agent, and maintaining the sundry machines in extended-stay motels, handling guest requests, late registrations, and early check-out procedures; cashing checks for guests; and taking any reservations that come in during the night. Depending on the size of the property, the auditing may take an hour a night, with the rest of the time spent at the front desk, or it may take an entire evening, with very little time dealing with hotel guests. The Night Auditor reports to the auditor or head bookkeeper. Because so many hotel employees speak English as a second language, it is helpful if the Night Auditor can speak a foreign language to better communicate with other employees.

Unless a Night Auditor works several nights a week at several hotels, there is no travel officially associated with the job. A Night Auditor might attend conferences and professional seminars, requiring some travel. These skills are easily transferable, so an auditor wanting to relocate can do so easily. Relocation costs generally are not paid for auditors.

Salaries

Night Auditors are often hired on a part-time basis or are considered hourly employees when they are on a full-time basis. They can expect starting salaries in the range of $7 to $12 per hour, depending on the location and size of the property, experience, and responsibilities.

Full-time Night Auditors usually receive vacation and sick leave and life and medical insurance. They may also be eligible for retirement investment programs. They also receive free or discounted food and beverages at the hotel and lodging discounts within the chain of hotels.

Employment Prospects

Even with most hotels using computer programs to track expenses and guest charges (eliminating the need for using an old-fashioned 10-key calculator), the costs and expenses still have to be verified for accuracy. Figures must be entered, and someone must make sure they are in the right categories and charged to the right accounts. These functions are almost always done overnight when the front office business is relatively slow. Therefore, there is always a need for Night Auditors.

Advancement Prospects

Night Auditors can move up to become full-time auditors or bookkeepers and progress from a small motel to larger, more prestigious properties, then into supervisory positions. With additional education they may become certified public accountants.

Education and Training

A high school diploma is the minimum education required. Training in Lotus 1–2–3, Excel, and other software programs is helpful, particularly for those who aim to become full-time CPAs or accountants. In some older hotel or motel properties, the use of a 10-key calculator may be necessary. A foreign language is helpful.

Experience, Skills, and Personality Traits

Experience in a hotel or travel-related industry keeping books and tracking accounts is important. A good head for math and problem-solving is required. The ability to work nights, generally alone and unsupervised, is essential.

Unions and Associations

The American Institute of Certified Public Accountants (AICPA) provides information about career development and opportunities. It conducts regular regional and national meetings and seminars.

Tips for Entry

1. Meet Night Auditors for advice on internships and job openings.
2. Work as a Night Auditor on weekends for hotel, auditing, and guest relations experience.
3. Read about the hotel industry in trade publications, either by subscription or on-line.
4. Take courses leading to a certified public accountant degree.

PURCHASING AGENT

CAREER PROFILE

Duties: Purchases all food and controllable items

Alternate Title(s): Purchasing Manager; Purveyor Manager

Salary Range: $10 an hour to $55,000 a year

Employment Prospects: Good

Advancement Prospects: Good

Best Geographical Location(s): Anywhere there is a hotel, restaurant, casino, museum, or other business that purchases consumable and nonperishable items

Prerequisites:

Education and Training—High school diploma, but an associate or bachelor's degree in business management or hospitality is desirable; courses in purchasing, negotiations, and computer spreadsheet programs are essential

Experience—Work in a purchasing office, preferably in a hotel or similar business

Special Skills and Personality Traits—Good interpersonal skills; computer literacy; organization skills; flexible

CAREER LADDER

```
┌─────────────────────────────┐
│     Purchasing Director      │
└─────────────────────────────┘

┌─────────────────────────────┐
│      Purchasing Agent        │
└─────────────────────────────┘

┌─────────────────────────────┐
│  Assistant Purchasing Agent  │
└─────────────────────────────┘
```

Position Description

Purchasing Agents can specialize in one area, such as restaurants, room furnishings, or office supplies, or they can be responsible for all items purchased by a hotel, resort, museum, cruise line, or other business, including food and beverage, equipment, tools, linens, and furniture (furniture, fixtures and equipment, or FF&E).

A food and beverage agent purchases all food and controllable items; establishes procedures for purchase orders and inventory control; receives deliveries and approves the invoice; stocks, controls, and distributes the inventory; rotates the stock to ensure that all items are used on a first-in/first-out basis; and maintains sanitation standards. He or she may be in charge of other employees and have to interview, train, and schedule their hours.

The Purchasing Agent has to be able to communicate well with employees, guests, and vendors. He or she should be able to work in a fast-paced environment, pay great attention to details, and have good negotiating skills to help control costs while maintaining good relationships with the

vendors. Some Purchasing Agents now use a central purchasing operation on the Internet, such as Avendra.com, open to all purchasers, or ChoiceBuy.com, open only to Choice Hotels International franchises but soon to be available to other buyers.

Purchasing Agents must also develop a back-up plan in case items cannot be delivered on a timely basis. A prime requisite is knowledge of computer spreadsheet software programs. At times the Purchasing Agent works as the manager of the day or manager on duty (MOD), dealing with the hotel guests and resolving any problems that arise.

Because deliveries come in all weather, and because perishable items must be refrigerated, the Agent can be exposed to inclement and frequently changing temperature and weather conditions. As the Agent may have to lift packages weighing as much as 50 pounds, there is some chance of injury.

There may be very little or extensive travel involved in this position. A Purchasing Agent may attend trade shows and visit suppliers or purveyors. A cruise line or cruise ship Purchasing Agent may be onboard and therefore travel extensively. The cruise line pays for the airfare from home to ship and back home.

Salaries

A Purchasing Agent may be paid on an hourly basis, receiving $10 to $13 an hour, or on an annual basis, receiving $55,000 or more, plus bonuses. Full-time employees usually receive health and life insurance and sick and vacation leave. Some may be offered investment and retirement income packages.

Purchasing Agents working for hotels, resorts, cruise lines, and other travel-related industries usually receive free or reduced-cost travel accommodations.

Relocations expenses are paid only in rare cases. Remote lodging facilities and cruise ships provide room and board.

Employment Prospects

Effective Purchasing Agents can save a property a good deal of money by wise buying, so there are usually plenty of positions available.

Advancement Prospects

Purchasing Agents can advance to overseeing a number of buyers or go into other management positions. Advancement opportunities are good for those who know how to negotiate well and control inventory properly.

Education and Training

A degree is not necessary but is helpful, particularly in marketing, purchasing, and management.

Experience, Skills, and Personality Traits

Purchasing Agents should be flexible and able to react to emergencies and a fast-paced environment. They should be organized, have good interpersonal skills, and be extremely competent using computers and the Internet.

Unions and Associations

The International Society of Hospitality Purchasers provides efficiency, professional standards, etiquette, and educational information for Purchasing Agents.

Tips for Entry

1. Learn the purchasing business from the ground up, starting in a small purchasing office to learn the entire scope of the operation.
2. Talk with Purchasing Agents, asking their advice about career choices, internships, and apprenticeship programs.
3. Establish a network of people in the industry by attending local functions of the International Society of Hospitality Purchasers.
4. Subscribe to trade publications or read about current trends and developments on-line.

EXECUTIVE ASSISTANT

CAREER PROFILE

Duties: Oversees all administrative details and support for senior managers

Alternate Title(s): Administrative Assistant; Secretary

Salary Range: $20,000 to $100,000+

Employment Prospects: Good

Advancement Prospects: Good

Best Geographical Location(s): Major cities and areas with a large number of outstanding hotels, resorts, restaurants, and cruise ships

Prerequisites:

Education and Training—A high school diploma or equivalency is required; college business degree may be required or preferred; extensive knowledge of computer software programs; foreign language is helpful

Experience—Several years of progressively more responsible positions within a business office

Special Skills and Personality Traits—Must be able to multitask, assume responsibility, and be a team player

CAREER LADDER

```
┌─────────────────────────────────┐
│      Executive Assistant        │
└─────────────────────────────────┘

┌─────────────────────────────────┐
│  Junior Administrative Assistant │
└─────────────────────────────────┘

┌─────────────────────────────────┐
│          Secretary              │
└─────────────────────────────────┘
```

Position Description

Every office needs an Executive Assistant, whether it is a hotel or resort, corporate office, spa, or cruise line. Duties and knowledge vary with each type of office, so one office may demand heavy administrative functions and another need more clerical skills.

An Executive Assistant handles such matters as travel arrangements, appointments, correspondence, telephone screening and logging, sorting and screening incoming mail and visitors, filing, and data entry. The Assistant may make independent decisions regarding planning, organization, and scheduling of work.

Other duties may include making meeting arrangements, coordination and documentation of meetings, acting as liaison between a management committee and outside officials, drafting outgoing mail and memos, maintaining a budget and paying bills, and preparing monthly reports. Still other assignments may consist of scheduling appointments and arranging transportation for a boss or bosses and for incoming visitors, maintaining office equipment and supplies, maintaining personnel files, and preparing expense reports. The Executive Assistant works for one or more senior-level executives, and everything must be kept confidential. An Executive Assistant may be required to schedule other secretaries, support staff, and temporary hires and cover for them when necessary.

Among the software programs an Executive Assistant should know are Microsoft Word or WordPerfect; Excel, Lotus or other spreadsheet; Outlook; and PowerPoint in Windows (or similar programs in a MAC format). Knowledge of PageMaker, Dreamweaver, or similar software may also be needed. It is also important to have an excellent command of grammar, spelling, and punctuation. Although many offices have entered the computer age, with voice recognition software, executives who create their own documents on a word processor or computer, and others who use a tape recorder or dictating machine, some offices still require an Assistant to know shorthand for taking and transcribing dictation.

Depending on the job, there may be little or extensive travel. One office may want the Assistant to stay at the office when the executives are traveling to make sure everything runs smoothly. Another office may want the Assistant traveling with the executive to take care of any problems encountered along the way or to effectively run a meeting or other function. An Executive Assistant may travel to attend industry conferences and seminars. The expenses related to these meetings may or may not be paid by the company.

Although an Executive Assistant may work a 40-hour week, longer hours, including evenings and weekends, may be required in the hospitality industry. This could include participation in or coordination of special events for the executive staff or providing staff assistance for an after-hours board meeting. The Assistant may also be required to coordinate menu planning for meals served at board meetings.

Salaries

Salaries depend on location, size of the company, duties assigned, and experience and may range from $20,000 to $100,000 or more. Full-time Executive Assistants usually receive vacation and sick leave and life and medical insurance. Retirement and stock investment programs may be offered. When working for a chain of hotels or resorts or a cruise line, free or reduced-cost travel may be available.

Employment Prospects

Secretarial or Assistant jobs are always plentiful, but the focus is changing as more offices become automated and encompass technical equipment that frees an Assistant from much tedious clerical work. Consolidation of hotel companies further reduces job opportunities. The more skills and education a candidate has, the better the prospects for an excellent, well-paying position. Look for hotel or resort administrative positions wherever there are large properties or corporate headquarters. Many cruise lines have corporate offices in Florida.

Advancement Prospects

Advancements will depend on computer and administrative skills and experience, with most advancements being awarded to existing employees who understand corporate operations.

Education and Training

Although a high school diploma can be sufficient, a college degree in business or hospitality, with a strong focus on personnel management, is helpful. A foreign language is desirable for international companies that may have their headquarters in the United States or in other countries.

Experience, Skills, and Personality Traits

An Executive Assistant must have analytical skills, excellent interpersonal skills, and the ability to work unsupervised. He or she should be highly organized and have excellent communication skills. Knowledge of the industry is important.

Unions and Associations

The International Association of Administrative Professionals, representing some 40,000 members and affiliates worldwide, offers seminars and a Certified Professional Secretary (CPS) and a Certified Administrative Professional (CAP) review and exam.

Tips for Entry

1. Work in a hotel or resort office to learn what is required of various support staff members.
2. Meet administrative assistants who know about internships and can tell you about job openings.
3. Attend as many conferences and meetings of administrative assistants as possible.
4. Read trade publications, either by subscription or online, to keep abreast of industry news and trends.

AUDIOVISUAL SUPERVISOR

CAREER PROFILE

Duties: Coordinate all activities using audio and visual equipment for a hotel, resort, cruise ship, convention center, or other meeting facility

Alternate Title(s): Audiovisual Specialist; Director of Audiovisual Services

Salary Range: From $9.00 an hour; $22,000 to $59,000 annually

Employment Prospects: Excellent

Advancement Prospects: Good

Best Geographical Location(s): Any location with a hotel, resort, convention center, or other conference center

Prerequisites:

Education and Training—Bachelor's degree in visual communications or audiovisual production suggested for supervisory level; high school diploma (or GED) or technical training for other positions

Experience—Several years' experience in hotel, conference center, or convention audiovisual services

Special Skills and Personality Traits—Technical and interpersonal skills; flexible

CAREER LADDER

```
┌─────────────────────────────┐
│   Communications Manager     │
└─────────────────────────────┘

┌─────────────────────────────┐
│   Audiovisual Supervisor     │
└─────────────────────────────┘

┌─────────────────────────────┐
│   Audiovisual Technician     │
└─────────────────────────────┘

┌─────────────────────────────┐
│   Media Services Assistant   │
└─────────────────────────────┘
```

Position Description

Audiovisual Supervisors schedule, set up, and remove the audiovisual equipment for meetings and functions held at the property. This includes lighting; sound; recording; data display devices; audio reinforcement; uplinks and downlinks for teleconferencing; and projection equipment. There might be one presentation setup a day, or several setups per hour according to the number of seminars or presentations scheduled. They may work for the meeting facility or for an outside company that contracts with the property. They may also rent equipment from other companies when there is a demand for additional apparatus.

As many presentations are made with laptop computers using PowerPoint software, the Audiovisual Supervisor must be knowledgeable about laptops and the PowerPoint program. Also, since many presenters may be presenting for the first time, it is important that the audiovisual technician have great people skills (to reassure the presenter that all will go well) and have tested their system prior to their presentation.

Working independently or with the sales and marketing department, the Audiovisual Supervisor prepares proposals and negotiates with customers for the cost of the services. He or she coordinates the daily operations schedule, which includes long-range planning for facilities and systems upgrades, replacement, preventive maintenance, and repair. The supervisor interviews, hires, trains, and manages other employees and makes sure sufficient staff is available to handle all the bookings and requests.

Because many events take place in the evenings and on weekends, the Audiovisual Supervisor can expect to work evenings, weekends, and holidays. Audiovisual Supervisors have a great deal of contact with the client, so a neat professional appearance is expected. Audiovisual work is almost always indoors, but it may require standing and walking for extended periods of time. It also requires the ability to lift and move the equipment.

Generally, Audiovisual Supervisors do not travel extensively, other than locally from one venue to another. Those who work for contract companies may travel from one location to another. Because there is a fairly constant demand for good audiovisual personnel, relocating is rarely a problem.

Salaries

Audiovisual personnel may work hourly, starting at $9.00 per hour, or as full-time employees with salaries ranging from $22,000 to $59,000. Full-time employees generally receive life and health insurance and sick and annual leave. They may also be eligible for stock investment and retirement plans, continuing education tuition reimbursement, and free or discounted accommodations, food, and beverages. Relocation expenses usually are not covered.

Employment Prospects

Employment opportunities are readily available, particularly for those who are familiar with state-of-the-art equipment. As companies are moving toward more teleconferencing, they will need specialists who understand the complexities of this field.

Advancement Prospects

Audiovisual Supervisors can move into other management fields or start their own businesses, particularly in consulting or in setting up elaborate video studios.

Education and Training

Some positions require a bachelor's degree in communications or business administration. In other cases, a high school diploma, with excellent experience and training, is sufficient. Audiovisual personnel should be well-trained in teleconferencing and other aspects of the field.

Some audiovisual companies create entire studios, such as a television newsroom or the NASA mission control center. This takes more advanced technical training and experience, including familiarity with setting up satellite transmission equipment.

Experience, Skills, and Personality Traits

Several years of audiovisual work in supervisory positions is required. People skills and knowledge of PowerPoint presentations are helpful. Audiovisual Supervisors should be flexible with their time schedules.

Unions and Associations

The International Communications Industries Association, Inc., offers seminars and information about the audiovisual field.

Tips for Entry

1. Learn the audiovisual business by working for a conference center or meeting facility.
2. Become familiar with such programs as PowerPoint, laptop computers, and other audiovisual equipment.
3. Talk with Audiovisual Supervisors, asking their advice about career choices, internships, and apprenticeship programs.
4. Subscribe to trade publications or read about current trends and developments on-line.

DIRECTOR OF INFORMATION TECHNOLOGY

CAREER PROFILE

Duties: Oversees daily operation and supervision of all computerized telecommunication and data systems

Alternate Title(s): IT Manager; Information Technology Specialist; Technology Manager; Director of Technology Systems

Salary Range: $14.00 per hour to $122,000 per year, plus possible bonuses

Employment Prospects: Excellent

Advancement Prospects: Good to excellent

Best Geographical Location(s): Any place that has a resort, hotel, restaurant, or attraction with a computer system, and on cruise ships

Prerequisites:

Education and Training—Associate's or bachelor's degree in computer science or computer information systems is recommended; knowledge of management information systems (MIS) and such programs as Novell Network, Windows 2000 system, Microsoft Exchange, and computer reservation systems (CRS)

Experience—Several years working with computers and telecommunication systems

Special Skills and Personality Traits—Excellent written and oral communication skills; able to deal with people who are having problems with their computer system

Licensure/Certification—Microsoft Certified Systems Engineer (MCSE); Novell certification

CAREER LADDER

```
┌─────────────────────────────────────────┐
│   Director of Information Technology     │
└─────────────────────────────────────────┘

┌─────────────────────────────────────────┐
│              IT Manager                  │
└─────────────────────────────────────────┘

┌─────────────────────────────────────────┐
│             IT Assistant                 │
└─────────────────────────────────────────┘
```

Position Description

The Director of Information Technology (IT) is responsible for the daily operation and supervision of all computerized systems within a hotel, resort, restaurant, museum, or other attraction, or on a cruise ship. This may include databases and software programs; hardware systems and upgrades; evaluations, analysis, coordination, and installation of any new systems; handling current inventory of all system equipment and their maintenance contracts; and assisting the purchasing department for any special computer supplies required.

Other assignments may include responsibility for PBX (telephone), telephone call accounting, point-of-sale (POS) system, sales and marketing, time clock, back office accounting, internal and external e-mail, and credit card systems. He or she may also be responsible for the in-house television channel and personal computers.

For many IT personnel, much of the day is spent troubleshooting PCs and fixing errors, working on data backup and recovery, and making sure the firewall (computer security system) is maintained to prevent hackers from breaking into the system. They may also help guests with their computer systems or teach a guest how to use the property's system in the business office.

As a supervisor, the IT Director is responsible for interviewing, hiring, training, and scheduling other employees. With computers running all day, it is possible that he or she will have to be on call all hours or expect evening, weekend, and holiday shifts. Travel, other than from one company site to another or to trade and corporate conferences, is not a major factor in this position.

Salaries

Depending on the type of property and the scope of the work, a Director of Information Technology may be an hourly employee earning $14.00 an hour to help troubleshoot computer systems or earn an annual salary of up to $122,000 for someone who handles the entire computer system for a chain of hotels or restaurants. Full-time Directors of Information Technology working for a hotel chain usually receive free or reduced-cost accommodations and meals. Except for high-level executives, relocation costs are rarely covered.

Employment Prospects

With the demise of many dotcom companies, there have been many more people available than positions open. However, there are always jobs available for IT personnel who are personable and knowledgeable about various computer programs and operating systems and how to integrate everything to effect a bottom-line savings for a company.

Advancement Prospects

Advancement possibilities include overseeing the IT systems for more than one property in a chain of hotels or restaurants or starting a private company offering consulting services.

Education and Training

An associate's or bachelor's degree in computer science or computer information systems is recommended. It is important to know management information systems (MIS) and such programs as Novel Network, Windows 2000 system, Microsoft Exchange, and computer reservation systems (CRS). As many systems have been installed gradually over the years, it helps to have training with a variety of systems and programs to help integrate them into one system.

Experience, Skills, and Personality Traits

Several years' experience working with computer systems in the hospitality industry is essential. IT managers should be people-oriented to be able to deal with clients who are frustrated when their systems are not working properly.

Special Requirements

Microsoft Certified Systems Engineer (MCSE), Novell, and other certifications are helpful but not required.

Unions and Associations

There are dozens, if not thousands, of organizations and user groups for IT specialists and managers. One of the largest is the Information Technology Association of America.

Tips for Entry

1. Learn the computer business from the ground up, taking courses in software programs and maintenance.
2. Talk with Directors of Information Technology, asking their advice about career choices, internships, and apprenticeship programs.
3. Establish a network of people in the industry by attending local IT meetings and conferences.
4. Subscribe to trade publications or read about current trends and developments on-line.

HEALTH CARE

DIETITIAN

CAREER PROFILE

Duties: Oversees the preparation and serving of meals; promotes healthy eating; proposes diet adjustments to foster better health

Alternate Title(s): Nutritionist

Salary Range: $24,000 to $55,000

Employment Prospects: Good to excellent

Advancement Prospects: Good

Best Geographical Location(s): Wherever there are large hotels and resorts, particularly those with spa facilities, or airline or cruise ship corporate offices

Prerequisites:

Education and Training—Degree in dietetics, foods and nutrition, food service management, or similar field of study

Experience—Food service, nutritional analysis and planning, and public relations backgrounds are helpful

Special Skills and Personality Traits—Verbal and written communication skills; good interpersonal skills; ability to teach, not preach

Licensure/Certification—Approximately half of the 50 states require licensing, a third require certification, and almost all have some laws dealing with dietetics

CAREER LADDER

```
┌─────────────────────────────────────┐
│   Head Dietitian or Nutritionist    │
└─────────────────────────────────────┘

┌─────────────────────────────────────┐
│     Dietitian or Nutritionist       │
└─────────────────────────────────────┘

┌─────────────────────────────────────┐
│    Cook, Chef, or Menu Planner      │
└─────────────────────────────────────┘
```

Position Description

Dietitians help plan menus for restaurants and meal service facilities in hotels, resorts, spas, and on airlines (to a much lesser degree these days) and cruise ships. They supervise the preparation of dishes having reduced fat and sugar, instruct kitchen staff on methods to nutritionally lower the caloric content of foods through modified preparations (baked or roasted instead of fried) and integrate larger portions of fruits and vegetables into menus to replace items that are higher in calories and fat and lower in nutritional value. The Dietitian calculates the number of calories, grams of fat and protein, and other components of a meal or menu item to determine how healthy a dish is and who would benefit from it.

At spas and health centers, Dietitians consult with guests to determine their normal daily eating habits and perhaps recommend such alterations as a reduction of salt intake for those with hypertension (high blood pressure) or how to create a tasty, attractive, balanced, and nutritional diet while considering such problems as lactose or wheat intolerance. They may give lessons or suggestions about how to shop at a grocery store and on food presentation (smaller plates so smaller servings look larger) to achieve these goals. In some cases, Dietitians may consult with medical practitioners, either on staff or consultants, to help effect the desired results.

It is important that Dietitians work closely with the chef and other members of the staff to assure that there are no "friendly enemies" lurking, such as housekeepers who normally leave chocolates on bed pillows, and to remind restaurant serving staff not to refill bread baskets and butter plates and to serve salad dressing on the side instead of already on the salad. A Dietitian may suggest that a bowl of fruit be placed at the reception desk and perhaps elsewhere so guests who are hungry after a day of travel have a healthy snack awaiting them and can thereby resist the temptation to have a fat-laden nibble before dinner. Dietitians may also deal with dietary fiber and vitamin supplements. They may be charged with preparing literature for guests to take home explaining these supplements and how to create recipes of a size suitable for a family (rather than in institutional measurements).

Dietitians and nutritionists may work on staff on a full-time basis or as consultants working for one or more properties or for a chain of hotels or restaurants. Within this range, they may work a regular 40-hour week or may be called on to lecture or consult in the evenings and on weekends.

There usually is not much travel associated with this job other than to industry conferences and trade shows. However, as a Dietitian for a chain of hotels, resorts, spas, or cruise ships, it may be necessary to travel to these locations to instruct the kitchen and waitstaff on modifications and recommendations to the menu or to lecture and consult with guests. Some Dietitians have gone on to write books about diet, nutrition, or cooking, explaining the Dietitian's approach to healthy eating and living, with recipes and photographs to show the reader how a meal with portion-controlled servings looks.

Salaries

Starting salaries may be as low as $24,000, with higher salaries of up to $55,000 going to those with more experience and educational background, and at more prestigious hotels, resorts, spas, or corporations. Full-time Dietitians usually receive vacation and sick leave and life and medical insurance. They may also be eligible for retirement and stock investment plans. Relocation costs may be covered for well-qualified Dietitians.

Employment Prospects

As more people become aware of healthy eating, even when they are attending meetings or on vacation, the restaurants and catering operations that serve these people are going to require the services of a Dietitian. They may be employed as a full-time employee to maintain a program or as a consultant (part-time) to help set up a program and review it periodically.

Advancement Prospects

Dietitians and nutritionists can move to positions within corporations, work as sales agents for pharmaceutical or food manufacturing companies, or start their own consulting businesses.

Education and Training

A college degree in dietetics, with a focus on biology, chemistry, food service management, public relations, or related areas is essential. Postgraduate work may also be required.

Special Requirements

A certification as a registered dietitian is awarded following exam work by the Commission on Dietetic Registration of the American Dietetic Association (ADA). Approximately half of the 50 states require licensing, a third require certification, and almost all have some laws dealing with dietetics.

Experience, Skills, and Personality Traits

Progressively more important positions as a Dietitian or nutritionist, working in such public health facilities as hospitals, schools, senior citizen centers, or similar setting are helpful. Excellent verbal and written communication skills, good interaction with people, and the ability to teach the benefits of good nutrition are important skills for this career.

Unions and Associations

Dietitians do not have a union, but they can belong to the American Dietetic Association, which offers seminars, certification, publications, and a means to keep up with the industry and new findings and practices.

Tips for Entry

1. Study the hospitality industry to stay abreast of trends in healthy eating.
2. Meet as many Dietitians and nutritionists as possible to learn about internships and job openings.
3. Work in a food service operation, either in preparation or in a planning setting.
4. Develop your interpersonal skills.
5. Subscribe to trade publications or read about current trends and developments on-line.

SPA/HEALTH CLUB MANAGER

CAREER PROFILE

Duties: Oversees all functions and operations of a spa, health club, or fitness center

Alternate Title(s): Spa Director; General Manager of Spa

Salary Range: $25,000 to $63,000, plus bonuses

Employment Prospects: Excellent

Advancement Prospects: Excellent

Best Geographical Location(s): Major cities and areas with a large number of outstanding hotels, resorts, restaurants, cruise ships, and spas

Prerequisites:

Education and Training—College degree in business management, with courses in the hospitality industry, alternative medicine, massage therapies, health, nutrition, and fitness; foreign language training and computer literacy are helpful

Experience—Positions with progressively greater responsibilities in more prestigious spas or health clubs

Special Skills and Personality Traits—Must be a people person with great written and oral communication skills; should be able to handle a multiplicity of duties simultaneously; physically fit; good interpersonal skills

Licensing/Certification—Certified Club Manager

CAREER LADDER

```
┌─────────────────────────────────────┐
│      Spa/Health Club Manager         │
└─────────────────────────────────────┘

┌─────────────────────────────────────┐
│  Assistant Spa/Health Club Manager   │
└─────────────────────────────────────┘

┌─────────────────────────────────────┐
│        Fitness Instructor            │
└─────────────────────────────────────┘

┌─────────────────────────────────────┐
│        Massage Therapist             │
└─────────────────────────────────────┘
```

Position Description

A Spa or Health Club Manager oversees all functions of the facility, including fitness instruction, pampering treatments, food and beverage supplies, sales and marketing, accounting, personnel, recreation, housekeeping and laundry, lectures and special programs, and any other function of the spa or health club.

Spas generally have a specific focus, with the two primary themes of fitness and pampering. Because spas and health clubs can have both transient (guest) and permanent (local) members, the Manager must balance the special treatment shown toward each group of guests, sometimes allotting special times in the exercise room for local members who want to use the facilities before or after work hours with transient guests who might want to use the same equipment before a day of sightseeing, golf,

or other activities. Scheduling pampering appointments and assigning lockers to appease each group can also be a difficult task.

Health spas are being constructed in almost every four- and five-star/diamond resort, on almost every cruise ship, and even in upscale business hotels. Day spas are even more popular, usually as an extension of a beauty salon.

The most visible function of the Manager is to create a place that is warm, comfortable, inviting, and nurturing to the guests. They are at the spa to be pampered (massages, facials, pedicures, manicures, haircuts, treatments, etc.), to learn about fitness and exercise (aerobic and nonaerobic, weight training, and endurance), or to acquire knowledge about today's approach to nutrition, healthy living, and eating. Beyond that, the Manager is either responsible for or assigns responsibility for creating a budget and making sure it is met, developing a retail sales outlet to sell logo clothing items (robes, headbands, etc.) and cosmetics, building an interesting selection of exercise options, and preparing literature about the spa.

Spas are very labor-intensive, employing people who are very people-oriented and independent. Inherent in these duties is the necessity to hire, train, schedule these employees, and make the jobs interesting and rewarding (financially and emotionally) to help retain employees. Wet areas (showers, hot tubs, steam and sauna rooms, swimming pools), physical activity, and treatments offer a myriad of possible accidents, allergic reactions, and other health problems. The Manager should be familiar with all health department rules, emergency procedures, ADA (Americans With Disabilities Act) regulations, and all other measures that may have to be implemented and administered to a guest or an employee.

The Spa Manager must be familiar with all the equipment, treatments, exercise classes, and all other aspects of the spa or health club and be able to explain how they work and their benefits, both to employees and guests. The Manager is sometimes called on to take over instructing a class, administering a massage, or some other aspect of the spa or health club if necessary. He or she should also be able to motivate guests to participate in exercise and nutritional programs, so that the guest will continue a healthier lifestyle at home.

Finally, should there be a complaint or problem, the Manager must be able to resolve it to the satisfaction of the guest and the spa or health club.

Although a 40-hour week is possible, most spas and health clubs open early, stay open late, and are open seven days a week. Therefore, Managers can expect different shifts, including evenings and weekends.

Industry trade shows and conferences may require some travel, and a Manager on a cruise ship will have months of travel each year. Managers may also be asked to travel to other spa or health club locations for training sessions.

Salaries

Spa and Health Club Managers are very much in demand as the industry keeps reinventing itself, going through phases when it promoted massage therapists to the managerial position or when it promoted business majors to be managers, and almost everything in between. Individuals knowledgeable in both fields can command a very large salary. Smaller spas and health clubs may offer a salary in the mid-$20,000 range, but larger, more prestigious spas will continue to pay in the upper $60,000 bracket.

To some extent, salaries are larger in the areas with the most resort and spa concentrations, including Southern California and Florida, where the weather is almost always nice. On the other hand, there is also a large pool of candidates in these areas, so spas in other locales may offer a large salary and relocation fees to entice candidates to their geographic areas.

Many spas and health clubs offer a bonus based on spa performance. Full-time Health Club and Spa Managers usually receive vacation and sick leave and life and medical insurance. They may also be offered retirement and stock investment plans.

Employment Prospects

This is an excellent time to enter the spa and health club management field. The majority of most Americans are overweight, overstressed, and underexercised. As lifespans increase, people are becoming interested in modifying their lifestyles and improving longevity. Therefore, more spas and health clubs will open, thus providing an ample supply of jobs.

Advancement Prospects

With so many spas and health clubs opening and current employees being promoted, advancement opportunities are outstanding. Spa or Health Club Managers may advance by managing a second spa or health club, opening their own spa or health club, or moving into resort management.

Education and Training

A college degree in business management, physical education, health sciences, or hospitality is recommended. However, people who have an outstanding ability to motivate others will do well even without a college degree. Computer literacy and a foreign language are helpful. Those who enter the field as fitness instructors or massage therapists may need to seek specific certifications or licenses.

Special Requirements

Although not required by many spas or health clubs, a Certified Club Manager recognition at two levels, Honor Society and Master Club Manager, may be obtained through education credits and longevity in the field and is helpful in securing top positions. The Club Managers Association of America (CMAA) offers a Certified Club Manager program.

Experience, Skills, and Personality Traits

Spa and health club experience is extremely helpful. Spa Managers should be able to multitask, be creative, and be detail oriented. Good written and oral communication skills are desirable. They should be personable, fit, and maintain a positive attitude.

Unions and Associations

Several organizations, including ISPA (International Spa Association), the Day Spa Association, and the Club

Managers Association of America (CMAA) provide seminars and conferences about the industry and projected trends.

Tips for Entry

1. Work in your local day spa or health club to learn about the various services and programs available.

2. Meet Spa and Health Club Managers who can help you learn about internships and tell you about job openings.

3. Attend as many conferences and meetings of spa personnel as possible.

4. Read trade publications, either by subscription or on-line, to keep abreast of industry news and trends.

TRAVELING NURSE

CAREER PROFILE

Duties: Performs medical duties at various health facilities on a temporary basis; administers to passengers on an airline or cruise ship; attends to residents at a summer camp

Alternate Title(s): A title that reflects a specialty such as Summer Camp Nurse, Cruise Nurse, or Airline Nurse Companion

Salary Range: $20 to $40 an hour, plus bonuses

Employment Prospects: Excellent

Advancement Prospects: Fair to good

Best Geographical Location(s): Almost anywhere in the United States

Prerequisites:

Education and Training—Must be a Registered Nurse or Licensed Practical Nurse

Experience—At least a year working as a nurse in fields from pediatrics to gerontology, with an emphasis on critical care

Special Skills and Personality Traits—Able to adapt to new situations easily; interpersonal skills

Licensure/Certification—State license as registered nurse; Registered Nurse (RN); Licensed Practical Nurse (LPN); Advanced Cardiac Life Support (ACLS) for cruise ships

CAREER LADDER

```
┌─────────────────────────────────────┐
│          Traveling Nurse            │
└─────────────────────────────────────┘


┌─────────────────────────────────────┐
│  Registered Nurse, Private Practice │
└─────────────────────────────────────┘


┌─────────────────────────────────────┐
│    Registered Nurse, Hospital or    │
│           Health Facility           │
└─────────────────────────────────────┘
```

Position Description

Traveling Nurses are employed in a variety of settings. Some administer to passengers on airline flights or cruises, while others may work at summer or residential camps. The most common is a Nurse who travels from one location to another as jobs demand, staying at one place for eight to 13 weeks or longer.

Nurses employed by airlines function as nurse companions for passengers. A passenger can contact an airline to request a nurse companion at an hourly fee plus a reduced-cost airline ticket. This Nurse then contacts the passenger's physician to learn about the passenger's medical needs and to make sure the passenger can handle flying. The passenger may suffer from Alzheimer's, need help with meals or getting around, or potentially need emergency medical aid.

Nurses work on cruise ships in permanent and temporary positions. A permanent position may mean sailing for four months at a time with two months off between workshifts. Others may work as little as two weeks at a time or as a Traveling Nurse with 13-week tours of duty. They are considered officers and interact with passengers on a social basis as well as in the infirmary. A *Cruise Nurse* assists the doctor in tending to the passengers and crewmembers. Most of their ill passengers have gastrointestinal discomfort, motion sickness, sunburn, or colds, although some will have cardiac problems, respiratory problems, trauma or orthopedic incidents, difficulties with hypertension (high blood pressure), or diabetes.

A *Camp Nurse* works at a summer camp (some camps are scheduled year-round), evaluating and treating campers' minor injuries and illnesses, keeping a log of the visits to the health center, and identifying any health problems serious enough to require a physician's attention. Their duties also include stocking first aid supplies, providing staff orientation in preventive health care, safeguarding and administering campers' prescription medications, and completing and maintaining paperwork about each camper. Camps may specialize in an area (horseback riding, archery, tenting, music, etc.) and be located anywhere from the mountains to the seashore, so a Nurse can essentially choose the activity and geographic area in which she or he wants to work. This is a great job for school nurses who want to work during the summer while school is not in session.

Traveling Nurses generally take assignments for 13 weeks at hospitals or health facilities that need staffing that cannot be completed through regular hiring. They perform regular nursing duties, depending on the area in which they work. These assignments can be almost anywhere in the country. If the health facility and the Nurse agree, the contract can be extended for another 13 weeks, or it could become a permanent position.

The Nurse has some choice in the shifts, which can be eight, 10, or 12 hours long, so three 12-hour days means someone can work Monday, Tuesday, and Wednesday, take off for eight days, and then work Friday, Saturday, and Sunday. One exception to this type of contract is when staff nurses go on strike, and Traveling Nurses are brought in to keep the hospital open. In that case, the assignment ceases when the staff nurses return to work.

To apply for one of these positions, a Nurse can contact one of more than 100 nurse staffing companies in the United States and submit a résumé and letters of recommendation. Following an interview, the Nurse may be offered the position.

Usually Traveling Nurses are young and without a family or older people who do not have many commitments to such things as family, children, and house payments. Both may want to see the country or visit a part of the country where friends and family are nearby.

Salaries

Summer Camp Nurses either work in exchange for having their children as residents at the camp or for pay (or both), which ranges from $250 to $700 per week for two weeks to three months. Room and board is provided along with health and malpractice insurance, although it is recommended that nurses carry their own malpractice insurance. Transportation to and from the camp is paid for.

Cruise Nurses may earn $110 per day with room and board, uniforms, and transportation to and from the ship provided. Sometimes the cruise line offers passage in trade for service.

Traveling Nurses can earn up to $40 an hour, plus overtime and bonuses for completing a full contract of eight to 13 weeks, plus lodging (and sometimes utilities) or a housing allowance, travel allowances, and rental car reimbursement. Traveling Nurses sometimes receive health and life insurance, but rarely do they receive accrued vacation leave. They may be eligible for retirement and investment programs.

Employment Prospects

With the current critical shortage of Nurses, employment prospects are excellent, especially since hospitals and health facilities would rather pay the price of hiring Traveling Nurses than lose revenue because a ward or wing has to be closed due to lack of staffing. Some areas of the country are more desperate and more desirable, with Northern California meeting both these criteria.

Advancement Prospects

Traveling Nurses can take a full-time position and then go into management (usually a permanent position, rather than a traveling situation).

Education and Training

A nursing degree from an accredited school is the minimum requirement. Specialized training, particularly in critical care, is particularly desirable.

Experience, Skills, and Personality Traits

Most Traveling Nurses have at least a year of nursing experience. A Traveling Nurse must be flexible and adapt easily to different locations and different modes of operation at each facility. Nurses good at mentoring are appreciated, since they can make suggestions about how other facilities handle certain situations.

Special Requirements

Traveling Nurses are required to be at least Registered Nurses. Eighteen states (Arizona, Arkansas, Delaware, Idaho, Indiana, Iowa, Maine, Maryland, Mississippi, Nebraska, New Jersey, North Carolina, North Dakota, South Dakota, Tennessee, Texas, Utah, and Wisconsin) have reciprocal arrangements to honor licensure from the other states in this group. If a Nurse lives in a state that is not part of this compact, then she or he must apply and pay the fees for a license in any of the other states.

Some states require fingerprinting and a criminal background check prior to issuing a license. When there is a fee for state licensure, most Traveling Nurse agencies will reimburse that fee after the Nurse has worked for them for a year.

Unions and Associations

The Association of Camp Nurses, the National Association of Traveling Nurses, the National Association for Practical

Nurse Education and Service, the National Council of State Boards of Nursing, Inc., the National League for Nursing, and the Nursing Licensure Compact Administrators provide information about nursing. The American Nurses Association and its labor arm, United American Nurses, lobby governmental bodies and provide other services and information of interest to Nurses.

Tips for Entry

1. Become familiar with the nursing industry, particularly critical care practices.

2. Talk with Traveling Nurses, asking their advice about career choices, internships, and apprenticeship programs.

3. Establish a network of people in the industry by attending local association and union functions.

4. Subscribe to trade publications or read about current trends and developments on-line.

MARITIME PHYSICIAN

CAREER PROFILE

Duties: Diagnoses and treats a variety of diseases and injuries experienced by crew and passengers on a ship

Alternate Title(s): Ship's Doctor

Salary Range: $0 (service in exchange for passage) to $8,000 per month

Employment Prospects: Good

Advancement Prospects: Fair to good

Best Geographical Location(s): Any port with passenger or cargo ships

Prerequisites:

Education and Training—Medical degree

Experience—Background in emergency medical care, cardiac care, minor surgery, and primary care

Special Skills and Personality Traits—Good interpersonal skills; excellent diagnostic skills; genuine concern and sympathy

Licensure/Certification—Medical degree; advanced life support certification; advanced trauma life support certification; advanced cardiac life support certification

CAREER LADDER

```
┌─────────────────────────────┐
│  Senior Maritime Physician  │
└─────────────────────────────┘

┌─────────────────────────────┐
│     Maritime Physician      │
└─────────────────────────────┘

┌─────────────────────────────┐
│     Emergency Physician     │
└─────────────────────────────┘
```

Position Description

A Maritime Physician examines patients; orders or performs necessary tests, analyses, and diagnostic images relating to a patient's condition; and administers or prescribes the necessary treatments and medications. At times, the physician may be required to perform minor surgery. When necessary, the physician may vaccinate patients to immunize them against communicable diseases.

Newer cruise ships have medical centers that are equipped to handle common medical emergencies until the patient can be transferred to an appropriate shore-side medical facility, if necessary. Some ships have a staff of one or more physicians, a dentist (particularly for crewmembers), and nurses to help rotate the hours the staff is on duty.

Cruise lines affiliated with the International Council of Cruise Lines, a trade association, cooperate with the Centers for Disease Control and Prevention and the U.S. Department of Agriculture to ensure high public health standards. These cruise lines have agreed to meet or exceed medical guidelines

established by the American College of Emergency Physicians. The number of physicians and nurses aboard a ship can depend on the size of the ship, the number of crewmembers and passengers (ships may carry as many as 3,400 passengers and 1,000 crewmembers) and the length of the voyage.

A Maritime Physician rarely handles prenatal and postnatal care, but the type of patients they see can vary in age from infants to senior citizens. Those who tend to crewmembers may see patients who have received very little medical attention prior to serving on the ship and those who are injured in ship-related accidents. At other times, the physician may have to deal with passengers and crewmembers who are homesick.

The physician reports any births, deaths, or outbreaks of contagious disease to the appropriate authorities. The physician also files a report with the ship's captain or other designated personnel regarding any follow-up services that should be performed on crewmembers and writes a note to the sick passenger's physician detailing what was done under the doctor's care. Some ships are equipped with telemedicine (the technology that allows the transfer of digitized X-ray images and other medical data) to connect with medical consultants ashore who have specialized medical experience and advice.

Maritime Physicians travel extensively and, depending on the itinerary of the ship, may visit exotic ports around the world. Other ships travel the same routes for extended periods of time. Depending on the ship's policy, the physician should have ample time for sightseeing while in these ports. They may be onboard for several months at a time and have extended periods when they are not needed onboard. Maritime Physicians will have a great deal of interaction with the passengers at meal time and during other functions aboard ship. Although a ship's physician may have scheduled medical hours for treating such basic problems as motion sickness, he or she is on call at all hours of the day during the voyage.

An alternative to working on a cruise ship is the job of an airline physician. There are a limited number of these positions, with American Airlines and United Airlines together employing fewer than 36 doctors. Airline physicians are land-based and provide medical advice to airline crews via communication links when a passenger is having such emergencies as a heart attack or asthma attack.

Salaries

Some passenger cruise lines hire a physician on a short-term basis or a "services in exchange for passage" basis, while others have full-time shipboard practitioners licensed in the country of the ship's registry or other countries. These positions pay between $4,000 and $8,000 per month, with contracts running from one to six months.

As part of their contracts, permanent Maritime Physicians will receive airfare between the ship and home, paid for by the ship's owners. They may be eligible for investment and retirement plans. Physicians generally receive discounts on purchases aboard ship and during shore visits.

Employment Prospects

Employment prospects continue to grow as a growing number of cruise ships are placed into service and as medical facilities onboard cruise and cargo ships improve. As some doctors become Maritime Physicians late in their career, there is a fair amount of turnover, allowing room for other doctors to secure these positions.

Advancement Prospects

There is some room for advancement, as a ship-based Maritime Physician may be promoted to a land-based position overseeing all the medical facilities and staff of a cruise line. Those doctors who start their career as a Maritime Physician may move on to positions within hospitals or other medical facilities on shore, start their own practices, or join private practices.

Education and Training

Maritime Physicians must have a medical degree and may be required to have at least three years of postgraduate medical training in primary care, minor surgery, emergency medical care, and cardiac care. Many physicians are required to participate in continuing medical education each year. The medical staff aboard a ship may be called on to use X-ray and laboratory equipment, defibrillators, external pacemakers, EKG machines, mechanical ventilators, cardiac monitors, infusion pumps, blood pressure monitors, pulse oximeters, respirators, and equipment to complete a blood transfusion.

A four-week course in cruise medicine—learning hands-on under the supervision of a ship's physician—may also be required.

Special Requirements

A medical degree is required, and some cruise lines require a certificate in advanced life support, advanced trauma life support, and advanced cardiac life support.

Experience, Skills, and Personality Traits

Fluency in English is required, and proficiency in another language is helpful, particularly for treating crewmembers who are not fluent in English. As many cruise passengers are middle-aged or older, experience in treating diseases and medical conditions of this age group is desirable. Some cruise lines attract families with children, so a background in pediatrics can be helpful, also. Maritime Physicians should be excellent diagnosticians and have good interpersonal skills.

They should have good oral and written communication skills. They should demonstrate genuine concern and sympathy, particularly toward crewmembers who spend many months away from home and loved ones.

Unions and Associations

The American Medical Association and other associations provide information and seminars of interest to Maritime Physicians. The American College of Emergency Physicians has a Cruise Ship and Maritime Medicine Section.

Tips for Entry

1. At medical school, specialize in emergency medical care or geriatric care.
2. Talk with physicians and other cruise or cargo ship personnel about career choices, internships, and apprenticeship programs.
3. Establish a network of people in the industry by attending local American Medical Association, American College of Emergency Physicians, and other association functions.
4. Subscribe to medicine and health publications or read about current trends and developments on-line.

SPECIALTIES

TRAVEL PHOTOGRAPHER

CAREER PROFILE

Duties: Shoots still pictures or video of domestic and international interest to readers or viewers to be used in editorial content or collateral material; cruise photographer takes portraits of passengers aboard a ship

Alternate Title(s): Travel Videographer; Photojournalist; Staff Photographer; Freelance Photographer; Cruise Photographer; Resort or Attraction Photographer; Commercial Photographer

Salary Range: $10,000 to $100,000

Employment Prospects: Fair to good

Advancement Prospects: Fair

Best Geographical Location(s): Any cities or areas with a large number of advertising and public relations agencies; aboard cruise ships; at attractions and resorts

Prerequisites:

Education and Training—Degree in photography, specializing in editorial, commercial, or portrait; computer literacy

Experience—Work on a newspaper or magazine, or for an advertising or public relations firm, hospitality corporation, or television station

Special Skills and Personality Traits—Creativity; an "eye" for a pictorial story; reliable; good interpersonal skills; excellent technical photography skills

CAREER LADDER

```
┌─────────────────────────────────┐
│   Photographer/Videographer     │
└─────────────────────────────────┘

┌─────────────────────────────────┐
│    Assistant Photographer       │
└─────────────────────────────────┘

┌─────────────────────────────────┐
│    Photographic Researcher      │
└─────────────────────────────────┘

┌─────────────────────────────────┐
│     Photo Lab Technician        │
└─────────────────────────────────┘
```

Position Description

There are several avenues Photographers can choose from within the travel industry, including videography, editorial, portrait, and commercial. This profile does not include hard news coverage or a career as a war correspondent/Photographer that could find a Photographer traveling to exotic but not necessarily safe destinations around the world.

Still Photographers can use a number of different camera formats, including 35 mm, digital, medium format ($2\frac{1}{4}$" × $2\frac{1}{4}$" negative size), and large format (4" × 5" or 8" × 10"). The smaller format cameras are easier to work with, but the larger formats produce sharper images. A professional lab, the Photographer, or a photographer's assistant may develop their images. Those who use digital must be competent in photo imaging software.

Videographers use motion picture film or videotape to provide coverage of a destination for a television show or a videotape cassette for promotional and advertising use. Sometimes these videos are called a B roll and are used as background to a travel story on a television show.

A Travel Photographer who shoots stills takes editorial photos for a newspaper, magazine, or website. These pictures are used to enhance an article about a destination or an activity and should help entice people to visit the destination or attend the activity. Photographers can be on staff or work on a freelance basis. New *Freelance Photographers* must spend a great deal of time looking for assignments, sometimes more time than in actual photography. If good enough, a freelancer can use the services of a stock agency that will sell his or her photographs for a commission.

The Photographer may stay in a small geographic area, say New England or the Northwest, or travel extensively. The latter would be particularly true when shooting a cruise ship at sea, visiting the various ports of call and taking interior shots of the ship and of people enjoying the onboard activities. A Travel Photographer can be on the road three or four months of the year, often spread out over the course of a year, or they can be away for months at a time.

A *Cruise Photographer* takes portrait photographs of passengers as they board the ship, as the captain at a formal event greets them, and as they are engaged in other onboard activities (e.g., a "jousting" competition, lounging by the pool, or enjoying a late night buffet). These photographs are processed immediately, aboard ship, and usually posted for sale within 24 hours. The darkroom staff makes duplicates if they are ordered, so an immediate and efficient filing system has to be established so the negatives can be retrieved for instant duplication. The Photographer travels with the ship, but with darkroom duties there may not be time to go sightseeing. *Resort* or *Attraction Photographers* also take photos of guests involved in such activities as a dolphin swim, making crafts, or competitive events.

Commercial photography is used for advertising and publicity. A *Commercial Photographer,* either on staff or as a freelancer, takes pictures of a hotel, resort, cruise ship, destination, or attraction that will be used in an ad or a brochure produced by or for the client. At times this may include food photography, highlighting the achievements of a noted chef. These photos may also be used on websites.

Salaries

Depending on whether a Photographer is freelance or on staff and the type of photography, an annual salary can be as low as $10,000 (freelance editorial) to $50,000 (staff of an advertising company) to $100,000 for a glossy magazine. Full-time staff Photographers usually receive vacation and sick leave and life and medical insurance. They may also be eligible for retirement and stock investment programs.

Freelance Travel Photographers who specialize in editorial content generally have to pay their own way on assignments and hope to be reimbursed for their travel expenses. They may also be invited on media trips that include transportation, lodging, and meals, leaving little in the way of expenses. A publication or advertising or public relations firm will pay all expenses for a Photographer on assignment.

Employment Prospects

Editorial freelance photography varies with the economy. In a good economy, people travel more and publications sell more advertising (to offset the cost of publishing), so more freelance work is purchased. Commercial Photographers should be in good demand because there are so many aspects to a good commercial photograph (lighting, timing, composition) that can not be duplicated by anyone with a point and shoot camera. Staff Travel Photographers may find they are handling assignments other than travel when the economy and advertising are in a down cycle.

Advancement Prospects

Freelance Photographers can advance to become Staff Photographers. Staff Photographers may be promoted to photo editor. When the economy is good and more magazines and advertising brochures are produced, advancement will be easier. Videographers can progress to become television producers and directors.

Education and Training

A degree in photography is helpful. Computer literacy is important, particularly with respect to digital photography programs.

Experience, Skills, and Personality Traits

Experience as a Photographer for newspapers or magazines is helpful, as is work at a television station. Experience assisting established Photographers is useful. Travel Photographers must be reliable and able to work on short notice. Those seeking freelance work should be comfortable with gaps in employment.

Unions and Associations

The American Society of Media Photographers, Inc. is a trade association of more than 5,000 members that promotes Photographers' rights, educates Photographers in better business practices, and produces business publications of interest to Photographers.

Tips for Entry

1. Attend Photographer workshops to learn about the latest news and trends within the industry.
2. Meet as many Photographers as you can to develop a network that will let you know about internships and apprenticeships.
3. Read trade publications either by subscription or online.

TRAVEL WRITER

CAREER PROFILE

Duties: Researches and writes travel articles that are succinct and informative, painting word pictures that will persuade someone to visit a destination or feel like they have visited it

Alternate Title(s): Travel Journalist; Staff Writer; Freelance Writer

Salary Range: $10,000 to $76,000

Employment Prospects: Fair to excellent

Advancement Prospects: Good

Best Geographic Location(s): Almost anywhere; but because extensive travel can be involved, living near a major airport can be an important factor in saving travel time and expense

Prerequisites:

Education and Training—A high school diploma is desirable, with a strong focus on English, geography, journalism, communications, business, accounting, computer literacy, and photography; a college degree in one of these areas is helpful

Experience—General experience in writing for newspapers, magazines, and the Internet, whether as a general assignment writer or one who has specialized in such fields as sports, arts, business, or other areas

Special Skills and Personality Traits—Creativity; natural curiosity; ability to interact well with other people and spend significant amount of time alone; self-disciplined; detail-oriented; able to handle emergencies, crises, and deadlines without undue stress; business management skills

CAREER LADDER

```
┌─────────────────────────────┐
│      Senior Writer          │
└─────────────────────────────┘

┌─────────────────────────────┐
│    Travel Writer, Staff      │
└─────────────────────────────┘

┌─────────────────────────────┐
│   Travel Writer, Freelance   │
└─────────────────────────────┘
```

Position Description

There are two general types of Travel Writers—*Staff Writers* and *Freelance Writers*. Either may write articles for newspaper, magazine, or other print or electronic publication or for radio or TV. While many newspapers have travel sections and many magazines are dedicated to some aspect of travel (such as cruising), many more special-interest publications run travel-related articles. For example, a magazine about NASCAR racing might carry a monthly column or section about the areas where the races are held. Other career opportunities can be found in trade journals, company newsletters, and copywriting for advertising agencies.

Generally, a newspaper Staff Writer works with the travel editor and from a calendar of special sections, often generated by or in connection with a special advertising focus. Determining this editorial calendar also involves the consideration of destinations within a two-hour drive or flight from a nearby airport. Sometimes local destinations (within a short drive) will be covered in the metro or lifestyle section of the paper, while destinations that are farther away will be in the travel section.

A Freelance Writer, obtaining an editorial calendar from the travel editor or from the advertising department, submits written articles (for newspapers) or queries (magazines) about a specific destination or topic. Such articles may be as short as 300 words (called front-of-the-book or back-of-the-book matter in magazines), as long as 2,000 words (thorough magazine-article), or 30,000 to 40,000 words for a guide-book. Once an article is submitted to the editor, it may come back to the Writer for additional or different information.

Usually a travel article includes details on how to get to the destination (which airlines fly there, what highways to take), how much a trip will cost (price of hotel, airfares, special packages, meals), and often a map of the area covered. Although a staff researcher might gather this information for a Staff Writer, it is the freelancer's responsibility to find and provide the material.

Beyond destination-centered articles and service pieces (e.g., 10 exercises before you start skiing), there are also pieces that cover the various aspects of the travel industry, including business travel, and news about hotels, cruising, airlines, travel agencies, and tour companies.

Readership demographics, particularly for magazines, play a part in deciding what destinations will be covered, whether it's travel for seniors, families, outdoors types, or those with other interests. The Writer and editor, and sometimes a travel photographer, will decide what aspect of a destination will be covered. At other times, a round-up article will be written, highlighting ten or twelve places to go for specific activities.

The allure of being a Travel Writer is the ability and need to travel to personally research interesting sites and interview people who live and work there. Publications with Staff Writers generally pay for these trips. Freelancers have to find their own way there, either through a media trip sponsored by a resort or travel and visitors bureau or by paying for the trip in hopes of selling the article enough times to recoup the costs. Many destinations require a "letter of assignment" from an editor saying the editor has asked the Writer to research the article and that the publication is planning to run it.

Travel Writers often take many pictures, both to sell to the publication and as a memory aide. Film is cheap, but getting back to a destination for specific information is not. With digital and point-and-shoot cameras, one does not have to be a stellar photographer just for memory jogging. If the photos will be submitted for publication, it is important to have a mix of vertical and horizontal aspects.

Most full-time Travel Writers are on the road three to four months a year, sometimes spread evenly throughout the year and at other times taking consecutive trips week after week. It requires a great deal of flexibility and patience to schedule airline flights, and train timetables, book hotel reservations, and tackle other problems experienced by "road warriors."

Salaries

There are some Travel Writers who earn incomes in the upper five digits, but they are few and far between. More likely, a Freelance Travel Writer will earn $10,000 annually. This is compensated for by the free or reduced-fare travel they enjoy. Full-time magazine Travel Writers and newspaper Staff Travel Writers earn as much as $75,000. Staff Travel Writers generally receive health, life, and, often, dental and optical insurance. Freelance Writers have to arrange for their own insurance either as an individual or a member of a writing association or union.

Employment Prospects

Travel writing job opportunities vary, to some extent, with the economy. As more people travel because of a good economy, there are more publications looking for more content. However, when there is an economic downturn, publications are looking for articles about economical ways to travel. Being a generalist Travel Writer has its benefits, but developing a specialty can mean a career will continue despite the economic situation.

There is a lot of competition in the travel writing industry because most people who have ever taken a trip feel they can write about "my summer vacation." There are also many people who will write travel articles for free. Additionally, a newspaper can ask reporters on other beats to write about where they have been on vacation. Still other competition comes from articles carried over the wire services and copy submitted by public relations agencies and tourism bureaus.

Advancement Prospects

Staff Travel Writers have an excellent opportunity to advance to higher positions, including assistant editor or editor, or transfer to regional, national, or international travel-related publications. Freelance Writers can advance to become a full-time Staff Travel Writer.

Education and Training

Although a college degree in communications, journalism, or geography and experience on a weekly or college newspaper are helpful, a college degree is not crucial for someone with talent, dedication, and a passion for writing.

Experience, Skills, and Personality Traits

Writing skills are essential for this job. Also important is the ability to interview people, visit a location for two or three days and grasp what an average tourist might take a week or more to see and enjoy, and withstand the rigors and possible snafus encountered in extensive traveling. A Freelance Writer must be able to work with a number of editors and deal with periods with a great number of assignments as well as times without any work. Bookkeeping, time management, and self-motivation are essential skills for the freelancer. Computer skills are indispensable for today's job market.

Unions and Associations

Travel Writers may join any number of associations, including the Society of American Travel Writers (SATW). They offer periodic publications, seminars, meetings, and other assistance. Other associations include the International Food, Wine and Travel Writers Association (IFW&TWA), International Travel Media (ITM), Midwest Travel Writers Association (MTWA), North American Ski Journalists Association (NASJA), North American Travel Journalists Association (NATJA), Outdoor Writers Association of America (OWAA), Outdoor Writers Guild (OWG), Periodical Writers Association of Canada (PWAC), Southeastern Outdoor Press Association (SEOPA), and Texas Outdoor Writers Association (TOWA).

Professional associations and unions include the American Society of Journalists and Authors (ASJA), which provides sample contracts, advice, details about issues of concern to writers, national meetings, and other assistance. The National Writers Union (NWU) offers sample contracts and helps writers negotiate complaints with major publications.

Tips for Entry

1. Collect the articles you have had published and photocopy them (print the ones that have been posted on the Internet) so you will have "clips" to send to editors, even if they are not about travel or the industry.
2. Internships are available at most newspapers, magazines, and other publications that offer good experience in a number of writing areas.

TRAVEL ATTORNEY

CAREER PROFILE

Duties: Handles legal matters pertaining to travel and hospitality issues, either as a corporate attorney or as one who handles cases dealing with travel-related injuries

Alternate Title(s): Travel Lawyer; a title that reflects a specialization such as Hospitality Lawyer, Trial Attorney

Salary Range: $28,000 to $150,000

Employment Prospects: Good to excellent

Advancement Prospects: Good

Best Geographical Location(s): Major cities with travel and tourism corporate offices (hotels, cruise lines, airlines); areas with law firms that handle travel-related lawsuits

Prerequisites:

Education and Training—Law degree from an accredited law school, with special courses in commercial, antitrust, labor, and liability law

Experience—Work in a travel-related field

Special Skills and Personality Traits—Strong oral and written communication skills; analytical and research skills; public speaking skills

Licensure/Certification—Admission to bar; state license

CAREER LADDER

```
┌─────────────────────────────┐
│      Travel Attorney        │
└─────────────────────────────┘

┌─────────────────────────────┐
│        Legal Intern         │
└─────────────────────────────┘

┌─────────────────────────────┐
│         Law Clerk           │
└─────────────────────────────┘
```

Position Description

A Travel Attorney can specialize in a variety of legal issues within the travel industry. He or she may represent clients (passengers or employees) who have been injured on a cruise ship, airplane, train, bus, or other public conveyance. There are legal considerations depending on where the incident happened, the nationality of the carrier, and the terms and conditions of the passenger's ticket or the employee's contract, and a Travel Attorney must be familiar with all these criteria.

An Attorney for a transportation provider (e.g. travel agency or tour operator) or a hotel or other lodging facility follows pending legislation and recommends any testimony or action deemed necessary. He or she prepares materials necessary for any action brought against the airline, hotel, resort, cruise ship, train, or bus company and represents the company in the lawsuit. A Travel Attorney may assist travel agencies in their dealings with airlines, hotels, car rental companies, computer reservation system (CRS) companies, and other travel suppliers. They may also assist travel agencies in their dealings with corporate clients. Hospitality Lawyers deal with insurance concerns, hospitality premises liability issues, wage and hour disputes, immigration processes, legal employee selection, franchising, food and beverage issues, and safety and security.

Travel and hospitality Attorneys may battle in court. A traveler might sue a hotel and travel agent after falling off a balcony that was below waist height, arguing that the hotel and travel agent should have been aware that the property did not meet U.S. safety standards, or a client might sue a travel agency because the hotel staff was surly, citing the agency should have known what type of hotel was being booked. A tour company might be sued if the bus they operate is involved in an accident that could have been avoided.

The Attorney starts by researching existing laws and the way they have been interpreted in earlier cases. In addition to injury cases, the problem may concern accessibility, discrimination, licensing, bonding, or other matters. Once the Attorney has determined the status of the issue in that and other jurisdictions, he or she gives the client the best information available, and, if necessary, they agree to go to the courts for resolution. The Attorney, with or without a trial Attorney, then represents the client in court, preparing the best offense or defense possible.

Other Travel Attorneys deal with mergers and acquisitions among travel agencies, a huge field these days as airlines are eliminating commissions and more people are booking travel accommodations on-line and skipping the work formerly done by travel agents. Among the duties involved in such consolidations is determining the value of the agency being acquired.

A very specialized field for Travel Attorneys is with small travel companies that do business with the government. The Attorney helps the client prepare proposals (to provide travel services to government agencies) and handle bid protests for clients where one bidder objects to the contract going to another bidder. A Travel Attorney could handle either side of this suit (i.e., the winner or the loser in the bidding process). The General Accounting Office (GAO) of the U.S. government usually hears these cases. At other times, the Attorney may help the client file a claim against the government if the contract is not followed or if the government demands that the client provide services beyond the scope of the contract. A board of contract appeals (BCA) usually hears these cases.

Travel Attorneys may travel little or extensively in the performance of their duties. They may have to go to another jurisdiction for research, testimony, or a trial. As an in-house Attorney, relocation may be necessary when switching from one company to another. Numerous legal meetings may also require some travel.

Salaries

A first-year lawyer working in a small firm in a small town may earn as little as $28,000 a year, but within a few years or when employed by a major law firm or company, may earn $150,000 or more a year. Attorneys who work for firms as in-house counsel to a travel provider company may work a 40-hour week, but in preparation and during a trial they may work many more hours, including evenings and weekends, for which they are paid overtime. Full-time Travel Attorneys usually receive vacation and sick leave and life and medical insurance. They may be eligible for retirement and stock investment plans.

Employment Prospects

Attorneys who specialize in the travel industry should find ample employment, particularly as people become more litigious in travel matters and as the number of travel agencies declines. There are very few Attorneys currently practicing specifically in travel-related law.

Advancement Prospects

The field of travel law is relatively new, but growing, so there should be ample opportunity to become a specialist in negligence cases or an in-house Attorney for a travel supplier. Within a firm, depending on the size and promotion policy, an Attorney could become a partner or start a separate law firm specializing in travel law.

Education and Training

A law degree from an accredited law school is necessary. A foreign language is helpful if the practice will include international clients. Computer skills are also helpful.

Special Requirements

All Attorneys must pass a state bar examination to be admitted to the bar and be licensed to practice. Many states have reciprocity agreements for admitting out-of-state attorneys without requiring them to take a separate bar exam.

Experience, Skills, and Personality Traits

If a Travel Attorney is going to be a trial Attorney, good public speaking skills and a persuasive manner are essential. Determination and an analytical mind are also important traits for this career.

Unions and Associations

Attorneys may belong to travel industry–related unions as an associate member, but membership in a bar association, either the American Bar Association or the National Bar Association, is helpful. Both associations have seminars, regional and national meetings, and publications and provide assistance to attorneys.

Tips for Entry

1. Intern for a law firm, either one that specializes in travel law or one in general practice.
2. Attend court trials for a better knowledge of the talents needed to be a Trial Attorney.
3. Meet as many Attorneys as possible to establish a network of people who can offer career advice and who know when and where there are openings.
4. Read trade publications, either by subscription or on-line.

PROFESSOR OF TRAVEL, TOURISM, AND HOSPITALITY

CAREER PROFILE

Duties: Instructs students in the various areas of travel, tourism, and hospitality

Alternate Title(s): Assistant Professor, Associate Professor, Instructor

Salary Range: $25,000 to $117,000

Employment Prospects: Good to excellent

Advancement Prospects: Fair

Best Geographic Location(s): All areas

Prerequisites:

Education and Training—Almost all postsecondary educational facilities require at least a master's degree (and some a doctorate) in a tourism, travel, or hospitality field; some schools invite experts from the field in as visiting professors and do not require advanced degrees; a foreign language is helpful

Experience—Work experience in the travel, tourism, or hospitality field; teaching experience

Special Skills and Personality Traits—Must relate well to people; basic computer skills; excellent oral and written communication skills

CAREER LADDER

```
┌─────────────────────────────────┐
│   Dean or Department Chair       │
└─────────────────────────────────┘

┌─────────────────────────────────┐
│          Professor               │
└─────────────────────────────────┘

┌─────────────────────────────────┐
│      Associate Professor         │
└─────────────────────────────────┘

┌─────────────────────────────────┐
│      Assistant Professor         │
└─────────────────────────────────┘

┌─────────────────────────────────┐
│          Instructor              │
└─────────────────────────────────┘
```

Position Description

Schools that offer courses and degrees in the fields of travel, tourism, and hospitality cover a huge range of topics, encompassing hotel management and travel supplier careers, including parks and recreation, therapeutic recreation, tourism and events management, exercise science, health promotion, sport management, food service management (quantity food and fine dining), and club management. Within tourism, a professor may also teach the ethics, philosophy, and history of the travel industry, as well as its current scope.

Generally, professors are expected to develop one or more courses at the associate, baccalaureate, or graduate level and teach the classes (sometimes with a teaching or graduate assistant). They also do research, prepare grant proposals, advise students, evaluate and grade student performance, assist in internship location and placement, work within the local community to establish a good rapport between local hospitality providers and students, and publish pertinent articles about the industry. Professors also mentor student dissertations, theses, and research projects. As a member of the college community, professors are expected to serve on graduate student committees and on departmental academic committees.

The students who take these courses may go into careers in such industries as commercial airlines, resorts and hotels, tour companies, theme parks, traveler information and interpretation programs, travel marketing and sales operations, hotel management, design, nutrition, communications, public relations and advertising, and other areas. Any given course may actually be of an interdisciplinary structure covering a variety of aspects of the travel industry.

With the increased growth of distance learning, professors may be required to develop, teach, grade, and administer one or more on-line courses (including on-line discussions), either on a credit or continuing education basis. These positions may be full- or part-time and may be at the school or at a remote location. Professors may be required to supervise other personnel including clerical staff, teaching assistants, and researchers.

As a full-time professor, employment may be on a nine- or 10-month basis with summers free or may include the summer semester. In schools where there are trimesters or quarters, vacation may be at other times of the year or simply between terms.

Most professors will stay on campus during the school year except to travel to professional meetings and conferences. However, they may travel extensively, with or without their students, to study travel, tourism, and hospitality practices in other parts of the country or world. This may take place during the school year or during term breaks.

Salaries

The pay scale for college-level travel and tourism faculty depends on academic rank (instructor, assistant professor, associate professor, professor), experience (in education and in the tourism field), whether a school is private or public, and the location of the school. A starting salary for a full-time instructor may be as low as $22,000 and progress to $67,000; salaries for an assistant professor generally start at $39,000; an associate professor at $38,000; and a professor at $51,000.

Full-time professors usually receive vacation and sick leave and life and medical insurance. Those paid on a yearly basis generally work nine or 10 months and have the other months for vacation. They may also be eligible for a retirement investment program and other benefits.

Employment Prospects

As tourism continues to increase in importance in the U.S. economy and the providers of travel and tourism services continue to demand more education and professionalism from their employees, the need for travel and tourism curric-

ula will continue to grow. Therefore, employment options should be good to excellent, with a choice of geographical location, private or public school, institution size, and liberal arts or specialized field of study.

Advancement Prospects

Other than new schools or new courses being offered in the travel and tourism field, which will create openings as instructors are promoted or choose to transfer to other schools, advancement in the education field tends to be limited due to low turnover. Professors may be promoted to such administrative functions as dean or chair of their department.

Education and Training

Almost all postsecondary educational facilities require at least a Master's (and some a doctorate) in a tourism, travel, or hospitality field (or education with a minor in one of those fields). Some schools will invite experts from the field to be visiting professors and not require the advanced degrees. A foreign language is helpful.

Experience, Skills, and Personality Traits

Work experience in a travel, tourism, or hospitality situation is preferred. The ability to work with students is essential, as are good oral and written communication skills. Computer skills are also necessary.

Unions and Associations

The International Society of Travel and Tourism Educators (ISTTE) provides seminars, guidance, and training programs for people in this profession.

Tips for Entry

1. Work in a travel-related industry to develop real-life skills and knowledge that can be taught in a classroom setting.
2. Meet with professors and instructors in the travel, tourism, and hospitality fields to establish a network of people who know about internships and job openings.
3. Read trade publications, either by subscription or on-line, to keep up with industry trends and statistics.

INTERPRETER/TRANSLATOR

CAREER PROFILE

Duties: Interprets and translates spoken or written words from one language to another

Alternate Title(s): None

Salary Range: $11 to $66 per hour; $21,000 to $100,000 per year

Employment Prospects: Good

Advancement Prospects: Good

Best Geographical Location(s): Washington, D.C.; New York City; urban areas of California; and other popular tourist destinations

Prerequisites:

Education and Training—Fluency in foreign language(s); training through course(s) in interpreting or translation

Experience—Work as an assistant interpreter or translator

Special Skills and Personality Traits—Exacting; analytical; objective; patient; interpreters should possess good social and interpersonal skills, be excellent listeners, and be able to think on their feet

Licensure/Certification—Accreditation as an Interpreter or Translator is suggested, but not required

CAREER LADDER

```
┌─────────────────────────────────┐
│   Chief Interpreter/Translator  │
└─────────────────────────────────┘

┌─────────────────────────────────┐
│         Staff Director          │
└─────────────────────────────────┘

┌─────────────────────────────────┐
│      Interpreter/Translator     │
└─────────────────────────────────┘
```

Position Description

The terms Interpreter and Translator are often used interchangeably, but generally, an Interpreter works with the spoken language and a Translator works with written language. Interpreters are most often needed to translate "PFIGS" languages: Portuguese, French, Italian, German, and Spanish. The next highest languages in demand are Chinese, Korean, and Japanese.

In translating conversations, the Interpreter must listen to the speaker to determine what is being said, remember what has been said, and convert the meaning from one language to another. The Interpreter must then translate the subsequent response from the second party's language to the first.

At times the translation will take place simultaneously (while the speaker talks—usually among large groups) or consecutively (when the speaker pauses after a sentence or two—usually among two or three people). Simultaneous interpretation can be difficult because it means listening and speaking at the same time. Consecutive interpretation also can be difficult because it means remembering what was said, and although it is generally just one or two sentences at a time, it can be more than that. Consecutive Interpreters may develop a private shorthand to take notes to help remember what is being said. In interpreting serious negotiations or international conferences that require intense concentration, Interpreters may work in pairs, with each working for 20 or 30 minutes at a time. At international conferences, Interpreters may sit in soundproof booths using a headphone to hear what is being said and a microphone to relate the interpretation.

Growing up in a bilingual or multilingual family helps because one acquires a familiarity with the vernacular and common phrases that one might not learn in formal education. Other Interpreters may interpret the spoken word into sign language for the hearing impaired. In working as a conversation

Interpreter, it helps to review the topic or itinerary to be translated prior to the session to become familiar with the names of the participants and any idiomatic language.

Although many jobs are indoors, working with tour groups may mean traveling around the country or city. Other jobs may be done over the telephone, but usually it is important to see the communicators for body language and other clues to the correct interpretation of the conversation. Many Interpreters work on a part-time or freelance basis and may work irregular and extended hours, including evenings and weekends.

Another source of jobs for Interpreters is as an English teacher in a foreign country or camp programs. Generally such teachers have an assistant proficient in the resident language, but it helps to have some competency in that language to support and reinforce the learning experience. They should have a TEFL (Teaching English as a Foreign Language) Certificate.

When translating documents, a Translator must read the material in its' original language and then rewrite it in one or more languages, using proper grammatical form for each language. Translators work for publishers, bilingual newspapers, law firms, and international companies and associations. They may work in offices or, as freelancers, work from home.

Salaries

Many Interpreters and Translators work on an hourly basis, with pay ranging from $11.00 to $66.00 an hour, depending on the location and complexity of the interpreting. A tour interpreter probably will not earn as much as someone working for a major international conference. Annual pay can range up to $100,000. Full-time Interpreters and Translators may receive sick and vacation leave and other benefits. Part-time Interpreters and Translators rarely do.

Teachers of English in a foreign country may receive as little as $1,000 a month in compensation, but they receive transportation to and from the country (as long as they complete their contract), lodging with a local family or in a dorm (or a housing subsidy), most meals, and paid training.

Employment Prospects

As more foreign-speaking people move into the country and more foreigners tour the United States, the prospects for employment will increase. Furthermore, as more foreigners move into the heartland rather than the coastal cities, the projections for employment in these areas should also increase. Other Interpreter jobs will arise in governmental and court settings to comply with the provisions of the Americans With Disabilities and the Rehabilitation Act which guarantee an Interpreter will be available to the hearing-impaired in certain situations.

Advancement Prospects

Many Interpreters and Translators work for the federal government or the United Nations and are promoted regularly, depending on their skills and the number of years on the job.

Education and Training

Very few jobs in this field require a college degree, but Georgetown University's certificate in translating and interpreting from the School of Languages and Linguistics, or a degree in American Sign Language Interpretation from an accredited college makes it easier to get a better-paying job. The knowledge of one or more foreign languages, including meaning and spelling, as well as an excellent command of English, are required. Interpreters and Translators should know about the culture and customs of the country of the language being interpreted. Courses in literature and cultural studies are helpful. Those interpreting for the hearing-impaired must know American Sign Language. Interpreters who specialize in certain areas, whether it is taking tour groups through art galleries and museums, to sporting events, or other place subjects, should have a thorough knowledge of that subject. Extensive foreign travel helps an Interpreter or Translator understand the language and its nuances and the culture of the country.

Special Requirements

There is no licensure or certification required to be a Translator or Interpreter, but the American Translators Association offers accreditation in 30 language pairs. The Translators and Interpreters Guild also offers accreditation programs.

Experience, Skills, and Personality Traits

An Interpreter must speak clearly, listen carefully, and possess gracious social and interpersonal skills. Interpreters should be able to concentrate and focus on what is being said to ensure they are accurately interpreting meaning, not just the literal conversation. They should have good public speaking skills. Translators and Interpreters should possess patience and self-discipline.

Unions and Associations

The American Translators Association offers services and accreditation programs of interest to Interpreters and Translators. The Translators and Interpreters Guild, part of the Newspaper Guild–Communications Workers of America union, runs a referral service and a certification program. They have Translators and Interpreters working in more than 30 languages, from Afrikaans to Ukrainian.

Tips for Entry

1. Learn a foreign language, from proper grammar to geographically specific idiomatic phrases.
2. Talk with Interpreters and Translators, asking their advice about career choices, internships, and apprenticeship programs.
3. Establish a network of people in the industry by attending local functions.
4. Subscribe to trade publications or read about current trends and developments on-line.

ENTERTAINER

CAREER PROFILE

Duties: Performs in resorts, casinos, theme parks, and road companies

Alternate Title(s): A title that reflects a specific talent area, such as Comedian, Dancer, Magician, Musician, Singer

Salary Range: $350 to $500 a week

Employment Prospects: Good

Advancement Prospects: Good

Best Geographical Location(s): Las Vegas, Reno, and other gaming locations; resorts; theme parks

Prerequisites:

Education and Training—Performing arts

Experience—Performances in school, community theater, or professional theater

Special Skills and Personality Traits—Talent; good interpersonal skills; charismatic; able to perform in front of large groups; foreign language knowledge helpful

CAREER LADDER

```
┌─────────────────────────────┐
│   Entertainment Director    │
└─────────────────────────────┘

┌─────────────────────────────┐
│       Show Producer         │
└─────────────────────────────┘

┌─────────────────────────────┐
│        Entertainer          │
└─────────────────────────────┘
```

Position Description

Entertainers are employed at resorts, casinos, theme parks, and in road shows in a variety of venues including showrooms, bars or lounges, nightclubs, and theaters. They may be actors, dancers, singers, magicians, jugglers, musicians (Rock 'n' Roll, Motown, popular, country, blues, classical, show, or other type), puppeteers, comedians, ice or roller skaters, or some other type of performer. Singers and dancers usually start in a revue then progress to a solo act or as part of a small group and progress to headliner status.

As part of the ensemble company, a show director usually coordinates all the acts, scheduling who will appear in what order and for how long. The director coordinates with musicians, lighting, technicians, special effects technicians, and costume designers to create an entire theme throughout the evening's entertainment. In the case of singers and dancers, the show producer, director, or choreographer creates the production numbers, teaches them to the performers, and guides them through rehearsals until the show is ready to present to an audience.

At resorts and casinos, performances usually are scheduled in the evening, with some specialty Entertainers (balloon artists, magicians, jugglers) performing and interacting with spectators during the day. Theme parks offer entertainment all day.

Performers in road companies (often referred to as a bus and truck company) tour the country, performing in each city from as little as one day or as long as a week or more. They are on the road (usually in a motorcoach) for months at a time, traveling one day and performing the next. The hours are long and the work can be grueling, but it is a terrific way to see the country and get experience as a performer.

There may be a rehearsal a day and a performance in the evening. This allows some time for sightseeing or pursuing other leisure activities. Theme parks may have as many as three, four, or more shows a day for contract performers. Other entertainment jobs for those who juggle, water ski, mime, or do acrobatics can be found in vacation and resort areas throughout the country.

Although many shows are in climate-controlled theaters, others, particularly at theme parks, may be outdoors. They are rarely performed during inclement weather, but the shows may be performed in hot, humid conditions.

As with any physical activity, there is a small possibility of injury. The entertainment venue may have insurance, but Entertainers should also carry insurance if possible. Musicians should have insurance on their instruments. Many showrooms, bars and lounges (particularly in Nevada), and other entertainment venues still allow guests to smoke, so the Entertainer has to be willing to be exposed to second-hand smoke.

Salaries

Salaries vary and depend on the Entertainer's experience and reputation, the venue, the length of the contract, and other factors. A bandleader may earn from $500 to $750 a week at a resort, while a sideman may earn from $350 to $500 a week. Salaries for dancers and other performers may range from $350 to $400 a week. Headliners can earn from $800 to $2,000 a week or more. Some companies provide relocation expenses. Many venues provide meals and accommodations, but others require Entertainers to provide their own room and board.

Most Entertainers are considered independent contractors and may not be eligible for any benefits. Additionally, only a relatively small percentage work full-time jobs all year, which explains why most theme park Entertainers are students. Many theme parks offer such benefits as free passes to the park, housing, scholarships, and discounts on park merchandise. Some theme parks pay for relocation expenses.

Employment Prospects

With the increase in the number of casinos, resorts, and theme parks, employment prospects for Entertainers are good. Many jobs can be found in Las Vegas, Reno, Laughlin, Atlantic City, Detroit, California, Florida, Missouri, and other areas with casinos, resorts, and theme parks. Jobs may be obtained through union halls, companies that hire entertainers for resorts, or on union, guild, or similar websites.

Advancement Prospects

Entertainers can advance by being moved from the chorus to featured performer status and from smaller venues to larger ones. From there, they can advance to film and television, become a show producer, or advance to some other management position within an entertainment venue.

Education and Training

A formal education is not required to be an Entertainer. However, specialized training in the specific talent area is important. This may include classes in theater, dance, music, or the performer's specialty. In areas where foreign languages are spoken, a foreign language is helpful.

Experience, Skills, and Personality Traits

Previous experience in a performing venue with a wide variety of experiences is helpful. Musicians should be able to sight-read. Performers should have excellent interpersonal skills and be able to connect with the audience easily. Performers should be physically fit, although there are some jobs for performers with physical and mental disabilities.

Unions and Associations

Associations and unions for Entertainers include the American Federation of Musicians (AFM), the American Federation of TV and Radio Artists (AFTRA), and the Screen Actors Guild (SAG). Each provides information about the industry, offers advice and seminars, and works to protect their members regarding pay and benefits. Not all venues sign union contracts.

Tips for Entry

1. Learn the entertainment business from the ground up, perhaps starting at a community theater, college, or other venues.
2. Have a videotape created of performances to present to casting directors or show producers, as a personal audition is not always possible.
3. Talk with Entertainers, asking their advice about career choices and possible openings.
4. Subscribe to trade publications or read about industry news on-line.

WEB DESIGNER

CAREER PROFILE

Duties: Creates, designs, and may also maintain Internet websites

Alternate Title(s): Webmaster, Web Developer

Salary Range: $20,000 to $100,000

Employment Prospects: Good to excellent

Advancement Prospects: Good

Best Geographical Location(s): Anywhere; often a job done off-site

Prerequisites:

Education and Training—Some companies may require a college degree, but a superb education in Web design, by class or experience, is generally sufficient

Experience—Designing and creating websites for other companies, preferably in a travel-related industry; courses in commercial art, advertising, or marketing

Special Skills and Personality Traits—Technical and artistic skills; able to function with little supervision; good oral and written communication skills

CAREER LADDER

```
┌─────────────────────────────┐
│         Webmaster           │
└─────────────────────────────┘

┌─────────────────────────────┐
│  Web Designer or Developer   │
└─────────────────────────────┘

┌─────────────────────────────┐
│    Web Content Provider     │
└─────────────────────────────┘
```

Position Description

A Web Designer creates and frequently maintains a website for Internet and Intranet retrieval and use. It requires a thorough knowledge of such web design programs as Dreamweaver, PhotoShop, Flash, HTML, java, javascript, applescript, C/C++, and digitizing video techniques.

Meeting with representatives from a hotel, resort, chain, airline, train, auto rental, or other company, the Web Designer determines what the website should contain. This might include reservation bookings, fare structure, flight schedules, descriptions and photos of hotels or resorts, nearby attractions and current events, news releases, company profiles, job openings and descriptions, sweepstakes or contests, and logo items (baseball caps, robes, key chains, china, bedding, etc.) customers can purchase from the company. The information has to be up-to-date, and most of it must be contained on secure pages so customers will feel comfortable giving their credit card information for a confirmed reservation or purchase.

Another area of the website may be for employees or members only, and this area of the website must also be protected from hackers so the content is not compromised or altered. Copyrighted material must be protected so online users cannot plagiarize the material. When such items as photographs and print articles are incorporated into the website, the Web Designer or Webmaster may be responsible for obtaining the copyright permission to use the image or text. An area for contacting company personnel usually is included, with e-mail addresses, regular addresses, and telephone numbers included so people can submit complaints, compliments, questions, or suggestions to the appropriate personnel.

The website must be easily navigable and quick to upload and download. If the company desires, it may provide a regular newsletter, bulletin, or announcement of specials that is mailed to subscribers, and the Web Designer or Webmaster may be charged with maintaining the subscriber list. Generally, an editor will be responsible for the content of these mailings, although the Web Designer may create the format.

In a large company, the Web Designer or Webmaster may supervise others, and may be called upon to interview, train, schedule hours, assign duties to employees, and review work for quality control and consistency. The Web Designer or Webmaster may be charged with developing and maintaining a budget. Additionally, the Web Designer may instruct other employees in creating Web content so authorized personnel can change the content from their area of the company without going through the Webmaster.

Generally, the job of a Web Designer or Webmaster does not include travel other than to industry conferences and seminars. However, there may be some meetings within the company that will require some travel. Because a Web Designer can work off-site via telecommuting or from the company's headquarters, there are rarely any company-paid relocation expenses when moving from one job to another. Many of these jobs are freelance or contract, while others are full-time positions.

Salaries

The salaries for Web Designers and Webmasters run a wide gamut as companies are still trying to determine the value and use of websites. Some Designers are considerably overpaid because companies have not been able to figure out how much their talents are worth. Other Designers, particularly those working on a freelance basis, also do not know how much they are worth and undercharge for their services.

A good Web Designer may earn $100,000 a year or more if he or she is designing and managing large, active websites, while someone starting in the business may earn less than $20,000 depending on education, experience, and clients. Urban area businesses tend to pay more, particularly on the East and West Coasts, to compensate for higher living expenses.

Full-time Web Designers and Webmasters may receive vacation and sick leave and life and medical insurance. Freelance positions do not include benefits.

Employment Prospects

Web Designer and Webmaster jobs should be plentiful in the years to come as companies refine their Website products and pursue quality of content over quality.

Advancement Prospects

With the growth of the Internet, the advancement possibilities are almost unlimited. Independent designers can see their companies grow, adding additional employees. Company Web Designers may be promoted to Webmaster or go on to larger companies that require larger and more significant websites or may start their own Web design businesses.

Education and Training

A college degree in marketing, business, or design and graphic arts is helpful, but the core need is for courses in Web design and the various languages used in producing attractive and effective websites.

Experience, Skills, and Personality Traits

Experience in Web design is essential. Because many designers telecommute, the designer must be able to work alone and with very little supervision. Despite the solitude, designers must have excellent oral and written communication skills. They should have extensive knowledge of computers and an eye for detail and design.

Unions and Associations

There are no unions for Web Designers. The Web Design and Developers Association and the National Web Design Association provide some information for people in this profession.

Tips for Entry

1. Learn as many software programming operations as possible.
2. Meet as many Web Designers and developers and Webmasters as possible to learn about internships and jobs available.
3. Read software programming publications, either by subscription or on-line.

INTERIOR DESIGNER

CAREER PROFILE

Duties: Creates and helps implement the interior design and decor of a hotel, resort, cruise ship, casino, restaurant, bar, retail establishment, museum, or other commercial property

Alternate Title(s): Registered Interior Designer

Salary Range: $19,000 to $67,000+

Employment Prospects: Good

Advancement Prospects: Good

Best Geographical Location(s): Any area with architectural firms that deal with hotels, resorts, casinos, restaurants, museums, or other commercial designs

Prerequisites:

Education and Training—Bachelor's degree or higher, particularly in interior design; furniture, fixtures and equipment (FF&E) knowledge; operational supplies and equipment (OS&E) knowledge

Experience—Previous work in a design capacity for a company that creates hotel and lodging or other public space interiors

Special Skills and Personality Traits—Creativity; computer literacy; able to think three-dimensionally; excellent communication skills

Licensure/Certification—National Council for Interior Design Qualification (NCIDQ) certification required in 22 states, Puerto Rico, and the District of Columbia

CAREER LADDER

```
┌─────────────────────────────┐
│      Chief Designer         │
└─────────────────────────────┘

┌─────────────────────────────┐
│     Interior Designer       │
└─────────────────────────────┘

┌─────────────────────────────┐
│  Assistant Interior Designer │
└─────────────────────────────┘
```

Position Description

An Interior Designer creates the feel and look of the public spaces in a hotel, resort, spa, cruise ship, museum, and other commercial properties, or they update the interior look of a property. This may take place before or during construction or renovation to assure that measurements are to industry standard (such as hallways that are 12 or 15 feet wide), and that all Americans with Disabilities Act (ADA) compliances and other industry standards are met.

Together with the owners and managers of the property, the architects, and others who are involved in the creation or renovation of the property, the Interior Designer discusses what is wanted and the uses of the property. Among the considerations are the cost of textiles, accessories, and furniture; their wear; ease of maintenance; safety of fabrics and finishes (flammability ratings and slip resistance); ergonomics; indoor air quality; conservation; illumination; acoustics; and color. This may be for an entire hotel, from ceiling color and materials to the floor coverings and everything in between, including bed and dining room linens, or it may be for just one project, such as a redesign of the carpet.

The Designer then prepares sketches, either by hand or with a CAD (computer aided design) software program, that are shown to the client for approval. Three-dimensional models may be made, either to scale or full-sized to show how a guest room will look and feel when completed. This will assure that table lamps fit on the tables, that desks and chairs are conveniently placed, and that bathroom lighting is appropriate; or that all seats in a lecture or meeting space have a clear view of the stage or individual access to electric and telephone hookups for laptop computers.

Some Interior Designers may specialize in one area, such as floral design, lighting, or acoustics. Others may concentrate on kitchen and restaurant design to ensure ease of use in the kitchen and serving in the restaurant. All Designers must be aware of load-bearing walls and federal, state, and local laws and building codes.

Designers supervise assistants who may carry out one or more elements of the design. The Designers may also solicit new business, create and approve contracts, and review catalogs and supply samples.

Interior Designers may work a standard 40-hour week, but they may also have to work evenings, weekends, and holidays to meet deadlines, or to make last-minute changes, and to attend meetings with clients. They may also have to travel to attend design shows and visit design centers and manufacturing facilities. Interior Designers who work for a hotel chain may have to visit the properties to make allowances for difference in structural design and location (some furnishings, for example, may be suited for tropical climates but not for cold-weather areas, and vice versa). Floral and other specialty Designers are more likely to work standard hours unless they are involved with creating unique arrangements for weddings, banquets, and other special events.

Interior Designers may work for a general design firm that includes architecture, landscaping, and lighting. Others may be self-employed. In either case, the designer must have a portfolio of earlier work assignments, perhaps showing proposal drawings and photographs of the completed work.

Salaries

Interior Designers earn from $19,000 to more than $67,000. Owners of interior design firms may earn $100,000 or more. Benefits for full-time Interior Designers usually include health and life insurance and sick and vacation leave. They may also include retirement and investment programs. Those working for hotels receive free or reduced-cost travel accommodations. Relocation expenses may be covered.

Employment Prospects

As new hotels, resorts, museums, cruise ships, casinos, and other commercial public spaces are created or renovated (hotels usually renovate every five years), Interior Designers are in constant demand.

Advancement Prospects

Interior Designers can advance to chief Interior Designer overseeing other Interior Designers, or start their own firm. Advancement prospects are good.

Education and Training

A bachelor's degree or higher, particularly in interior design, is required. Knowledge of furniture, fixtures, and equipment (FF&E) and operational supplies and equipment (OS&E) is desirable.

Experience, Skills, and Personality Traits

Past work experience in a design firm specializing in hotels, resorts, casinos, museums, and other commercial public buildings is required. The ability to visualize three-dimensionally, to convert that vision to a computer, and to communicate it to the client is essential. Good interpersonal skills are mandatory.

Special Requirements

Twenty-two states (Alabama, Arkansas, California, Colorado, Connecticut, Florida, Georgia, Illinois, Kentucky, Louisiana, Maine, Maryland, Minnesota, Missouri, Nevada, New Jersey, New Mexico, New York, Tennessee, Texas, Virginia, and Wisconsin) and Puerto Rico and the District of Columbia require licensing of Interior Designers. The National Council for Interior Design Qualification (NCIDQ) exam is the standard, with continuing education required in most jurisdictions for renewal of certification.

Unions and Associations

The American Society of Interior Designers, the Industrial Designers Society of America, and the International Interior Design Association all work toward promoting the trade, offering educational seminars and other items of interest to Designers.

Tips for Entry

1. Become familiar with interior design practices and software, by taking related courses or obtaining a B.A. in interior design.
2. Talk with Interior Designers, asking their advice about career choices, internships, and apprenticeship programs.
3. Establish a network of people in the industry by attending local Interior Designer functions.
4. Subscribe to trade publications or read about current trends and developments on-line.

LANDSCAPE ARCHITECT

CAREER PROFILE

Duties: Designs the outdoor components of a building

Alternate Title(s): None

Salary Range: $36,000 to $80,000+

Employment Prospects: Good

Advancement Prospects: Good

Best Geographical Location(s): Wherever hotels, resorts, casinos, golf courses, zoos, museums, shopping malls, and other public commercial properties exist or are being built

Prerequisites:

Education and Training—Bachelor's or master's degree in landscape architecture; knowledge of Photo-Shop, QuarkExpress, PageMaker, Land Development Desktop R-3, and AutoCad computer software programs

Experience—Internship with a landscape firm

Special Skills and Personality Traits—Effective communicator; good interpersonal skills; foreign language sometimes required; creative; graphics skills

Licensure/Certification—All states except Colorado, New Hampshire, North Dakota, and Vermont require a license to be a Landscape Architect. Some states require additional testing beyond the Registered Landscape Architect designation

CAREER LADDER

```
┌─────────────────────────────────┐
│        Project Manager          │
└─────────────────────────────────┘

┌─────────────────────────────────┐
│   Senior Landscape Architect    │
└─────────────────────────────────┘

┌─────────────────────────────────┐
│       Landscape Architect       │
└─────────────────────────────────┘

┌─────────────────────────────────┐
│  Assistant Landscape Architect  │
└─────────────────────────────────┘
```

Position Description

A Landscape Architect designs the outdoor component of a building, including landscapes (trees, bushes, flowers, grasses) and hardscapes (retaining walls, walkways, driveways, curbs, steps, ramps, fences, pergolas, fountains, etc.) for the exterior grounds, atria, patios, terraces, and pool areas to assure a positive first impression to visitors and a pleasing visual environment for employees. Meeting with the building architect, interior and lighting designers, security staff, the client, and others involved in the planning or renovation of a building, the Landscape Architect reviews the site and the proposed use.

Among the Landscape Architect's concerns are making sure that the landscape and hardscape work with the lighting to create a hazard-free site, optimizes the orientation of the building and plantings for energy and maintenance cost savings, and avoids plantings that might be adversely affected by diseases and local weather and soil conditions. He or she looks for a design that optimizes the use of a site while enhancing its aesthetics and that sustains the environment rather than imposes designs on it.

The Landscape Architect may be responsible for obtaining land analysis and permits and providing impact statements. He or she then creates a site planning and planting design, considering stormwater drainage, erosion, sedimentation control, irrigation, and grading. The plan might include pedestrian and bike paths, horse trails, sitting niches, patios, pergolas, fountains, and other features. The plan is created by using computer aided drawing (CAD) programs such as PhotoShop, QuarkExpress, PageMaker,

Land Development Desktop R-3, and AutoCad. That plan (including drawings and specifications) and a model (with estimated construction costs) are presented to the client for approval.

Once this is accomplished, the Landscape Architect meets with the landscape contractor and oversees the implementation and completion of the plan, including notification to and meeting with regulatory governmental bodies when it is time for inspections. He or she also monitors expenses to ensure the project stays on budget or consults with the client if there is a possible expense overrun. The Landscape Architect may be responsible for hiring, training, performance appraisals, promotions, and scheduling of others working on the project.

When a golf course is being planned or is going to be renovated, a Landscape Architect meets with the client and the golf course design team to ensure that the course will be attractive, challenging, and environmentally sound. A Landscape Architect creating a site plan for a zoo provides for comfortable visitor access to the various animal exhibits and helps re-create appropriate habitats for the animals.

As landscaping is outdoors, there may be some occasions when the Landscape Architect has to be outdoors in inclement weather. Extensive travel may be included in this position if a project is not in the home office area. Other travel possibilities might arise to attend industry conferences and visit manufacturers' display centers.

Salaries

A Landscape Architect can earn from $36,000 to $80,000 or more a year. Full-time employees usually receive health and life insurance and sick and annual leave plus investment and retirement plan options. When working for a hotel or lodging chain, free or reduced-cost travel accommodations should be included.

Employment Prospects

As more companies become aware of the benefits of environmentally sound landscaping and hardscaping, they will call on Landscape Architects to create and implement these factors in their construction or renovation plans. Therefore, employment prospects are good.

Advancement Prospects

A Landscape Architect can advance to overseeing a number of other Architects or start his or her own business.

Education and Training

A bachelor's and often a master's degree in Landscape Architecture are required. Other courses in botany, geology, and related sciences are helpful.

Experience, Skills, and Personality Traits

Past work experience on landscaping projects, even starting as a groundskeeper, is desirable. A Landscape Architect should have excellent computer and communication skills and love to work outdoors to create tranquil and functional settings.

Special Requirements

Only Colorado, New Hampshire, North Dakota, and Vermont do not require a license to be a Landscape Architect. All other states require Landscape Architects to be licensed. Some states require additional testing beyond the registered Landscape Architect designation. This designation ensures the Architect has had a minimum education in an appropriate field and several years of experience.

Unions and Associations

The American Society of Landscape Architects works to promote the profession with seminars, publications, and other services of interest to Landscape Architects.

Tips for Entry

1. Learn the landscape business from the ground up, perhaps starting as a groundskeeper or interning at a Landscape Architect office.
2. Talk with Landscape Architects, asking their advice about career choices, internships, and apprenticeship programs.
3. Establish a network of people in the industry by attending local functions of the American Society of Landscape Architects.
4. Subscribe to trade publications or read about current trends and developments on-line.

ANIMAL KEEPER

<table>
<tr><td></td><td></td></tr>
</table>

CAREER PROFILE

Duties: Cares for animals in zoological parks, aquaria, circuses, and other locations

Alternate Title(s): Animal Attendant; Zookeeper; Animal Curator

Salary Range: $10,000 to $66,000

Employment Prospects: Good

Advancement Prospects: Fair

Best Geographical Location(s): Any area with a zoo; aquarium; animal park; circus; stable; or resort with animals

Prerequisites:

Education and Training—Bachelor's degree in zoology; biology; wildlife biology; wildlife management; animal behavior; marine biology; animal husbandry; or exotic animal management

Experience—Work or volunteer experience in a zoo or at a veterinary clinic

Special Skills and Personality Traits—Able to lift at least 50 pounds

Licensure/Certification—Scuba certification for aquarium work

CAREER LADDER

```
┌─────────────────────────────────┐
│          Zookeeper              │
└─────────────────────────────────┘

┌─────────────────────────────────┐
│       Head Animal Keeper        │
└─────────────────────────────────┘

┌─────────────────────────────────┐
│   Assistant Head Animal Keeper  │
└─────────────────────────────────┘

┌─────────────────────────────────┐
│         Animal Keeper           │
└─────────────────────────────────┘
```

Position Description

An Animal Keeper cares for animals, and he or she must clean, groom, exercise, feed, water, monitor, and administer medical treatments to them. They may be mammals, birds, reptiles, amphibians, or invertebrates.

The Animal Keeper is generally employed by a zoo, stable, animal park, aquarium, game preserve, or resort with animals where he or she interacts with visitors, answering their questions and furthering their knowledge of the animal and its habitat.

On a daily basis, the animals must be tended to, weighed, fed, and cleaned; and their enclosures cleaned and sterilized. Direct close contact between the animals and the Animal Keeper, such as hand-feeding, is kept to a minimum to avoid potential injury and to make sure the young animals learn important social interactions and appropriate behavior from their parents. The Animal Keeper may also help veterinarians with their procedures.

Among other possible responsibilities, Animal Keepers may help design, build, and repair animal enclosures and care for the plants in and around the exhibits. They may develop and present educational programs using the animals and contribute to the educational themes of the exhibits; answer animal-related telephone calls; and provide customer service.

Animal Keepers in managerial positions interview, hire, train, and supervise department employees and volunteers. They either plan or help plan an annual and projected budget of expenses and revenues. They must comply with regulations mandated by the Animal Welfare Act and take part in U.S. Department of Agriculture inspections.

Because animals need care around the clock in most situations, Animal Keepers work around the clock, so shifts may include evening and weekend work. As many animals are kept in outdoor settings, work can be required in any weather in any season.

Animal Keepers who work with circuses travel extensively while the circus is touring the country. Those who work in zoos and aquaria may visit the savannas of Africa, the rainforests of South America, and the tropics of India, all without leaving home. They also may travel to other zoos or attractions and attend industry conferences.

Salaries

Animal Keepers may earn a starting salary of $22,000 a year, while more experienced personnel can earn $60,000 a year. They generally receive sick and vacation leave and health and life insurance. Other benefits may include investment and retirement programs. Those who work in theme and animal parks and aquaria usually receive free or reduced-cost admission to their park and others within the chain.

Employment Prospects

General employment in animal keeping is fairly good, particularly for entry-level positions. Although some new zoological and theme parks are opening, they are not numerous.

Advancement Prospects

Animal Keepers seeking advancement may move up to such positions as assistant head Animal Keeper, head Animal Keeper, or Zookeeper. However, there are few upper-level management position openings each year.

Education and Training

A bachelor's degree in zoology, biology, wildlife biology, wildlife management, animal behavior, marine biology, animal husbandry, or exotic animal management is usually required for all but entry-level, volunteer, and internship positions. An Advanced degree is helpful for those who want to become a head Animal Keeper.

Special Requirements

Animal Keepers who plan to work at aquaria or zoological parks with water-based animals should have a scuba certification.

Experience, Skills, and Personality Traits

Some volunteer or paid work experience in an animal setting is required, whether at a veterinarian clinic, zoological park, aquarium, or other place.

Animal Keepers must be excellent observers, learning the habits and behaviors of individual animals and groups. They must be able to detect subtle changes in an animal's physical or psychological condition and react accordingly.

Animal Keepers must love and understand animals. They must also have good public speaking skills for dealing with visitors. Aquarium Animal Keepers should be excellent swimmers. Stable workers should have a solid command of horsemanship.

Unions and Associations

The American Zoo and Aquarium Association (AZA) and the American Association of Zoo Keepers are organizations that promote animal care education and provide information about animal keeping.

Tips for Entry

1. Become familiar with animals by volunteering at a veterinarian clinic, zoo, game preserve, stable, or other place where animals are kept.
2. Talk with Animal Keepers, asking their advice about career choices, internships, and apprenticeship programs.
3. Establish a network of people in the industry by attending local functions of the American Zoo and Aquarium Association and the American Association of Zoo Keepers.
4. Subscribe to trade publications or read about current trends and developments on-line.

ASTRONOMER

CAREER PROFILE

Duties: Teaches students and adults about the heavens

Alternate Title(s): Planetarian

Salary Range: $25 per hour to $75,000 annually

Employment Prospects: Fair

Advancement Prospects: Fair

Best Geographical Location(s): Resorts in areas without a lot of light pollution; planetaria and science centers; universities with astronomy studies programs; remote areas with observatories

Prerequisites:

Education and Training—Bachelor's degree or higher in physics and astronomy

Experience—At least three years' experience teaching astronomy

Special Skills and Personality Traits—Knowledge of Digistar, Spice automation system, Zeiss Jena star projector, laser programming, and Bowen audio system is helpful; good public speaking skills are essential; computer literacy

CAREER LADDER

```
┌─────────────────────────────┐
│    Planetarium Manager      │
└─────────────────────────────┘

┌─────────────────────────────┐
│   Star Show Modeler/Animator │
└─────────────────────────────┘

┌─────────────────────────────┐
│       Planetologist         │
└─────────────────────────────┘

┌─────────────────────────────┐
│ Astronomy/Physics Instructor │
└─────────────────────────────┘
```

Position Description

Although many Astronomers work to solve problems in navigation, space flight, and satellite communications, some work to teach others about the wonders of the stars, planets, galaxies, Sun, and Moon. They work at schools and universities, in planetaria, and at science centers, and some work at resorts where they lead evening star walks. This profile will focus on Astronomers employed by planetaria and resorts, given their role in travel and tourism.

Astronomers who work at planetaria develop new and adapt existing sky programs to present to the public. They may supervise undergraduate participation in outreach activities to the public and grades K to 12. They may also collaborate with local school districts, and conduct research into science education. As the director of a planetarium, an Astronomer may be responsible for developing external funding for the facility in general or a specific show or exhibit in particular. When a planetarium is connected to a university, the Astronomer may also teach one or more courses each year, both at the university and the planetarium, and work as a liaison between the two institutions.

Although many planetarium presentations are made commercially, many new shows are created at the planetarium using 3-D models, animations, and Digistar systems. Other creations may include hands-on activities kits and educational games. As some of these programs may be presented at other locales, some travel may be included.

At other times, the Astronomer may be asked to write articles for the institution's publication or website or for an astronomy magazine or to appear on radio and television to talk about such astronomical events as a meteor shower or comet. He or she may also be required to recruit, train, schedule, and supervise other employees. Astronomers working in research may temporarily work away from home at national or international observatories. Planetarium astronomers generally work daytime hours, but there are also a number of evening and weekend presentations.

Resort Astronomers show the evening skies to resort guests using a telescopes to point out significant events each evening. They usually have day job working at a nearby observatory or university teaching astronomy and lead star walks in the evenings.

Salaries

The area of employment determines the salary range for Astronomers. High school science teachers earn less than college instructors, and planetarium Astronomers earn less than government employees. Astronomers who lead star walks at resorts may earn $25 per hour or more (or as part of an agreement for a grant from the resort to the observatory or college or university), while Astronomers with multiple postgraduate degrees may earn annual salaries of $75,000 or more. Full-time Astronomers should receive health and life insurance and sick and annual leave. Retirement and investment programs usually are available. Relocation assistance may be included.

Employment Prospects

Competition for employment is stiff, with more graduates with astronomy degrees than positions available. However, because astronomy is a multidisciplinary field, it lends itself to work in optics, chemistry, atomic physics, computer science, mechanical and electrical engineering, biology, and fluid dynamics—all interesting areas to explore until the right astronomy position comes along. Typical astronomy positions can be found in secondary schools, colleges and universities, observatories, laboratories, federal agencies, and science centers. Resort astronomy positions can be found at upscale resorts in Hawaii, Alaska, Arizona, New Mexico, Australia, and other places near observatories.

Advancement Prospects

Astronomers may advance from planetaria program coordinators to managers or go into government and university research and teaching. With astronomy jobs fairly limited, advancement prospects are only fair.

Education and Training

A bachelor's degree in physics and astronomy is the minimum requirement for planetaria jobs, with higher degrees required to work for colleges, universities, and the government. Often, other science degrees and a passion for astronomy as a hobby are sufficient for some positions.

Experience, Skills, and Personality Traits

Astronomers should be excellent observers and possess problem-solving, analytical, and communication skills. For those who produce star shows, creativity is a plus, as is a mechanical aptitude to repair theater equipment. Astronomers should understand the workings of various telescopes and other astronomical equipment to be able to make minor repairs and adjustments as needed.

Unions and Associations

The American Association of Variable Star Observers, the Astronomical League, the Astronomical Society of the Pacific, and the Royal Astronomical Society of Canada are four major organizations that pursue the interests of astronomy.

Tips for Entry

1. Become familiar with general sciences, including astronomy and physics.
2. Talk with Astronomers, asking their advice about career choices, internships, and apprenticeship programs.
3. Establish a network of people in the industry by attending local astronomy organization functions.
4. Subscribe to trade publications or read about current trends and developments on-line.

APPENDIXES

APPENDIX I
ASSOCIATE'S DEGREE PROGRAMS IN TRAVEL, TOURISM, AND HOSPITALITY

ALABAMA

Faulkner State Community College
Hotel and Restaurant Management
1900 U.S. Highway 31 South
Bay Minette, AL 36507
Phone: (257) 580-2100 or (800) 231-3752
www.faulkner.cc.al.us

Southern Institute
Travel and Tourism Department
2015 Highland Avenue, South
Birmingham, AL 35205

ALASKA

Alaska Pacific University
Hotel, Food Service and Tourism
4101 University Drive
Anchorage, AK 99508
Phone: (907) 564-8234
Fax: (907) 562-4276
http://www.alaskapacific.edu

ARIZONA

Central Arizona College
Hotel and Restaurant Management
8470 North Overfield Road
Coolidge, AZ 85228
Phone: (520) 426-4403
http://www.cac.cc.az.us

Pima Community College
Hospitality and Tourism
1255 North Stone Avenue
Tucson, AZ 85709-3030
Phone: (520) 206-6278
Fax: (520) 206-6162
http://www.dtc.pima.edu

ARKANSAS

Garland County Community College
Hospitality and Tourism
101 College Drive
Hot Springs, AR 71913
Phone: (501) 760-4155 or (501) 760-4100
http://www.gccc.cc.ar.us

CALIFORNIA

Butte Community College
Tourism and Travel Department
3536 Butte Campus Drive
Oroville, CA 95965-8303
Phone: (530) 895-2396
Fax: (530) 895-2411
http://www.butte.cc.ca.us

City College of San Francisco
Hotel and Restaurant Department
50 Phelam Avenue
San Francisco, CA 94112
Phone: (415) 239-3152
http://www.ccsf.edu

Coastline Community College
Travel and Tourism Department Costa
    Mesa Center
2990 Mesa Verde Drive, East
Costa Mesa, CA 92626
Phone: (714) 241-6213
Fax: (714) 751-3806
http://www.coastline.cced.edu

**The Collins School of Hospitality
    Management**
California State Polytechnic University
3801 West Temple Avenue
Pomona, CA 91768
Phone: (909) 869-2275
http://www.csupomona.edu/~cshm

Condie Junior College
Travel and Airline
One West Campbell Avenue
Campbell, CA 95008
Phone: (408) 866-6666

Empire Business College
Hospitality and Tourism
3035 Cleveland Avenue
Suite 102
Santa Rosa, CA 95403
Phone: (707) 546-4000
Fax: (707) 546-4058
http://www.empcol.com

Foothill College
Travel Careers Program
12345 El Monte Road
Los Altos Hills, CA 94022-4599
Phone: (650) 949-7263
Fax: (650) 949-7287
bss.foothill.fhda.edu/tc

Long Beach City College
Hospitality and Tourism
4901 East Carson Street
Long Beach, CA 90808
Phone: (562) 938-4325
Fax: (562) 938-4118
http://www.lbcc.cc.ca.us

Miracosta College
Hospitality and Tourism
One Barnard Drive
Oceanside, CA 92056-3899
Phone: (760) 757-2121, ext. 6404
Fax: (760) 795-6804
http://www.miracosta.edu/Travel

Mission College
Hospitality Management
3000 Mission College Boulevard
Santa Clara, CA 95054
Phone: (408) 855-5252 or (888) 509-
    7040
Fax: (408) 855-5452
http://www.missioncollege.org

Palomar College
Hospitality and Tourism
Vocational Programs
1140 West Mission Road
San Marcos, CA 92069
Phone: (760) 744-1150, ext. 2286
Fax: (760) 591-9108
http://www.palomar.edu

Rancho Santiago College
Travel and Tourism
8045 East Chapman Avenue
Orange, CA 92869
Phone: (714) 564-4528
http://www.rsccd.org/rsccd/scc/scc_home

San Bernadino Valley College
Hospitality and Tourism
701 South Mt. Vernon Avenue
San Bernadino, CA 92410-2798
Phone: (909) 888-6511

San Diego Mesa College
Hospitality and Tourism
School of Health Science/Public Service
7250 Mesa College Drive
San Diego, CA 92111
Phone: (619) 388-2370
http://www.sdmesa.sdccd.net

Santa Barbara City College
Hotel and Restaurant Management
721 Cliff Drive
Santa Barbara, CA 93109
Phone: (805) 965-0581
http://www.sbcc.cc.ca.us

Santa Monica College
Tourism, Hospitality, Leisure Services
    and College Recreational Activities
1900 Pico Boulevard
Santa Monica, CA 90405-1628
Phone: (310) 434-4315
Fax: (310) 434-3652
http://www.smc.edu

Travel University
Hospitality and Tourism
3870 Murphy Canyon Road
Suite 310
San Diego, CA 92123
Phone: (858) 292-9755
Fax: (858) 292-8008
http://www.traveluniversity.edu

West Los Angeles College
Department of Travel
4800 Freshman Drive
Culver City, CA 90230
Phone: (310) 287-4369
Fax: (310) 841-0396
http://www.wlac.cc.ca.us

COLORADO

Art Institute, School of Culinary Arts
Culinary Department
675 South Broadway
Denver, CO 80209
Phone: (303) 824-4954
Fax: (303) 778-8312
http://www.aic.edu

Blair Junior College
Travel and Tourism
828 Wooten Road
Colorado Springs, CO 80915
Phone: (719) 574-1082

Mesa State College/UTEC
Culinary Arts
2508 Blichmann Avenue
Grand Junction, CO 81505
Phone: (970) 255-2632
Fax: (970) 255-2650
http://www.mesastate.edu

Metropolitan State College
HMTA Department
P.O. Box 173362
Campus Box 60, PL 124
Denver, CO 80217-3362
Phone: (303) 556-3152
http://www.mscd.edu

Northeastern Junior College
Travel and Tourism Management
    Program
100 College Drive
Sterling, CO 80751
Phone: (303) 522-6600
http://www.njc.edu

Parks Junior College
Travel and Tourism
9065 Grant
Denver, CO 80229-4339
Phone: (303) 430-8511

CONNECTICUT

Briarwood College
Department of Travel and Tourism
2279 Mt. Vernon Road
Southington, CT 06790
Phone: (860) 628-4751
Fax: (860) 628-6444
http://www.briarwood.edu

Gateway Community College
Management Programs
Hospitality and Tourism
60 Sargent Drive
New Haven, CT 06511
Phone: (203) 285-2175
Fax: (203) 285-2180
http://www.gwctc.commnet.edu

**International College of Hospitality
    Management**
Hospitality Management
101 Wykeham Road

Washington, CT 06793
Phone: (860) 868-9555 or (800) 955-0809
Fax: (860) 868-2114
http://www.ichm.ritz.edu

**Naugatuck Valley Community
    Technical College**
Hospitality Management
750 Chase Parkway
Waterbury, CT 06708
Phone: (203) 578-8175
http://www.nvcc.commnet.edu

Norwalk Community College
Hospitality and Tourism
188 Richards Avenue
Norwalk, CT 06854-1655
Phone: (203) 857-7355
Fax: (203) 857-3327
http://www.nctc.commnet.edu

University of New Haven
School of Hospitality and Tourism
Room 223, Harugari Hall
300 Orange Avenue
West Haven, CT 06516
Phone: (203) 932-7413
http://www.newhaven.edu/tourism

DELAWARE

**Delaware Technical and Community
    College**
Hospitality and Tourism
P.O. Box 610
Georgetown, DE 19947
Phone: (302) 856-5400
http://www.dtcc.edu

FLORIDA

Art Institute–Ft. Lauderdale
Travel and Tourism
1799 Southeast 17th Street
Ft. Lauderdale, FL 33316-3000
Phone: (305) 463-3000
http://www.aifl.artinstitutes.edu

Broward Community College
Hospitality and Tourism
3501 Southwest Davie Road
Ft. Lauderdale, FL 33314
Phone: (954) 475-6710
Fax: (954) 475-6594
http://www.broward.cc.fl.us

Central Florida Community College
P.O. Box 1388
Ocala, FL 34478-1388

Phone: (352) 873-5848
Fax: (352) 873-5883
http://www.gocfcc.com

Daytona Beach Community College
Hospitality Management
P.O. Box 2811
1200 International Speedway Boulevard
Daytona Beach, FL 32120-2811
Phone: (386) 254-3051
http://www.dbcc.cc.fl.us

**Florida Community College at
    Jacksonville**
Hotel and Restaurant/Travel Agency
    Operations
4501 Capper Road
Jacksonville, FL 32218
Phone: (904) 766-6603
Fax: (904) 766-6654
http://www.fccj.org

Florida Culinary Institute
Admissions Department
2400 Metrocentre Boulevard
West Palm Beach, FL 33407
Phone: (800) 826-9986
Fax: (561) 842-9503
http://www.floridaculinary.com

Florida National College
Hospitality and Tourism
4162 West 12th Avenue
Hialeah, FL 33012
Phone: (305) 821-3333, ext. 1002
Fax: (305) 362-0595
http://www.fnc.edu

**International School of Tourism and
    Hospitality Management**
Schiller International University
251 Lyndhurst Street
Dunedin, FL 34698
Phone: (727) 736-5082
Fax: (727) 736-6263
http://www.schiller.edu

Keiser College
Travel and Hospitality
1500 Northwest 49th Street
Ft. Lauderdale, FL 33309
Phone: (954) 776-4456
Fax: (954) 489-2974
http://www.keisercollege.cc.fl.us

**Miami-Dade Community College
    Wolfson Campus**
Hospitality Management
300 Northeast Second Avenue

Room 3704
Miami, FL 33132-2297
Phone: (305) 237-3044
Fax: (305) 237-7074
http://www.mdcc.edu

Palm Beach Community College
Hospitality Department
4200 Congress Avenue
Lake Worth, FL 33461
Phone: (561) 868-3330
Fax: (561) 868-3379
http://www.pbcc.cc.fl.us

Seminole Community College
Hospitality and Tourism
100 Weldon Boulevard
Sanford, FL 32773
Phone: (407) 328-2050
http://www.seminole.cc.ff.us

Webber International University
International Tourism Management
P.O. Box 96
1201 North Scenic Highway
Babson Park, FL 33827
Phone: (863) 638-2942
Fax: (863) 638-2823
http://www.webber.edu

GEORGIA

North Metro Technical Institute
Hospitality and Tourism
5198 Ross Road
Acworth, GA 30102
Phone: (404) 975-4058

HAWAII

Brigham Young University–Hawaii
Hospitality and Tourism
55220 Kulanuist Street
Laie, HI 96762
Phone: (808) 293-3591
http://www.byuh.edu

Kapiolani Community College
Food Service and Hospitality Education
4303 Diamond Head Road
Honolulu, HI 96816
Phone: (808) 734-9716
Fax: (808) 734-9212
http://www.kcc.hawaii.edu

Travel University International
Hospitality and Tourism
Ala Moana Building
Suite 2000

1441 Kapiolani Boulevard
Honolulu, HI 96814
Phone: (808) 946-3535
Fax: (808) 942-1660
http://www.traveluniversity.edu

IDAHO

College of Southern Idaho
Hospitality and Tourism
Evergreen A-34
315 Falls Avenue
Twin Falls, ID 83303
Phone: (208) 735-9554, ext. 2407
Fax: (208) 736-2136
http://www.csi.edu/ip/mandm/faculty/
    bpappas

North Idaho College
Culinary Department
1000 West Garden Avenue
Hedlund Building
Coeur d'Alene, ID 83814-2199
Phone: (208) 666-8004
Fax: (208) 769-3459
http://www.NorthIdahoCollege.edu

ILLINOIS

Chicago Citywide College
Hospitality and Tourism
226 West Jackson Boulevard
4th Floor
Chicago, IL 60606-6997
Phone: (312) 855-8235

College of Dupage
Travel and Tourism
425 Fawell Boulevard
Glen Ellyn, IL 60137-6599
Phone: (630) 942-2556
Fax: (630) 858-7263
http://www.cod.edu

Elgin Community College
Hospitality and Tourism
Office ABT 109
Elgin, IL 60123
Phone: (847) 214-7912
Fax: (847) 214-1879
http://www.elgin.edu

Kendall College
Hotel/Restaurant and Culinary
    Management
2408 Orrington Avenue
Evanston, IL 60201
Phone: (847) 866-1300, ext. 1692
Fax: (847) 866-9346
http://www.kendall.edu

Lexington College
10840 South Western Avenue
Chicago, IL 60643
Phone: (773) 779-3800
Fax: (773) 779-7450
http://www.lexingtoncollege.edu

Lincoln College
School of Travel
510 Wellselley Drive
Normal, IL 61761
Phone: (309) 452-0724
http://www.lincoln.mclean.il.us

Moraine Valley Community College
Hospitality and Tourism
10900 South 88th Avenue
Palos Hills, IL 60465
Phone: (708) 974-5708
http://www.morainevalley.edu

Northwestern Business College
Travel and Hospitality Department
8020 West 87th Street
Hickory Hills, IL 60457
Phone: (708) 430-0990
Fax: (708) 430-0995
http://www.northwesternbc.edu

Northwestern Business College
Travel and Hospitality
4829 North Lipps Avenue
Chicago, IL 60630
Phone: (773) 777-4220, ext. 423
Fax: (773) 777-2861
http://www.northwesternbc.edu

Parkland College
Hospitality Industry
2400 West Bradley Avenue
Champaign, IL 61821
Phone: (800) 346-8089
Fax: (217) 373-3896
http://www.parkland.cc.il.us

Robert Morris College
Hospitality and Tourism
401 South State Street
Chicago, IL 60605
Phone: (312) 935-6835
http://www.rmcil.edu

Triton College
Hospitality Industry Administration
1405 Central Road 102A
Arlington Heights, IL 60005
Phone: (312)456-0300
http://www.triton.cc.il.us

United American College of Travel and Tourism Careers
Hospitality and Tourism
10006 Kimberly Way
Lisle, IL 60532-3174
Phone: (708) 250-8866

William Rainey Harper College
Hospitality Management
1200 West Algonquin Road
Palatine, IL 60067-7398
Phone: (847) 925-6874 or (847) 925-6057
http://www.harpercollege.com

INDIANA

Indiana University Purdue University–Ft. Wayne
Hospitality Management Program
Neff Hall, Room 330B
Ft. Wayne, IN 46805-1499
Phone: (219) 481-6562 or (219) 481-5767
http://www.ipfw.edu/cfs/dinner1.htm

Indiana University Purdue University Indianapolis
Tourism, Conventions and Event Management
901 West New York Street
Indianapolis, IN 46202
Phone: (317) 274-7649
Fax: (317) 278-2041
http://www.iupui.edu/~indyhper

Indiana Vocational Technical College
Hospitality and Tourism
Culinary Arts
5727 Sohl Avenue
Hammond, IN 46320
Phone: (219) 937-9422
http://www.ivytech.edu

Ivy Tech
Hospitality and Tourism
P.O. Box 1763
Indianapolis, IN 46206
Phone: (317) 921-4797
http://www.ivytech.edu

Purdue University
Department of Hospitality and Tourism Management
1266 Stone Hall, Room 106
West Lafayette, IN 47907-1266
Phone: (765) 494-4643
Fax: (765) 494-0327
http://www.cfs.purdue.edu/HTM

IOWA

American Institute of Business–College of Business
Hospitality and Tourism
2500 Fleur Drive
Des Moines, IA 50321
Phone: (515) 244-4221
Fax: (515) 244-6773
http://www.aib.edu

Iowa Lakes Community College
Hospitality and Tourism
3200 College Drive
Emmetsburg, IA 50536
Phone: (712) 852-3554
http://www.ilcc.cc.ia.us

Kaplan College
Hospitality and Tourism
801 East Kimberly Road
Davenport, IA 52807
Phone: (563) 355-3500
Fax: (563) 355-1320
http://www.kaplancollegeia.com

Kirkwood Community College
Culinary Arts
6301 Kirkwood Blvd, SW
P.O. Box 2068
Cedar Rapids, IA 52406
Phone: (319) 398-5411
http://www.kirkwoodcollege.com

KANSAS

Johnson County Community College
Hospitality Management
12345 College Boulevard
Overland Park, KS 66210-1299
Phone: (913) 469-8500
Fax: (913) 469-2560
http://www.jccc.edu

KENTUCKY

Sullivan College–Louisville
Hospitality and Tourism
3101 Bardstown Road
Louisville, KY 40205
Phone: (502) 456-6504
http://www.sullivan.edu

LOUISIANA

Culinary Arts Institute of Louisiana
Hospitality and Tourism
2857 Perkins Road
Baton Rouge, LA 70808
Phone: (225) 343-6233 or (800) 927-0829

Fax: (225) 336-4880
http://www.caila.com

Delgado Community College
Culinary Arts/Occupational Studies
Building 11
615 City Park Avenue
New Orleans, LA 70119-4399
Phone: (504) 483-4208
http://www.dcc.edu

MAINE

Andover College
Travel and Tourism
901 Washington Avenue
Portland, ME 04103
Phone: (207) 774-6126
Fax: (207) 774-1715
http://www.andovercollege.com

Beal College
Hospitality and Tourism
629 Main Street
Bangor, ME 04401
Phone: (207) 947-4591
http://www.bealcollege.com

Southern Maine Vocational Technical Institute
Hospitality and Tourism
Ford Road
South Portland, ME 04106
Phone: (207) 799-7303

MARYLAND

Anne Arundel Community College
Food Service and Lodging
101 College Parkway
Arnold, MD 21012
Phone: (410) 777-2390
http://www.aacc.cc.md.us

Baltimore International College
Hospitality and Tourism
25 South Calvert Street
Baltimore, MD 21202-4066
Phone: (800) 752-4710
http://www.bic.edu

Chesapeake College
Box 8
Wye Mills, MD 21679
Phone: (410) 822-5400, ext. 234
Fax: (410) 827-9222
http://www.chesapeake.edu

Montgomery College
Hospitality and Tourism

51 Mannakee Street
Rockville, MD 20850
Phone: (301) 251-7191
http://www.montgomerycollege.edu

Villa Julie College
Travel and Tourism Department
Greenspring Valley Road
Stevenson, MD 21153
Phone: (301) 486-7000
http://www.vjc.edu

MASSACHUSETTS

Bay State College
Travel and Tourism Department
122 Commonwealth Avenue
Boston, MA 02116
Phone: (617) 450-8325
Fax: (617) 236-8023
http://www.baystate.edu

Becker College
Travel and Tourism Department
Three Paxton Street
Leicester, MA 01524
Phone: (508) 791-9241
http://www.beckercollege.edu

Cape Cod Community College
Hospitality and Tourism
2240 Iyanough Road
West Barnstable, MA 02668
Phone: (508) 362-2131
http://www.capecod.mass.edu

Lasell College
Hotel and Travel/Tourism Administration
1844 Commonwealth Avenue
Newton, MA 02166
Phone: (617) 964-4280
http://www.lasell.edu

Marian Court Junior College
Travel and Tourism
35 Little's Point Road
Swampscott, MA 01907-2840
Phone: (617) 595-6768
http://www.mariancourt.edu

Massachusetts Bay Community College
Business and Management
   Department/Tourism
50 Oakland Street
Wellesley, MA 02481
Phone: (781) 239-2207
Fax: (781) 416-1607
http://www.mbcc.mass.edu

Massasoit Community College
Travel and Tourism Department
One Massasoit Boulevard
Brockton, MA 02302
Phone: (508) 588-9100
Fax: (508) 497-1250
http://www.massasoit.mass.edu

Newbury College
Department of Hospitality Management
129 Fisher Avenue
Brookline, MA 02146
Phone: (617) 730-7182
http://www.newbury.edu

Quinsigamond Community College
Travel Agent Training
670 West Boylston Street
Worcester, MA 01606-2031
Phone: (508) 853-2300
http://www.qcc.mass.edu

MICHIGAN

Ferris State University
Hospitality and Tourism
1319 Cramer Circle
Big Rapids, MI 49307-2736
Phone: (231) 591-2382
Fax: (231) 591-2998
http://www.ferris.edu

Grand Rapids Community College
Hospitality Education Division
151 Fountain, NE
Grand Rapids, MI 49503
Phone: (616) 234-GRCC
http://www.grcc.cc.mi.us

Henry Ford Community College
Hospitality Studies
Dearborn, MI 48128
Phone: (313) 845-9651
Fax: (313) 845-9784
http://www.hfcc.net

Jackson Community College
Hospitality Management
2111 Emmons Road
Jackson, MI 49201
Phone: (517) 787-0800
http://www.jackson.cc.mi.us

Lansing Community College
Hospitality and Travel/Tourism
P.O. Box 40010
Lansing, MI 48901-7210
Phone: (517) 483-1542
Fax: (517) 483-1535
http://www.lansing.cc.mi.us

Mott Community College
Culinary Arts/Hospitality Management
1401 East Court Street
Flint, MI 48503
Phone: (313) 762-0448
http://www.mcc.edu

Northern Michigan University
Food Service Management
1401 Presque Isle Avenue
Marquette, MI 49855
Phone: (906) 227-1544 or (800) 682-9797
http://www.nmu.edu

Northwestern Michigan College
Food Services/Hospitality Management
1701 East Front Street
Traverse City, MI 49684
Phone: (616) 922-1197
http://www.nmc.edu

Oakland Community College
Hospitality and Tourism
27055 Orchard Lake Road
Farmington Hills, MI 48018
Phone: (248) 522-3700
Fax: (248) 522-3706
http://www.occ.cc.mi.us

Siena Heights College
Hotel, Restaurant and Industrial
    Management
1247 East Siena Heights Drive
Adrian, MI 49221
Phone: (517) 263-0073
http://www.sienahts.edu

Suomi College
Travel Services
Quincy Avenue
Hancock, MI 49930-1882
Phone: (906) 482-5300
http://www.suomi.edu

MINNESOTA

Alexandria Technical College
Hospitality and Tourism
1601 Jefferson Street
Alexandria, MN 56308
Phone: (320) 762-0221 or (888) 234-1222
http://www.act.tec.mn.us

Central Lakes College
Travel Planning Program
501 West College Drive
Brainerd, MN 56401-4096
Phone: (800) 933-0346
http://www.clc.mnscu.edu

Dakota City Technical College
Travel and Tourism Program
1300 East 145th Street
Rosemount, MN 55068-2932
Phone: (651) 423-8397
Fax: (651) 423-8558
http://www.dctc.mnscu.edu

Minneapolis Business College
Hospitality and Tourism
1711 West County Road B
Roseville, MN 55113
Phone: (800) 279-5200 or (651) 636-7406
http://www.mplsbusinesscollege.com

National College
Hospitality and Tourism
1380 Energy Lane, Suite 13
St. Paul, MN 55108
Phone: (612) 644-1265

Normandale Community College
Hospitality Department
9700 France Avenue South
Bloomington, MN 55431
Phone: (952) 787-8209 or (952) 487-
    8230 or (866) 880-8740
http://www.normandale.edu

Riverland Community College
Travel Planner Program
2200 Tech Drive
Albert Lea, MN 56007-3499
Phone: (800) 333-2584
http://www.riverland.cc.mn.us

MISSOURI

Maple Woods Community College
Hospitality and Tourism
2601 Northeast Barry Road
Kansas City, MO 64156
Phone: (816) 437-3252
http://www.kcmetro.cc.mo.us

Penn Valley Community College
Lodging and Food Service Management
3201 Southwest Trafficway
Kansas City, MO 64111
Phone: (816) 759-4089
http://kcmetro.edu/pennvalley

**St. Louis Community College at Forest
Park**
Hospitality Studies/Tourism Department
5600 Oakland Avenue
St. Louis, MO 63110-1393
Phone: (314) 644-9274
http://www.stlcc.cc.mo.us/fp

MONTANA

Flathead Valley Community College
Hospitality Management
777 Grandview
Kalispell, MT 59901
Phone: (406) 756-3862
Fax: (406) 756-3351
http://www.fvcc.cc.mt.us

University of Montana–Western
Tourism and Recreation
Business and Technology
710 South Atlantic Street
Box 120
Dillon, MT 59725-3598
Phone: (406) 683-7111
Fax: (406) 683-7816
http://www.umwestern.edu

NEBRASKA

Central Community College
Hospitality and Tourism
P.O. Box 1024
Hastings, NE 68902
Phone: (402) 461-2458
Fax: (402) 461-2506
http://www.cccneb.edu

Lincoln School of Commerce
Tour and Travel Department
1831 K Street
Lincoln, NE 68508
Phone: (402) 474-5315
Fax: (402) 474-5302
http://www.lincolnschoolofcommerce.com

Metropolitan Community College
Hospitality and Tourism
P.O. Box 3777
Omaha, NE 68103
Phone: (402) 457-2400 or (800) 228-
    9553
http://www.mccneb.edu

Southeast Community College
Food Service
8800 O Street
Lincoln, NE 68520
Phone: (402) 471-3333
http://www.southeast.edu

NEVADA

**Community College of Southern
    Nevada**
Department of Resorts and Gaming, Z-1A
3200 East Cheyenne Avenue
North Las Vegas, NV 89030

Phone: (702) 651-4827
Fax: (702) 651-4558
http://www.ccsn.nevada.edu

NEW HAMPSHIRE

Hesser College
Travel Department
3 Sundial Avenue
Manchester, NH 03103
Phone: (800) 526-9231
Fax: (603) 666-4722
http://www.hesser.edu

New Hampshire Community Technical College
Hospitality and Tourism
2020 Riverside Drive
Berlin, NH 03570
Phone: (603) 752-1113
http://www.berlin.tec.nh.us

New Hampshire Technical Institute
Hospitality and Tourism
31 College Drive
Concord, NH 03301
Phone: (603) 271-6963
Fax: (603) 271-8883
http://nhti.net

NEW JERSEY

Atlantic Cape Community College
Academy of Culinary Arts
5100 Black Horse Pike
Mays Landing, NJ 08330-9888
Phone: (609) 343-4938
Fax: (609) 343-5122
http://www.atlantic.edu

Bergen Community College
Travel and Tourism
400 Paramus Road
Paramus, NJ 07652-1595
Phone: (201) 447-0525
Fax: (973) 423-3776
http://www.bergen.edu

Berkeley College
Hospitality and Tourism
44 Rifle Camp Road
West Paterson, NJ 07424
http://www.berkeleycollege.edu

Hudson Valley Community College
The Culinary Arts Institute
161 Newkirk Street
Jersey City, NJ 07306
Phone: (201) 714-2193

Fax: (201) 656-1522
http://www.hudson.cc.nj.us

Middlesex County College
Hospitality and Tourism
P.O. Box 3050
Edison, NJ 08818-3050
http://www.middlesex.cc.nj.us

County College of Morris
Hospitality and Tourism
214 Center Grove Road
Randolph, NJ 07869-2086
Phone: (888) 226-8001 or (973) 328-5000
http://www.ccm.edu

NEW MEXICO

Dona Ana Branch Community College
Business and Information Systems—
    Hospitality Services
3400 South Espina
MSC 3DA
P.O. Box 30001
Las Cruces, NM 88003
Phone: (505) 527-7518
Fax: (505) 527-7515
http://dabcc-www.nmsu.edu

New Mexico State University
Hotel, Restaurant and Tourism
    Management
Box 30003, MSC 3HRTM
Las Cruces, NM 88003-0003
Phone: (505) 646-8099
Fax: (505) 646-8100
http://www.nmsu.edu/~hrtm

NEW YORK

Adirondack Community College
Hospitality and Tourism
Bay Road
Queensbury, NY 12804
Phone: (518) 743-2267
Fax: (518) 745-1433
http://www.sunyacc.edu

American Institute of Tourism
1001 Avenue of the Americas
11th Floor
New York, NY 10018
Phone: (646) 366-8500
Fax: (646) 366-8505
http://www.nitgroup.com

Bryant and Stratton Business Institute
Hospitality and Tourism
200 Bryant and Stratton Way

Williamsville, NY 14221
Phone: (716) 631-0260
http://www.bryantstratton.edu

Culinary Institute of America
Culinary and Baking and Pastry Arts
1946 Campus Drive
Hyde Park, NY 12538
Phone: (800) CULINARY
http://www.ciachef.edu

Culinary Institute of America
Hospitality and Tourism
433 Albany Post Road
Hyde Park, NY 12538-1499
Phone: (914) 452-9600
Fax: (914) 451-1076
http://www.culinary.edu

Erie Community College North
Hospitality and Tourism
Main and Youngs Road
Williamsville, NY 14221
Phone: (716) 634-0800
http://www.ecc.edu

Finger Lakes Community College
Travel and Tourism
4355 Lake Shore Drive
Canandaigua, NY 14424
Phone: (716) 394-3500
http://www.fingerlakes.edu

Genesee Community College
Hospitality Management
1 College Road
Batavia, NY 14020
Phone: (716) 343-0055
http://www.sunygenesee.cc.ny.us

Herkimer County Community College
Business/Travel and Tourism
100 Reservoir Road
Herkimer, NY 13350
Phone: (315) 866-0300, ext. 235
Fax: (315) 866-7253
http://www.hccc.ntcnet.com

Jefferson Community College
Hospitality and Tourism
Outer Coffeen Street
Watertown, NY 13601
Phone: (315) 646-1420
http://www.sunyjefferson.edu

Kingsborough Community College
Hospitality and Tourism
2001 Oriental Boulevard
Brooklyn, NY 11235

Phone: (718) 368-5143
Fax: (718) 368-4880
http://www.kbcc.cuny.edu

LaGuardia Community College
Hospitality and Tourism
31-10 Thomson Avenue
Long Island City, NY 11101
Phone: (718) 482-5600
http://www.lagcc.suny.edu

Monroe Community College
Hospitality and Tourism
1000 East Henrietta Road
Rochester, NY 14623
Phone: (716) 292-2598
http://www.monroecc.edu

Nassau Community College
Hospitality and Tourism
1 Education Drive
Garden City, NY 11530
Phone: (516) 222-7344
http://www.sunynassau.edu

Paul Smith's College of Arts and Science
Hospitality Management
Routes 86 and 30
P.O. Box 265
Paul Smiths, NY 12970-0265
Phone: (518) 327-6218 or (800) 421-2605
Fax: (518) 327-6016
http://www.paulsmiths.edu

Rochester Institute of Technology
School of Food, Hotel and Travel
14 Lomb Memorial Drive
Rochester, NY 14623
Phone: (716) 475-2063
http://www.rit.edu

Rockland Community College
Hospitality and Tourism
145 College Road
Suffern, NY 10901
Phone: (914) 574-4786
Fax: (914) 574-4153
http://www.sunyrockland.edu

Schenectady County Community College
Hospitality and Tourism
78 Washington Avenue
Schenectady, NY 12305
Phone: (518) 381-1200
Fax: (518) 346-0379
http://www.sunysccc.edu

State University of New York Agricultural and Technical College
Hotel/Restaurant Management
Cornell Drive
Canton, NY 13617
Phone: (315) 386-7011
http://www.canton.edu

State University of New York at Cobleskill
Travel and Resort Marketing
College of Agriculture and Technology
Cobleskill, NY 12043
Phone: (518) 255-5525 or (800) 295-8988
Fax: (518) 255-6325
http://www.cobleskill.edu

State University of New York
Hospitality and Tourism
College of Technology
124 MacDonald Hall
Delhi, NY 13753
Phone: (607) 746-4189
http://www.delhi.edu

State University of New York
Hospitality and Tourism
School of Business
Brooks Hall, 320
Morrisville, NY 13408
Phone: (315) 684-6017
Fax: (315) 684-6225
http://www.morrisville.edu

Suffolk Community College
Hospitality and Tourism
Crooked Hill Road
Brentwood, NY 11717-1092
Phone: (516) 851-6848
Fax: (516) 851-6340
http://www.sunysuffolk.edu

Sullivan County Community College
Department of Travel and Tourism
P.O. Box 269
Loch Sheldrake, NY 12759
Phone: (914) 434-5750
Fax: (914) 434-4806
http://www.sullivan.suny.edu

NORTH CAROLINA

Asheville-Buncombe Technical Community College
Hospitality Education
340 Victoria Road
Asheville, NC 28801
Phone: (828) 254-1921
http://www.asheville.cc.nc.us

Blue Ridge Community College
Travel and Tourism Department
College Drive
Flat Rock, NC 28731
Phone: (828) 692-3572, ext. 257
Fax: (828) 692-2441
http://www.blueridge.cc.nc.us

Cape Fear Community College
Hotel/Restaurant Management
411 North Front Street
Wilmington, NC 28401-3993
Phone: (910) 362-7072
Fax: (910) 362-7497
http://www.cfcc.net

Central Piedmont Community College
Hospitality and Tourism
P.O. Box 35009
Charlotte, NC 28235-5009
Phone: (704) 330-4639
Fax: (704) 330-4637
http://www.cpcc.edu

Hardbarger Junior College
Travel and Tourism Department
1920 North Boulevard
Raleigh, NC 27604
Phone: (919) 828-7291

Southwestern Community College
Hospitality Management
275 Webster Road
Sylva, NC 28779
Phone: (704) 586-4091
http://www.southwest.cc.nc.us

Wake Technical Community College
Hospitality and Tourism
9101 Fayetteville Road
Raleigh, NC 27603-5696
Phone: (919) 662-3417
http://www.waketech.edu

Wilkes Community College
Hospitality and Tourism
P.O. Box 120
Wilkesboro, NC 28967-0120
Phone: (919) 667-7136
http://www.wilkes.cc.nc.us

OHIO

Columbus State Community College
Hospitality Management Department
550 East Spring Street
P.O. Box 1609
Columbus, OH 43216
Phone: (614) 287-5126

Fax: (614) 287-5973
http://www.cscc.edu

Cuyahoga Community College
Lodging and Tourism Management
    Program
2900 Community College – Concourse 87
Cleveland, OH 44115
Phone: (216) 987-4085
Fax: (216) 987-4086
http://www.tri-c.edu

Lakeland Community College
Travel and Tourism
7700 Clocktower Drive
Kirtland, OH 44094-5198
Phone: (440) 953-7000
http://www.lakeland.cc.oh.us

Ohio University
Travel and Tourism
Southern Campus
1804 Liberty Avenue
Ironton, OH 45638
Phone: (740) 533-4559
Fax: (740) 533-4590
http://www.Southern.ohiou.edu/tat

Sinclair Community College
Travel and Tourism Department
444 West Third Street, 13-426
Dayton, OH 45402-1421
Phone: (937) 512-4587
Fax: (937) 512-5396
http://www.sinclair.edu

OKLAHOMA

Oklahoma Junior College
Hospitality and Tourism
7330 East 71st Street
Tulsa, OK 74133
Phone: (918) 459-0200

Tulsa Junior College
Hospitality and Tourism
Cultural and Social Services
909 South Boston Avenue
Tulsa, OK 74119
Phone: (918) 587-6561

OREGON

Central Oregon Community College
Hotel/Restaurant Management
2600 Northwest College Way
Bend, OR 97701
Phone: (541) 383-7700
http://www.cocc.edu

Chemeketa Community College
Hospitality and Tourism
4000 Lancaster Drive NE
P.O. Box 14007
Salem, OR 97309
Phone: (503) 399-5000
http://www.chemek.cc.or.us

Mt. Hood Community College
Hospitality and Tourism
26000 Southeast Stark Street
Gresham, OR 97030
Phone: (503) 491-7486
Fax: (503) 491-7618
http://www.mhcc.edu

Portland Community College
Hospitality and Tourism
12000 Southeast 49th Avenue
Portland, OR 97219
Phone: (503) 244-6111
http://www.pcc.edu

PENNSYLVANIA

Bucks County Community College
Department of Business
Swamp Road
Newtown, PA 18940
Phone: (215) 968-8241
Fax: (215) 504-8509
http://www.bucks.edu

Central Pennsylvania College
College Hill Road
Summerdale, PA 17093-0309
Phone: (800) 759-2727
Fax: (717) 732-5254
http://www.centralpenn.edu

Delaware County Community College
Hospitality
901 South Media Line Road
Media, PA 19063-1094
Phone: (610) 359-5267
http://www.dccc.edu

Harcum College
Hospitality/Tourism
750 Montgomery Avenue
Bryn Mawr, PA 19010
Phone: (610) 526-6073
Fax: (610) 526-6031
http://www.harcum.edu

Harrisburg Area Community College
Hospitality and Tourism
One HACC Drive
Harrisburg, PA 17110-2999

Phone: (717) 780-2495
Fax: (717) 231-7670
http://www.hacc.edu

ICM School of Business
Hospitality and Tourism
10 Wood Street
Pittsburgh, PA 15222
Phone: (412) 261-2647 or (800) 441-
5222
http://www.icmschool.com

Keystone Junior College
Travel and Tourism Program
P.O. Box 50
La Plume, PA 18440-0200
Phone: (717) 945-5141, ext. 6004
http://www.keystone.edu

Lehigh Carbon Community College
Hospitality and Tourism
600 Hayden Circle
Allentown, PA 18103
Phone: (610) 264-4081

Luzerne County Community College
Tourism/Travel Management
1333 South Prospect
Nanticoke, PA 18634
Phone: (570) 740-0517
Fax: (570) 740-0553
http://www.luzerne.edu

Mansfield University
Hospitality and Tourism
104 Elliott Hall
Mansfield, PA 16933
Phone: (570) 662-4519
Fax: (570) 662-4111
http://www.mnsfld.edu

Mercyhurst College
Hospitality and Tourism
HRIM
501 East 38th Street
Erie, PA 16546
Phone: (814) 824-2356
http://www.mercyhurst.edu

Northampton Community College
Hospitality and Tourism
3835 Green Pond Road
Bethlehem, PA 18017-7568
Phone: (610) 861-5357
Fax: (610) 691-8489
http://www.northampton.edu

Reading Area Community College
Travel and Tourism
10 South Second Street
Reading, PA 19603-1706
Phone: (610) 372-4721
http://www.racc.cc.pa.us

Restaurant School at Walnut Hill
College
4207 Walnut Street
Philadelphia, PA 19104
Phone: (215) 222-4200 or (877) 925-6994
Fax: (215) 222-4219
http://www.therestaurantschool.com

Westmoreland County Community
College
Hospitality and Tourism
Armbrust Road
Youngwood, PA 15697
Phone: (412) 925-4235
http://www.wccc-pa.edu

York Technical Institute
Travel/Tourism
1405 Williams Road
York, PA 17402
Phone: (717) 757-1100 or (800) 227-9675
Fax: (717) 757-4964
http://www.yti.edu

RHODE ISLAND

Johnson and Wales University
The Center for International Travel
and Tourism Studies
8 Abbott Park Place
Providence, RI 02903
Phone: (401) 598-4639
Fax: (401) 598-4764
http://www.jwu.edu

SOUTH CAROLINA

Horry Georgetown Technical College
Hospitality and Tourism
743 Hemlock Street
Myrtle Beach, SC 29577
Phone: (843) 477-2000
Fax: (843) 477-0775
http://www.hor.tec.sc.us/hospitality

Johnson and Wales University—
Charleston
701 East Bay Street
Charleston, SC 29403
Phone: (800) 723-3429 or (800) 598-2667
http://www.jwu.edu/charles/index.htm

Technical College of the Lowcountry
921 South Ribault Road
P.O. Box 1288
Beaufort, SC 29901-1288
Phone: (843) 525-8235
Fax: (843) 525-8330
http://www.tcl-tec-sc-us.org

Trident Technical College
Hospitality, Tourism and Culinary Arts
P.O. Box 118067
7118 Rivers Avenue 29418
Charleston, SC 29423-8067
Phone: (843) 722-5542
http://www.trident.tec.sc.us

SOUTH DAKOTA

Black Hills State University
Hospitality and Tourism
College of Business and Technology
1200 University Street
Spearfish, SD 57799-9106
Phone: (605) 642-6702
Fax: (605) 642-6273
http://www.bhsu.edu

TENNESSEE

Southwest Tennessee Community
College
Hospitality and Tourism
5983 Macon Cove
Memphis, TN 38134
Phone: (877) 717-STCC
http://www.stcc.cc.tn.us

Volunteer State Community College
1480 Nashville Pike
Gallatin, TN 37066
Phone: (615) 452-8600
Fax: (615) 230-3317
http://www.vscc.cc.tn.us

TEXAS

Del Mar College
Department of Hospitality Management
West Campus
101 Baldwin Boulevard
Corpus Christi, TX 78404-3897
Phone: (361) 698-1734 or (800) 652-3357
Fax: (361) 698-1829
http://www.delmar.edu

El Paso Community College
Hospitality and Travel Services
P.O. Box 20500

El Paso, TX 79998
Phone: (915) 831-2217
Fax: (915) 831-2155
http://www.epcc.edu

Richland College
Travel, Exposition, and Meeting
   Management
12800 Abrams Road, Room S-230
Dallas, TX 75243-2199
Phone: (972) 238-6097
Fax: (972) 238-6333
http://www.rlc.dcccd.edu

Richland College
Hospitality and Tourism
12800 Abrams Road
Dallas, TX 75243-2199
Phone: (972) 238-6106
http://www.rlc.dcccd.edu

St. Philips College
Hospitality and Tourism
1801 Martin Luther King Drive
San Antonio, TX 78203
Phone: (210) 531-3298
Fax: (210) 531-3351
http://www.accd.edu/spc/spcmain/spc.htm

Tarrant County College—Southeast
Hospitality Management, Culinary Arts,
   Dietetics
2100 Southeast Parkway
Arlington, TX 76018
Phone: (817) 515-3608
Fax: (817) 515-3172
http://www.tccd.net

Texas State Technical College—Waco
Food Service/Culinary Arts
3801 Campus Drive
Waco, TX 76705
Phone: (254) 867-4868
http://www.waco.tstc.edu

UTAH

Mountain West College
Travel and Tourism
3280 West 3500 South
West Valley City, UT 84119
Phone: (801) 840-4800
http://www.mwcollege.com

Utah Valley State College
Hospitality Management
800 West University Parkway
Orem, UT 84058-5999

Phone: (801) 222-8234
http://www.uvsc.edu

VERMONT

Champlain College
Tourism and Event Management Program
163 South Willard Street
Burlington, VT 05402-0670
Phone: (802) 865-6438
Fax: (802) 860-2763
http://www.champlain.edu/majors/
    hospitality

New England Culinary Institute
Hospitality and Tourism
RR #1, 250 Main Street
Montpelier, VT 05602
Phone: (802) 223-6324
http://www.neculinary.com

VIRGINIA

Commonwealth College
Travel/Hospitality
301 Centre Pointe Drive
Virginia Beach, VA 23462-4419

Northern Virginia Community College
Hospitality and Tourism
Annandale Campus
8333 Little River Turnpike
Annandale, VA 22003
Phone: (703) 323-3457
http://www.nv.cc.va.us

Tidewater Community College
Hospitality Management
1700 College Crescent
Virginia Beach, VA 23456
Phone: (757) 321-7173
Fax: (757) 468-3077
http://www.tc.cc.va.us

WASHINGTON

Art Institute of Seattle
Culinary Arts
2323 Elliott Avenue
Seattle, WA 98121
Phone: (206) 448-0900
http://www.ais.edu

Seattle Central Community College
Culinary Arts/Hospitality
1701 Broadway
Seattle, WA 98122
Phone: (206) 344-4310
Fax: (206) 587-3868
http://www.seattlecentral.org

Spokane Community College
Hospitality and Tourism
1810 Greene Street, North
Spokane, WA 99207
Phone: (509) 536-7337
http://www.scc.spokane.cc.wa.us

WISCONSIN

Gateway Technical College
Hospitality and Tourism
3520 30th Avenue
Kenosha, WI 54144-1690
Phone: (414) 656-6936
http://www.gateway.tec.wi.us

Madison Area Technical College
Business Technology, Culinary Trades
    and Leisure Services
3550 Anderson Street
Madison, WI 53704-2599
Phone: (608) 243-4455
Fax: (608) 246-6316
http://www.matcmadison.edu

Moraine Park Technical College
Hospitality and Tourism

P.O. Box 1940
Fond du Lac, WI 54936-1940
Phone: (414) 929-2116
http://www.moraine.tec.wi.us

Milwaukee Area Technical College
Hospitality and Tourism
700 West State Street
Milwaukee, WI 53233
Phone: (414) 297-6600
http://www.milwaukee.tec.wi.us

Nicolet Area Technical College
Culinary Arts
P.O. Box 518
Rhinelander, WI 54501
Phone: (715) 365-4410
http://www.nicolet.tec.wi.us

Waukesha Co. Tech College
Hospitality and Tourism
800 Main Street
Pewaukee, WI 53072
Phone: (262) 691-5566
Fax: (262) 691-5254
http://www.waukesha.tec.wi.us

WYOMING

Northwest College
231 West Sixth Street
Powell, WY 82435
Phone: (307) 754-6101
Fax: (307) 754-6249
http://www.northwestcollege.org

Sheridan College
Hospitality Program
P.O. Box 1500
Sheridan, WY 82801
Phone: (800) 913-9139, ext. 6223
Fax: (307) 674-2013
http://www.sc.cc.wy.us

APPENDIX II
BACHELOR'S DEGREE PROGRAMS IN TRAVEL, TOURISM, AND HOSPITALITY

ALABAMA

Alabama State University
Department of Health and Physical
   Education
915 South Jackson Street
Montgomery, AL 36195-0301
Phone: (334) 229-4502
http://www.alasu.edu

Auburn University
Hotel and Restaurant Management
328 Spidle Hall
Auburn, AL 36849
Phone: (334) 844-1333
Fax: (334) 844-3268
http://www.auburn.edu

University of South Alabama
Department of HPELS
307 University Boulevard
Mobile, AL 36688
Phone: (334) 460-7131
http://www.southalabama.edu

ALASKA

Alaska Pacific University
Hotel, Food Service and Tourism
4101 University Drive
Anchorage, AK 99508
Phone: (907) 564-8234
Fax: (907) 562-4276
http://www.alaskapacific.edu

University of Alaska–Fairbanks
Hospitality and Tourism
School of Management
P.O. Box 757520
Fairbanks, AK 99775
Phone: (907) 474-6525
http://www.uaf.edu

ARIZONA

Arizona State University
Hospitality and Tourism
Moeur #131
Tempe, AZ 85287-4905
Phone: (602) 965-4630
http://www.asu.edu

Northern Arizona University
School of Hotel and Restaurant
   Management
P.O. Box 5638
Flagstaff, AZ 86011-5638
Phone: (928) 523-1705
Fax: (928) 523-5233
http://www.nau.edu/hrm

ARKANSAS

Arkansas Tech University
Hospitality Administration
100 Williamson Hall
Russellville, AR 72801
Phone: (501) 968-0687
Fax: (501) 968-0600
http://www.atu.edu

Henderson State University
Health, Physical Education and
   Recreation Department
HSU Box 7552
Arkadelphia, AR 71999-0001
Phone: (870) 230-5192
Fax: (870) 230-5073
http://www.hsu.edu

University of Arkansas
Hospitality and Tourism
University of Business and Economic
   Research
BADM 443
Fayetteville, AR 72701
Phone: (501) 575-4151
http://www.uark.edu

CALIFORNIA

Alliant International University
School of Hospitality Management
10455 Pomerado Road
San Diego, CA 92131
Phone: (858) 635-4627
Fax: 858-635-4794
http://www.alliant.edu

California State University at Chico
Resort and Lodging Management
400 West First Street
Chico, CA 95929-0560
Phone: (530) 898-4855
Fax: (530) 898-6557
http://www.csuchico.edu

**California State University, Long
   Beach**
Department of Recreation and Leisure
   Studies
1250 Bellflower Boulevard
Long Beach, CA 90840-4903
Phone: (562) 985-4071
http://www.csulb.edu

California State University, Northridge
Leisure Studies and Recreation
18111 Nordhoff Street
Northridge, CA 91330-8269
Phone: (818) 677-3202
Fax: (818) 677-2695
http://www.csun.edu

**Collins School of Hospitality
   Management**
California State Polytechnic University
3801 West Temple Avenue
Pomona, CA 91768
Phone: (909) 869-2275
http://www.csupomona.edu/~cshm

Golden Gate University
Hotel, Restaurant and Tourism
   Management
536 Mission Street, Room 493
San Francisco, CA 94105
Phone: (415) 442-6508
Fax: (415) 442-7049
http://www.ggu.edu

Loyola Marymount University
Ed and Lynn Hogan Program in Travel
   and Tourism
7900 Loyola Boulevard
Los Angeles, CA 90045-8395
Phone: (310) 338-3798
Fax: (310) 338-3000
http://www.lmu.edu

San Francisco State University
Hospitality and Tourism
P.O. Box 27188
San Francisco, CA 94127
Phone: (415) 586-6888
http://www.sfsu.edu

University of California at Irvine
Hospitality and Tourism
School of Social Sciences
765 SST
Irvine, CA 92717
Phone: (714) 824-3144
http://www.uci.edu

University of San Francisco
Hospitality Management
2130 Fulton Street MCL 115
San Francisco, CA 94117-1080
Phone: (415) 422-6236
http://www.usfca.edu

COLORADO

Art Institute, School of Culinary Arts
Culinary Department
675 South Broadway
Denver, CO 80209
Phone: (303) 824-4954
Fax: (303) 778-8312
http://www.culinary.arts-usa.com

Colorado State University
The College of Natural Resources
Natural Resource Recreation and Tourism
300 West Drake
Ft. Collins, CO 80523-1480
Phone: (970) 491-6591
Fax: (970) 491-2255
http://www.cnr.colostate.edu

Fort Lewis College
Tourism and Resort Management
1000 Rim Drive
Durango, CO 81301
Phone: (970) 247-7550
http://www.fortlewis.edu

Mesa State College/UTEC
Culinary Arts
2508 Blichmann Avenue
Grand Junction, CO 81505
Phone: (970) 255-2632
Fax: (970) 255-2650
http://www.mesastate.edu

University of Colorado at Boulder
Tourism Management Program
College of Business

Campus Box 420
Boulder, CO 80309-0420
Phone: (303) 492-4267
Fax: (303) 492-3620
http://bus.colorado/homeworking.html

University of Denver
School of Hotel, Restaurant and Tourism
    Management
2030 East Evans Avenue
Denver, CO 80208
Phone: (303) 871-4275
Fax: (303) 871-4260
http://www.dcb.du.edu/hrtm

CONNECTICUT

**International College of Hospitality
    Management**
Tourism Administration
101 Wykeham Road
Washington, CT 06793
Phone: (860) 868-9555 or (800) 955-0809
Fax: (860) 868-2114
E-mail: admissions@ichm.cc.ct.us
http://www.ichm.ritz.edu

University of New Haven
School of Hospitality and Tourism
Room 223, Harugari Hall
300 Orange Avenue
West Haven, CT 06516
Phone: (203) 932-7413
http://www.newhaven.edu/tourism

DELAWARE

Delaware State University
Hospitality Management Program
1200 North Dupont Highway
Dover, DE 19901
Phone: (302) 857-6980
Fax: (302) 857-6983
http://www.dsc.edu

University of Delaware
Hotel, Restaurant and Institutional
    Management
321 South College Avenue
Newark, DE 19716
Phone: (302) 831-6077
Fax: (302) 831-6395
http://www.udel.edu/hrim

DISTRICT OF COLUMBIA

George Washington University
MTA Program

600 21st Street, NW
Washington, DC 20052
Phone: (202) 994-8740
Fax: (202) 994-1630
http://www.gwutourism.org

Howard University
Hospitality Management Program
2400 Sixth Street, NW
Washington, DC 20059
Phone: (202) 806-1535 or (202) 986-
    4132
E-mail: cthaysbert@howard.edu

FLORIDA

Bethune-Cookman College
Hospitality Management
640 Dr. Mary McLeod Bethune
    Boulevard
Daytona Beach, FL 32114
Phone: (386) 481-2871
Fax: (386) 481-2895
http://www.bethune.cookman.edu

Florida Atlantic University
Hospitality and Tourism
777 Glades Road
P.O. Box 3091
Boca Raton, FL 33431
Phone: (561) 297-3666
Fax: (561) 297-3935
http://www.fau.edu

Florida International University
School of Hospitality Management
North Miami Campus HM 215
3000 Northeast 151st Street
North Miami, FL 33181
Phone: (305) 919-4539
Fax: (305) 919-4513
http://hospitality.fiu.edu

Florida State University
Hospitality and Tourism
Dedman School of Hospitality
1 Champions Way, Room 4110
Tallahassee, FL 32306-2541
Phone: (850) 644-8244
Fax: (850) 644-5565
http://www.cob.fsu.edu/ha

**International School of Tourism and
    Hospitality Management**
Schiller International University
251 Lyndhurst Street
Dunedin, FL 34698
Phone: (727) 736-5082
Fax: (727) 736-6263
http://schiller.edu

Nova Southeastern University
Hotel and Tourism
1244 Northwest 117th Avenue
Coral Springs, FL 33071
Phone: (954) 262-8105
Fax: (954) 262-3810
http://www.nova.edu/

Orlando College/Melbourne
Hospitality and Tourism
2401 North Harbor City Boulevard
Melbourne, FL 32935
Phone: (407) 254-6459

Saint Thomas University
Hotel Management Accounting
16400 Northwest 32nd Avenue
Miami, FL 33054
Phone: (305) 625-6623
Fax: (305) 628-6504
http://www.stu.edu

Saint Thomas University
Tourism and Hospitality Management
16400 Northwest 32nd Avenue
Miami, FL 33054
Phone: (305) 628-6535
Fax: (305) 628-6504
http://www.stu.edu

University of Central Florida
Rosen School of Hospitality Management
Office CH-302
Orlando, FL 32816-1450
Phone: (407) 823-2188
Fax: (407) 823-5696
http://www.hospitality.ucf.edu

Webber International University
International Tourism Management
P.O. Box 96
1201 North Scenic Highway
Babson Park, FL 33827
Phone: (863) 638-2942
Fax: (863) 638-2823
http://www.webber.edu

GEORGIA

Georgia Southern University
Hotel and Restaurant Management
P.O. Box 8034
Statesboro, GA 30460-8034
Phone: (912) 681-5345
Fax: (912) 681-0276
http://www.gasou.edu

Georgia State University
Hospitality and Tourism

Cecil B. Day School of Hospitality
  Administration
35 Broad Street, Suite 1215/University
  Plaza
Atlanta, GA 30303
Phone: (404) 651-3512
Fax: (404) 651-3670
http://www.robinson.gsu.edu/hospitality

Savannah State College
Hospitality and Tourism
P.O. Box 20359
Savannah, GA 31404
Phone: (912) 356-2838
http://www.savstate.edu

HAWAII

Brigham Young University–Hawaii
Hotel and Restaurant Management
BYU – Box 1773
Laie, HI 96762
Phone: (808) 293-3594
http://www.byuh.edu

Hawaii Pacific University
Hospitality and Tourism
1164 Bishop Street
Honolulu, HI 96813
Phone: (808) 544-0287
Fax: (808) 544-1136
http://www.hpu.edu

University of Hawaii at Manoa
Hospitality, Tourism and Transportation
2560 Campus Road
Honolulu, HI 96822
Phone: (808) 956-4892
Fax: (808) 956-5378
http://www.tim.hawaii.edu

IDAHO

University of Idaho
Department of Resource Recreation and
  Tourism
975 West Sixth Street
Moscow, ID 83844-1139
Phone: (208) 885-7911 or (888) 884-
  3246
Fax: (208) 885-6226
http://www.its.uidaho.edu/rrt

ILLINOIS

Bradley University
Family and Consumer Science
B Hall 206
Peoria, IL 61625

Phone: (309) 677-2433
Fax: (309) 677-3813
http://www.bradley.edu

Chicago State University
Hospitality
9501 South Martin Luther King Drive
BHS 430
Chicago, IL 60628
Phone: (773) 995-3968
Fax: (773) 995-2269
http://www.csu.edu

Kendall College
Hotel/Restaurant and Culinary
  Management
2408 Orrington Avenue
Evanston, IL 60201
Phone: (847) 866-1304 or (877) 588-8860
Fax: (847) 733-7450
http://www.kendall.edu

Northern Illinois University
Department of HFR
Dietetics, Nutrition and Food Systems
  Administration
Dekalb, IL 60115
Phone: (815) 753-6385
http://www.niu.edu

Northwestern University
Hospitality and Tourism
Transportation Library
633 Clark Street
Evanston, IL 60208
Phone: (312) 491-5275
http://www.northwestern.edu

Robert Morris College
Hospitality and Tourism
401 South State Street
Chicago, IL 60605
Phone: (312) 935-6835
http://www.rmcil.edu

**Southern Illinois University at
  Carbondale**
Food and Nutrition
Quigley Hall, Room 209
Carbondale, IL 62901
Phone: (618) 453-5193
Fax: (618) 453-7517
http://www.siu.edu

**University of Illinois at
  Urbana–Champaign**
Food Science and Human Nutrition
905 South Goodwin Avenue
Urbana, IL 61801

Phone: (217) 333-2024
Fax: (217) 265-0929
http://www.ag.uiuc.edu/~food-
  lab/index.html

Western Illinois University
Recreation, Park and Tourism
  Administration
Currens Hall 400
Macomb, IL 61455
Phone: (309) 298-1967
Fax: (309) 298-2967
http://www.wiu.edu/users/mirpta

INDIANA

Ball State University
Geography Department
2000 West University Drive
Muncie, IN 47306
Phone: (765) 285-1776
Fax: (765) 285-2351
http://www.bsu.edu/geog/

Indiana University
Tourism Management
Recreation and Park Administration
School of Health, Physical Education and
  Recreation
1025 East Seventh Street
Bloomington, IN 47405-4801
Phone: (812) 855-4711
Fax: (812) 855-3998
http://www.indiana.edu/~recpark

**Indiana University Purdue
  University–Fort Wayne**
Hospitality Management Program
Neff Hall, Room 330B
Ft. Wayne, IN 46805-1499
Phone: (219) 481-6562
Fax: (219) 481-5767
E-mail: knight@ipfw.edu
http://www.ipfw.edu/cfs/dinner1.htm

**Indiana University Purdue University
  Indianapolis**
Tourism, Conventions and Event
  Management
901 West New York Street
Indianapolis, IN 46202
Phone: (317) 274-7649
Fax: (317) 278-2041
http://www.iupui.edu/~indyhyper/

Purdue University
Department of Hospitality and Tourism
  Management
1266 Stone Hall, Room 106

West Lafayette, IN 47907-1266
Phone: (765) 494-4643
Fax: (765) 494-0327
E-mail: kavanaur@cfs.purdue.edu
http://www.cfs.purdue.edu/HTM

IOWA

Iowa State University
Hotel and Restaurant Management
1055 Le Baron Hall
Ames, IA 50011-1120
Phone: (515) 294-7474
Fax: (515) 294-8551
http://www.fcs.iastate.edu/hrim

KANSAS

Kansas State University
Hotel and Restaurant Management
103 Justin Hall
Department of HRIMD
Manhattan, KS 66506-1404
Phone: (785) 532-2210

KENTUCKY

Eastern Kentucky University
Department of Geography and Planning
201 Roark Building
Richmond, KY 40475
Phone: (859) 622-1418

Morehead State University
Department of Human Sciences
325 Read Hall
Morehead, KY 40351
Phone: (800) 585-6781
http://www.morehead-st.edu

Transylvania University
Hospitality and Tourism
300 North Broadway
Lexington, KY 40508-1797
Phone: (859) 233-8249
Fax: (859) 233-8749
http://www.transylvaniauniversity.edu

University of Kentucky
Hospitality Management
120 Erikson Road
Lexington, KY 40506-0050
Phone: (859) 257-3829
Fax: (859) 257-1275

Western Kentucky University
Consumer and Family Sciences
  Department
#1 Big Red Way, AC 302F

Bowling Green, KY 42101-3576
Phone: (270) 745-4031
Fax: (270) 745-3999
http://www.wku.edu/hospitality

LOUISIANA

Grambling State University
Hotel and Restaurant Management
P.O. Box 1190
Grambling, LA 71245
Phone: (318) 274-2249
Fax: (318) 274-6049
http://www.gram.edu

Southwestern Louisiana University
Hospitality and Tourism
Home Economics
ULA Box 40399
Lafayette, LA 70504
Phone: (318) 231-6644

Tulane University
Hospitality and Tourism
Freeman School of Business
6823 Saint Charles Avenue
New Orleans, LA 70118
Phone: (504) 865-5668
http://www.tulane.edu

University of Louisiana at Lafayette
Hospitality Management
P.O. Box 40399
Lafayette, LA 70504-0399
Phone: (337) 482-1015
Fax: (337) 482-5395
E-mail: jagrusa@louisiana.edu
http://www.louisiana.edu

University of New Orleans
School of Hotel, Restaurant and Tourism
  Administration
5919 Pratt Drive
New Orleans, LA 70122
Phone: (504) 286-6385

MAINE

University of Maine
Parks, Recreation and Tourism
221 Nutting Hall
Orono, ME 04469
Phone: (207) 581-2850

MARYLAND

Morgan State University
Hospitality and Tourism Management
McMechen Building, Room 114

1700 East Cold Spring Lane
Baltimore, MD 21251
Phone: (443) 885-4587
Fax: (410) 319-4034
http://www.morgan.edu

University of Maryland–Eastern Shore
Hotel and Restaurant Management
Henson Center, Room 2000
Princess Anne, MD 21853
Phone: (410) 651-6567
Fax: (410) 651-6273

MASSACHUSETTS

Boston University
Hotel and Food Administration
808 Commonwealth Avenue
Boston, MA 02215
Phone: (413) 545-9495

Framingham State College
Hospitality and Tourism
Home Economics
Hemenway Hall, State Street
Framingham, MA 01701
Phone: (508) 620-1220
http://www.framingham.edu/

Northeastern University
356 Richards Hall
360 Huntington Avenue
Boston, MA 02115
Phone: (617) 373-2000
http://www.northeastern.edu

Salem State College
Travel and Tourism Concentration
352 Lafayette Street
Salem, MA 01970-5353
Phone: (978) 542-6225
Fax: (978) 542-6269
http://www.dgl.salem.mass.edu

University of Massachusetts
Hotel, Restaurant and Travel
    Administration
107 Flint Lab
Amherst, MA 01003-2710
Phone: (413) 545-4041
Fax: (413) 545-1235
http://www.umass.edu

Westfield State College
Hospitality and Tourism
Department of Economics/Business
577 Western Avenue
Westfield, MA 01086
Phone: (413) 572-5313

MICHIGAN

Central Michigan University
Hospitality Services Administration
MKT/HSA Department–CMU
Mount Pleasant, MI 48653
Phone: (989) 774-4000
Fax: (989) 774-7406

Eastern Michigan University
Department of Geography and Geology
203 Strong Hall
Ypsilanti, MI 48197
Phone: (734) 487-7575
Fax: (734) 487-6979
http://www.emich.edu

Ferris State University
Hospitality and Tourism
901 South State Street
Big Rapids, MI 49307-2736
Phone: (231) 591-2382
Fax: (231) 591-2998
http://www.ferris.edu

Grand Valley State University
Hospitality and Tourism Management
2249 Mackinac Hall
Allendale, MI 49401
Phone: (616) 895-3118
Fax: (616) 875-3115
http://www.gvsu.edu

Michigan State University
School of Hospitality Business
232 Eppley Center
East Lansing, MI 48824
Phone: (517) 355-5080
Fax: (517) 432-1170
http://www.bus.msu.edu/shb/

Northern Michigan University
Hospitality Management
1401 Presque Isle Avenue
Marquette, MI 49855
Phone: (906) 227-1544
http://www.nmu.edu

Western Michigan University
Tourism and Travel
148 East Michigan
Kalamazoo, MI 49001
Phone: (269)387-3530
http://www.mich.edu/

MINNESOTA

Rasmussen Business College
Travel and Tourism Department

12450 Wayzata Boulevard
Minnetonka, MN 55343
Phone: (888) 549-6755
http://www.rasmussen.edu

Southwest State University
Hotel, Restaurant and Institutional
    Management
1501 State Street
Marshall, MN 56258
Phone: (507) 537-7670
Fax: (507) 537-7179
http://www.southwest.msus.edu

St. Cloud State University
Geography Department
720 Fourth Avenue South
St. Cloud, MN 56301-4498
Phone: (320) 255-2271
Fax: (320) 529-1660
http://www.stcloudstate.edu

University of Minnesota
Hotel, Restaurant and Institution
    Management
2900 University Avenue
Crookston, MN 56716
Phone: (218) 281-8200
Fax: (218) 281-8250
http://www.crk.umn.edu

MISSISSIPPI

University of Mississippi
Department of Exercise Science and
    Leisure Management
222 Turner Complex
University, MS 38677
Phone: (601) 232-7573
Fax: (601) 232-5525
E-mail: tkaufman@olemiss.edu

University of Southern Mississippi
Department of Hospitality Management
155 Madison Place
Hattiesburg, MS 39402
Phone: (601) 266-6762
Fax: (601) 266-6707

University of Southern Mississippi
Hospitality Management and Culinary
    Arts
730 East Beach Boulevard
Long Beach, MS 39560
Phone: (228) 214-3226
Fax: (228) 214-3223
http://www.usm.edu

MISSOURI

Central Missouri State University
Hotel and Restaurant Management
Hudson Building
Warrensburg, MO 64093
Phone: (660) 543-4362
Fax: (660) 543-8295
http://www.cmsu.edu

Southwest Missouri University
Hospitality and Restaurant
    Administration
901 South National Avenue
Springfield, MO 65804-0094
Phone: (417) 836-6042

University of Missouri–Columbia
Hotel and Restaurant Management
122 Eckles Hall
Columbia, MO 65211
Phone: (573) 882-4114

MONTANA

University of Montana
Recreation and Nature-Based Tourism
    Management
32 Campus Drive
Missoula, MT 59812-0576
Phone: (406) 243-5107
Fax: (406) 243-6656
http://www.forestry.umt.edu/degrees/
    undergraduate/rrmgt

University of Montana–Western
Business and Technology
710 South Atlantic Street, Box 120
Dillon, MT 59725-3598
Phone: (406) 683-7111
Fax: (406) 683-7816
http://www.umwestern.edu

NEBRASKA

University of Nebraska Omaha
The School of Health, Physical Education
    and Recreation
6001 Dodge Street
Omaha, NE 68132
Phone: (402) 554-2670
E-mail: unoadm@unomaha.edu
http://www.unomaha.edu

University of Nebraska Kearney
Tourism Program
C 208 West Center
Kearney, NE 68849
Phone: (308) 865-8331

NEVADA

Sierra Nevada College Lake Tahoe
Hospitality and Tourism
800 College Drive
P.O. Box 4269
Incline Village, NV 89450-4269
Phone: (800) 332-8666

University of Nevada Las Vegas
William F. Harrah College of Hotel
    Administration
Department of Tourism and Convention
    Administration
4505 Maryland Parkway, Box 456013
Las Vegas, NV 89154-6013
Phone: (702) 895-3161
Fax: (702) 895-4109
http://hotel.unlv.edu/Tourism

University of Nevada, Reno
Director of Hospitality
Hospitality and Tourism
1664 North Virginia Street
Economics Department
Reno, NV 89557
Phone: (775) 784-1110
http://www.unr.edu

NEW HAMPSHIRE

Plymouth State College
Hospitality and Tourism
17 High Street
Plymouth, NH 03264
Phone: (603) 536-1550
http://www.plymouth.edu

University of New Hampshire
Hotel Administration
Durham, NH 03824
Phone: (603) 659-3321
Fax: (603) 862-3383
http://orbit.unh.edu/dhm

University of New Hampshire
Hospitality Management
McConnel Hall
Durham, NH 03824
Phone: (603) 862-3458
Fax: (603) 862-3383
http://orbit.unh.edu/dhm

NEW JERSEY

Fairleigh Dickinson University
School of Hotel, Restaurant and Tourism
    Management
1000 River Road H-DH2-I4

Teaneck, NJ 07666-1914
Phone: (201) 692-7271
Fax: (201) 692-7279
http://www.fdu.edu

Georgian Court College
Hospitality and Tourism
900 Lakewood Avenue
Lakewood, NJ 08701
Phone: (732) 364-2200
Fax: (732) 431-3173
http://www.georgian.edu

Montclair State University
Commercial Recreation and Tourism
    Program
Upper Montclair, NJ 07043-1624
Phone: (973) 655-4000

NEW MEXICO

New Mexico Highlands University
Department HPLS
Las Vegas, NM 87701
Phone: (505) 454-3287

New Mexico State University
Hotel, Restaurant and Tourism
    Management
Box 30003, MSC 3HRTM
Las Cruces, NM 88003-0003
Phone: (505) 646-8099
Fax: (505) 646-8100
http://www.nmsu.edu/~hrtm

University of New Mexico
Travel and Tourism Management
Anderson School of Management
MSC05 3090
Albuquerque, NM 87131-0001
Phone: (505) 277-6471
Fax: (505) 277-7108
http://www.unm.edu

NEW YORK

Buffalo State
Hospitality and Tourism
207 Caudell Hall
1300 Elmwood Avenue
Buffalo, NY 14222
Phone: (716) 878-5913, ext. 3359
Fax: (716) 878-5834
http://www.buffalostate.edu

Cornell University
School of Hotel Administration
174 Statler Hall
Ithaca, NY 14853-6902
Phone: (607) 255-6376

Fax: (607) 254-5121
http://hotelschool.cornell.edu

Culinary Institute of America
Hospitality and Tourism
433 Albany Post Road
Hyde Park, NY 12538-1499
Phone: (914) 452-9600
Fax: (914) 451-1076

Keuka College
Hospitality and Tourism
Keuka Park
New York, NY 14478
Phone: (315) 536-5324 or (800)
33KEUKA
http://www.keuka.edu

Mercy College
Hotel and Restaurant Management
555 Broadway
Dobbs Ferry, NY 10522
Phone: (914) 693-4500

New York Institute of Technology
Hospitality and Tourism
P.O. Box 9029
Central Islip, NY 11722-4597
Phone: (516) 348-3210

New York University
Tisch Center for Hospitality, Tourism and
Travel Administration
10 Astor Place, Suite 504
New York, NY 10003-7154
Phone: (212) 998-9107
Fax: (212) 995-4676
http://www.scps.nyu.edu/tischcenter

Niagara University
College of Hospitality and Tourism
Management
Niagara University, NY 14109-2012
Phone: (716) 286-8270
Fax: (716) 286-8277
http://www.niagara.edu/hospitality

Plattsburgh State University
Hospitality and Tourism
235 Redcay Hall, School of Business and
Economics
Plattsburgh, NY 12901
Phone: (518) 564-4214
Fax: (518) 564-4215
http://www.plattsburgh.edu

Rochester Institute of Technology
School of Food, Hotel and Travel
14 Lomb Memorial Drive

Rochester, NY 14623
Phone: (716) 475-2063

**State University of New York at
Oneonta**
Food Service and Restaurant
Administration
Department of Human Ecology
Ravine Parkway
Oneonta, NY 13820-4015
Phone: (607) 436-2705
Fax: (607) 436-2051
http://www.oneonta.edu

St. Johns University
Hospitality and Tourism
800 Utopia Parkway
Jamaica, NY 11439
Phone: (718) 990-6137
Fax: (718) 990-1882
http://www.stjohns.edu

Syracuse University
Hospitality and Food Service
Management
College for Human Development
034 Slocum Hall
Syracuse, NY 13244
Phone: (315) 443-1870
http://www.syr.edu

NORTH CAROLINA

Appalachian State University
Department of Management
Boone, NC 28608
Phone: (828) 262-2000
http://www.appstate.edu

Barber Scotia College
Hospitality Management
145 Cabarrus Avenue West
Concord, NC 28025
Phone: (704) 789-2900
http://www.b-sc.edu

East Carolina University
Department of Nutrition and Hospitality
Management
School of Human Environmental
Sciences
East Fifth Street
Greenville, NC 27858-4353
Phone: (252) 328-6917
Fax: (252) 328-4276
http://www.ecu.edu/hes/NUHMhome.htm

North Carolina Central University
Hospitality and Tourism Administration

1801 Fayetteville Street
Durham, NC 27707
Phone: (919) 560-6488
Fax: (919) 220-5455

North Carolina State University
Recreation Resource Administration
4008 Biltmore Hall
Raleigh, NC 27695
Phone: (919) 737-3276

North Carolina Wesleyan College
Hotel and Food Management
College Station
Rocky Mount, NC 27801
Phone: (252) 985-5100

Southwestern Community College
Hospitality Management
275 Webster Road
Sylva, NC 28779
Phone: (704) 586-4091

University of North Carolina
Hospitality and Tourism
250 East Franklin Street
CB #3938, Davis Library
Chapel Hill, NC 27514
Phone: (919) 962-2211
http://www.unc.edu

**University of North Carolina at
Greensboro**
Recreation, Parks and Tourism
P.O. Box 26169
Greensboro, NC 27402-6169
Phone: (336) 334-3041
Fax: (336) 334-3238
http://www.uncg.edu/rpt

**University of North Carolina at
Wilmington**
Department of Health and Applied
Human Sciences
Parks and Recreation Management
601 South College Road
Wilmington, NC 28403-3297
Phone: (910) 962-3283
Fax: (910) 962-7073
http://www.uncwil.edu/hahs

Western Carolina University
Hospitality and Tourism
Cullowhee, NC 28753
Phone: (828) 227-2148
Fax: (828) 227-7705
http://www.wcu.edu

NORTH DAKOTA

North Dakota State University
Hotel, Motel and Restaurant Management
State University Station
1301 12th Avenue North
Fargo, ND 58105
Phone: (701) 231-7356
Fax: (701) 231-7174
http://www.ndsu.nodak.edu/instruct/
    grossnick/foodnutr

OHIO

Bowling Green State University
Sport Management, Recreation and
    Tourism
School of Human Movement, Sport and
    Leisure Studies
Bowling Green, OH 43403-0248
Phone: (419) 372-6902
Fax: (419) 372-0383
http://www.bgsu.edu

Central State University
Smith Hall, 309
P.O. Box 1004
Wilberforce, OH 45384
Phone: (937) 376-6204
Fax: (937) 376-6206
http://www.centralstate.edu

Kent State University
Recreational and Leisure Service Unit
265 Macc Annex
Kent, OH 44242
Phone: (330) 672-2015
http://www.kent.edu

Ohio State University
Hospitality Management
2914 Granada Hills Drive
Columbus, OH 43231
Phone: (614) 292-5034

Ohio University
Travel and Tourism
Southern Campus
1804 Liberty Avenue
Ironton, OH 45638
Phone: (740) 533-4559
Fax: (740) 533-4590
http://web2.southern.ohiou.edu/tat

Tiffin University
Hospitality and Tourism
155 Miami Street
Tiffin, OH 44883
Phone: (800) 968-6446
Fax: (419) 443-5002
http://www.tiffin.edu

OKLAHOMA

Northeastern State University
Meetings and Destination Management
Hospitality and Tourism
600 North Grand Avenue
Tahlequah, OK 74464
Phone: (918) 456-5511, ext. 3086
Fax: (918) 458-2337
http://www.nsuok.edu

Oklahoma State University
School of Hotel and Restaurant
    Administration
210 Human Environmental Services West
Stillwater, OK 74078
Phone: (405) 744-6713
Fax: (405) 744-6299
http://osuhrad.org

OREGON

Oregon State University
Hotel/Restaurant Management
College of Business
104 Kent Administration Building
Corvallis, OR 97331
Phone: (503) 754-3693
http://oregonstate.edu

Southern Oregon State
Hospitality and Tourism
School of Business
1250 Siskiyou Boulevard
Ashland, OR 97520
Phone: (503) 552-6716

PENNSYLVANIA

California University of Pennsylvania
Hospitality and Tourism
250 University Avenue
California, PA 15419
Phone: (724) 938-4531
Fax: (724) 938-5780
http://www.cup.edu

Drexel University
Hotel, Restaurant and Institutional
    Management
33rd and Market Streets
Philadelphia, PA 19104
Phone: (215) 895-2411
Fax: (215) 895-2426
http://www.drexel.edu

East Stroudsburg University
Department of Hotel, Restaurant and
    Tourism Management
Hospitality Management Building
200 Prospect Street

East Stroudsburg, PA 18301
Phone: (717) 422-3762
Fax: (717) 422-3777

Indiana University of Pennsylvania
Hotel, Restaurant, and Institutional
    Management Department
10 Ackerman Hall
911 South Drive
Indiana, PA 15705
Phone: (724) 357-4440
Fax: (724) 357-7582
http://www.iup.edu/hrim

Mansfield University
Hospitality and Tourism
104 Elliott Hall
Mansfield, PA 16933
Phone: (570) 662-4519
Fax: (570) 662-4111
http://www.mnsfld.edu

Marywood College
Hospitality and Tourism
2300 Adams Avenue
Scranton, PA 18509
Phone: (570) 348-6274
Fax: (570) 961-4762
http://www.marywood.edu/

Mercyhurst College
Hospitality and Tourism
Hotel, Restaurant, and Institutional
    Management Department
501 East 38th Street
Erie, PA 16546
Phone: (814) 824-2356
http://www.mercyhurst.edu

Pennsylvania State University
School of Hotel Restaurant and
    Recreation Management
201 Mateer Building
University Park, PA 16802-6501
Phone: (814) 863-7255
http://www.psu.edu

Robert Morris College
Hospitality Management
Narrows Run Road
Corapolis, PA 15108-1189
Phone: (412) 262-8636
Fax: (412) 262-8494
http://www.Robert-Morris.edu

Temple University
School of Tourism and Hospitality
    Management
112 Pearson Hall (048-00)
Broad Street and Montgomery Avenue

Philadelphia, PA 19122
Phone: (215) 204-6297
Fax: (215) 204-8705
http://www.temple.edu/sthm

Widener University
School of Hospitality Management
One University Place
Chester, PA 19013
Phone: (610) 499-1103
Fax: (610) 499-1106
http://www.widener.edu/hospitality/sohm.
   html

RHODE ISLAND

Johnson and Wales University
Center for International Travel and
   Tourism Studies
8 Abbott Park Place
Providence, RI 02903
Phone: (401) 598-4639
Fax: (401) 598-4764
http://www.jwu.edu

University of Rhode Island
Food Science
17 Woodward Hall
Kingston, RI 02881
Phone: (401) 792-5869
http://www.uri.edu

SOUTH CAROLINA

Clemson University
Parks, Recreation and Tourism
   Management
263 Lehotsky Hall
Clemson, SC 29634-0735
Phone: (864) 656-3400
Fax: (864) 656-2226
http://www.clemson.edu

**Johnson and Wales
   University–Charleston**
701 East Bay Street
Charleston, SC 29403
Phone: (800) 723-3429 or (800) 598-2667
http://www.jwu.edu/charles/index.htm

University of South Carolina
Hotel, Restaurant, and Tourism
   Administration
Institute for Tourism Research
Columbia, SC 29208
Phone: (803) 777-2764
Fax: (803) 777-1224
http://www.hrsm.sc.edu.html

Winthrop College
Food Systems Management

Rock Hill, SC 29733
Phone: (803) 323-2101
http://www.winthrop.edu

SOUTH DAKOTA

Black Hills State University
Hospitality and Tourism
College of Business and Technology
1200 University Street
Spearfish, SD 57799-9106
Phone: (605) 642-6702
Fax: (605) 642-6273
http://www.bhsu.edu

National American University
Hospitality and Tourism
321 Kansas City Street
Rapid City, SD 57709
Phone: (605) 394-4820
http://www.national.edu

TENNESSEE

Belmont University
Hospitality and Tourism
1900 Belmont Boulevard
Nashville, TN 37212-3757
Phone: (615) 460-6000 or (615) 383-7001
http://www.belmont.edu

University of Tennessee
Department of Nutrition
1215 West Cumberland Avenue, Room
   230 JHB
Knoxville, TN 37996-1900
Phone: (865) 974-6831
Fax: (865) 974-5236
http://trcs.he.utk.edu

TEXAS

**Conrad Hilton College of Hotel and
   Restaurant Management**
Hospitality and Tourism
University of Houston
4800 Calhoun Road
Houston, TX 77204-3902
http://www.hrm.uh.edu

Southern Methodist University
Department of Anthropology
Dallas, TX 75275
Phone: (214) 692-2926
http://www.smu.edu

Texas A & M University
Recreation, Parks and Tourism Sciences
2261 Texas A & M University
College Station, TX 77843-2261
Phone: (979) 845-5411

Fax: (979) 845-0446
http://www.rpts.tamu.edu

Texas Tech
Restaurant, Hotel and Institutional
   Management
2500 Broadway
Lubbock, TX 79409-1162
Phone: (409) 845-6454
Fax: (409) 845-0446
http://www.ttu.edu

University of North Texas
Hospitality Management
P.O. Box 311100
Denton, TX 76203
Phone: (940) 369-8207
Fax: (940) 565-4348
http://www.scs.unt.edu/smhm

University of Texas at San Antonio
Tourism Management Program
6900 North Loop 1604 West
San Antonio, TX 78249-0679
Phone: (210) 458-7100
Fax: (210) 458-5783
http://www.utsa.edu

Wiley College
Hotel and Restaurant
711 Rosbourough Springs Road
Marshall, TX 75670
Phone: (214) 938-8341
http://www.wileyc.edu

UTAH

Brigham Young University
Geography Department
690 Spencer W. Kimball Tower
Provo, UT 84602
Phone: (801) 422-3852
http://www.byu.edu

University of Utah
Parks, Recreation and Tourism
   Department
College of Health
1901 E. South Campus Drive, Room
   1085
Salt Lake City, UT 84112
Phone: (801) 581-8542
Fax: (801) 581-4930
http://www.health.utah.edu/prt

Utah Valley State College
Hospitality Management
800 West University Parkway
Orem, UT 84058-5999
Phone: (801) 222-8234
http://www.uvsc.edu

VERMONT

Champlain College
Tourism and Event Management Program
163 South Willard Street
Burlington, VT 05402-0670
Phone: (802) 865-6438
Fax: (802) 860-2763
http://www.champlain.edu/majors/
 hospitality

University of Vermont
Hospitality and Tourism
School of Natural Resources
George B. Aiken Center #357
Burlington, VT 05405
Phone: (802) 656-0652

VIRGINIA

College of William and Mary
Hospitality and Tourism
School of Business Administration
P.O. Box 8795
Williamsburg, VA 23187
Phone: (757) 221-2911
Fax: (757) 221-2937
http://www.wm.edu

James Madison University
Hotel and Restaurant Management
366 Franklin Street
Harrisonburg, VA 22801
Phone: (540) 568-6211
http://www.jmu.edu

George Mason University
Tourism and Events Management
Room 312, PW1, Mail Stop 4E5
10900 University Boulevard
Manassas, VA 20110-2203
Phone: (703) 993-4698
Fax: (703) 998-2025
http://www.gmu.edu/departments/hfrr

Old Dominion University
Recreation and Tourism Studies
Hampton Boulevard
Health and Physical Education Building,
 Room 124
Norfolk, VA 23529
Phone: (757) 683-3000
http://www.odu.edu/recreation

Virginia Commonwealth University
Division of Health, Physical Education
 and Recreation
School of Education
P.O. Box 842037
Richmond, VA 23284-2037

Phone: (804) 828-0100
Fax: (804) 828-1946
http://www.vcu.edu/

Virginia Polytechnic Institute and State University
Hospitality and Tourism
Virginia Tech College of Human
 Resources
351 Wallace Hall
Blacksburg, VA 24061-0462
Phone: (540) 231-5515
Fax: (540) 231-8313
http://www.chre.vt.edu/admin/HTM/htm.
 htm

Virginia State University
Hospitality Management
P.O. Box 9211
Petersburg, VA 23806
Phone: (804) 524-6753
Fax: (804) 524-5048
http://www.vsu.edu

WASHINGTON

Central Washington University
Recreation and Tourism Program
400 East 8th Avenue
Mail Stop 7572
Ellensburg, WA 98926
Phone: (509) 963-1968
Fax: (509) 963-1848
http://www.cwu.edu

University of Washington
Marine Tourism
School of Marine Affairs
3707 Brooklyn Avenue NE
Seattle, WA 98195
Phone: (206) 543-0106
Fax: (206) 543-1417
http://www.sma.washington.edu

Washington State University
Hotel and Restaurant Administration
Todd Addition
P.O. Box 644742
Pullman, WA 99164
Phone: (509) 335-5766
http://www.cbe.wsu.edu/departments/hra/
 index

WEST VIRGINIA

Concord College
Travel and Tourism
Box D-137
Athens, WV 24712
Phone: (888) 344-6679 or (304) 384-5249
http://www.concord.edu

Davis and Elkins College
Hospitality and Tourism
100 Campus Drive
Elkins, WV 26241-3996
Phone: (304) 637-1802
http://www.dne.edu

Fairmont State College
Family Consumer Science
1201 Locust Avenue
Fairmont, WV 26554
Phone: (304) 367-4271
Fax: (304) 367-4587
http://www.fscwv.edu

West Liberty State College
Hospitality and Tourism
Department of Management and
 Administrative Systems
School of Business Administration
P.O. Box 295
West Liberty, WV 26074
Phone: (304) 336-8053 or (800) 732-6204
http://www.wlsc.edu

West Virginia State College
Hospitality Management
Campus Box 183, P.O. Box 1000
Institute, WV 25112-1000
Phone: (304) 766-3213
http://www.wvsc.edu

WISCONSIN

University of Wisconsin
Hospitality and Tourism
Parkside, Center for Survey
P.O. Box 2000
Kenosha, WI 53141
Phone: (414) 553-2105
http://www.uwp.edu

University of Wisconsin-Stout
Department of Hospitality and Tourism
UW-Stout, Home Economics 442
Menomonie, WI 54751
Phone: (715) 232-2339
http://www.uwstout.edu

WYOMING

University of Wyoming
Geography and Recreation
University Station
Laramie, WY 82701
Phone: (307) 766-3311
http://www.uwyo.edu

APPENDIX III
M.A. AND PH.D. PROGRAMS IN TRAVEL, TOURISM, AND HOSPITALITY

A. MASTER'S DEGREE PROGRAMS

ALABAMA

Auburn University
Hotel and Restaurant Management
328 Spidle Hall
Auburn, AL 36849
Phone: (334) 844-1333
Fax: (334) 844-3268
http://www.auburn.edu

ARIZONA

Arizona State University
Hospitality and Tourism
P.O. Box 874905
Tempe, AZ 85287-4905
Phone: (480) 965-7291
Fax: (480) 965-5664
http://www.asu.edu

CALIFORNIA

California State University, Long Beach
Department of Recreation and Leisure Studies
1250 Bellflower Boulevard
Long Beach, CA 90840-4903
Phone: (562) 985-4071
http://www.csulb.edu

California State University, Northridge
Recreation Administration
18111 Nordhoff Street
Northridge, CA 91330-8269
Phone: (818) 677-3202
Fax: (818) 677-2695
http://www.csun.edu

Golden Gate University
Hotel, Restaurant and Tourism Management
536 Mission Street, Room 493
San Francisco, CA 94105
Phone: (415) 442-6508
Fax: (415) 442-7049
http://www.ggu.edu/

COLORADO

Colorado State University
Natural Resource Recreation and Tourism
233 Forestry Building
Fort Collins, CO 80523-1480
Phone: (970) 491-6591
Fax: (970) 491-2255
http://www.cnr.colostate.edu

University of Denver
School of Hotel, Restaurant and Tourism Management
2030 East Evans Avenue
Denver, CO 80208
Phone: (303) 871-4275
Fax: (303) 871-4260
http://www.dcb.du.edu/hrtm

CONNECTICUT

University of New Haven
School of Hospitality and Tourism
Room 223, Harugari Hall
300 Orange Avenue
West Haven, CT 06516
Phone: (203) 932-7412
http://www.newhaven.edu/tourism

DELAWARE

University of Delaware
Hospitality Information Management
321 South College Avenue
Newark, DE 19716
Phone: (302) 831-6077
Fax: (302) 831-6395
http://www.udel.edu/hrim

DISTRICT OF COLUMBIA

George Washington University
Masters of Tourism Administration Program
600 21st Street, NW
Washington, DC 20052
Phone: (202) 994-4456
Fax: (202) 994-1630
http://www.gwutourism.org

FLORIDA

Florida International University
School of Hospitality Management
North Miami Campus HM 215
3000 Northeast 151st Street
North Miami, FL 33181
Phone: (305) 919-4539
Fax: (305) 919-4513
http://www.hospitality.fiu.edu

Florida Metropolitan University/Melbourne
Hospitality and Tourism
2401 North Harbor City Boulevard
Melbourne, FL 32935
Phone: (321) 253-2929
http://www.fmu.edu

Florida State University
Hospitality and Tourism
Dedman School of Hospitality
1 Champions Way, Room 4110
Tallahassee, FL 32306-2541
Phone: (850) 644-8244
Fax: (850) 644-5565
http://www.cob.fsu.edu/ha

Schiller International University
International School of Tourism and Hospitality Management
251 Lyndhurst Street
Dunedin, FL 34698
Phone: (727) 736-5082
Fax: (727) 736-6263
http://www.schiller.edu

University of Central Florida
Rosen School of Hospitality Management
Classroom Building One
Suite 302
Orlando, FL 32816-1450
Phone: (407) 823-2188
Fax: (407) 823-5696
http://www.hospitality.ucf.edu

GEORGIA

Georgia State University
Hospitality and Tourism
Cecil B. Day School of Hospitality
    Administration
35 Broad Street, Suite 1215/ University
    Plaza
Atlanta, GA 30303
Phone: (404) 651-3512
Fax: (404) 651-3670
http://www.robinson.gsu.edu/hospitality

HAWAII

University of Hawaii at Manoa
Hospitality, Tourism and Transportation
2560 Campus Road
Honolulu, HI 96822
Phone: (808) 956-4892
Fax: (808) 956-5378
http://www.tim.hawaii.edu

IDAHO

University of Idaho
Department of Resource Recreation &
    Tourism
975 West Sixth Street
Moscow, ID 83844-1139
Phone: (208) 885-7911 or (888) 884-3246
Fax: (208) 885-6226
http://www.its.uidaho.edu/rrt

ILLINOIS

Western Illinois University
Recreation, Parks and Tourism
    Administration
Currens Hall 400
Macomb, IL 61455
Phone: (309) 298-1967
Fax: (309) 298-2967
http://www.wiu.edu/users/mirpta

INDIANA

Indiana University
Tourism Management
Recreation and Parks Administration
School of Health, Physical Education and
    Recreation
Bloomington, IN 47405-4801
Phone: (812) 855-2672
Fax: (812) 855-3998
http://www.indiana.edu/~hperweb

Purdue University
Department of Hospitality and Tourism
    Management
1266 Stone Hall, Room 106

West Lafayette, IN 47907-1266
Phone: (765) 494-4643
Fax: (765) 494-0327
http://www.cfs.purdue.edu

IOWA

Iowa State University
Hotel and Restaurant Management
11 Mackay Hall
Ames, IA 50011-1120
Phone: (515) 294-1730
Fax: (515) 294-8551
http://www.fcs.iastate.edu/hrim

LOUISIANA

University of Louisiana at Lafayette
Hospitality Management
P.O. Box 40399
Lafayette, LA 70504-0399
Phone: (337) 482-1015
Fax: (337) 482-5395
http://www.louisiana.edu

MASSACHUSETTS

University of Massachusetts
Hotel, Restaurant and Travel
    Administration
107 Flint Lab
Amherst, MA 01003-9247
Phone: (413) 545-4049
Fax: (413) 545-1235
http://www.umass.edu/hrta

MICHIGAN

Michigan State University
School of Hospitality Business
232 Eppley Center
East Lansing, MI 48824
Phone: (517) 355-5080
Fax: (517) 432-1170
http://www.bus.msu.edu/shb

MINNESOTA

St. Cloud State University
Geography Department
720 4th Avenue South
St. Cloud, MN 56301-4498
Phone: (320) 255-2271
Fax: (320) 529-1660
http://www.stcloudstate.edu

MISSISSIPPI

University of Mississippi
Department of Exercise Science and
    Leisure Management

222 Turner Complex
University, MS 38677
Phone: (601) 232-7573
Fax: (601) 232-5525
http://www.olemiss.edu

MISSOURI

University of Missouri–Columbia
Hotel and Restaurant Management
122 Eckles Hall
Columbia, MO 65211
Phone: (573) 882-4114
http://www.missouri.edu

MONTANA

University of Montana
Recreation and Nature-Based Tourism
    Management
32 Campus Drive
Missoula, MT 59812-0576
Phone: (406) 243-5107
Fax: (406) 243-6656
http://www.forestry.umt.edu/degrees/
    undergraduate/rrmgt

NEVADA

University of Nevada Las Vegas
College of Hotel Administration
4505 Maryland Parkway
Las Vegas, NV 89154-6023
Phone: (702) 895-0875
Fax: (702) 895-4870
http://www.unlv.edu/Tourism

University of Nevada Las Vegas
Department of Tourism and Convention
    Administration
William F. Harrah College of Hotel
    Administration
4505 Maryland Parkway, Box 456023
Las Vegas, NV 89154-6023
Phone: (702) 895-3720
Fax: (702) 895-4870
http://www.tca.unlv.edu

NEW JERSEY

Fairleigh Dickinson University
School of Hotel, Restaurant and Tourism
    Management
1000 River Road, H-DH2-I4
Teaneck, NJ 07666-1914
Phone: (201) 692-7271
Fax: (201) 692-7279
http://www.fdu.edu

NEW YORK

Cornell University
School of Hotel Administration
174 Statler Hall
Ithaca, NY 14853-6902
Phone: (607) 255-6376
Fax: (607) 254-5121
http://www.hotelschool.cornell.edu

New York University
Tisch Center for Hospitality, Tourism and
    Travel Administration
10 Astor Place, Suite 504
New York, NY 10003-7154
Phone: (212) 998-9107
Fax: (212) 995-4676
http://www.scps.nyu.edu/tischcenter

NORTH CAROLINA

East Carolina University
Department of Nutrition and Hospitality
    Management
School of Human Environmental
    Sciences
Rivers Building
Greenville, NC 27858-4353
Phone: (252) 328-6917
Fax: (252) 328-4276
http://www.ecu.edu/hes

**University of North Carolina at
    Greensboro**
Recreation, Parks and Tourism
P.O. Box 26169
Greensboro, NC 27402-6169
Phone: (336) 334-3041
Fax: (336) 334-3238
http://www.uncg.edu/rpt

OHIO

Ohio State University
Hospitality Management
2914 Granada Hills Drive
Columbus, OH 43231
Phone: (614) 292-5034
http://www.osu.edu

OKLAHOMA

Oklahoma State University
School of Hotel and Restaurant
    Administration
210 Human Environmental Services West
Stillwater, OK 74078
Phone: (405) 744-6713
Fax: (405) 744-6299
http://www.osuhrad.org

PENNSYLVANIA

Pennsylvania State University
School of Hotel, Restaurant and
    Recreation Management
201 Mateer Building
University Park, PA 16802-6501
Phone: (814) 863-7255

Robert Morris College
Hospitality Management
Narrows Run Road
Corapolis, PA 15108-1189
Phone: (412) 262-8636
Fax: (412) 262-8494
http://www.Robert-Morris.edu

Temple University
School of Tourism and Hospitality
    Management
1801 North Broad Street
Philadelphia, PA 19122
Phone: (215) 204-8701
Fax: (215) 204-8705
http://www.temple.edu/sthm

Widener University
School of Hospitality Management
One University Place
Chester, PA 19013
Phone: (610) 499-1103
Fax: (610) 499-1106
http://www.widener.edu/hospitality/sohm

SOUTH CAROLINA

Clemson University
Parks, Recreation and Tourism
    Management
263 Lehotsky Hall
Clemson, SC 29634-0735
Phone: (864) 656-3400
Fax: (864) 656-2226
http://www.clemson.edu

University of South Carolina
Hotel, Restaurant, and Tourism
    Administration
Institute for Tourism Research
Columbia, SC 29208
Phone: (803) 777-2764
Fax: (803) 777-1224
http://www.sc.edu

SOUTH DAKOTA

Black Hills State University
Hospitality and Tourism
College of Business and Technology
1200 University Street

Spearfish, SD 57799-9106
Phone: (605) 642-6702
Fax: (605) 642-6273
http://www.bhsu.edu

TENNESSEE

University of Tennessee
Department of Nutrition
1215 West Cumberland Avenue, Room
    230 JHB
Knoxville, TN 37996-1900
Phone: (865) 974-6831
Fax: (865) 974-5236
http://trcs.he.utk.edu

TEXAS

Texas A&M University
Recreation, Park and Tourism Sciences
2261 Texas A&M University
College Station, TX 77843-2261
Phone: (979) 845-5411
Fax: (979) 845-0446
http://www.rpts.tamu.edu

Texas Tech University
Education, Nutrition and
    Restaurant/Hotel Management
Box 41162
2500 Broadway
Lubbock, TX 79409-1162
Phone: (806) 742-3068
Fax: (806) 742-3042
http://www.hs.ttu.edu/enrhm

University of Houston
Conrad N. Hilton College of Hotel and
    Restaurant Management
229 Conrad N. Hilton Hotel and College
Houston, TX 77204-3902
Phone: (713) 743-2408
Fax: (713) 743-2581
http://www.hrm.uh.edu

University of North Texas
Hospitality Management
P.O. Box 311100
Denton, TX 76203
Phone: (940) 369-8207
Fax: (940) 565-4348
http://www.scs.unt.edu/smhm

UTAH

University of Utah
Parks, Recreation and Tourism
    Department
College of Health

1901 E. South Campus Drive, Room
    1085
Salt Lake City, UT 84112
Phone: (801) 581-8542
Fax: (801) 581-4930
http://www.health.utah.edu/prt

VERMONT

University of Vermont
Hospitality and Tourism
School of Natural Resources
George B. Aiken Center #357
Burlington, VT 05405
Phone: (802) 656-0652
http://www.uvm.edu

VIRGINIA

Old Dominion University
Recreation and Tourism Studies

Hampton Boulevard
Health and Physical Education Building,
    Room 124
Norfolk, VA 23529
Phone: (757) 683-3000
http://www.odu.edu/recreation

Virginia Commonwealth University
Division of Health, Physical Education,
    and Recreation
School of Education
P.O. Box 842037
Richmond, VA 23284-2037
Phone: (804) 828-1948
Fax: (804) 828-1946
http://www.vcu.edu

**Virginia Polytechnic Institute and State
    University**
Hospitality and Tourism

Virginia Tech College of Human
    Resources
351 Wallace Hall
Blacksburg, VA 24061-0462
Phone: (540) 231-5515
Fax: (540) 231-8313
http://www.chre.vt.edu/admin

WISCONSIN

University of Wisconsin–Stout
Department of Hospitality and Tourism
College of Human Development
415 Home Economics Building
Menomonie, WI 54751-0790
Phone: (715) 232-2089
Fax: (715) 232-2588
http://www.uwstout.edu

B. DOCTORAL DEGREE PROGRAMS

ALABAMA

Auburn University
Hotel and Restaurant Management
328 Spidle Hall
Auburn, AL 36849
Phone: (334) 844-1333
Fax: (334) 844-3268
http://www.auburn.edu

CALIFORNIA

California State University, Long Beach
Department of Recreation and Leisure
    Studies
1250 Bellflower Boulevard
Long Beach, CA 90840-4903
Phone: (562) 985-4071
http://www.csulb.edu

COLORADO

Colorado State University
Natural Resource Recreation and Tourism
Colorado State University
Fort Collins, CO 80523-1480
Phone: (970) 491-6591
Fax: (970) 491-2255
http://www.cnr.colostate.edu

DISTRICT OF COLUMBIA

George Washington University
Masters of Tourism Administration
    Program

600 21st Street, NW
Washington, D.C. 20052
Phone: (202) 994-8740
Fax: (202) 994-1630
http://www.gwutourism.org

IDAHO

University of Idaho
Department of Resource Recreation and
    Tourism
P.O. Box 441139
Moscow, ID 83844-1139
Phone: (208) 885-7911
Fax: (208) 885-6226
http://www.its.uidaho.edu/rrt

INDIANA

Indiana University
Tourism Management
Recreation and Park Administration
School of Health, Physical Education and
    Recreation
Bloomington, IN 47405-4801
Phone: (812) 855-2672
Fax: (812) 855-3998
http://www.indiana.edu

Purdue University
Department of Hospitality and Tourism
    Management
1266 Stone Hall, Room 106
West Lafayette, IN 47907-1266

Phone: (765) 494-4643
Fax: (765) 494-0327
http://www.cfs.purdue.edu

IOWA

Iowa State University
Hotel and Restaurant Management
11 Mackay Hall
Ames, IA 50011-1120
Phone: (515) 294-1730
Fax: (515) 294-8551
http://www.fcs.iastate.edu/hrim

KANSAS

Kansas State University
Hotel and Restaurant Management
103 Justin Hall
Department of Hotel, Restaurant,
    Institution Management and Dietetics
Manhattan, KS 66506-1404
Phone: (785) 532-2210
http://www.ksu.edu

MISSISSIPPI

University of Southern Mississippi
Department of Hospitality Management
155 Madison Place
Hattiesburg, MS 39402
Phone: (601) 266-6762
Fax: (601) 266-6707
http://www.usm.edu

MONTANA

University of Montana
Recreation and Nature-Based Tourism
    Management
32 Campus Drive
Missoula, MT 59812-0576
Phone: (406) 243-5107
Fax: (406) 243-6656
http://www.forestry.umt.edu/degrees/
    undergraduate/rrmgt

NEVADA

University of Nevada Las Vegas
Department of Tourism and Convention
    Administration
William F. Harrah College of Hotel
    Administration
4505 Maryland Parkway
P.O. Box 456023
Las Vegas, NV 89154-6023
Phone: (702) 895-3930
Fax: (702) 895-4870
http://www.unlv.edu/Tourism

NEW YORK

Cornell University
School of Hotel Administration
255 Statler Hall
Ithaca, NY 14853-6902
Phone: (607) 255-3932
Fax: (607) 255-9540
http://www.hotelschool.cornell.edu

OKLAHOMA

Oklahoma State University
School of Hotel and Restaurant
    Administration
210 Human Environmental Studies West
Stillwater, OK 74078

Phone: (405) 744-6713
Fax: (405) 744-6299
http://www.osuhrad.org

PENNSYLVANIA

Pennsylvania State University
School of Hotel, Restaurant and
    Institutional Management
201 Mateer Building
University Park, PA 16802-6501
Phone: (814) 863-7255
http://www.psu.edu

SOUTH CAROLINA

Clemson University
Parks, Recreation and Tourism
    Management
263 Lehotsky Hall
Clemson, SC 29634-0735
Phone: (864) 656-3400
Fax: (864) 656-2226
http://www.clemson.edu

TENNESSEE

University of Tennessee
Department of Nutrition
1215 West Cumberland Avenue, Room
    230
Knoxville, TN 37996-1900
Phone: (865) 974-2141
Fax: (865) 974-5236
http://www.utk.edu

TEXAS

Texas A&M University
Recreation, Parks and Tourism Sciences
2261 Texas A&M University
College Station, TX 77843-2261

Phone: (979) 845-5411
Fax: (979) 845-0446
http://www.rpts.tamu.edu

Texas Tech University
Restaurant/Hotel Institutional Management
506 Human Science Building
Lubbock, TX 79409-1162
Phone: (806) 742-3068
Fax: (806) 742-3042
E-mail: betty.stout@ttu.edu
http://www.hs.ttu.edu/enhrm/rhim

UTAH

University of Utah
Parks, Recreation and Tourism Department
190 E. South Campus Drive, Room 1085
Salt Lake City, UT 84112
Phone: (801) 581-8542
Fax: (801) 581-4930
http://www.health.utah.edu/prt

VIRGINIA

**Virginia Polytechnic Institute and State
    University**
Hospitality and Tourism
Virginia Tech College of Human
    Resources
351 Wallace Hall
Blacksburg, VA 24061-0462
Phone: (540) 231-5515
Fax: (540) 231-8313
http://www.chre.vt.edu/admin

APPENDIX IV
CERTIFICATE PROGRAMS IN TRAVEL, TOURISM, AND HOSPITALITY

ARIZONA

American Express Travel School
Hospitality and Tourism
3600 East University, Building G, Suite 1220
Phoenix, AZ 85034
Phone: (602) 470-3330
http://www.azohwy.com/h/hx103972.htm

Central Arizona College
Hotel and Restaurant Management
8470 North Overfield Road
Coolidge, AZ 85228
Phone: (520) 426-4403
http://www.cac.cc.az.us

Northern Arizona University
P.O. Box 5638
Flagstaff, AZ 86011-5638
Phone: (928) 523-1705
Fax: (928) 523-5233
http://www.nau.edu/hrm

Pima Community College
Hospitality and Tourism
1255 North Stone Avenue
Tucson, AZ 85709-3030
Phone: (520) 206-6278
Fax: (520) 206-6162
http://www.dtc.pima.edu

ARKANSAS

Garland County Community College
Hospitality and Tourism
101 College Drive
Hot Springs, AR 71913
Phone: (501) 760-4155 or (501) 760-4100
http://www.gccc.cc.ar.us

CALIFORNIA

Butte Community College
Tourism and Travel Department
3536 Butte Campus Drive
Oroville, CA 95965-8303
Phone: (530) 895-2396
Fax: (530) 895-2411
http://www.butte.cc.ca.us

California State University, Long Beach
Recreation and Leisure Studies
Department of Family and Consumer Sciences
Long Beach, CA 90840-4903
Phone: (562) 985-4071
http://www.csulb.edu/

Carmel Unified School District
Hospitality and Tourism
P.O. Box 222780
Carmel, CA 93922
Phone: (408) 624-3544

Coastline Community College
Travel and Tourism Department, Costa Mesa Center
2990 Mesa Verde Drive, East
Costa Mesa, CA 92626
Phone: (714) 241-6213
Fax: (714) 751-3806
http://www.coastline.cccd.edu

Foothill College
Travel Careers Program
12345 El Monte Road
Los Altos Hills, CA 94022-4599
Phone: (650) 949-7263
Fax: (650) 949-7287
http://bss.foothill.fhda.edu/tc/

Long Beach City College
Hospitality and Tourism
4901 East Carson Street
Long Beach, CA 90808
Phone: (562) 938-4325
Fax: (562) 938-4118
http://www.lbcc.cc.ca.us

Los Medanos College
Center for Travel Marketing
2700 East Leland Road
Pittsburg, CA 94565
Phone: (925) 439-2181, ext. 3349
Fax: (925) 427-1599
http://www.losmedanos.net/travel

Miracosta College
Hospitality and Tourism

One Barnard Drive
Oceanside, CA 92056-3899
Phone: (760) 757-2121, ext.6404
Fax: (760) 795-6804
http://www.miracosta.edu/Travel

Mission College
Hospitality Management
3000 Mission College Boulevard
Santa Clara, CA 95054
Phone: (408) 855-5252 or (888) 509-7040
Fax: (408) 855-5452
http://www.missioncollege.org/

Palomar College
Hospitality and Tourism
Vocational Programs
1140 West Mission Road
San Marcos, CA 92069
Phone: (760) 744-1150, ext. 2286
Fax: (760) 591-9108
http://www.palomar.edu

San Bernardino Valley College
Hospitality and Tourism
701 South Mt. Vernon Avenue
San Bernardino, CA 92410-2798
Phone: (909) 888-6511
http://sbvc.sbccd.cc.ca.us/sbvc_htm/index.php?page=main.htm

San Diego Mesa College
Hospitality and Tourism
School of Health Science/Public Service
7250 Mesa College Drive
San Diego, CA 92111
Phone: (619) 388-2370
http://www.sdmesa.sdccd.net

San Francisco State University
Hospitality and Tourism
P.O. Box 27188
San Francisco, CA 94127
Phone: (415) 586-6888
http://www.sfsu.edu/

Santa Monica College
Tourism, Hospitality, Leisure Services and College Recreational Activities

1900 Pico Boulevard
Santa Monica, CA 90405-1628
Phone: (310) 434-4315
Fax: (310) 434-3652
http://www.smc.edu

Western College of Travel Careers, Inc.
Hospitality and Tourism
1350 Carlback Avenue, Suite 310
Walnut Creek, CA 94596
Phone: (510) 945-0790

West Los Angeles College
Department of Travel
4800 Freshman Drive
Culver City, CA 90230
Phone: (310) 287-4369
Fax: (310) 841-0396
http://www.wlac.cc.ca.us

COLORADO

Art Institute, School of Culinary Arts
Culinary Department
675 South Broadway
Denver, CO 80209
Phone: (303) 824-4954
Fax: (303) 778-8312
http://www.aic.artinstitutes.edu

CONNECTICUT

American Educational Institute
Hospitality and Tourism
3851 Main Street
Bridgeport, CT 06606
Phone: (203) 371-0088

Gateway Community College
Management Programs
Hospitality and Tourism
60 Sargent Drive
New Haven, CT 06511
Phone: (203) 285-2175
Fax: (203) 285-2180
http://www.gwctc.commnet.edu

Grasso Southeastern Regional Technical School
Hotel Department
189 Fort Hill Road
Groton, CT 06340
Phone: (860) 441-0340
Fax: (860) 446-9895
http://www.cttech.org/grasso/index.htm

Huntington Institute
Hospitality and Tourism
193 Broadway

Norwich, CT 06360
Phone: (203) 886-0507

International College of Hospitality Management
Hospitality Management
101 Wykeham Road
Washington, CT 06793
Phone: (860) 868-9555 or (800) 955-0809
Fax: (860) 868-2114
http://www.ichm.ritz.edu

Norwalk Community College
Hospitality and Tourism
188 Richards Avenue
Norwalk, CT 06854-1655
Phone: (203) 857-7355
Fax: (203) 857-3327
http://www.nctc.commnet.edu

Stone Academy
Hospitality and Tourism
1315 Dixwell Avenue
Hamden, CT 06514-4136
Phone: (203) 288-7474
Fax: (203) 288-8869

DISTRICT OF COLUMBIA

George Washington University
Masters in Tourism Administration Program
600 21st Street, NW
Washington, DC 20052
Phone: (202) 994-8740
Fax: (202) 994-1630
http://www.gwutourism.org

FLORIDA

Broward Community College
Hospitality and Tourism
3501 Southwest Davie Road
Ft. Lauderdale, FL 33314
Phone: (954) 475-6710
Fax: (954) 475-6594
http://www.broward.edu/

Florida Community College at Jacksonville
Hotel and Restaurant/Travel Agency Operations
4501 Capper Road
Jacksonville, FL 32218
Phone: (904) 766-6603
Fax: (904) 766-6654
http://www.fccj.org

Florida International University
School of Hospitality Management

North Miami Campus HM 215
3000 Northeast 151st Street
North Miami, FL 33181
Phone: (305) 919-4539
Fax: (305) 919-4513
http://www.hospitality.fiu.edu

Keiser College
Travel and Hospitality
1500 Northwest 49th Street
Ft. Lauderdale, FL 33309
Phone: (954) 776-4456
Fax: (954) 489-2974
http://www.keisercollege.cc.fl.us

Miami-Dade Community College
Hospitality Management
300 Northeast Second Avenue, Room 3704
Miami, FL 33132-2297
Phone: (305) 237-3044
Fax: (305) 237-7074
http://www.mdcc.edu

Mid-Florida Tech
Travel and Tourism
2900 West Oakridge Road
Orlando, FL 32809
Phone: (407) 855-5880, ext. 2282
Fax: (407) 251-6009
http://www.mft.ocps.k12.fl.us/traveltour.htm

Southeast Institute of Culinary Arts
Culinary Arts
St. Augustine Technical Center
2980 Collins Avenue
St. Augustine, FL 32084
Phone: (904) 824-4401

GEORGIA

Georgia State University
Hospitality and Tourism
Cecil B. Day School of Hospitality Administration
35 Broad Street, Suite 1215
University Plaza
Atlanta, GA 30303
Phone: (404) 651-3512
Fax: (404) 651-3670
http://www.robinson.qsu.edu/hospitality

HAWAII

Brigham Young University–Hawaii
Hospitality and Tourism
55220 Kulanuist Street
Laie, HI 96762

Phone: (808) 293-3591
http://www.byuh.edu/

Kapiolani Community College
Food Service and Hospitality Education
4303 Diamond Head Road
Honolulu, HI 96816
Phone: (808) 734-9716
Fax: (808) 734-9212
http://www.kcc.hawaii.edu

Travel Institute of the Pacific
Hospitality and Tourism
1314 South King Street, Suite 1164
Honolulu, HI 96814
Phone: (808) 531-2708
http://www.tiphawaii.com

Travel University International
Hospitality and Tourism
Ala Moana Building, Suite 2000
1441 Kapiolani Boulevard
Honolulu, HI 96814
Phone: (808) 946-3535
Fax: (808) 942-1660
http://www.traveluniversity.edu

ILLINOIS

College of Dupage
Travel and Tourism
425 Fawell Boulevard
Glen Ellyn, IL 60137-6599
Phone: (630) 942-2556
Fax: (630) 858-7263
http://www.cod.edu

Elgin Community College
Hospitality and Tourism
1700 Spartan Drive
Elgin, IL 60123
Phone: (847) 697-1000
http://www.elgin.edu/

Harper College
Travel Academy
1375 South Wolf Road
Prospect Heights, IL 60070
Phone: (847) 925-6009
Fax: (847) 925-6020
http://www.harpercollege.com

Joliet Junior College
Hotel, Restaurant and Food Service
    Management
214 North Ohawa Street
Joliet, IL 60431
http://www.jjc.cc.il.us/

Kendall College
2408 Orrington Avenue
Evanston, IL 60201
Phone: (847) 866-1304 or (877) 588-8860
Fax: (847) 733-7450
http://www.kendall.edu

Parkland College
Hospitality Industry
2400 West Bradley Avenue
Champaign, IL 61821
Phone: (800) 346-8089
Fax: (217) 373-3896
http://www.parkland.cc.il.us

William Rainey Harper College
Hospitality Management
1200 West Algonquin Road
Palatine, IL 60067-7398
Phone: (847) 925-6874
Fax: (847) 925-6057
http://www.harpercollege.edu/

INDIANA

**Indiana University Purdue University
    Indianapolis**
Tourism, Conventions and Event
    Management
901 West New York Street
Indianapolis, IN 46202
Phone: (317) 274-7649
Fax: (317) 278-2041
http://www.iupui.edu/~indyhper

IOWA

Hamilton Business College
Hospitality and Tourism
1924 D Street, SW
Cedar Rapids, IA 52404
Phone: (319) 363-0481
http://www.hamiltonia.edu/

Iowa Western Community College
2700 College Road, A013
Council Bluffs, IA 51503
Phone: (712) 325-3378 or (800) 452-
    5852, ext. 3378
http://www.iwcc.edu

Kaplan College
Hospitality and Tourism
Travel Department
1807 East Kimberly Road
Davenport, IA 52807
Phone: (563) 355-3500
Fax: (563) 355-1320

KENTUCKY

Sullivan College–Louisville
Hospitality and Tourism
3101 Bardstown Road
Louisville, KY 40205
Phone: (502) 456-6504

Sullivan University–Lexington
Hospitality and Tourism
2355 Harrodsburg Road
Lexington, KY 40504
Phone: (859) 276-4357

LOUISIANA

Cameron College
Hospitality and Tourism
P.O. Box 19288
New Orleans, LA 70179
Phone: (504) 821-5881
http://www.cameroncollege.com/

Delgado Community College
Culinary Arts/Occupational Studies
Building 11
615 City Park Avenue
New Orleans, LA 70119-4399
Phone: (504) 483-4208
http://www.dcc.edu

MAINE

Andover College
Travel and Tourism
901 Washington Avenue
Portland, ME 04103
Phone: (207) 774-6126
Fax: (207) 774-1715
http://www.andovercollege.com

MARYLAND

Chesapeake College
P.O. Box 8
Wye Mills, MD 21679
Phone: (410) 822-5400, ext. 234
Fax: (410) 827-9222
http://www.chesapeake.edu/

Essex Community College
HMRC Department
7201 Roseville Road
Baltimore, MD 21237
Phone: (301) 522-1456
http://www.ccbc.cc.md.us/essex

MASSACHUSETTS

Massachusetts Bay Community College
Business and Management
    Department/Tourism

50 Oakland Street
Wellesley, MA 02481
Phone: (781) 239-2207
Fax: (781) 416-1607
http://www.mbcc.mass.edu

Massasoit Community College
Travel and Tourism Department
One Massasoit Boulevard
Brockton, MA 02302
Phone: (508) 588-9100
Fax: (508) 497-1250
http://www.massasoit.mass.edu

Quinsigamond Community College
Travel Agent Training
670 West Boylston Street
Worcester, MA 01606-2031
Phone: (508) 853-2300
http://www.qcc.mass.edu/

MICHIGAN

Ferris State University
Hospitality and Tourism
106 West Commons
1319 Cramer Drive
Big Rapids, MI 49307-2736
Phone: (231) 591-2382
Fax: (231) 591-2998
http://www.ferris.edu

Jackson Community College
Hospitality Management
2111 Emmons Road
Jackson, MI 49201
Phone: (517) 787-0800
http://www.jackson.cc.mi.us/

Lansing Community College
Hospitality and Travel/Tourism
P.O. Box 40010
Lansing, MI 48901-7210
Phone: (517) 483-1542
Fax: (517 483-1535
http://www.lansing.cc.mi.us

Northern Michigan University
Culinary Arts
1401 Presque Isle Avenue
Marquette, MI 49855
Phone: (906) 227-1544 or (800) 682-9797
http://www.nmu.edu/

MINNESOTA

Central Lakes College
Travel Planning Program
501 West College Drive
Brainerd, MN 56401-4096

Phone: (800) 933-0346
http://www.clc.mnscu.edu/

Dakota City Technical College
Travel and Tourism Program
1300 East 145th Street
Rosemount, MN 55068-2932
Phone: (651) 423-8397
Fax: (651) 423-8558
http://www.dctc.mnscu.edu

Rasmussen Business College
Travel and Tourism Department
12450 Wayzata Boulevard
Minnetonka, MN 55343
Phone: (952) 545-2000 or (800) 852-0929
http://www.rasmussen.edu/

MISSOURI

Patricia Stevens College
Hospitality and Tourism
1415 Olive Street
St. Louis, MO 63103
Phone: (314) 421-0949
http://www.patriciastevenscollege.com/

MONTANA

Flathead Valley Community College
Hospitality Management
777 Grandview
Kalispell, MT 59901
Phone: (406) 756-3862
Fax: (406) 756-3351
http://www.fvcc.cc.mt.us

NEBRASKA

Central Community College
Hospitality and Tourism
P.O. Box 1024
Hastings, NE 68902
Phone: (402) 461-2458
Fax: (402) 461-2506
http://www.cccneb.edu

NEVADA

Community College of Southern Nevada
Travel and Tourism
Department of Resorts and Gaming, Z-1A
3200 East Cheyenne Avenue
North Las Vegas, NV 89030
Phone: (702) 651-4827
Fax: (702) 651-4558
http://www.ccsn.nevada.edu

University of Nevada Las Vegas
Department of Tourism and Convention
   Administration
William F. Harrah College of Hotel
   Administration
4505 Maryland Parkway, Box 456023
Las Vegas, NV 89154-6023
Phone: (702) 895-3930
Fax: (702) 895-4870
http://www.unlv.edu/Tourism

NEW JERSEY

Atlantic Cape Community College
Hospitality Management
5100 Black Horse Pike
Mays Landing, NJ 08330
Phone: (609) 343-4972
Fax: (609) 343-5122
http://www.atlantic.edu

Bergen Community College
Travel and Tourism
400 Paramus Road
Paramus, NJ 07652-1595
Phone: (201) 447-0525
Fax: (973) 423-3776
www.bergen.edu

Hudson Valley Community College
Culinary Arts Institute
161 Newkirk Street
Jersey City, NJ 07306
Phone: (201) 714-2193
Fax: (201) 656-1522
http://www.hudson.cc.nj.us

Mercer County Community College
Hospitality and Tourism
1200 Old Trenton Road
Trenton, NJ 08690
Phone: (609) 586-4800, ext. 3436
Fax: (609) 586-5602
http://www.mccc.edu

NEW YORK

American Institute of Tourism
1001 Avenue of the Americas, 11th Floor
New York, NY 10018
Phone: (646) 366-8500
Fax: (646) 366-8505
http://www.nitgroup.com

French Culinary Institute
462 Broadway
New York, NY 10013
http://www.frenchculinary.com/

Jefferson Community College
Hospitality and Tourism
Outer Coffeen Street
Watertown, NY 13601
Phone: (315) 646-1420
http://www.sunyjefferson.edu/

New York University
Tisch Center for Hospitality, Tourism and
    Travel Administration
10 Astor Place, Suite 504
New York, NY 10003-7154
Phone: (212) 998-9107
Fax: (212) 995-4676
http://www.scps.nyu.edu/tischcenter

**Ridley-Lowell Business & Technology
    Institute**
Hospitality and Tourism
116 Front Street
Binghamton, NY 13905
Phone: (607) 724-2941
Fax: (607) 724-0799
http://www.ridley.edu

**Schenectady County Community
    College**
Hospitality and Tourism
78 Washington Avenue
Schenectady, NY 12305
Phone: (518) 381-1200
Fax: (518) 346-0379
http://www.sunysccc.edu

Suffolk Community College
Hospitality and Tourism
Crooked Hill Road
Brentwood, NY 11717-1092
Phone: (516) 851-6848
Fax: (516) 851-6340
http://www.sunysuffolk.edu

Sullivan County Community College
Department of Travel and Tourism
P.O. Box 269
Loch Sheldrake, NY 12759
Phone: (914) 434-5750
Fax: (914) 434-4806
http://www.sullivan.suny.edu

NORTH CAROLINA

**Asheville-Buncombe Technical
    Community College**
Hospitality Education
340 Victoria Road
Asheville, NC 28801
Phone: (828) 254-1921
http://www.asheville.cc.nc.us

Blue Ridge Community College
Travel and Tourism Department
College Drive
Flat Rock, NC 28731
Phone: (828) 692-3572, ext. 257
Fax: (828) 692-2441
http://www.blueridge.cc.nc.us

Cape Fear Community College
Hotel/Restaurant Management
411 North Front Street
Wilmington, NC 28401-3993
Phone: (410) 362-7072
Fax: (910) 362-7497
http://cfcc.net/

Central Piedmont Community College
Hospitality and Tourism
P.O. Box 35009
Charlotte, NC 28235-5009
Phone: (704) 330-4639
Fax: (704) 330-4637
http://www.cpcc.edu

OHIO

Columbus State Community College
Hospitality Management Department
550 East Spring Street
P.O. Box 1609
Columbus, OH 43216
Phone: (614) 287-5126
Fax: (614) 287-5973
E-mail: msteiska@cscc.edu
http://www.cscc.edu

Ohio University
Travel and Tourism
Southern Campus
1804 Liberty Avenue
Ironton, OH 45638
Phone: (740) 533-4559
Fax: (740) 533-4590
http://web2.southern.ohiou.edu/tat

OKLAHOMA

Demarge College
Hospitality and Tourism
9301 South Western
Oklahoma City, OK 73139
Phone: (405) 947-1425
http://www.demarge.edu/

OREGON

Chemeketa Community College
Hospitality and Tourism
P.O. Box 14007

Salem, OR 97309
http://www.chemek.cc.or.us/

Mt. Hood Community College
Hospitality and Tourism
26000 Southeast Stark Street
Gresham, OR 97030
Phone: (503) 491-7486
Fax: (503) 491-7618
http://www.mhcc.edu/

Western Culinary Institute
Hospitality and Tourism
1316 Southwest 13th Avenue
Portland, OR 97201
Phone: (800) 666-0312
http://www.westernculinary.com

PENNSYLVANIA

Harrisburg Area Community College
Hospitality and Tourism
One HACC Drive
Harrisburg, PA 17110-2999
Phone: (717) 780-2495
Fax: (717) 231-7670
http://www.hacc.edu

Mercyhurst College
Hospitality and Tourism
Hotel, Restaurant and Institutional
    Management
501 East 38th Street
Erie, PA 16546
Phone: (800) 825-1926
http://www.mercyhurst.edu

Northampton Community College
Hospitality and Tourism
3835 Green Pond Road
Bethlehem, PA 18017-7568
Phone: (610) 861-5357
Fax: (610) 691-8489
http://www.northampton.edu

**Restaurant School at Walnut Hill
    College**
4207 Walnut Street
Philadelphia, PA 19104
Phone: (215) 222-4200 or (877) 925-
    6994
Fax: (215) 222-4219
http://www.therestaurantschool.com

York Technical Institute
Travel/Tourism
1405 Williams Road
York, PA 17402
Phone: (717) 757-1100

Fax: (717) 757-4964
http://www.yti.edu

SOUTH CAROLINA

Technical College of the Lowcountry
921 South Ribault Road
P.O. Box 1288
Beaufort, SC 29901-1288
Phone: (843) 525-8235
Fax: (843) 525-8330
http://www.tcl-tec-sc-us.org

TENNESSEE

Belmont University
Hospitality and Tourism
1900 Belmont Boulevard
Nashville, TN 37212-3757
Phone: (615) 460-6000
Fax: (615) 383-7001
http://www.belmont.edu

TEXAS

American Airlines Travel Academy
Hospitality and Tourism
P.O. Box 155391
Fort Worth, TX 76155-5391
Phone: (817) 963-3480

Del Mar College
Department of Hospitality Management
101 Baldwin Boulevard
West Campus
Corpus Christi, TX 78404-3897
Phone: (361) 698-1734 or (800) 652-3357
Fax: (361) 698-1829
http://www.delmar.edu

El Paso Community College
Hospitality and Travel Services
P.O. Box 20500
El Paso, TX 79998
Phone: (915) 831-2217
Fax: (915) 831-2155
http://www.epcc.edu

Richland College
Hospitality and Tourism
12800 Abrams Road
Dallas, TX 75243-2199
Phone: (972) 238-6106
http://www.rlc.dcccd.edu

Richland College
Travel, Exposition, and Meeting
   Management

12800 Abrams Road, Room S-230
Dallas, TX 75243-2199
Phone: (972) 238-6097
Fax: (972) 238-6333
http://www.rlc.dcccd.edu

Tarrant County College
Hospitality Management, Culinary Arts,
   Dietetics
2100 Southeast Parkway
Arlington, TX 76018
Phone: (817) 515-3608
Fax: (817) 515-3172
http://www.tccd.net

Texas A&M University
Recreation, Park and Tourism Sciences
2261 Texas A&M University
College Station, TX 77843-2261
Phone: (979) 845-5411
Fax: (979) 845-0446
http://www.rpts.tamu.edu

Texas State Technical College–Waco
Food Service/Culinary Arts
3801 Campus Drive
Waco, TX 76705
Phone: (245) 867-4868 or (800) 792-
   8784
http://www.waco.tstc.edu

UTAH

Utah Valley State College
Hospitality Management
800 West University Parkway
Orem, UT 84058-5999
Phone: (801) 222-8234
http://www.uvsc.edu

VIRGINIA

Northern Virginia Community College
Hospitality and Tourism
Annandale Campus
8333 Little River Turnpike
Annandale, VA 22003
Phone: (703) 323-3457
http://www.nv.cc.va.us

Tidewater Community College
Hospitality Management
1700 College Crescent
Virginia Beach, VA 23456
Phone: (757) 321-7173
Fax: (757) 468-3077
http://www.tc.cc.va.us

WASHINGTON

Bellingham Technical College
Hospitality and Tourism
3028 Lindbergh Avenue
Bellingham, WA 98225
Phone: (360) 738-3105
http://www.beltc.ctc.edu

Clover Park Technical College
Hospitality and Tourism
4500 Stellacoom Boulevard, SW
Tacoma, WA 98499-4098
Phone: (253) 589-5649
Fax: (253) 589-5849
http://www.cptc.ctc.edu

Seattle Central Community College
Culinary Arts/Hospitality
1701 Broadway
Seattle, WA 98122
Phone: (206) 344-4310
Fax: (206) 587-3868
http://www.seattlecentral.com

Washington State University
Hotel and Restaurant Administration
P.O. Box 644756
Pullman, WA 99165
Phone: (509) 335-5766 or (888) 585-5433
http://www.cbe.wsu.edu/departments/hra/
   index.html

WISCONSIN

Madison Area Technical College
Business Technology, Culinary Trades
   and Leisure Services
3550 Anderson Street
Madison, WI 53704-2599
Phone: (608) 243-4455
Fax: (608) 246-6316
http://www.matcmadison.edu

Milwaukee Area Technical College
Hospitality and Tourism
700 West State Street
Milwaukee, WI 53233
Phone: (414) 297-6600
http://www.milwaukee.tec.wi.us

Waukesha County Tech College
Hospitality and Tourism
800 Main Street
Pewaukee, WI 53072
Phone: (414) 691-5322
Fax: (262) 691-5254
http://www.waukesha.tec.wi.us

APPENDIX V
PROFESSIONAL ASSOCIATIONS AND UNIONS

Accessible Journeys
35 West Sellers Avenue
Ridley Park, PA 19078
Phone: (610) 521-0339 or (800) 846-4537
Fax: (610) 521-6959
http://www.disabilitytravel.com

Actors Equity
165 West 46th Street
New York, NY 10036
Phone: (212) 869-8530
Fax: (212) 719-9815
http://www.actorsequity.org

Aerobics and Fitness Association of America
15250 Ventura Boulevard, Suite 200
Sherman Oaks, CA 91403
Phone: (818) 905-0040; or (800) 225-2322
Fax: (818) 990-5468
http://www.afaa.com

Air Couriers Association
350 Indiana Street, Suite 300
Golden, CO 80401
Phone: (800) 282-1202
http://www.aircourier.org

Aircraft Mechanics Fraternal Association
P.O. Box 1221
Laconia, NH 03247-1221
Phone: (800) 520-2632
Fax: (603) 524-1331
http://www.the-mechanic.com/amfapages

Air Line Pilots Association International
535 Herndon Parkway
Herndon, VA 20170
Phone: (703) 689-2270
http://www.alpa.org

Airline Professionals Association
Teamsters Local 1224
2754 Old State Route 73
Wilmington, OH 45177
Phone: (937) 383-2500

Fax: (937) 383-0902
http://www.apa1224.org

Airline Reporting Corporation
1530 Wilson Boulevard, Suite 800
Arlington, VA 22209-2448
Phone: (703) 816-8000
Fax: (703) 816-8104
http://www.arccorp.com

Airport Consultants Council
908 King Street, Suite 100
Alexandria, VA 22314
Phone: (703) 683-5908
Fax: (703) 683-2564
http://www.acconline.org

Airport Ground Transportation Association
8001 National Bridge Road
St. Louis, MO 63121-4499
Phone (314) 516-7271
Fax: (314) 516 7272
http://agtaweb.org

Airports Council International
1775 K Street, NW, Suite 500
Washington, DC 20006
Phone: (202) 293-8500
Fax: (202) 331-1362
http://www.aci-na.org

Air Transport Association of America
1301 Pennsylvania Avenue, NW, Suite 1110
Washington, DC 20006
Phone: (202) 626-4000
http://www.airlines.org

Allied Pilots Association
14600 Trinity Boulevard
O'Connell Building, Suite 500
Fort Worth, TX 76155-2512
Phone: (817) 302-2272
http://www.alliedpilots.org

Amalgamated Transit Union
5025 Wisconsin Avenue, NW
Washington, D.C. 20016-4139

Phone: (202) 537-1645
Fax: (202) 244-7824
http://www.atu.org

American Academy of Physician Assistants Information Center
950 North Washington Street
Alexandria, VA 22314-1552
Phone: (703) 836-2272
Fax: (703) 684-1924
http://www.aapa.org

American Advertising Federation
1101 Vermont Avenue, NW, Suite 500
Washington, DC 20005-6306
Phone: (202) 898-0089
Fax: (202) 898-0159
http://www.aaf.org

American Assembly of Collegiate Schools of Business
600 Emerson Road, Suite 300
St. Louis, MO 63141-6762
Phone: (314) 872-8461
Fax: (314) 872-8495
http://www.aacsb.edu

American Association of Advertising Agencies
405 Lexington Avenue, 18th Floor
New York, NY 10174-1801
Phone: (212) 682-2500
Fax: (212) 682-8391
http://www.aaaa.org

American Association of Airport Executives
601 Madison Street
Alexandria, VA 22314
Phone: (703) 824-0500
Fax: (703) 820-1395
http://www.airportnet.org

American Association of Medical Assistants
20 North Wacker Drive, Suite 1575
Chicago, IL 60606-2903
Phone: (312) 899-1500
http://www.aama-ntl.org

American Association of Zoo Keepers
3601 Southwest 29th, Suite 133
Topeka, KS 66614
Phone: (785) 273-9149
http://www.aazk.org

American Astronomical Society
2000 Florida Avenue, NW, Suite 400
Washington, DC 20009-1231
Phone: (202) 328-2010
Fax: (202) 234-2560
http://www.aas.org

American Bar Association
750 North Lake Shore Drive
Chicago, IL 60611
Phone: (312) 988-5000
http://www.abanet.org

American Bus Association
1100 New York Avenue, NW
Washington, DC 20005-3934
Phone: (202) 842-1645
Fax: (202) 842-0850
http://www.buses.org

American Camping Association
5000 State Road 67 North
Martinsville, IN 46151
Phone: (765) 342-8456
http://www.acacamps.org

American College of Emergency Physicians
1125 Executive Circle
Irving, TX 75038-2522
Phone: (972) 550-0911 or (800) 798-1822
Fax: (972) 580-2816
http://www.acep.org

American Culinary Federation
10 San Bartola Drive
St. Augustine, FL 32085
Phone: (904) 824-4468 or (800) 624-9458
Fax: (904) 825-4758
http://www.acfchefs.org

American Dietetic Association
216 West Jackson Boulevard, Suite 800
Chicago, IL 60606-6995
Phone: (312) 899-0040 or (800) 877-1600
http://www.eatright.org

American Federation of Musicians
1501 Broadway
New York, NY 10036
Phone: (212) 869-1330
http://www.amf.org

American Federation of TV and Radio Artists
260 Madison Avenue
New York, NY 10016-2402
Phone: (212) 532-0800
Fax: (212) 532-2242
5757 Wilshire Boulevard, 9th Floor
Los Angeles, CA 90036-3689
Phone: (323) 634-8100
Fax: (323) 634-8194
http://www.aftra.org

American Hotel and Lodging Association (AHLA)
1201 New York Avenue, NW
Washington, DC 20005-3931
Phone: (202) 289-3100
http://www.ahla.com

American Institute of Architects
1735 New York Avenue, NW
Washington, DC 20006
Phone: (800) AIA-3837
Fax: (202) 626-7547
http://www.aia.org

American Institute of Certified Public Accountants (AICPA)
1211 Avenue of the Americas
New York, NY 10036
Phone: (212) 596-6200
Fax: (212) 596-6213
http://www.aicpa.org

American Maritime Officers
2 West Dixie Highway
Dania Beach, FL 33004
Phone: (954) 921-2221 or (800) 362-0513
Fax: (954) 926-5112
http://www.amo-union.org

American Marketing Association (AMA)
311 South Wacker Drive, Suite 500
Chicago, IL 60606
Phone: (312) 542-9000 or (800) AMA-1150
http://www.marketingpower.com

American Nurses Association
(United American Nurses)
600 Maryland Avenue, SW, Suite 100 West
Washington, DC 20024
Phone: (202) 651-7000 or (800) 274-4ANA (4262)
Fax: (202) 651-7347
http://www.nursingworld.org

American Physical Society
One Physics Ellipse
College Park, MD 20740-3844
Phone: (301) 209-3200
Fax: (301) 209-0865
http://www.aps.org

American Public Transportation Association
1666 K Street, NW, Suite 1100
Washington, DC 20006
Phone: (202) 496-4800
http://www.apta.com

American Society of Association Executives
1575 Eye Street, NW
Washington, DC 20005-1103
Phone: (202) 626-2723 or (202) 626-2803 (TDD)
Fax: (202) 371-8825
http://www.asaenet.org

American Society of Interior Designers
608 Massachusetts Avenue, NE
Washington, DC 20002-6006
Phone: (202) 546-3480
http://www.asid.org

American Society of Journalists and Authors (ASJA)
1501 Broadway, Suite 302
New York, NY 10036
Phone: (212) 997-0947
Fax: (212) 768-7414
http://www.asjc.org

American Society of Landscape Architects
636 Eye Street, NW
Washington, DC 20001-3736
Phone: (202) 898-2444
Fax: (202) 898-1185
http://www.asla.org

American Society of Media Photographers, Inc. (ASMP)
150 North Second Street
Philadelphia, PA 19106
Phone: (215) 451-ASMP (2767)
Fax: (215) 451-0880
http://www.asmp.org

American Society of Travel Agents
1101 King Street, Suite 200
Alexandria, VA 22314
Phone: (703) 739-2782
Fax: (703) 684-8319
http://www.asta.org

American Translators Association
225 Reinekers Lane, Suite 590
Alexandria, VA 22314
Phone: (703) 683-6100
Fax: (703) 683-6122
http://www.atanet.org

**American Zoo and Aquarium
    Association**
8403 Colesville Road, Suite 710
Silver Spring, MD 20910-3314
Phone: (301) 562-0777
Fax: (301) 452-0888
http://www.aza.org

**Association for Car and Truck Rental
    Independents and Franchisees**
125 Fairfield Way, Suite 200
Bloomingdale, IL 601808-1584
Phone: (888) 200-2795
Fax: (630) 307-8515
http://www.actif.org

Association Management Companies
414 Plaza Drive, Suite 209
Westmont, IL 60559
Phone: (630) 655-4611
Fax: (630) 655-0391
http://www.amcinstitute.org

Association of American Railroads
50 F Street, NW
Washington, DC 20001
Phone: (202) 639-2100
Fax: (202) 639-2558
http://www.aar.org

Association of Aviation Psychologists
Department of Psychology
San Francisco University
1600 Holloway Avenue
San Francisco, CA 94132
http://online.sfsu.edu/~kmosier/aap

Association of Camp Nurses
8504 Thorsonveien, NE
Bemidji, MN 56601
Phone: (218) 586-2633
http://www.campnurse.org

**Association of Corporate Travel
    Executives (ACTE)**
515 King Street, Suite 340
Alexandria, VA 22314
Phone: (703) 683-5322
Fax: (703) 683-2720
http://www.acte.org

Association of Flight Attendants
1275 K Street, NW, Suite 500
Washington, DC 20005

Phone: (202) 712-9799
Fax: (202) 712-9792 (fax/Human
    Resources)
http://www.afanet.org

**Association of Professional Flight
    Attendants**
1004 West Euless Boulevard
Euless, TX 76040
Phone: (817) 540-0108 or (800) 395-2732
http://www.apfa.org

Association of Retail Travel Agents
2692 Richmond Road, Suite 202
Lexington, KY 40509
Phone: (859) 296-9739
Fax: (859) 266-9396
http://www.artaonline.com

Astronomical Society of the Pacific
390 Ashton Avenue
San Francisco, CA 94112
Phone: (415) 337-1100
Fax: (415) 337-5205
http://www.astrosociety.org

**Building Officials Code
    Administrators, Inc.**
4051 West Flossmoor Road
Country Club Hills, IL 60478
Phone: (708) 799-2300
Fax: (708) 799-4981
http://www.bocai.org

Circus Education Specialists
56 Lion Lane
Westbury, NY 11590
Phone: (516) 334-2123
Fax: (516) 334-2249
http://www.circusfans.org

**Club Managers Association of America
    (CMAA)**
1733 King Street
Alexandria, VA 22314
Phone: (703) 739-9500
Fax: (703) 739-0124
http://www.cmaa.org

Coalition of Airline Pilots Associations
1101 Pennsylvania Avenue, NW, Suite
    6612
Washington, DC 20004
Phone: (202) 756-2956
Fax: (202) 756-7509
http://www.capapilots.org

Council of Public Relations Firms
90 Park Avenue, 16th Floor
New York, NY 10016

Phone: (877) 773-4767
http://www.prfirms.org

Courier Travel
CT Web Technologies, Inc.
P.O. Box 3051
Nederland, CO 80466
Phone: (303) 570-7586 or (866) 470-3061
Fax: (313) 625-6106
http://www.couriertravel.org

**Cruise Lines International Association
    (CLIA)**
500 Fifth Avenue, Suite 1407
New York, NY 10110
Phone: (212) 921-0066
Fax: (800) 372-2542
http://www.cruising.org

Day Spa Association
310 17th Street
Union City, NJ 07087
Phone: (201) 865-2065
http://www.dayspaassociation.com

Federal Aviation Administration
800 Independence Avenue, SW
Washington, DC 20591
Phone: (202) 336-4000
http://www.faa.gov

Federal Railroad Administration
1120 Vermont Avenue, NW
Washington, D.C. 20590
Phone: (202) 493-6024
http://www.fra.dot.gov

**Hospitality Sales and Marketing
    Association International**
8201 Greensboro Drive
McLean, VA 22102
Phone: (703) 610-9024
Fax: (703) 610-9005
http://www.hsmai.org

**Hotel and Catering International
    Management Association**
Trinity Court
34 West Street
Sutton, Surrey
England SM1 1SH
Phone: +44 (0) 870 0106689
Fax: +44 (0) 20 8772 7500
http://www.hcima.org.uk

**Hotel Employees and Restaurant
    Employees International Union
    (HERE)**
1219 28th Street, NW
Washington, DC 20007
Phone: (202) 393-4373

Fax: (202) 333-0468
http://www.hereunion.org

Independent Pilots Association
200 High Rise Drive, Suite 199
Louisville, KY 40202
Phone: (800) 285-4472
Fax: (502) 968-0470
http://www.ipapilot.org

Industrial Designers Society of America
1142 Walker Road
Great Falls, VA 22066
Phone: (703) 707-6000
Fax: (703) 787-8501
http://www.idsa.org

Information Technology Association of America
1401 Wilson Boulevard, Suite 1100
Arlington, VA 22209
Phone: (703) 522-5055
Fax: (703) 525-2279
http://www.itaa.org

Institute of Certified Travel Agents
148 Linden Street
P.O. Box 812059
Wellesley, MA 02482
Phone: (781) 237-0280 or (800) 542-4282
Fax: (781) 237-3860
http://www.icta.com

Institute of Internal Auditors
249 Maitland Avenue
Altamonte Springs, FL 32701-4201
Phone: (407) 830-7600
http://www.theiia.org

Institute of Management Accountants
10 Paragon Drive
Montvale, NJ 07645-1760
Phone: (201) 573-9000 or (800) 638-4427
Fax: (201) 474-1600
http://www.imanet.org

International Airlines Travel Agent Network
300 Garden City Plaza, Suite 342
Garden City, NY 11530-3302
Phone: (516) 663-6000
Fax: (516) 747-4462
http://www.iatan.org

International Association of Administrative Professionals
10502 Northwest Ambassador Drive

P.O. Box 20404
Kansas City, MO 64195-0404
Phone: (816) 891-6600
Fax: (816) 891-9118
http://www.iaap-hq.org

International Association of Air Travel Carriers
P.O. Box 847
Scottsbluff, NE 69363-0847
Phone: (308) 632-3273
Fax: (308) 632-8261
http://www.courier.org

International Association of Amusement Parks and Attractions
1448 Duke Street
Alexandria, VA 22314
Phone: (703) 836-4800
Fax: (703) 836-9675
http://www.iaapa.org

International Association of Convention and Visitors Bureaus (IACVB)
2025 M Street, NW, Suite 500
Washington, DC 20036
Phone: (202) 296-7888
Fax: (202) 296-7889
http://www.iacvb.org

International Association of Machinists and Aerospace Workers
9000 Machinists Place
Upper Marlboro, MD 20772-2687
Phone: (301) 967-4500
http://www.goiam.org

International Association of Security and Investigative Regulators
8300 Colesville Road, Suite 750
Silver Spring, MD 20910
Phone: (301) 585-1844
Fax: (301) 585-4442
http://www.iasir.org

International Brotherhood of Electrical Workers
1125 15th Street, NW
Washington, DC 20005
Phone: (202) 833-7000
Fax: (202) 467-6316
http://www.ibew.org

International Brotherhood of Teamsters
25 Louisiana Avenue, NW
Washington, DC 20001
Phone: (202) 624-6800
http://www.teamster.org

International Caterers Association
1200 17th Street, NW
Washington, DC 20036
Phone: (888) 604-5844
http://hcacater.org

International Communications Industries Association, Inc.
11242 Waples Mill Road, Suite 200
Fairfax, VA 22030
Phone: (703) 273-7200 or (800) 659-7469
http://www.infocomm.org

International Concierge Institute
The Breakers Hotel
County Road
Palm Beach, FL 33480
Phone: (407) 655-5611
http://www.acfchefs.org

International Council of Cruise Lines
2111 Wilson Boulevard, 8th Floor
Arlington, VA 22201
Phone: (703) 522-8463 or (800) 595-9338
Fax: (703) 522-3811
http://www.iccl.org

International Council on Hotel, Restaurant, and Institutional Education (CHRIE)
2613 North Parham Road, 2nd Floor
Richmond, VA 23294
Phone: (804) 346-4800
Fax: (804) 346-5009
http://www.chrie.org

International Executive Housekeepers Association (I.E.H.A.)
10001 Eastwind Drive, Suite 301
Westerville, OH 43081-3361
Phone: (614) 895-7166 or (800) 200-6342
Fax: (614) 895-1248
http://www.ieha.org

International Federation of Women's Travel Organizations
304 Gateway Drive
Enterprise, AL 36330
Phone: (334) 393-4431
Fax: (530) 686-8891
http://www.ifwto.org

International Festivals and Events Association
2601 Eastover Terrace
Boise, ID 83706
Phone: (208) 433-0950

Fax: (208) 433-9812
http://www.ifea.com

**International Food, Wine and Travel
    Writers Association (IFW&TWA)**
P.O. Box 8249
Calabasas, CA 91372
Phone: (818) 999-9959
Fax: (818) 347-7545
http://www.ifwtwa.org/

**International Interior Design
    Association**
13-122 Merchandise Mart
Chicago, IL 60654-1104
Phone: (312) 467-1950 or (888) 799-4432
Fax: (312) 467-0779
http://www.iida.org

**International Organization of Masters,
    Mates, and Pilots**
700 Maritime Boulevard
Linthicum Heights, MD 21090-1941
Phone: (410) 850-8700 or (877) 667-5522
Fax: (410) 850-0973
http://www.bridgedeck.org

International Planetarium Society, Inc.
Rauch Planetarium
108 West Brandeis Avenue
Louisville, KY 40292
Contact information transfers with
    Membership Chair
Phone: (502) 852-5855
Fax: (502) 852-0831
http://www.ips-planetarium.org

**International Society of Hospitality
    Purchasers**
300 Montgomery Street
San Francisco, CA 94104
Phone: (415) 399-0995
Fax: (415) 399-0935
http://www.ishp.org

**International Society of Travel and
    Tourism Educators**
23220 Edgewater
St. Clair Shores, MI 48082
Phone: (586) 294-0208 (voice and fax)
http://www.istte.org

**International Society of Women Airline
    Pilots**
24 West Mall Drive
Huntington, NY 11743
http://www.iswap.org

International Spa Association
2365 Harrodsburg Road, Suite A325
Lexington, KY 40504

Phone: (859) 226-4372
Fax: (859) 226-4445
http://www.experienceispa.com

Leading Caterers of America
216 South Bayshore Drive
Miami, FL 33133
Phone: (305) 285-1362 or (800) 743-6660
Fax: (305) 858-6660
http://www.leadingcaterers.com

Les Clefs d'Or USA, Ltd.
24088 North Bridle Trail Road
Lake Forest, IL 60045
Phone: (847) 247-4285
http://www.lesclefsdorusa.com

**Marine Engineer's Beneficial
    Association**
Hall of States Building
444 North Capitol Street, Suite 800
Washington, D.C. 20001
Phone: (202) 638-5355
Fax: (202) 638-5369
http://www.dimeba.org

Marketing Research Association
1344 Silas Deane Highway, Suite 306
P.O. Box 230
Rocky Hill, CT 06067-0230
Phone: (860) 257-4008
Fax: (860) 257-3990
http://www.mra-net.org

Meeting Professionals International
4455 LBJ Freeway, Suite 1200
Dallas, TX 75244-5903
Phone: (972) 702-3000
Fax: (972) 702-3070
http://www.mpiweb.org

**Midwest Travel Writers Association
    (MTWA)**
P.O. Box 83552
Lincoln, NE 68501-3542
Phone: (402) 438-2253 (voice and fax)
http://www.mtwa.org

**National Air Traffic Controllers
    Association**
1325 Massachusetts Avenue, NW
Washington, DC 20005
Phone: (202) 628-5451
Fax: (202) 628-5767
http://www.natca.org

**National Association for Practical
    Nurse Education and Service, Inc.**
1400 Spring Street, Suite 310
Silver Spring MD 20910

Phone: (301) 588-2491
Fax: (301) 588-2839
http://www.napnes.org

**National Association of Catering
    Executives**
5565 Sterrett Place, Suite 328
Columbia, MD 21044
Phone: (410) 997-9055
Fax: (410) 997-8834
http://www.nace.net

**National Association of Credit
    Management**
8840 Columbia 100 Parkway
Columbia, MD 21045
Phone: (410) 740-5560
Fax: (410) 740-5574
http://www.nacm.org

**National Association of Institutional
    Linen Management (NAILM)**
2130 Lexington Road, Suite H
Richmond, KY 40475
Phone: (859) 624-0177 or (800) 669-0863
Fax: (859) 624-3580
http://www.nailm.com

**National Association of Plumbing-
    Heating-Cooling Contractors**
180 South Washington Street
P.O. Box 6808
Falls Church, VA 22040
Phone: (703) 237-8100 or (800) 533-
7694
Fax: (703) 237-7442
http://www.naphcc.org

National Association of Sports Officials
2017 Lathrop Avenue
Racine, WI 53405
Phone: (262) 632-5448
Fax: (262) 632-5460
http://www.naso.org

**National Association of Traveling
    Nurses**
P.O. Box 35189
Chicago, IL 60707-0189
Phone: (708) 453-0080
Fax: (708) 453-0083
http://www.travelingnurse.org

National Athletic Trainers Association
2952 Stemmons Freeway
Dallas, TX 75247-6916
Phone: (214) 637-6282 or (800) TRY-
NATA (879-6282)
Fax: (214) 637-2206
http://www.nata.org

National Bar Association
1225 11th Street, NW
Washington, DC 20001
Phone: (202) 842-3900
Fax: (202) 289-6170
http://www.nationalbar.org

National Business Travel Association
  (NBTA)
110 North Royal Street, 4th Floor
Alexandria, VA 22314
Phone: (703) 684-0836
Fax: (703) 684-0263
http://www.nbta.org

National Coalition of Black Meeting
  Planners
8630 Fenton Street, Suite 126
Silver Spring, MD 20910
Phone: (202) 628-3952
Fax: (301) 588-0011
http://www.ncbmp.com

National Collegiate Athletic
  Association
700 West Washington Street
P.O. Box 6222
Indianapolis, IN 46206-6222
Phone: (317) 917-6222
http://www.ncaa.org

National Concierge Association
120 South Sixth Street, Suite 1700
Minneapolis, MN 55402
Phone: (612) 317-2932
Fax: (612) 317-2910
http://www.conciergeassoc.org

National Council of State Boards of
  Nursing, Inc.
676 North St. Clair Street, Suite 550
Chicago, IL 60611-2921
Phone: (312) 787-6555
http://www.ncsbn.org

National Flight Paramedics
  Association
383 F Street
Salt Lake City, UT 84103-2756
Phone: (800) 381-6372
Fax: (801) 534-0434
http://www.nfpa.rotor.com

National High School Athletic Coaches
  Association
P.O. Box 4342
Hamden, CT 06514
Phone: (203) 288-7473
Fax: (203) 288-8224
http://www.hscoaches.org

National League for Nursing
61 Broadway
New York, NY 10006
Phone: (212) 363-5555 or (800) 669-1656
Fax: (212) 989-2272
http://www.nln.org

National Motorcoach Network
P.O. Box 7430
Fairfax Station, VA 22039
Phone: (703) 250-7897
Fax: (703) 250-1477
http://www.motorcoach.com

National Park Service
1849 C Street, NW
Washington, DC 20240
Phone: (202) 208-6843
Fax: (202) 219-0910
http://www.nps.gov

National Pilots Association
Suite 275, South Atlanta Air Center
3401 Norman Berry Drive
Atlanta, GA 30344
Phone: (404) 599-7700
Fax: (404) 559-7735
http://www.npa-atl.org

National Press Photographers
  Association
3200 Croasdaile Drive, Suite 306
Durham, NC 7713
Phone: (919) 383-7246
Fax: (919) 383-7261
http://www.nppa.org

National Recreation and Parks
  Association
22377 Belmont Ridge Road
Ashburn, VA 20148-4501
Phone: (703) 858-0784
Fax: (703) 858-0794
http://www.nrpa.org

National Restaurant Association
1200 17th Street, NW
Washington, DC 20036
Phone: (202) 331-5900 or
  (800) 424-5156
Fax: (202) 331-2429
http://www.restaurant.org

National Retail Federation
325 7th Street, NW, Suite 1100
Washington, DC 20004
Phone: (202) 783-7971 or (800) NRF-
  HOW2
Fax: (202) 737-2849
http://www.nrf.com

National Ski Patrol
133 South Van Gordon Street, Suite 100
Lakewood, CO 80228
Phone: (303) 998-1111
Fax: (303) 988-3005
http://www.nsp.org

National Society of Accountants
1010 North Fairfax Street
Alexandria, VA 22314
Phone: (703) 549-6400 or (800) 966-
  6679
Fax: (703) 549-2984
http://www.nsacct.org

National Tour Association
546 East Main Street
Lexington, KY 40508
Phone: (800) 682-8886
Fax: (859) 226-4404
http://www.ntaonline.com

National Tourism Foundation
546 East Main Street
Lexington, KY 40508
Phone: (800) 682-8886
http://www.ntfonline.org

National Trust for Historic
  Preservation
1785 Massachusetts Avenue, NW
Washington, DC 20036
Phone: (202) 588-6000
Fax: (202) 588-6038
http://www.nationaltrust.org

National Web Design Association
http://www.2webs.com

National Writers Union (NWU)
National Office East
113 University Place, 6th Floor
New York, NY 10003
Phone: (212) 254-0279
Fax: (212) 254-0673
National Office West
337 17th Street, #101
Oakland, CA 94612
Phone: (510) 839-0110
Fax: (510) 839-6097
http://www.nwu.org

North American Snowsports
  Journalists Association (NASJA)
http://www.nasja.org

North American Travel Journalists
  Association (NATJA)
531 Main Street, #902
El Segundo, CA 90245

Phone: (310) 836-8712
Fax: (310) 836-8769
http://www.natia.org

Nursing Licensure Compact Administrators
Utah Board of Nursing
160 East 300 South
Salt Lake City, UT 84111-2316
Phone: (801) 530-6628 or (866) 275-3675 (in Utah)
Fax: (801) 530-6511
http://www.dopl.utah/gov/licensing/nurse

Outdoor Guides Association
P.O. Box 12996
Tallahassee, Fl 32317
Phone: (850) 671-4409
Fax: (850) 668-2340
http://worldwidewilderness.com

Outdoor Writers Association of America (OWAA)
121 Hickory Street, Suite 1
Missoula, MT 59801
Phone: (406) 728-7434
Fax: (406) 728-7445
http://www.owaa.org

Professional Aviation Maintenance Association
Ronald Reagan Washington National Airport
Washington, DC 20001
Phone: (703) 417-8800
Fax: (703) 417-8801
http://www.pama.org

Professional Convention Management Association
2301 South Lake Shore Drive, Suite 1001
Chicago, IL 60616-1419
Phone: (312) 434-7262
Fax: (312) 423-7222
http://www.pcma.org

Public Relations Society of America (PRSA)
33 Irving Place, 3rd Floor
New York, NY 10003
Phone: (212) 460-1474
Fax: (212) 995-0757
http://www.prsa.org

Receptive Services Association, Inc.
17000 Commerce Parkway, Suite C
Mt. Laurel, NJ 08054
Phone: (856) 638-0423
Fax: (856) 439-0525
http://www.rsana.com

Recreation Vehicle Industry Association
P.O. Box 2999
Reston, VA 20795
Phone: (703) 620-6003
Fax: (703) 620-5071
http://www.rvia.org

Regional Airline Association
2025 M Street, NW
Washington, DC 20036
Phone: (202) 367-1170
Fax: (202) 367-2170
http://www.raa.org

Resort and Commercial Recreation Association
P.O. Box 2437
Aurora, IL 60507
Phone: (630) 892-2175
Fax: (630) 801-4202
http://www.r-c-r-a.org

Sales and Marketing Executives International, Inc.
P.O. Box 1390
Sumas, WA 98295-1390
Phone: (312) 893-0751
Fax: (604) 855-0165
http://www.smei.org

Screen Actors Guild
5757 Wilshire Boulevard
Los Angeles, CA 90036-3600
Phone: (323) 954-1600 or (323) 549-6648 (TTD)
Fax: (323) 549-6603
http://www.sag.org

Seafarers International Union
5201 Auth Way
Camp Springs, MD 20746
Phone: (301) 899-0675 or (877) 235-3275
Fax: (301) 899-7355
http://www.seafarers.org

Select Registry
P.O. Box 150
Marshall, MI 49068
Phone: (616) 789-0393 or (800) 344-5244
Fax: (616) 789-0970
http://www.selectreqistry.com

Society for Human Resources Management (SHRM)
1800 Duke Street
Alexandria, VA 22314-3499
Phone: (703) 548-3440
Fax: (703) 535-6490
http://www.shrm.org

Society for the Advancement of Travel for the Handicapped
347 Fifth Avenue, Suite 610
New York, NY 10016
Phone: (212) 447-7284
Fax: (212) 725-8253
http://www.sath.org

Society of American Travel Writers (SATW)
1500 Sunday Drive, Suite 102
Raleigh, NC 27607
Phone: (919) 787-5181
Fax: (919) 787-4916
http://www.satw.org

Society of Corporate Meeting Professionals
217 Ridgemont Avenue
San Antonio, TX 78209
Phone: (210) 822-6522
Fax: (210) 822-9838
http://www.sqmp.org

Society of Government Meeting Planners
908 King Street, Lower Level
Alexandria, VA 22314
Phone: (703) 549-0892
Fax: (703) 549-0708
http://www.sgmp.org

Society of Incentive and Travel Executives
401 North Michigan Avenue
Chicago, IL 60611
Phone: (312) 321-5148
Fax: (312) 527-6783
http://www.site-intl.org

Southeastern Outdoor Press Association (SEOPA)
105 Ninth Street
Slidell, LA 70458-1417
Phone: (800) 849-7367
http://www.seopa.org

Southwest Airlines Pilots' Association
Exchange Park, American General Tower
6363 Forest Park Road, Suite 800
Dallas, TX 75235
Phone: (214) 350-9237 or (800) 969-7972
Fax: (214) 350-0647
http://www.swapa.org

Student and Youth Travel Association of North America
1520 South Lapeer Road
Lake Orion, MI 48360

Phone: (248) 814-7982
Fax: (248) 814-7150
http://www.syta.com

**Texas Outdoor Writers Association
    (TOWA)**
7503 Bayswater
Amarillo, TX 79119
Phone: (806) 376-4488
http://www.towa.org

Translators and Interpreters Guild
962 Wayne Avenue, Suite 500
Silver Spring, MD 20910
Phone: (301) 563-6450 or (800) 992-0367
Fax: (301) 563-6020
http://www.ttig.org

Transport Workers Union of America
80 West End Avenue
New York, NY 10023
Phone: (212) 873-6000
Fax: (212) 721-1431
http://www.twu.com

**Travel and Tourism Research
    Association**
P.O. Box 2133
Boise, ID 83701
Phone: (208) 429-9511
Fax: (208) 429-9511
http://www.ttra.com

Travel Industry Association of America
1100 New York Avenue, NW, Suite 450
Washington, DC 20005-3934
Phone: (202) 408-8422
Fax: (202) 408-1255
http://www.tia.org

Travel Journalists Guild
P.O. Box 10643
Chicago, IL 60610
Phone: (312) 664-9279
Fax: (312) 664-9701
http://www.tigonline.com

**United American Nurses
(American Nurses Association)**
600 Maryland Avenue, SW, Suite 100
    West
Washington, DC 20024
Phone: (202) 651-7000 or (877) ANA-
    ORGANIZE (262-6742)
Fax: (202) 651-7347
http://www.nursingworld.org/uan

**United Association of Journeymen and
    Apprentices of the Plumbing,
    Pipefitting, Sprinkler Fitting
    Industry of the United States and
    Canada**
815 16th Street, NW
Washington, DC 20006
Phone: (202) 637-5000

Fax: (202) 637-5058
http://www.ua.org

United Motorcoach Association
113 South West Street, 4th Floor
Alexandria, VA 22314
Phone: (703) 838-2929 or (800) 424-
8262
Fax: (703) 838-2950
http://www.uma.org

**United States Tour Operators
    Association**
275 Madison Avenue, Suite 2014
New York, NY 10016
Phone: (212) 599-6599
Fax: (212) 599-6744
http://www.ustoa.com

United Transportation Union
14600 Detroit Avenue
Cleveland, OH 44107-4250
Phone: (216) 521-1161
http://www.utu.org

**Web Design and Developers
    Association (WDDA)**
8515 Brower
Houston, TX 77017
Phone: (435) 518-9784
http://www.wdda.org

APPENDIX VI
PROFESSIONAL PERIODICALS

Air Line Pilot
Air Line Pilots Association
535 Herndon Parkway
P.O. Box 1169
Herndon, VA 22070
Phone: (703) 689-2270
http://www.alpa.org

Airliners
World Transport Press Inc.
P.O. Box 20189
Castro Valley, CA 94546
Phone: (510) 732-2747
Fax: (510) 732-2699
http://www.airliners.viaweb.com

Airport Business
Cygnus Business Media
1233 Janesville Avenue
Fort Atkinson, WI 53538
Phone: (920) 563-6388 or (800) 547-7377
Fax: (920) 563-1700
http://www.airportbusiness.com

Airport Magazine
American Association of Airport
    Executives
601 Madison Street, Suite 400
Alexandria, VA 22314-1756
Phone: (703) 824-0500
Fax: (703) 820-1395
http://www.airportnet.org

Air Transport World
1350 Connecticut Avenue, NW, Suite 902
Washington, DC 20036
Phone: (202) 659-8500
Fax: (202) 659-1554
http://www.atwonline.com

AOPA Pilot
AOPA
421 Aviation Way
Frederick, MD 21701-4756
Phone: (301) 695-2350
Fax: (301) 695-2180
http://www.aopa.org

Association Meetings
Corporate Meetings & Incentives
PRIMEDIA Business Magazines &
    Media, Inc.

9800 Metcalf Avenue
Overland Park, KS 66212
Phone: (913) 341-1300
Fax: (913) 967-1898
http://www.primediabusiness.com

Aviation Week
McGraw-Hill Companies
1200 G Street, NW, Suite 200
Washington, DC 20005
Phone: (202) 383-2403
Fax: (202) 383-7956
http://www.aviationnow.com

Business Travel News
VNU Business Publications USA
770 Broadway
New York, NY 10003
Phone: (646) 654-5000
http://www.btonline.com

Bus Tours Magazine
9698 West Judson Road
Polo, IL 61064
Phone: (815) 946-2341
Fax: (815) 946-2347
http://www.busmag.com

Casino Journal
Nevada Hospitality
New Jersey Casino Journal
Casino Journal Publishing Group
8025 Black Horse Pike, Suite 470
West Atlantic City, NJ 08232
Phone: (609) 484-8866 or (800) 486-7529
Fax: (609) 645-1661
http://www.casinocenter.com/nh

Catering Industry Employee
Hotel Employees and Restaurant
    Employees International Union
1219 28th Street, NW
Washington, DC 20007-3389
Phone: (202) 393-4373
Fax: (202) 965-2958
http://www.hereunion.org

Corporate and Incentive Travel
Coastal Communications Corporation
2600 North Military Trail
Boca Raton, FL 33431-6309

Phone: (561) 989-0600
Fax: (561) 989-9509
http://www.corporate-inc-travel.com

Cruise and Vacation Views
Orban Communications, Inc.
25 Washington Street, 4th Floor
Morristown, NJ 07960
Phone: (973) 605-2442
Fax: (973) 605-2722
http://www.cruise-reports.com

Cruise Industry News
441 Lexington Avenue, Suite 1209
New York, NY 10017
Phone: (212) 986-1025
Fax: (212) 986-1033
http://www.cruiseindustrynews.com

Entree
Iowa Hospitality Association
8525 Douglas Avenue, Suite 47
Des Moines, IA 50322
Phone: (515) 276-1454
Fax: (515) 276-3660
http://www.iowahospitality.com

FIU Hospitality
Florida International University
151st Street and Biscayne Boulevard
North Miami, FL 33181
Phone: (305) 348-2235
http://www.fiu.edu

Frequent Flier
2 Penn Plaza
New York, NY 10121
Phone: (212) 292-5616
http://www.frequentflyer.oag.com

Group Tour Magazine Great Lakes
    Region, Mid-Atlantic Region, New
    England, Southeaster Region,
    Western Region
Shoreline Creations, Ltd.
2465 112th Avenue
Holland, MI 49424
Phone: (616) 393-2077 or (800) 767-3489
Fax: (616) 393-0085
http://magazines.grouptour.com

Hospitality Design
Bill Communications, Inc.

770 Broadway, 5th Floor
New York, NY 10003-9595
Phone: (646) 654-4500
Fax: (646) 654-7212
http://www.billcom.com

Hospitality News
Delmont Communications
1700 Livingston Avenue
St. Paul, MN 55118
http://hospitalitynews.com

*Hospitality Sales and Marketing
    Association International (HSMAI)*
8201 Greensboro Drive, Suite 300
McLean, VA 22102
Phone: (703) 610-9024
Fax: (703) 610-9005
http://www.hsmai.org

*Hotel & Motel Management Product
    News*
Advanstar Communications
201 Sandpointe Avenue
Suite 600
Santa Ana, CA 92707
Phone: (714) 513-8400 or (800) 854-3112
Fax: (714) 513-8402
http://www.advanstar.com

Inn Times
Interbriefs, Inc.
2101 Crystal Plaza Arcade, No. 246
Arlington, VA 22202-4600
Phone: (202) 363-9305
Fax: (202) 686-3966

*International Journal of Hospitality and
    Tourism Administration; Journal of
    Convention and Exhibition
    Management; Journal of Human
    Resources in Hospitality and Tourism
    Services; Journal of Quality
    Assurance in Hospitality and
    Tourism; Journal of Teaching in
    Travel and Tourism; Journal of
    Travel and Tourism Marketing*
The Haworth Press, Inc.
10 Alice Street
Binghamton, NY 13904-1580
Phone: (607) 722-5857 or (800) 429-6784
Fax: (607) 722-6362
http://www.haworthpressinc.com

International Travel News
Martin Publications, Inc.
2120 28th Street
Sacramento, CA 95818
Phone: (916) 457-3643

Jax Fax Travel Marketing Magazine
Jet Airtransport Exchange, Inc.
48 Wellington Road
Milford, CT 06460
Phone: (203) 301-0255 or
    (800) 9-JAXFAX
Fax: (203) 301-0250
http://www.jaxfax.com

*Journal of Hospitality and Leisure
    Marketing*
The School of Hospitality Business
The Eli Broad College of
    Business/Management
Michigan State University
235 Eppley Center
East Lansing, MI 48824-1121
Phone: (517) 353-9211
Fax: (517) 484-1170
http://www.haworthpressinc.com

*Journal of Hospitality and Tourism
    Research*
Council on Hotel, Restaurant, and
    Institutional Education
1200 17th Street, NW
Washington, DC 20036-3097
Phone: (202) 331-5990
Fax: (202) 785-2511
http://www.chrie.org

LH (Lodging Hospitality)
Penton Media, Inc.
1300 East 9th Street
Cleveland, OH 44114-1503
Phone: (216) 696-7000
Fax: (216) 696-7658
http://www.lhonline.com

Lodging Magazine
American Hotel and Lodging Association
1201 New York Avenue, NW, Suite 600
Washington, DC 20005-3931
Phone: (202) 289-3100
Fax: (202) 289-3199
http://www.ahlaonline.org

Meeting News
Miller Freeman, Inc.
1 Penn Plaza
New York, NY 10119-1198
Phone: (212) 615-2247 or (800) 950-1314
Fax: (212) 643-5612
http://www.meetingnews.com
http://www.mfi.com

Meetings and Conventions
500 Plaza Drive

Secaucus, NJ 07094-3626
Phone: (201) 902-2000
Fax: (201) 902-1843
http://www.northstartravelmedia.com/
    pages/mc

Midwest Hospitality
Missouri Restaurant Association
9233 Ward Parkway, Suite 123
Kansas City, MO 64114-3312
Phone: (816) 753-5222
Fax: (816) 753-6993
http://www.morestaurants.com

Military Club and Hospitality
Executive Business Media, Inc.
825 Old Country Road
P.O. Box 1500
Westbury, NY 11590-0812
Phone: (516) 334-3030
Fax: (516) 334-3059

Northwest Hospitality News
Hospitality News Group
P.O. Box 21027
Salem, OR 97307-1027
Phone: (503) 390-8343 or (800) 685-1932
Fax: (503) 390-8344
http://www.hospitalitynewsgroup.com

Ohio Tavern News
The Daily Reporter, Inc.
580 South High Street, S-316
Columbus, OH 43215
Phone: (614) 224-4835
Fax: (614) 224-8649

*Open World for Disability and Mature
    Travel*
Society for Accessible Travel and
    Hospitality
347 Fifth Avenue, No. 610
New York, NY 10016-5010
Phone: (212) 447-7284
Fax: (212) 725-8253

*Progress in Tourism and Hospitality
    Research*
John Wiley and Sons, Inc.
605 Third Avenue
New York, NY 10158
Phone: (212) 850-6000 or (800) 225-
    5945

Recommend
Worth International Communications
    Corp.
5979 Northwest 151st Street, Suite 120
Miami Lakes, FL 33014

Phone: (305) 828-0123 or (800) 447-0123
Fax: (305) 826-6950
http://www.gotravel.com

Restaurant Hospitality
Penton Media, Inc.
1300 East 9th Street
Cleveland, OH 44114-1503
Phone: (216) 696-7000
Fax: (216) 696-7658

Restaurants, Resorts and Hotels
The Publishing Group
P.O. Box 566
Stratford, CT 06615-0566
Phone: (203) 279-0149

Seatrade Review
Seatrade North America
125 Village Boulevard, Suite 220
Princeton, NJ 08540
Phone: (609) 452-9414
Fax: (609) 452-9374

Successful Meetings
770 Broadway
New York, NY 10003

Phone: (212) 592-6403
Fax: (212) 592-6600
http://www.sucessmtgs.com

Timeshare Business
Resort Condominiums International, Inc.
9998 North Michigan Road
Carmel, IN 46032-9640
Phone: (317) 805-9641 or (800) 338-7777
Fax: (317) 805-9507
http://www.rci.com

Travel Agent Magazine
801 Second Avenue
New York, NY 10017
Phone: (212) 370-1047
http://www.travelagentcentral.com

Travel News
Travel Agents International, Inc.
11006 4th Street North, No. 27
St. Petersburg, FL 33716-2945
Phone: (813) 576-8241
Fax: (813) 579-0529

Travel Trade
15 West 44th Street, Sixth Floor

New York, NY 10036
Phone: (212) 730-6600
Fax: (212) 730-7137

Travel Weekly
Cahners Travel Group
500 Plaza Drive
Secaucus, NJ 07094
Phone: (201) 902-2000
Fax: (201) 902-1843
http://www.traveler.net/two

TravelAge West
9911 West Pico Boulevard
Los Angeles. CA 90035
Phone: (310) 772-7430
Fax: (310) 286-3530
http://www.travelagewest.com

Travel World News Magazine
Travel Industry Network, Inc.
50 Washington Street
South Norwalk, CT 06854
Phone: (203) 853-4955
Fax: (203) 866-1153

APPENDIX VII
MAJOR CRUISE LINES

American Cruise Lines
One Marine Park
Hadam, CT 06438
Phone: (860) 345-8005 or (800) 814-6880
Fax: (860) 345-4265
http://www.americancruiselines.com

Carnival Cruise Lines
3655 Northwest 87th Avenue
Miami, FL 33178-2428
Phone: (305) 599-2600 or (800) 438-6744
http://www.carnival.com

Celebrity Cruises Inc.
1050 Caribbean Way
Miami, FL 33132
Phone: (305) 539-6000
http://www.celebritycruises.com

Costa Cruise Lines
200 South Park Road, Suite 200
Hollywood, FL 33021
Phone: (800) 462-6782
http://www.costacruises.com

Crystal Cruises
2049 Century Park East, Suite 1400
Los Angeles, CA 90067
Phone: (310) 785-9300
Fax: (310) 785-0011
http://www.crystalcruises.com

Cunard Line Limited
6100 Blue Lagoon Drive, Suite 400
Miami, FL 33126
Phone: (305) 463-3000 or (305) 463-3010
http://www.curnard.com

Delta Queen Steamboat Company
30 Robin Street Wharf
New Orleans, LA 70130-1890

Phone: (504) 586-0631 or (504) 585-0630
http://www.deltaqueen.com

Disney Cruise Line
P.O. Box 10210
Lake Buena Vista, FL 32880
Phone: (407) 566-3500
Fax: (407) 566-3751
http://www.disneycruise.com

Holland America Line
300 Elliott Avenue West
Seattle, WA 98119
Phone: (206) 281-3535
Fax: (206) 281-7110
http://www.hollandamerica.com

Norwegian Cruise Line
7665 Corporate Center Drive
Miami, FL 33126-1201
Phone: (305) 436-4000
Fax: (805) 436-4120
http://www.ncl.com

Orient Lines, Inc.
1510 Southeast 17th Street, Suite 400
Ft. Lauderdale, FL 33316
Phone: (954) 527-6660
Fax: (954) 527-6657
http://www.orientlines.com

Princess Cruises
24303 Town Center Drive
Santa Clarita, CA 91355
Phone: (661) 753-0000
http://www.princesscruises.com

Radisson Seven Seas Cruises
600 Corporate Drive, Suite 410
Ft. Lauderdale, FL 33334
Phone: (954) 776-6123

Fax: (954) 772-3763
http://www.rssc.com

Royal Caribbean International
1050 Caribbean Way
Miami, FL 33132
Phone: (305) 539-6000
http://www.royalcaribbean.com

Royal Olympic Cruises
805 Third Avenue
New York, NY 10022
Phone: (212) 688-7555
http://www.royalolympiccruises.com

Seabourn Cruise Line
6100 Blue Lagoon Drive, Suite 400
Miami, FL 33126
Phone: (305) 463-3010
Fax: (305) 463-3010
http://www.seabourn.com

Silversea Cruises, Ltd.
110 East Broward Boulevard
Ft. Lauderdale, FL 33301
Phone: (954) 522-4477
Fax: (954) 522-4499
http://www.silversea.com

Windjammer Barefoot Cruises
1759 Bay Road
Miami Beach, Fl 33139-1413
Phone: (305) 672-6453
Fax: (305) 674-1219
http://www.windjammer.com

Windstar Cruises
300 Elliott Avenue West
Seattle, WA 98119
Phone: (800) 258-7245
http://www.windstarcruises.com

APPENDIX VIII
MAJOR HOTEL CHAINS

Aston Hotels & Resorts
2155 Kalakaua Avenue
Honolulu, HI 96815
Phone: (808) 944-4353
http://www.aston-hotels.com

Best Western International, Inc.
6201 North 24th Parkway
Phoenix, AZ 85016
Phone: (602) 957-5753
Fax: (602) 957-5641
http://www.bestwestern.com

Blair Hotels
P.O. Box 30
Cody, WY 82414
Phone: (307) 587-3654
Fax: (307) 587-2795
http://www.blairhotels.com

Carlson Hospitality Worldwide
P.O. Box 59159
Minneapolis, MN 5459-8204
Phone: (763) 212-5616
Fax: (763) 212-3400
http://www.countryinns.com,
http://www.parkinn.com,
http://www.parkplaza.com,
http://www.radisson.com,
http://www.regenthotels.com,
http://www.rssc.com

Castle & Cook Resorts
600 Iwilei Road
Honolulu, HI 96817
Phone: (808) 548-3700
Fax: (808) 548-3710
http://www.islandoflanai.com

Castle Resorts & Hotels
3 Waterfront Plaza
500 Ala Moana Boulevard
Honolulu, HI 96813
Phone: (808) 524-0900 or (808) 521-9994
http://www.castleresorts.com

Cendant Hotel Group
1 Sylvan Way
Parsippany, NJ 07054
Phone: (973) 496-0750 or (973) 496-
7307

http://www.cendant.com
Refer to the Cendant website for links to
these hotels: AmeriHost Inn, Days
Inn, Super 8, Travelodge, Wingate Inn,
Knights Inn, Villager, Ramada Inn,
and Howard Johnson.

Charles Group of Hotels
4101 Collins Avenue
Miami Beach, FL 33140
Phone: (305) 673-3337
Fax: (305) 538-2025
http://www.cghcorp.com

Choice Hotels International
10750 Columbia Pike
Silver Spring, MD 20901
Phone: (301) 592-5032
Fax: (301) 592-6177
http://www.choicehotels.com
Refer to the Choice Hotels website for
links to the following hotels: Comfort
Inn, Comfort Suites, Quality, Sleep
Inn, Clarion, MainStay Suites, Econo
Lodge, Rodeway Inn, and Flag.

Crestline Hotels & Resorts, Inc.
8405 Greensboro Drive, Suite 500
McLean, VA 22102
Phone: (571) 382-1800
Fax: (571) 382-1860
http://www.crestlinehotels.com

Destination Hotels and Resorts
10333 East Dry Creek Road
Englewood, CO 80102
Phone: (303) 799-3830
Fax: (303) 779-6011
http://www.destinationhotels.com

**Discover Resorts International and
Prestige Resorts and Destinations**
7150 East Camelback Road
Scottsdale, AZ 85251
Phone: (480) 421-6021
Fax: (480) 941-3900
http://www.discoverresorts.com

Empire Hotel Group
515 West 42nd Street
New York, NY 10036

Phone: (212) 694-7171
Fax: (212) 967-5025
http://www.newyorkhotel.com

Fairmont Hotels and Resorts
410 Park Avenue
New York, NY 10022
Phone: (212) 715-7098
Fax: (212) 371-2723
http://www.fairmont.com

Forever Resorts
P.O. Box 52038
Phoenix, AZ 85072
Phone: (480) 998-7199
Fax: (480) 998-9965
http://www.foreverresorts.com

Gaylord Opryland
2800 Opryland Drive
Nashville TN 37214
Phone: (615) 889-1000
http://www.gaylordhotels.com

Hampshire Hotels and Resorts
595 11th Avenue
New York, NY 101036
Phone: (212) 474-9898
Fax: (212) 474-9897
http://www.bestnyhotels.com

Hilton Hotels Corporation
9336 Civic Center Drive
Beverly Hills, CA 90210
Phone: (310) 205-4545
Fax: (310) 205-7880
http://www.hilton.com
Refer to the Hilton Hotels website for
links to the following hotels: Hilton,
Conrad Hotels, DoubleTree, Embassy
Suites Hotels, Hampton Inns and
Suites, Hilton Garden Inn, Homewood
Suites, and Scandic.

Historic Hotels of America
1785 Massachusetts Avenue, NW
Washington, DC 20036
Fax: (202) 588-6292
http://www.historichotels.org

Hyatt Hotels and Resorts
200 West Madison Street

Chicago, IL 60606
Phone: (312) 750-1234
Fax: (312) 920-2299
http://www.hyatt.com

Le Meridien
420 Lexington Avenue
New York, NY 10170
Phone: (212) 805-5000
Fax: (212) 697-1445
http://www.lemeridien.com

Loews Hotels
667 Madison Avenue
New York, NY 10021
Phone: (212) 521-2383
http://www.loewshotels.com

Mandarin Oriental Hotel Group
5000 Kahala Avenue
Honolulu, HI 96816-5498
Phone: (808) 739-8856
Fax: (808) 739-8800
http://www.mandarinoriental.com

Marriott International, Inc.
1 Marriott Drive
Washington, DC 20058
Phone: (301) 380-7796
Fax: (301) 380-4684
http://www.marriott.com
Refer to the Marriott website for links to the following hotels: Renaissance Hotels, Courtyard, Residence Inn, Fairfield Inn, Marriott Hotels, Resorts and Suites, Towne Place Suites, Springhill Suites, ExecuStay, Ritz Carlton, and Ramada Inn International.

Omni Hotels
420 Decker Drive

Irving, TX 75062
Phone: (972) 871-5623 or (972) 871-5665
http://www.omnihotels.com

Outrigger Hotels and Resorts
2375 Kuhio Avenue
Honolulu, HI 96815
Phone: (808) 921-6941
Fax: (808) 921-6901
http://www.outrigger.com

Park Inn Hotels
P.O. Box 59159
Minneapolis, MN 55459-8204
Phone: (763) 212-56 26
Fax: (763) 212-3400
http://www.parkinn.com

Prestige Resorts and Destinations
7750 East Camelback Road
Scottsdale, AZ 85251
Phone: (480) 421-6021
Fax: (480) 421-3900
http://www.prestigeresorts.com

Raffles International Hotels and Resorts
323 East Wacker Street
Chicago, IL 50501
Phone: (954) 447-2500
Fax: (954) 712-2937
http://www.raffles.com
http://www.swissotel.com

Six Continents Hotels
3 Ravinia Drive
Atlanta, GA 30346
Phone: (770) 604-2000
Fax: (770) 391-9632
http://www.6c.com
Refer to the Six Continents Hotels website for links to the following

hotels: Crowne Plaza Hotels and Resorts, Holiday Inn Express, Holiday Inn Hotels, and InterContinental Hotels and Resorts.

Sonesta International Hotels Corporation
116 Huntington Avenue
Boston, MA 02116
Phone: (617) 421-5400
Fax: (617) 421-5402
http://www.sonesta.com

Starwood Hotels and Resorts
1111 Westchester Avenue
White Plains, NY 10604
Phone: (914) 640-8167
Fax: (914) 640-2654
http://www.starwoodhotels.com
Refer to the Starwood Hotels website for links to the following hotels: Sheraton, Four Points Sheraton, W Hotels, Westin, St. Regis, and Luxury Collection.

Vagabond Inns
5933 West Century Boulevard
Los Angeles, CA 92262
Phone: (760) 318-0905
Fax: (760) 318-0908
http://www.vagabondinns.com

Wyndham Hotels and Resorts
1950 North Stemmons
Dallas, TX 75207
Phone: (214) 863-1000
Fax: (214) 863-1440
http://www.wyndham.com

APPENDIX IX
WEBSITES OF INTEREST

JOB BANKS

CareerBuilder
http://www.careerbuilder.com

FlipDog
http://www.FlipDog.com

Hotjobs
http://www.hotjobs.com

Monster
http://www.monster.com

United States Government Jobs
http://www.usajobs.com

Yahoo
http://careers.yahoo.com

HOTEL JOBS

http://www.hcareers.com/?source-goto

http://www.hospitalityonline.com

http://www.hoteljobs.com

**http://www.nationjob.com/community_
list.cgi/hotel**

CAREER DESCRIPTIONS
AND GUIDANCE

Aviation jobs
http://www.avscholars.com/avcareers.
phtml

Careers in Government
http://www.careersingovernment.com

Index of Occupational Profiles
http://careers.lancs.ac.uk/profiles

**Indiana Career and Postsecondary
Advancement Center**
http://Icpac.indiana.edu

**International, United States, State and
Local Labor Union Information**
http://union-organizing.com/unions

**National Association of Colleges and
Employers**
http://www.naceweb.org/jobwire/jobwire.
cfm

Nation Job
http://www.nationjob.com/links-art/
careerart

Nonprofit jobs around the world
http://www.ideallist.org/career/morejobs

**Occupational Outlook Handbook,
Bureau of Labor Statistics**
http://www.bls.gov/oco/home.htm

**Private Industry Council of San
Francisco**
http://www.picsf.org

**United Kingdom job descriptions and
information**
http://www.prospects.ac.uk/cms

**Upper Rio Grande Tech-Prep and
Youth Consortium**
http://www.careersprep.com

Wageweb
http://www.wageweb.com/jobdesc

BIBLIOGRAPHY

There are countless books regarding every aspect of travel-related careers. The books listed below are divided into general categories, but subjects often overlap. Several of these books are out of print but still available through special order, various websites, or at libraries. For other similar titles and subjects, check bookstore listings under travel, hospitality, business, management, marketing, and other specific career interests.

Accounting & Financial Management

Gray, William S. *Hospitality Accounting.* Upper Saddle River, N.J.: Prentice Hall, 1996.

Smidgall, Raymond S. *Hospitality Industry Managerial Accounting.* 4th edition. Orlando, Fla.: Educational Institute, 1997.

Advertising, Marketing & Public Relations

Abbey, James R. *Hospitality Sales and Advertising.* 3rd edition. Orlando, Fla.: Educational Institute, 1998.

Burke, James F., and Barry Resnick. *Marketing and Selling the Travel Product.* 2nd edition. Independence, Ky.: Delmar Learning Publishers, 1999.

Colbert, Judy, and Saul Fruchthendler. *Big Bang Marketing for Spas: See Your Profits Explode with These Easy and Effective Advertising and Publicity Ideas.* Crofton, Md.: Tuff Turtle Publishing, 2004.

Crotts, John C., Crotts and Chris A. Ryan, eds. *Marketing Issues in Pacific Area Tourism.* Binghamton, N.Y.: Haworth Hospitality Press, 1997.

Davidoff, Philip G. *Sales and Marketing for Travel and Tourism.* 2nd edition. Upper Saddle River, N.J.: Prentice Hall, 1994.

Dervaes, Claudine. *Sales and Marketing Skills.* Tampa, Fla.: Solitaire Publishing, 1998.

Fesenmaier, Daniel R.; Joseph T. O'Leary; and Muzaffer Uysal, eds. *Recent Advances in Tourism Marketing Research.* Binghamton, N.Y.: Haworth Hospitality Press, 1996.

Gartrell, Richard B. *Destination Marketing for Convention and Visitor Bureaus.* 2nd edition. Dubuque, Iowa: Kendall/Hunt Publishing Company, 1996.

Kotler, Philip, James C. Makens, and John R. Bowen. *Marketing for Hospitality and Tourism.* 3rd edition. Upper Saddle River, N.J.: Prentice Hall, 2002.

Kudrle, Albert E., and Melvin Sandler. *Public Relations for Hospitality Managers.* Hoboken, N.J.: John Wiley & Sons, 1995.

Lazer, William, and Roger A. Layton. *Contemporary Hospitality Marketing.* Orlando, Fla.: Educational Institute, 1999.

Lewis, Robert C., and Richard E. Chambers. *Marketing Leadership in Hospitality.* 3rd edition. Hoboken, N.J.: John Wiley & Sons, 1999.

Lewis, Robert C. *Cases in Hospitality Marketing and Management.* 2nd edition. Hoboken, N.J.: John Wiley & Sons, 1997.

Middleton, Victor T. C., and Jackie R. Clarke. *Marketing in Travel and Tourism.* 3rd edition. Burlington, Mass.: Butterworth-Heinemann, 2001.

Middleton, Victor T. C., and Rebecca Hawkins. *Sustainable Tourism: A Marketing Perspective.* Burlington, Mass.: Butterworth-Heinemann, 1998.

Morgan, Nigel, and Annette Pritchard. *Tourism, Promotion, and Power: Creating Images, Creating Identities.* Hoboken, N.J.: John Wiley & Sons, 1998.

Morrison, M. Alastair. *Hospitality and Travel Marketing.* 2nd edition. Independence, Ky.: Delmar Learning Publishers, 2001.

Moutinho, Luiz, Paulo Rita, and Bruce Cury. *Expert Systems in Tourism Marketing.* Farmington Hills, Mich.: International Thomson Business Press, 1996.

Nykiel, Ronald A., and Elizabeth Jascolt. *Marketing Your City, U.S.A.* Binghamton, N.Y.: Haworth Hospitality Press, 1998.

Nykiel, Ronald A. *Marketing in the Hospitality Industry.* 3rd edition. Orlando, Fla.: Educational Institute, 1997.

Seaton, A. V., and M. M. Bennett. *Marketing Tourism Products.* Farmington Hills, Mich.: International Thomson Business Press, 1996.

Williams, Anna Graf. *Hospitality Cases in Marketing and Operations.* Upper Saddle River, N.J.: Prentice Hall, 1997.

World Tourism Organization, ed. *Marketing the Mediterranean as a Region.* Madrid, Spain: WTO Publications, 1997.

World Tourism Organization, ed., *Shining in the Media Spotlight.* Madrid, Spain: WTO Publications, 1997.

Airlines and Flying

Davidoff, Philip G., and Davidoff, Doris S. *Air Fares & Ticketing.* 3rd edition. Upper Saddle River, N.J.: Prentice Hall, 1995.

Davidoff, Philip G., Doris S. Davidoff, and Donald M. Davidoff. *Apollo Reservations and Ticketing.* New York: Glencoe/McGraw-Hill, 1994.

March, Carol. *Choosing an Airline Career: In-Depth Descriptions of Entry-Level Positions, Travel Benefits, How to Apply and Interview.* New York: Capri Publishing, 1993.

Monahan, Kelly. *Air Courier Bargains.* Tampa, Fla.: Solitaire Publishing, 1998.

Muir, Pamela B. *Airline Reservations Systems Training: NATARS II.* Upper Saddle River, N.J.: Prentice Hall, 1994.

Rubin, Karen. *Flying High in Travel.* Hoboken, N.J.: John Wiley & Sons, 1993.

Salk, Ronald. *Airport Transit Guide.* 19th edition. Roanoke, Va.: (distributed by SFC Travel Publications), 2002.

Bed and Breakfast

Ryan, Ellen. *Innkeeping Unlimited: Practical, Low-Cost Ways to Improve Your B & B and Win Repeat Business.* Rockville, Md.: Can-Do Press, 1998.

Casinos & Gaming

Eade, Vincent H., and Raymond H. Eade. *Introduction to the Casino Entertainment Industry.* Upper Saddle River, N.J.: Prentice Hall, 1997.

Fenich, George G., and Kathryn Hashimoto. *Casino Gaming Dictionary: Terms and Language for Managers.* Dubuque, Iowa: Kendall/Hunt Publishing Company, 1996.

Field, Shelly. *Career Opportunities in Casinos and Casino Hotels.* New York: Facts On File, 2000.

Hashimoto, Kathryn, Sheryl Fried Kline, and George G. Fenich. *Casino Management: Past, Present, Future.* 2nd edition. Dubuque, Iowa: Kendall/Hunt Publishing Company, 1998.

Hsu, Cathy H. C., ed. *Legalized Casino Gaming in the United States.* Binghamton, N.Y.: Haworth Hospitality Press, 1999.

International Gaming Institute, Univ. of Nevada, Las Vegas, and William F. Harrah College of Hotel Administration. *The Gaming Industry: Introduction and Perspectives.* Hoboken, N.J.: John Wiley & Sons, 1996.

Kilby, Jim, and Jim Fox. *Casino Operations Management.* Hoboken, N.J.: John Wiley & Sons, 1997.

Lew, Alan A., and George A. Van Otten, eds. *Tourism and Gaming on American Indian Lands.* Elmsford, N.Y.: Cognizant Communications, 1998.

Meyer-Arendt, K. J., and Rudi Hartmann, eds. *Casino Gambling in America.* Elmsford, N.Y.: Cognizant Communications, 1998.

Rudd, Denis P., and Lincoln H. Marshall. *Introduction to Casino and Gaming Operations.* Upper Saddle River, N.J.: Prentice Hall, 1996.

Computers & Technology

Collins, Galen R., and Tarun Malik. *Hospitality Information Technology: Learning How to Use It.* 4th edition. Dubuque, Iowa: Kendall/Hunt Publishing Company, 1998.

Kasavana, Michael L., and John J. Cahill. *Managing Computers in the Hospitality Industry.* 3rd edition. Orlando, Fla.: Educational Institute, 1997.

Leshin, Cynthia B. *Internet Investigations in Hospitality, Travel, and Tourism.* 2nd edition. Upper Saddle River, N.J.: Prentice Hall, 1999.

Concierge

Stiel, Holly, and Delta Collins. *Ultimate Service; The Complete Handbook to the, World of the Concierge.* Upper Saddle River, N.J.: Prentice Hall, 1994.

Corporate Travel and Meetings

Hildreth, Richard A. *Essentials of Meeting Management.* Upper Saddle River, N.J.: Prentice Hall, 1990.

Montgomery, Rhonda J., and Sandra K. Strick. *Meetings, Conventions, and Expositions.* Hoboken, N.J.: John Wiley & Sons, 1994.

Poynter, James M. *Corporate Travel Management.* Upper Saddle River, N.J.: Prentice Hall, 1990.

Reiff, Annette. *Introduction to Corporate Travel.* Independence, Ky.: Delmar Learning Publishers, 1994.

Cruises

Dervaes, Claudine. *Selling Cruises.* Tampa, Fla.: Solitaire Publishing, 2000.

Dickinson, Bob, and Andy Vladimir. *Selling the Sea.* Hoboken, N.J.: John Wiley & Sons, 1996.

Mancini, Marc. *Cruising: A Guide to the Cruise Line Industry.* Independence, Ky.: Delmar/Thomson Learning, 2000.

Miller, Mary Fallon. *How to Get a Job with a Cruise Line.* St. Petersburg, Fla.: Ticket to Adventure, 2000.

Semer-Purzycki, Jeanne, and Robert H. Purzycki. *Sails for Profit: A Complete Guide to Selling and Booking Cruise Travel.* Upper Saddle River, N.J.: Prentice Hall, 1999.

Zvoncheck, Juls. *Cruises: Selecting, Selling and Booking.* Upper Saddle River, N.J.: Prentice Hall, 1994.

Dictionaries

Dervaes, Claudine. *The Travel Dictionary.* Tampa, Fla.: Solitaire Publishing, 1998.

Dervaes, Claudine, and John Hunter. *The U.K. to U.S. Dictionary.* Tampa, Fla.: Solitaire Publishing, 1994.

English, Richard, ed. *World Travel Dictionary.* 2nd edition. Roanoke, Va.: SF Communications, 1999.

Medlik, S. *Dictionary of Travel, Tourism, and Hospitality.* 2nd edition. Burlington, Mass.: Butterworth-Heinemann, 1996.

Economics

Cooke, Andrew. *The Economics of Leisure and Sport.* Farmington Hills, Mich.: International Thomson Business Press, 1994.

Dieke, Peter U., ed. *Political Economy of Tourism in Africa.* Elmsford, N.Y.: Cognizant Communications, 1999.

Tribe, John. *Economics of Leisure and Tourism.* Burlington, Mass.: Butterworth-Heinemann, 1995.

Education

Angelo, Rocco M., and Andrew Vladimir. *Hospitality Today: An Introduction.* 3rd edition. Orlando, Fla.: Educational Institute, 1998.

Chon, Kye-Sung, Ph.D., ed. *The Practice of Graduate Research in Hospitality and Tourism.* Binghamton, N.Y.: Haworth Hospitality Press, 1999.

Chon, Kye-Sung, Ph.D., and Ray Sparrowe, Ph.D. *Welcome to Hospitality: An Introduction.* 2nd Edition. Independence, Ky.: Delmar Learning, 1999.

Clark, Mona, Michael Riley, Roy C. Wood, and Ella Wilkie. *Research and Writing Dissertations in Hospitality and Tourism.* Farmington Hills, Mich.: International Thomson Business Press, 1998.

Dervaes, Claudine. *Teaching Travel: A Handbook for the Educator.* Tampa, Fla.: Solitaire Publishing, 1998.

Forrest, Lewis C. *Training for the Hospitality Industry.* 2nd edition. Orlando, Fla.: Educational Institute, 1996.

Poynter, James M. *How to Research and Write a Thesis in Hospitality and Tourism.* Hoboken, N.J.: John Wiley & Sons, 1993.

Ryan, Chris. *Researching Tourist Satisfaction: Issues, Concepts, Problems.* Farmington Hills, Mich.: International Thomson Business Press, 1995.

Thompson, Mary Anne. *The Global Resume and CV Guide.* Hoboken, N.J.: John Wiley & Sons, 2000.

Walker, John R. *Introduction to Hospitality.* 3rd edition. Upper Saddle River, N.J.: Prentice Hall, 2001.

Williams, Anna Graf, Ph.D., and Karen J. Hall. *Creating Your Career Portfolio: At a Glance Guide.* 3rd edition. Upper Saddle River, N.J.: Prentice Hall, 1997.

Environment

Foundation for Environmental Education World Tourism Organization, ed. *Awards for Improving the Coastal Environment: The Example of the Blue Flag.* Madrid, Spain: WTO Publications, 1997.

Singh, Tejvir, and Shalini Singh, eds. *Tourism Development in Critical Environments.* Elmsford, N.Y.: Cognizant Communications, 1999.

Williams, Stephen. *Outdoor Recreation and the Urban Environment.* Farmington Hills, Mich.: International Thomson Business Press, 1995.

World Tourism Organization. *Handbook on Natural Disaster Reduction in Tourist Areas.* Madrid, Spain: WTO Publications, 1998.

World Tourism Organization. *Rural Tourism—A Solution for Employment, Local Development, and Environment.* Madrid, Spain: WTO Publications, 1997.

Food Services and Catering

Baskette, Michael, and Eleanor M. Mainella. *Art of Nutritional Cooking.* 2nd edition. Upper Saddle River, N.J.: Prentice Hall, 1999.

Bax, Bryan. *National Assessment Institute Handbook for Safe Food Service Management.* 2nd edition. Upper Saddle River, N.J.: Prentice Hall, 1998.

Becker, Cheri, John Antun, and Thomas Lynch. *Synergistic Food Production Management: The Comprehensive Workbook.* Upper Saddle River, N.J.: Prentice Hall, 1999.

Charley, Helen, and Connie M. Weaver. *Foods: A Scientific Approach.* 3rd edition. Upper Saddle River, N.J.: Prentice Hall, 1998.

Cullen, Noel C. *The World of Culinary Supervision, Training, and Management.* Upper Saddle River, N.J.: Prentice Hall, 1999.

Drysdale, John A. *Profitable Menu Planning.* 2nd edition. Upper Saddle River, N.J.: Prentice Hall, 1998.

Freeland-Graves, Jeanne Himich, and Gladys Peckham. *Foundations of Food Preparation.* 6th edition. Upper Saddle River, N.J.: Prentice Hall, 1996.

Gielisse, Victor, Kathryn C. Gielisse, and Mary E. Kimbrough. *In Good Taste: A Contemporary Approach to Cooking.* Upper Saddle River, N.J.: Prentice Hall, 1999.

Ismail, Ahmed. *Catering and Convention Services.* Independence, Ky.: Delmar Learning Publishers/ITP, 1999.

Jones, Peter, and Paul Merricks, eds. *Management of Foodservice Operations,* New York: Continuum Publishing, 1995.

Keiser, James. *Contemporary Management Theory: Controlling and Analyzing Costs in Foodservice Operations.* 4th edition. Upper Saddle River, N.J.: Prentice Hall, 2000.

Kotschevar, Lendal Henry, and Richard Donnelly. *Quantity Food Purchasing.* 5th edition. Upper Saddle River, N.J.: Prentice Hall, 1999.

Labensky, Sarah R. *Applied Math for Food Service.* Upper Saddle River, N.J.: Prentice Hall, 1998.

Labensky, Sarah R., CCP, Alan M. Hause, and Steven Labensky. *On Cooking: A Textbook of Culinary Fundamentals.* 3rd edition. Upper Saddle River, N.J.: Prentice Hall, 2002.

Lattin, Gerald W. *The Lodging and Food Service Industry.* 4th edition. Orlando, Fla.: Educational Institute, 1998.

McSwane, David, and Nancy Rue. *Essentials of Food Safety and Sanitation.* Upper Saddle River, N.J.: Prentice Hall, 1998.

McVety, Paul J., Susan Desmond Marshall, and Bradley J. Ware. *The Menu and the Cycle of Cost Control.* Dubuque, Iowa: Kendall/Hunt Publishing Company, 1997.

McWilliams, Margaret. *Foods: Experimental Perspectives.* 4th edition. Upper Saddle River, N.J.: Prentice Hall, 2000.

Mill, Robert Christie. *Restaurant Management: Customers, Operations, and Employees.* Upper Saddle River, N.J.: Prentice Hall, 1998.

Miller, Jack E., David K. Hayes, and Lea R. Dopson. *Food and Beverage Cost Control.* Hoboken, N.J.: John Wiley & Sons, 2001.

Molt, Mary K. *Food for Fifty.* 11th edition. Upper Saddle River, N.J.: Prentice Hall, 2000.

Morr, Mary L., and Theodore F. Irmiter. *Introductory Foods: A Laboratory Manual.* 6th edition. Upper Saddle River, N.J.: Prentice Hall, 1995.

Ojugo, Clement, and Todd Rymer. *Practical Food & Beverage Cost Control.* Independence, Ky.: Delmar Learning Publishers/ITP, 1999.

Pavesic, David V. *Fundamental Principles of Restaurant Cost Control.* Upper Saddle River, N.J.: Prentice Hall, 1997.

Payne-Palacio, June, and Monica Theis, eds. *West's and Wood's Introduction to Foodservice.* 9th edition. Upper Saddle River, N.J.: Prentice Hall, 2001.

Sanders, Edward E., and Timothy H. Hill. *Foodservice Profitability: A Control Approach.* 2nd edition. Upper Saddle River, N.J.: Prentice Hall, 2000.

Spears, Marian C. *Foodservice Organizations: A Managerial and Systems Approach.* 3rd edition. Upper Saddle River, N.J.: Prentice Hall, 2000.

Spears, Marian C. *Foodservice Procurement: Purchasing for Profit.* Upper Saddle River, N.J.: Prentice Hall, 1998.

Strianese, Anthony J., and Pamela P. Strianese. *Dining Room and Banquet Management.* 2nd edition. Independence, Ky.: Delmar Learning Publishers, 1997.

Ulm, Robert A. *How Much to Buy: A Foodservice Purchasing Workbook.* Upper Saddle River, N.J.: Prentice Hall, 1994.

Wood, Roy C. *Working in Hotels and Catering.* 2nd edition. Farmington Hills, Mich.: International Thomson Business Press, 1997.

Group Travel

Dervaes, Claudine. *Hotels and Car Rentals, Packages and Tours, Motorcoach and Rail.* Tampa, Fla.: Solitaire Publishing, 1998.

Fielder, Anita L. *Managing Group Tours.* Holland, Mich.: Shoreline Creations, Ltd., 1995.

Goldsmith, Carol S., and Ann H. Waigand. *Building Profits with Group Travel.* Tampa, Fla.: Solitaire Publishing 1990.

Klender, Jeane S.; Amy Gustin (illustrator); and Amber Christman-Clark, ed. *Coach Full of Fun.* Holland, Mich.: Shoreline Creations, Ltd., 1995.

Laws, Eric. *Managing Packaged Tourism.* Farmington Hills, Mich.: International Thomson Business Press, 1997.

Mancini, Marc. *Conducting Tours.* 2nd edition. Independence, Ky.: Delmar Learning Publishers/ITP, 1996.

Poynter, James M. *Tour Design, Marketing, and Management.* Upper Saddle River, N.J.: Prentice Hall, 1993.

Hospitality Business, Management and Operations

Astroff, Milton T., and James R. Abbey. *Convention Management and Service.* 5th edition. Orlando, Fla.: Educational Institute, 1998.

Bardi, James A. *Hotel Front Office Management.* 3rd edition. Hoboken, N.J.: John Wiley & Sons, 2002.

Barrows, Clayton W., and Robert H. Boselman, eds. *Hospitality Management Education.* Binghamton, N.Y.: Haworth Hospitality Press, 1999.

Baum, Tom, and Ram Mudambi. *Economic and Management Methods for Tourism and Hospitality Research.* Hoboken, N.J.: John Wiley & Sons, 1999.

Borchgrevink, Carl P., ed. *Perspectives on the Hospitality Industry: An Introduction to Hospitality Management.* Dubuque, Iowa: Kendall/Hunt Publishing Company, 1999.

Brotherton, Bob, ed. *Handbook of Contemporary Hospitality Management.* Hoboken, N.J.: John Wiley & Sons, 1999.

Casado, Matt A. *Conversational Spanish for Hospitality Managers and Supervisors.* Hoboken, N.J.: John Wiley & Sons, 1995.

Casado, Matt A. *Housekeeping Management.* Hoboken, N.J.: John Wiley & Sons, 1999.

Clark, M. *Interpersonal Skills for Hospitality Management.* Farmington Hills, Mich.: International Thomson Business Press, 1995.

Dittmer, Paul R., and Gerald G. Griffin. *Dimensions of the Hospitality Industry.* 3rd edition. Hoboken, N.J.: John Wiley & Sons, 2002.

Educational Institute of the American Hotel and Lodging Association, ed. *Case Studies in Condominium and Vacation Ownership Management.* Orlando, Fla.: Educational Institute, 1998.

Educational Institute of the American Hotel and Lodging Association, ed. *Case Studies in Lodging Management.* Orlando, Fla.: Educational Institute, 1998.

Gee, Chuck Y. *International Hotel Development and Management.* Orlando, Fla.: Educational Institute, 1994.

Gentry, Robert A., Pedro Mandoki, and Jack Rush. *Resort Condominium and Vacation Ownership Management: A Hospitality Perspective.* Orlando, Fla.: Educational Institute, 1999.

Go, Frank. *Human Resource Management in the Hospitality Industry.* Hoboken, N.J.: John Wiley & Sons, 1996.

Gray, William S. *Hotel and Motel Management and Operations.* 3rd edition. Upper Saddle River, N.J.: Prentice Hall, 1994.

Hall, Stephen S.J., ed. *Ethics in Hospitality Management.* Orlando, Fla.: Educational Institute, 1994.

Hinkin, Timothy R. *Cases in Hospitality Management.* Hoboken, N.J.: John Wiley & Sons, 1995.

Hinton, Roy W. *Top of the House: A Hotel Management Simulation.* Dubuque, Iowa: Kendall/Hunt Publishing Company, 1996.

Howell, David W. *Principles and Methods of Scheduling Reservations.* 3rd edition. Upper Saddle River, N.J.: Prentice Hall, 1993.

Ismail, Ahmed. *Hotel Sales and Operations.* Independence, Ky.: Delmar Learning Publishers/ITP, 1999.

Kappa, Margaret M., Aleta Nitschke, and Patricia B. Schappert. *Managing Housekeeping Operations.* 2nd edition. Orlando, Fla.: Educational Institute, 1997.

Kasavana, Michael L. *Managing Front Office Operations.* 5th edition. Orlando, Fla.: Educational Institute, 1998.

Kavanaugh, Raphael R., and Jack D. Ninemeier. *Supervision in the Hospitality Industry.* 3rd edition. Orlando, Fla.: Educational Institute, 2001.

Lewis, Robert C. *Cases in Hospitality Strategy and Policy.* Hoboken, N.J.: John Wiley & Sons, 1998.

Miller, Jack E., John R. Walker, and Karen Eich Drummond. *Supervision in the Hospitality Industry.* 3rd edition. Hoboken, N.J.: John Wiley & Sons, 2002.

Moreo, Patrick J., Gail Sammons, and James Dougan. *Office Operations and Night Audit Workbook.* Upper Saddle River, N.J.: Prentice Hall, 1996.

Olsen, Michael D., Eliza Ching-Yick Tse, and Joseph J. West. *Strategic Management in the Hospitality Industry.* 2nd edition. Hoboken, N.J.: John Wiley & Sons, 1999.

Perdue, Joe, ed. *Contemporary Club Management.* Orlando, Fla.: Educational Institute, 1997.

Powers, Tom, Jo Marie Powers, and Clayton W. Barrows. *Introduction to Management in the Hospitality Industry.* 7th edition. Hoboken, N.J.: John Wiley & Sons, 2002.

Powers, Tom, Jo Marie Powers, and Clayton W. Barrows. *Introduction to the Hospitality Industry.* 5th edition. Hoboken, N.J.: John Wiley & Sons, 2002.

Renner, Peter. *Basic Hotel Front Office Procedures.* 3rd edition. Hoboken, N.J.: John Wiley & Sons, 1994.

Swarbrooke, John. *Development and Management of Visitor Attractions.* Burlington, Mass.: Butterworth-Heinemann, 1995.

Woods, Robert H., and Judy Z. King. *Quality Leadership and Management in the Hospitality Industry.* Orlando, Fla.: Educational Institute, 1996.

Human Resources

Woods, R. *Managing Hospitality Human Resources.* 3rd edition. Orlando, Fla.: Educational Institute, 2000.

Law and Legal Issues

Jarvis, Robert M., John R. Goodwin, and William D. Henslee. *Travel Law: Cases and Materials.* Durham, N.C.: Carolina Academic Press, 1998.

Morris, Karen. *Hotel, Restaurant, and Travel Law.* 5th edition. Independence, Ky.: Delmar Learning Publishers/ITP, 1998.

Leisure and Recreation

Gaskill, Paul L. *Introduction to Leisure Services in North Carolina.* 3rd edition. Dubuque, Iowa: Kendall/Hunt Publishing Company, 1998.

Greenberg, Peter S., and Ellen Beal, eds. *Learning Adventures Around the World.* Lawrenceville, N.J.: Peterson's Guides, 1998.

Hall, Colin Michael, and Stephen John Page. *Geography of Tourism and Recreation.* London: Routledge, 1999.

Haywood, Les, ed. *Community Leisure and Recreation.* Burlington, Mass.: Butterworth-Heinemann, 1994.

Lawson, Fred R. *Tourism and Recreation Handbook of Planning and Design.* Burlington, Mass.: Butterworth-Heinemann, 1998.

Leitner, Michael J., and Sara F. Leitner. *Leisure Enhancement.* 2nd edition. Binghamton, N.Y.: Haworth Hospitality Press, 1996.

Van Der Smissen, Betty, and Theodore Haskell, eds. *Recreation in Michigan: Great Professional Opportunities.* Dubuque, Iowa: Kendall/Hunt Publishing, 1995.

Mystery Shopping

Poynter, James M. *Mystery Shopping.* 4th edition. Dubuque, Iowa: Kendall/Hunt Publishing Company, 2002.

Security

Ellis, Raymond C. *Security and Loss Prevention Management.* 2nd edition. Orlando, Fla.: Educational Institute, 1999.

Special Events and Event Management

Getz, Donald. *Event Management & Event Tourism.* Elmsford, N.Y.: Cognizant Communications, 1997.

Tourism

Blank, Uel, and Blank, Vel. *The Community Tourism Industry Imperative—The Necessity, the Opportunities, Its Potential.* Venture Publishing, 1989.

Brunt, Paul. *Market Research in Travel and Tourism.* Burlington, Mass.: Butterworth-Heinemann, 1997.

Brymer, Robert A., ed. *Hospitality and Tourism: An Introduction to the Industry.* 8th edition. Dubuque, Iowa: Kendall/Hunt Publishing Company, 1998.

Burns, Peter M. *Introduction to Tourism and Anthropology.* London: Routledge, 1999.

Butler, Richard, and Thomas Hinch. *Tourism and Indigenous Peoples.* Farmington Hills, Mich.: International Thomson Business Press, 1996.

Crotts, John C., and W. Fred Van Raaij, eds. *Economic Psychology of Travel and Tourism.* Binghamton, N.Y.: Haworth Hospitality Press, 1995.

Gartner, William C. *Tourism Development: Principles, Processes, and Policies.* Hoboken, N.J.: John Wiley & Sons, 1996.

Getz, Don, and Stephen Page. *The Business of Rural Tourism; International Perspectives.* Farmington Hills, Mich.: International Thomson Business Press, 1997.

Getz, Donald. *Explore Wine Tourism.* Elmsford, N.Y.: Cognizant Communications, 2001.

Harris, Rob, and Neil Leiper, eds. *Sustainable Tourism: An Australian Perspective.* Burlington, Mass.: Butterworth-Heinemann, 1995.

Harrison, Lynn C., and Winston Husbands, eds. *Practicing Responsible Tourism: International Case Studies in Tourism Planning, Policy, and Development.* Hoboken, N.J.: John Wiley & Sons 1996.

Jenkins, John M., and Colin Michael Hall. *Tourism and Public Policy.* Farmington Hills, Mich.: International Thomson Business Press, 1996.

Landry, Janice L., and Anna H. Fesmire. *World Is Out There Waiting: An Introduction to Travel and Tourism.* Upper Saddle River, N.J.: Prentice Hall, 1994.

Medlik, S. *Understanding Tourism.* Burlington, Mass.: Butterworth-Heinemann, 1997.

Nickerson, Norma Polovitz. *Foundations of Tourism.* Upper Saddle River, N.J.: Prentice Hall, 1996.

Orams, Mark. *Marine Tourism.* London: Routledge, 1999.

Pizam, Abraham, and Yoel Mansfeld, eds. *Consumer Behavior in Travel and Tourism.* Binghamton, N.Y.: Haworth Hospitality Press, 1999.

Riegel, Carl, and Melissa Dallas. *Hospitality and Tourism Careers: A Blueprint for Success.* Upper Saddle River, N.J.: Prentice Hall, 1998.

Samuels, Jack B., and Reginald Foucar-Szocki. *Guiding Your Entry into the Hospitality and Tourism Mega-Profession.* Upper Saddle River, N.J.: Prentice Hall, 1999.

Shackley, Myra L. *Wildlife Tourism.* Farmington Hills, Mich.: International Thomson Business Press, 1996.

Sheperd, Rebecca A., John Westlake, and Christopher P. Cooper. *Educating the Educators in Tourism: A Manual of Tourism and Hospitality Education.* Madrid, Spain: WTO Publications, 1996.

Swarbrooke, John, and Susan Horner. *Consumer Behavior in Tourism.* Burlington, Mass.: Butterworth-Heinemann, 1999.

Tyler, Duncan, Yvonne Guerrier, and Martin Robertson, eds. *Managing Tourism in Cities.* Hoboken, N.J.: John Wiley & Sons, 1998.

Wheatcroft, Stephen, ed. *Aviation and Tourism Policies.* Farmington Hills, Mich.: International Thomson Business Press, 1994.

Williams, Allan M., and Gareth Shaw, eds. *Tourism and Economic Development: European Experience.* 3rd Edition. Hoboken, N.J.: John Wiley & Sons, 1999.

World Tourism Organization, ed. *International Tourism: A Global Perspective.* Madrid, Spain: WTO Publications. 1997.

Travel Agencies

Davidoff, Philip G., and Doris S. Davidoff. *Worldwide Tours: A Travel Agent's Guide to Selling Tours.* Upper Saddle River, N.J.: Prentice Hall, 1990.

Dervaes, Claudine. *Domestic Travel and Ticketing.* Tampa, Fla.: Solitaire Publishing, 2000.

Dervaes, Claudine. *International Travel & Ticketing.* Tampa, Fla.: Solitaire Publishing, 2000.

Dreith, Rae. *Computer Reservation Systems—Apollo.* 6th edition. New York: Education Systems, 1999.

Dreith, Rae. *Computer Reservation Systems—SABRE.* 5th edition. New York: Education Systems, 1999.

Dreith, Rae. *Computer Reservation Systems—WORLDSPAN.* 3rd edition. New York: Education Systems, 1999.

Gagnon, Patricia J. *Travel Career Development.* 6th edition. Wellesley, Mass.: Institute of Certified Travel Agents, 1998.

Gregory, Aryear. *The Travel Agent: Dealer in Dreams.* 4th edition. Upper Saddle River, N.J.: Prentice Hall, 1998.

Hood, Linda R., and Coates, Robert M. *Domestic Ticketing and Airfare.* Independence, Ky.: Delmar Learning Publishers, 1994.

Jung, Gerald P. *A Practical Guide to Selling Travel.* Upper Saddle River, N.J.: Prentice Hall, 1999.

Monaghan, Kelly. *Independent Agent Opportunities.* Tampa, Fla.: Solitaire Publishing, 2000.

Payette, Douglas A. *So You Want to Be a Travel Agent: An Introduction to Domestic Travel.* Upper Saddle River, N.J.: Prentice Hall, 1995.

Schwartz, Roberta, and Debra J. Macneill. *Travel Sales and Customer Service.* 2nd edition. Wellesley, Mass.: Institute of Certified Travel Agents, 1999.

Semer-Purzycki, Jeanne. *International Fares and Ticketing.* Upper Saddle River, N.J.: Prentice Hall, 1996.

Sorensen, Helle. *International Air Fares—Construction and Ticketing.* Independence, Ky.: Delmar Learning Publishers, 1995.

Syratt, Gwenda. *Manual of Travel Agency Practice.* 2nd edition. Burlington, Mass.: Butterworth-Heinemann, 1995.

Thompson, Douglas. *How to Open Your Own Travel Agency.* Tampa, Fla.: Solitaire Publishing, 1998.

Thompson, Douglas, and Alexander Anolik. *A Personnel and Operations Manual for Travel Agencies.* Tampa, Fla.: Solitaire Publishing, 1992.

Thompson, Douglas, and Mary Miller-Marshall. *Travel Agency Bookkeeping Made Simple.* Tampa, Fla.: Solitaire Publishing, 1991.

Todd, Ginger. *Travel Perspectives: A Guide to Becoming a Travel Agent.* 2nd edition. Independence, Ky.: Delmar Learning Publishers, 1996.

INDEX

Boldface page numbers denote main entries.

Woodland High School
800 N. Moseley Dr.
Stockbridge, GA 30281
770-389-2784